BLUE PERIOD

TSUBASA YAMAGUCHI

4

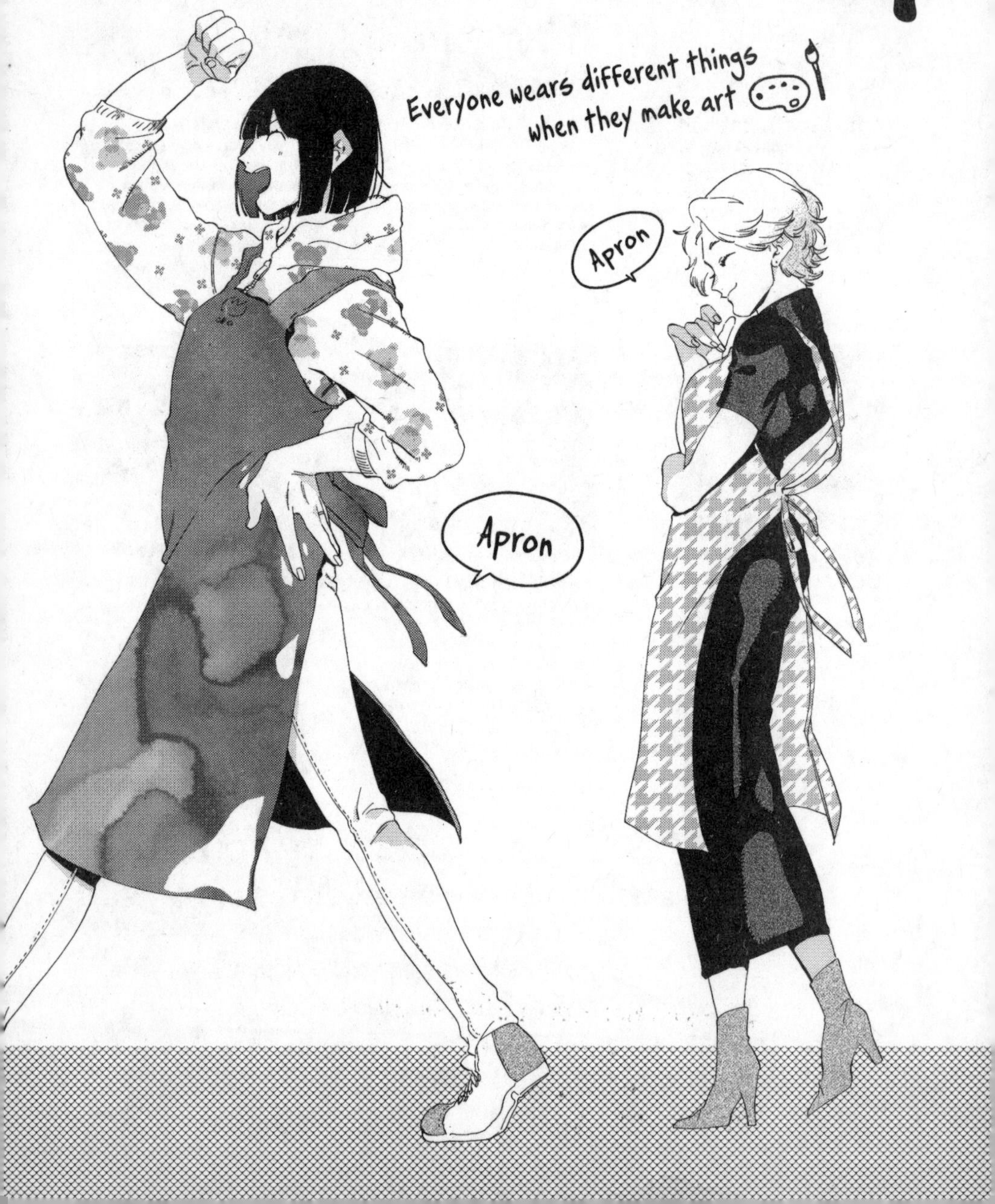
Everyone wears different things
when they make art
Apron
Apron

CHARACTERS

Yotasuke Takahashi
A third-year high school student who used to attend the same prep school as Yatora. His talent, skill, and unsociable character inspire Yatora to be a better artist.

Ryuji Ayukawa
Goes by the name Yuka. A boy who dresses in women's clothing. A member of the art club who's in the same class as Yatora. He invited Yatora to the Art Club.

Yatora Yaguchi
A third-year in high school. After seeing Mori-senpai's painting, he discovered the joy of making art and was hooked. He sets his sights on Tokyo University of the Arts, the most competitive of all Japanese art colleges.

Ooba-sensei
An instructor at the art prep school that Yatora attends. Her height matches the volume of her voice.

Maki Kuwana
A third-year in high school. She attends the same prep school as Yatora. Her parents are TUA alumni, and her older sister, who is a bit of a "campus celebrity," currently attends TUA.

Haruka Hashida
A student who's in the same year and school as Yotasuke. He attends the same prep school as Yatora. As an art connoisseur of sorts, he enjoys museum outings and the like.

TABLE OF CONTENTS

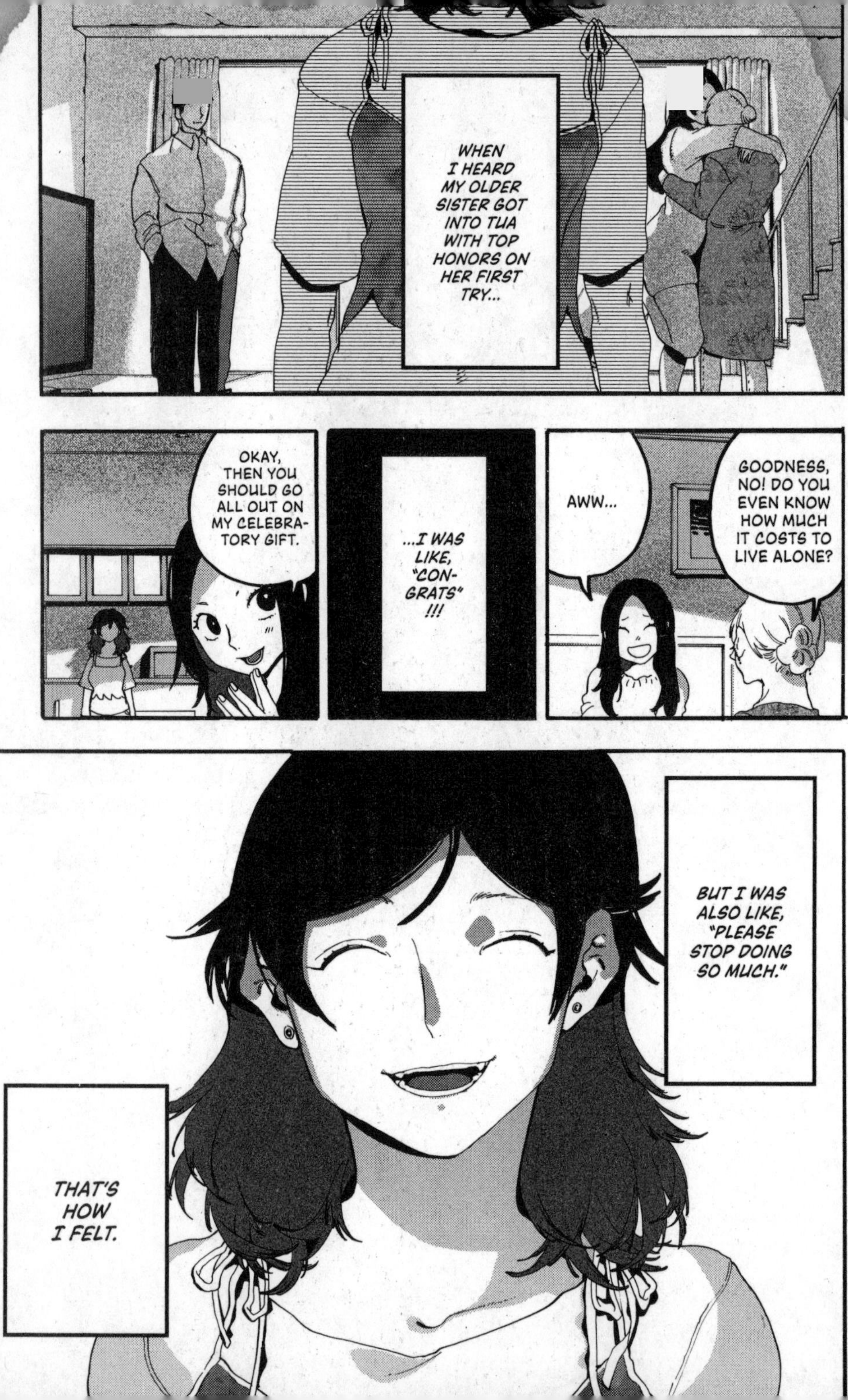
WHEN I HEARD MY OLDER SISTER GOT INTO TUA WITH TOP HONORS ON HER FIRST TRY...
GOODNESS, NO! DO YOU EVEN KNOW HOW MUCH IT COSTS TO LIVE ALONE?
AWW...
...I WAS LIKE, "CON-GRATS"!!!
OKAY, THEN YOU SHOULD GO ALL OUT ON MY CELEBRA-TORY GIFT.
BUT I WAS ALSO LIKE, "PLEASE STOP DOING SO MUCH."
THAT'S HOW I FELT.

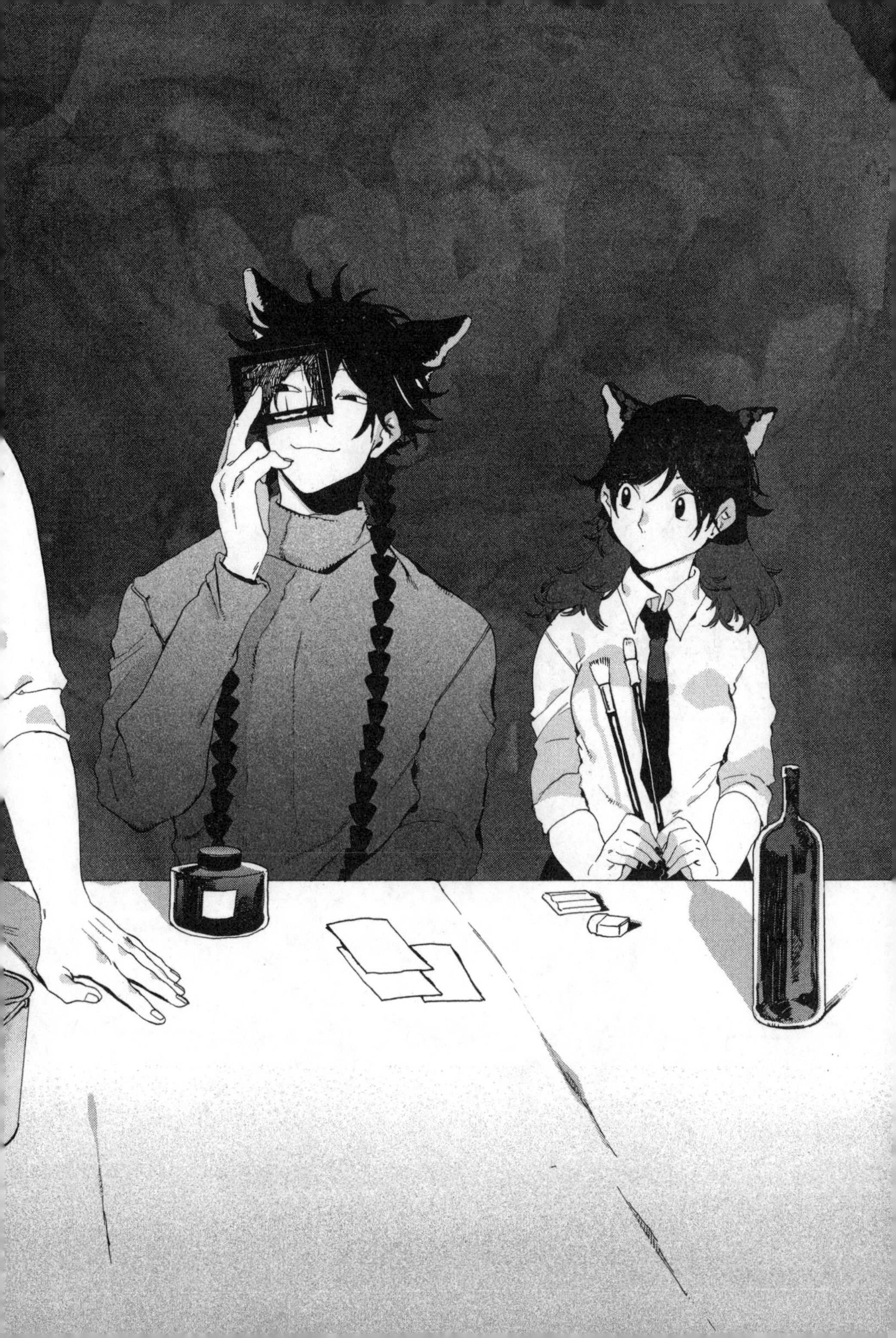

STROKE 13

MENTAL BREAKDOWNS ARE NO JOKE

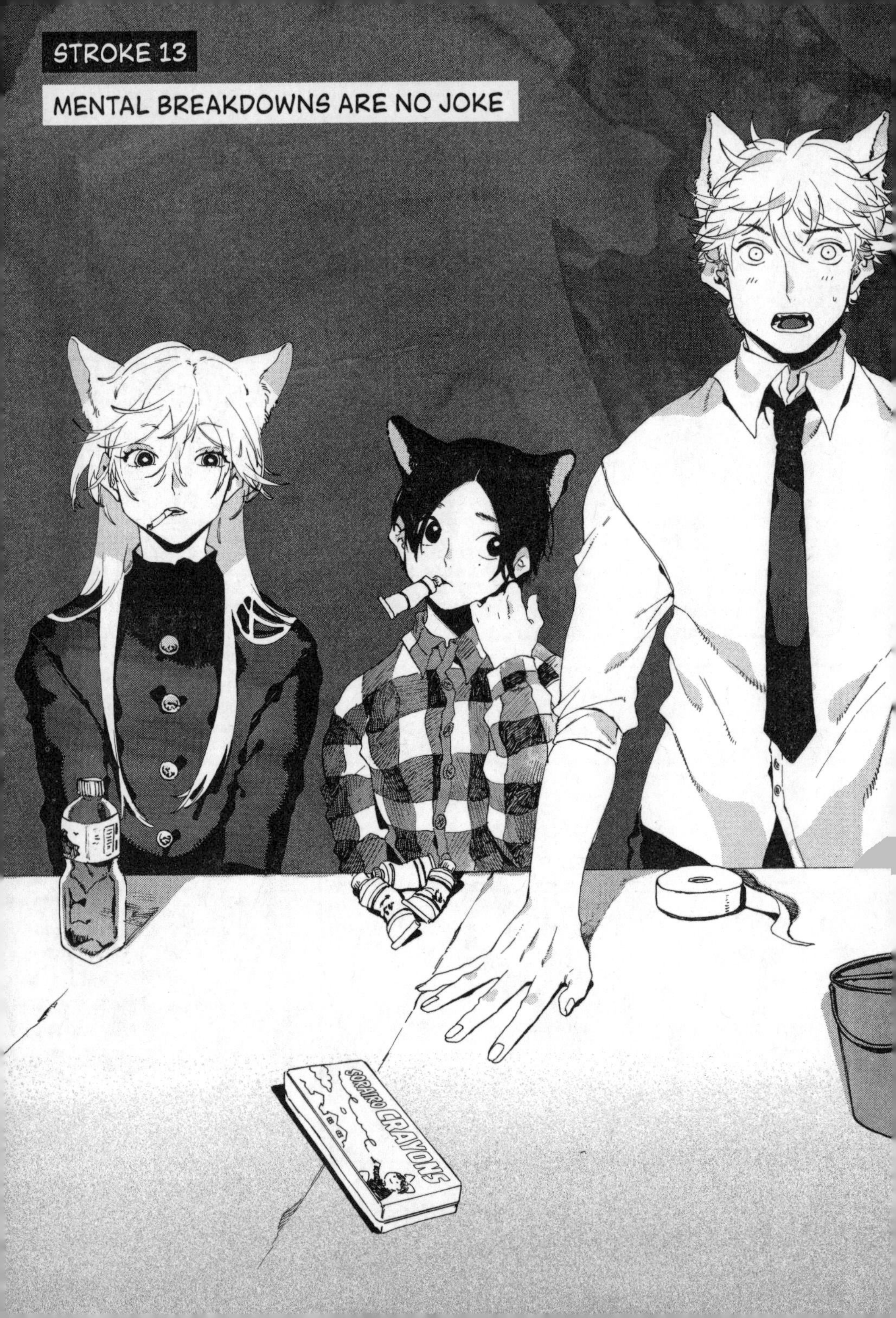
SORAIRO CRAYONS

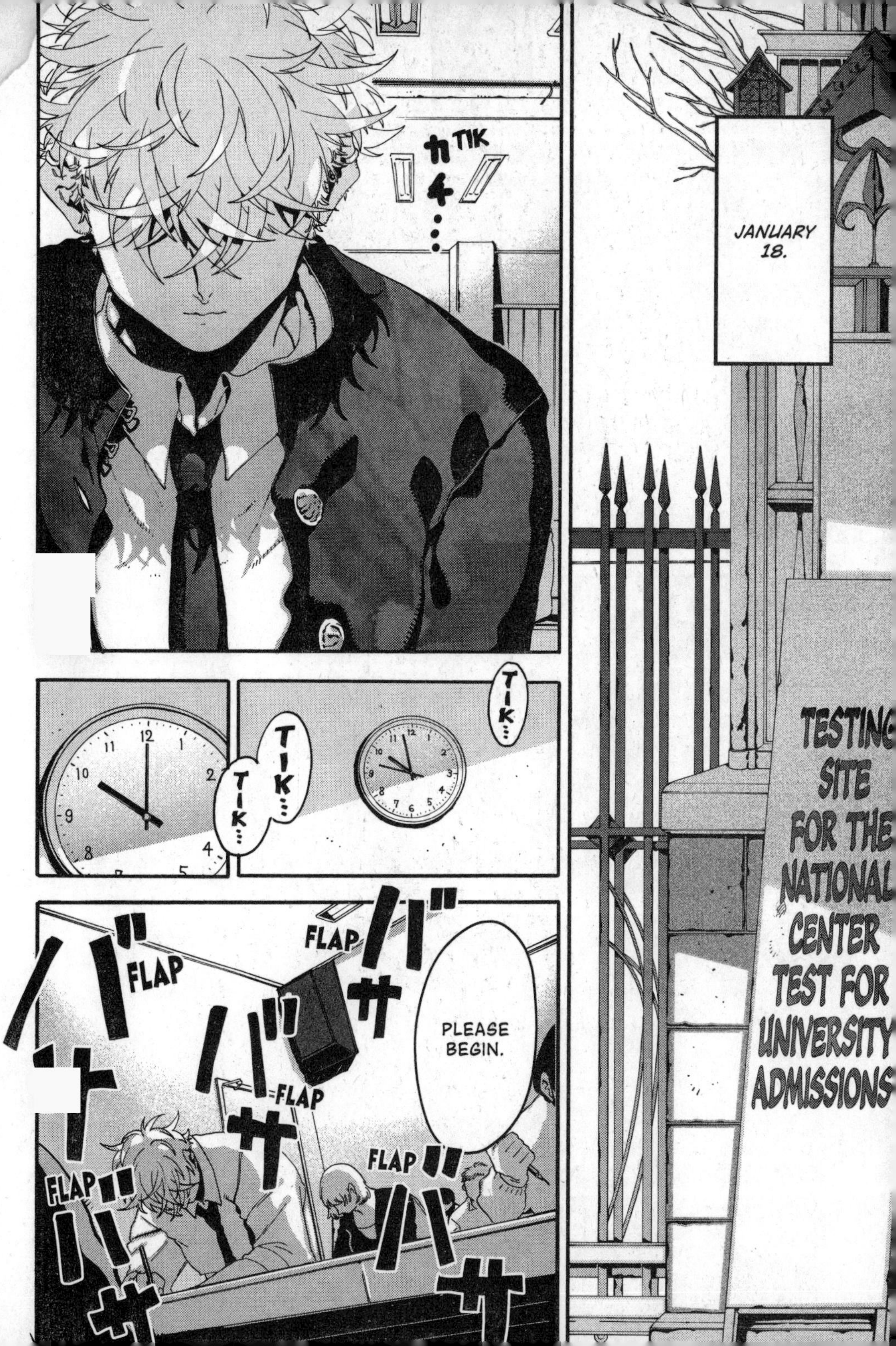

JANUARY 18.
TESTING SITE FOR THE NATIONAL CENTER TEST FOR UNIVERSITY ADMISSIONS
TIK
TIK...
TIK...
TIK...
PLEASE BEGIN.
FLAP
FLAP
FLAP
FLAP
FLAP

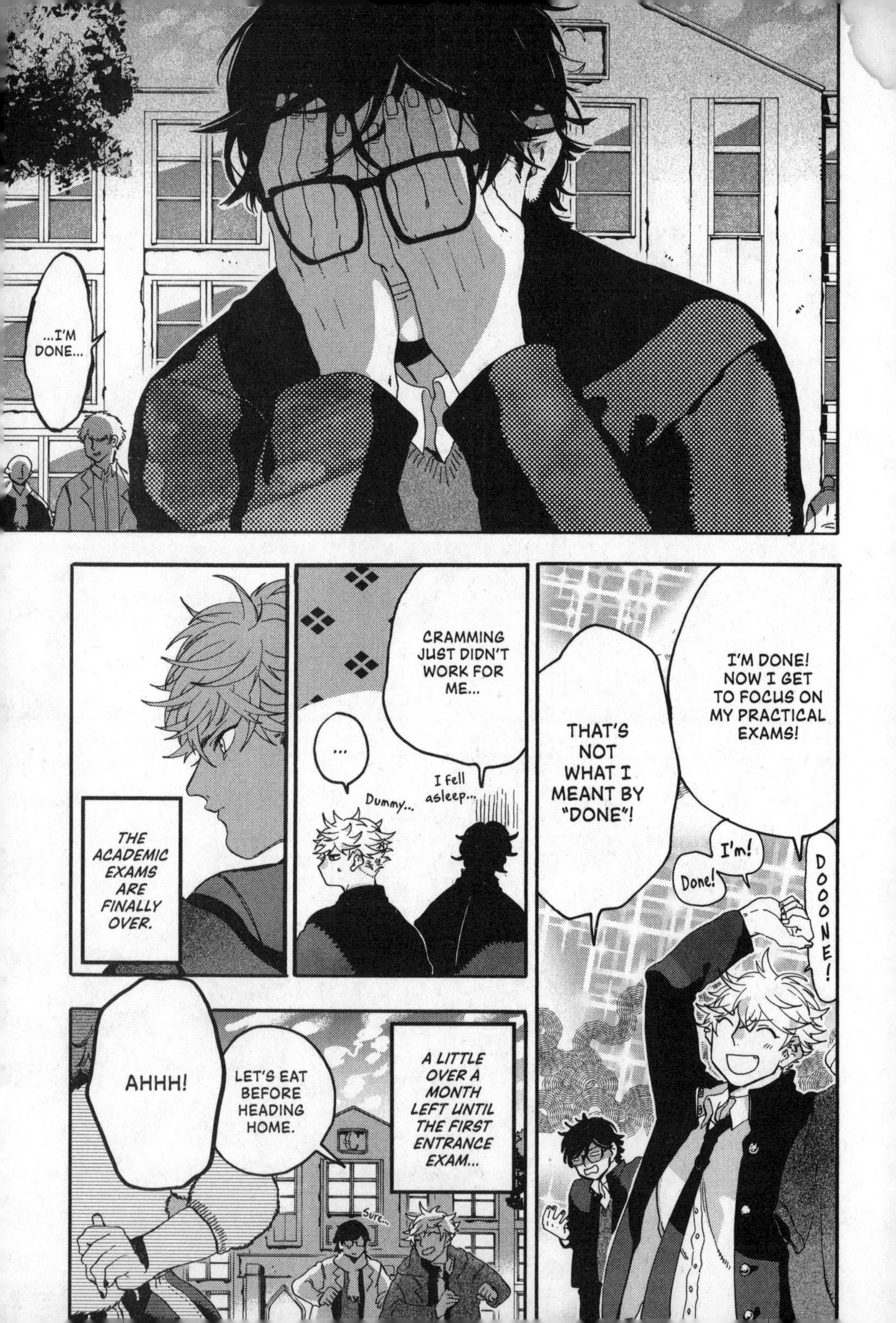
...I'M DONE...
I'M DONE! NOW I GET TO FOCUS ON MY PRACTICAL EXAMS!
DOOOONE!
I'm!
Done!
THAT'S NOT WHAT I MEANT BY "DONE"!
CRAMMING JUST DIDN'T WORK FOR ME...
I fell asleep...
...
Dummy...
THE ACADEMIC EXAMS ARE FINALLY OVER.
A LITTLE OVER A MONTH LEFT UNTIL THE FIRST ENTRANCE EXAM...
LET'S EAT BEFORE HEADING HOME.
Sure...
AHHH!

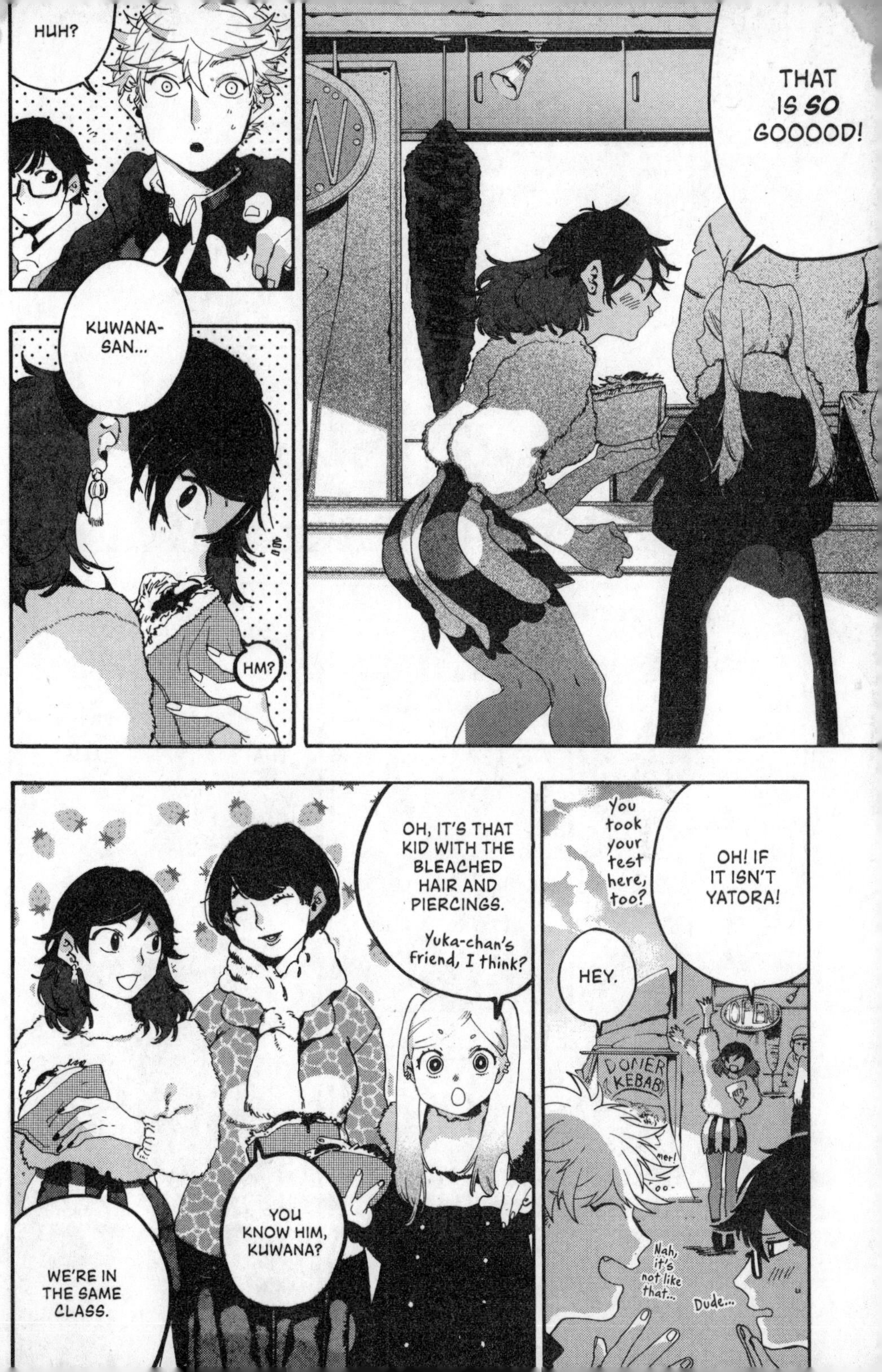
THAT IS SO GOOOOD!
HUH?
KUWANA-SAN...
HM?
OH! IF IT ISN'T YATORA!
You took your test here, too?
HEY.
OPEN
DONER KEBAB
Nah, it's not like that...
Dude...
OH, IT'S THAT KID WITH THE BLEACHED HAIR AND PIERCINGS.
Yuka-chan's friend, I think?
YOU KNOW HIM, KUWANA?
WE'RE IN THE SAME CLASS.

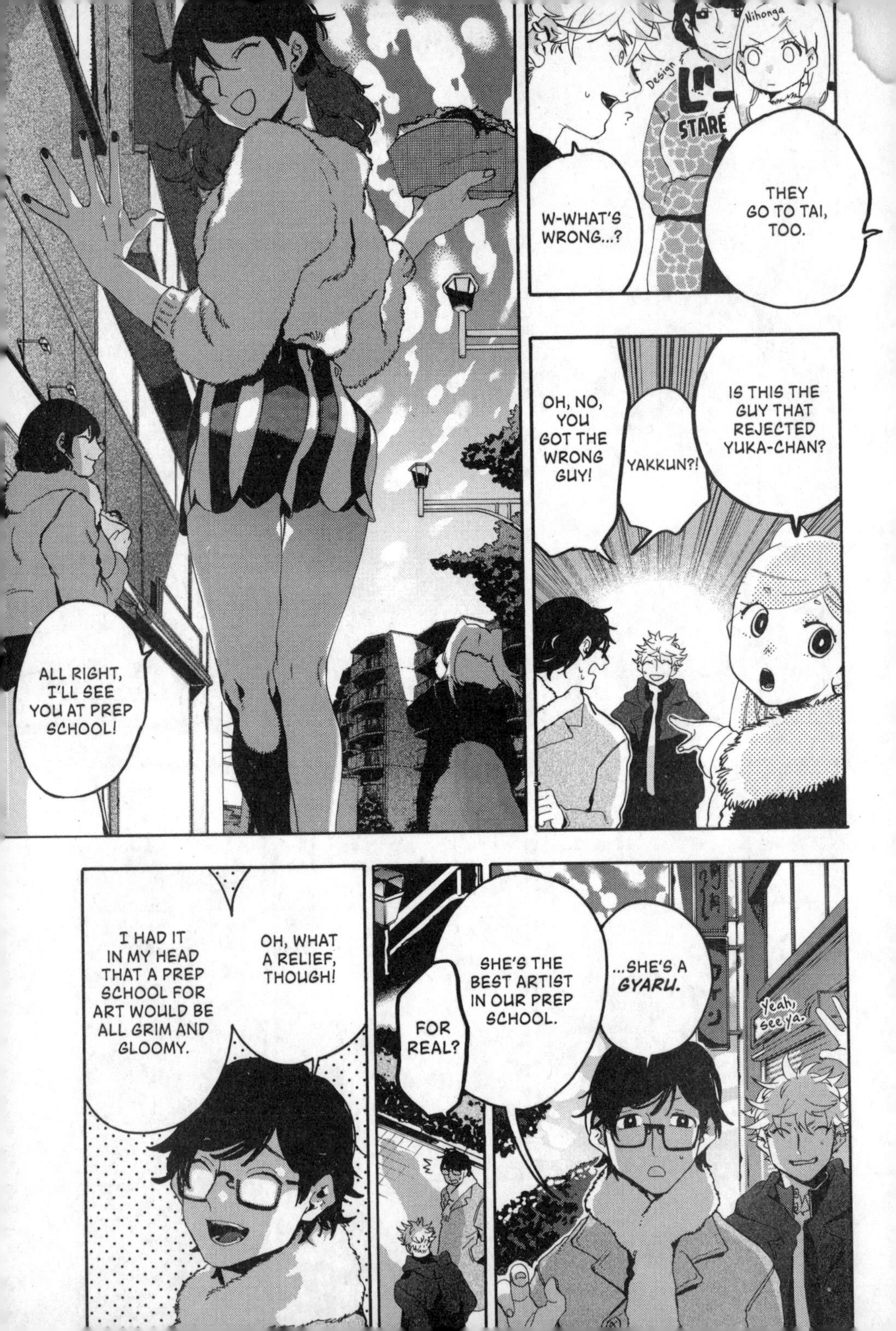
Nihonga
Design
STARE
THEY GO TO TAI, TOO.
W-WHAT'S WRONG...?
IS THIS THE GUY THAT REJECTED YUKA-CHAN?
YAKKUN?!
OH, NO, YOU GOT THE WRONG GUY!
ALL RIGHT, I'LL SEE YOU AT PREP SCHOOL!
Yeah, see ya.
...SHE'S A *GYARU.*
SHE'S THE BEST ARTIST IN OUR PREP SCHOOL.
FOR REAL?
OH, WHAT A RELIEF, THOUGH!
I HAD IT IN MY HEAD THAT A PREP SCHOOL FOR ART WOULD BE ALL GRIM AND GLOOMY.

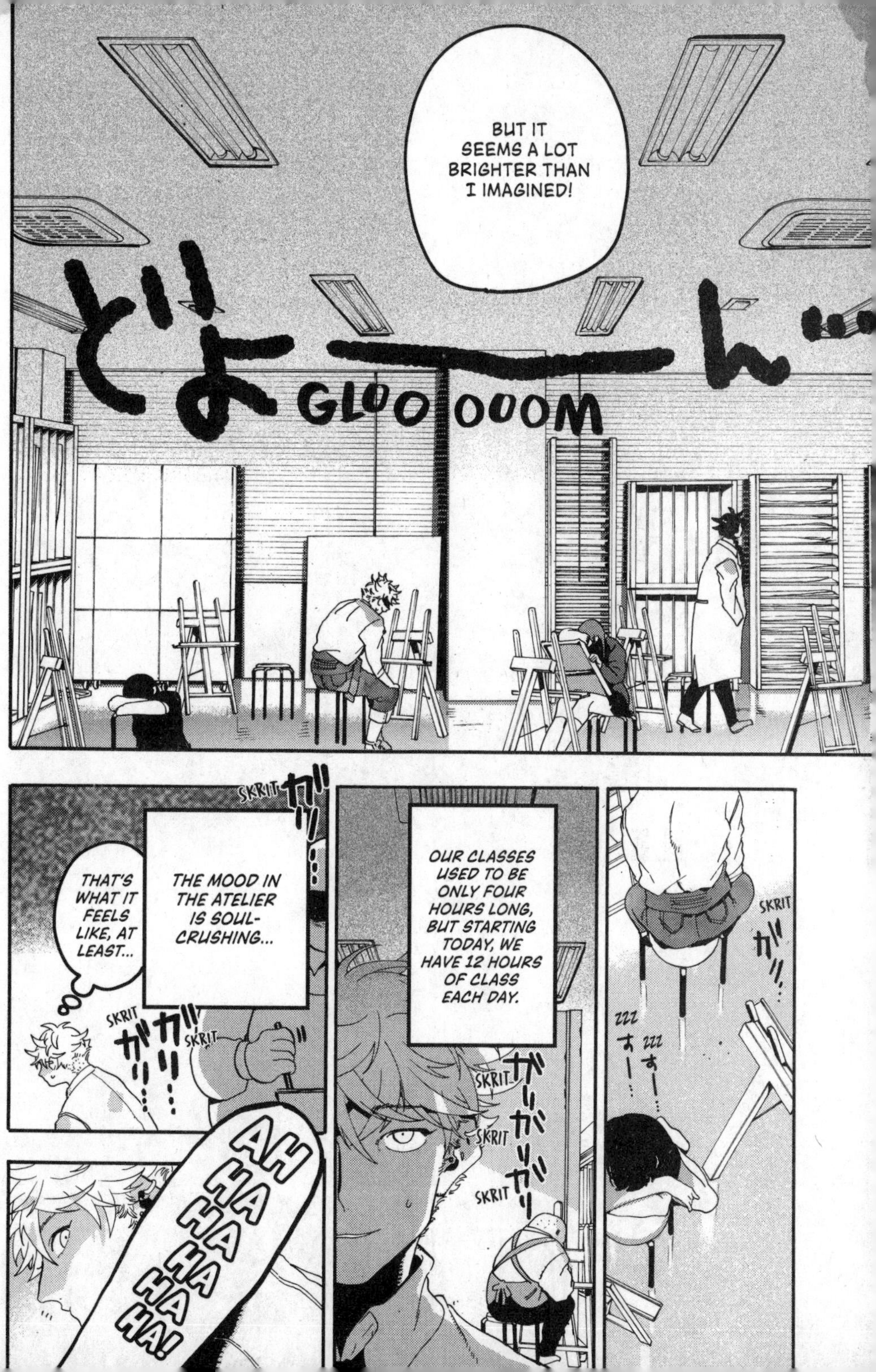
BUT IT SEEMS A LOT BRIGHTER THAN I IMAGINED!
どよーん…
GLOOOOOM
SKRIT
ガリ…
zzz
すー…
zzz
すー…
OUR CLASSES USED TO BE ONLY FOUR HOURS LONG, BUT STARTING TODAY, WE HAVE 12 HOURS OF CLASS EACH DAY.
SKRIT
SKRIT
SKRIT
ガリガリガリ
SKRIT
ガリ…
THE MOOD IN THE ATELIER IS SOUL-CRUSHING...
THAT'S WHAT IT FEELS LIKE, AT LEAST...
SKRIT
SKRIT
ガリガリ…
AH HA HA HA HA HA!

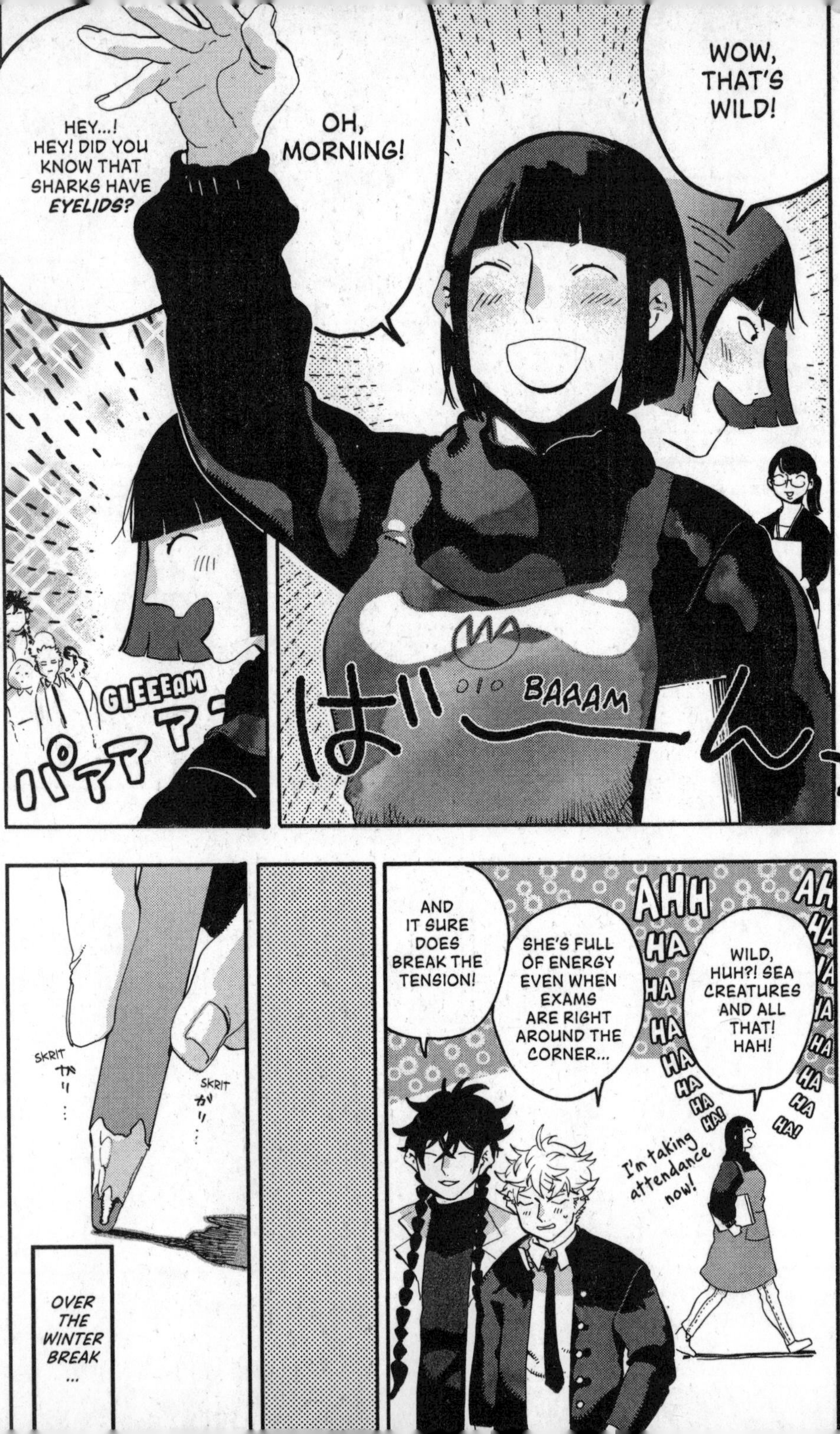
WOW, THAT'S WILD!
OH, MORNING!
HEY...! HEY! DID YOU KNOW THAT SHARKS HAVE *EYELIDS?*
BAAAM
GLEEEAM
AHH HA HA HA HA HA HA HA!
AH HA HA HA HA HA HA HA!
WILD, HUH?! SEA CREATURES AND ALL THAT! HAH!
SHE'S FULL OF ENERGY EVEN WHEN EXAMS ARE RIGHT AROUND THE CORNER...
AND IT SURE DOES BREAK THE TENSION!
I'm taking attendance now!
SKRIT
SKRIT
OVER THE WINTER BREAK ...

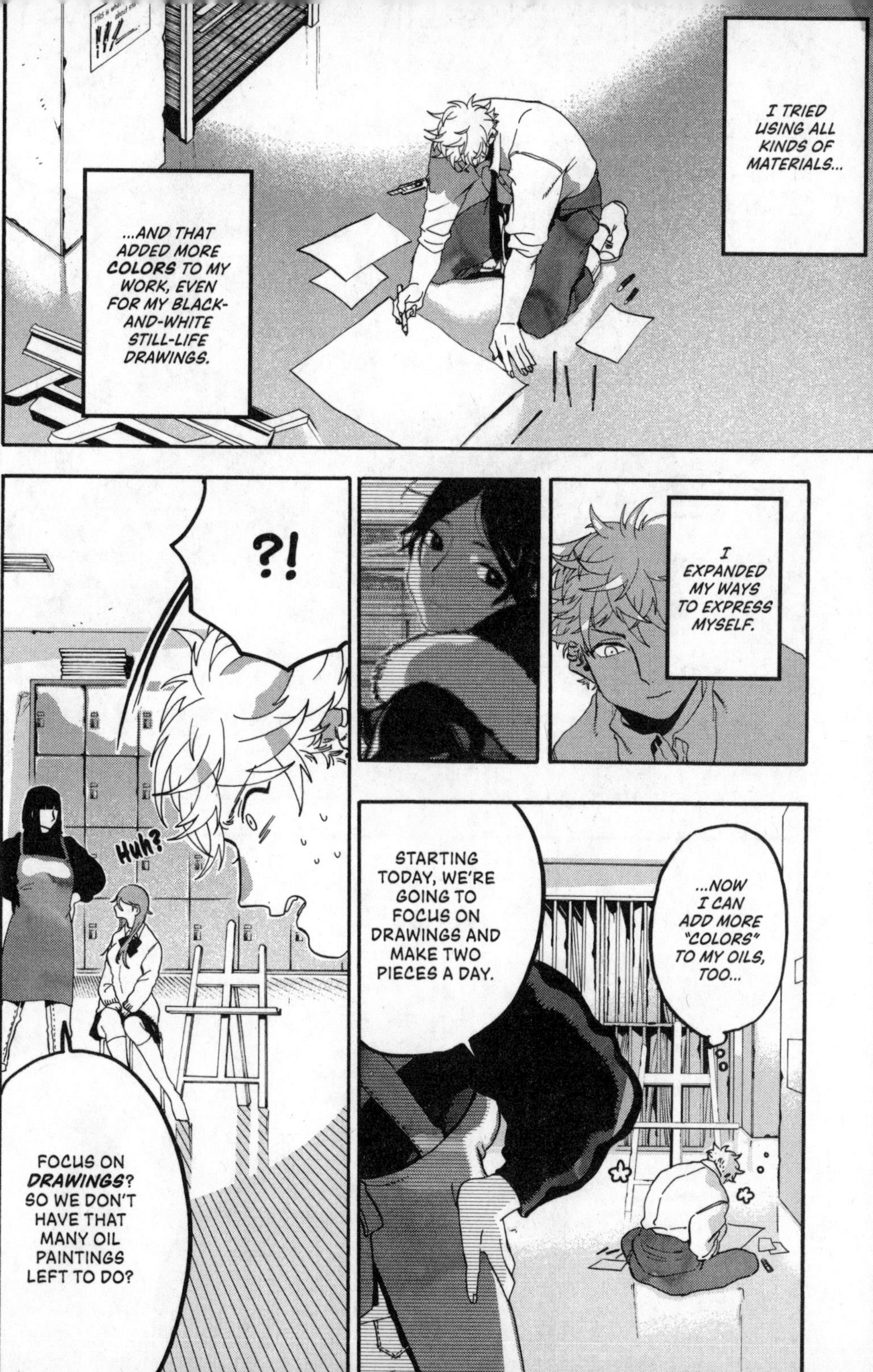
I TRIED USING ALL KINDS OF MATERIALS...
...AND THAT ADDED MORE COLORS TO MY WORK, EVEN FOR MY BLACK-AND-WHITE STILL-LIFE DRAWINGS.
I EXPANDED MY WAYS TO EXPRESS MYSELF.
...NOW I CAN ADD MORE "COLORS" TO MY OILS, TOO...
STARTING TODAY, WE'RE GOING TO FOCUS ON DRAWINGS AND MAKE TWO PIECES A DAY.
?!
Huh?
FOCUS ON DRAWINGS? SO WE DON'T HAVE THAT MANY OIL PAINTINGS LEFT TO DO?

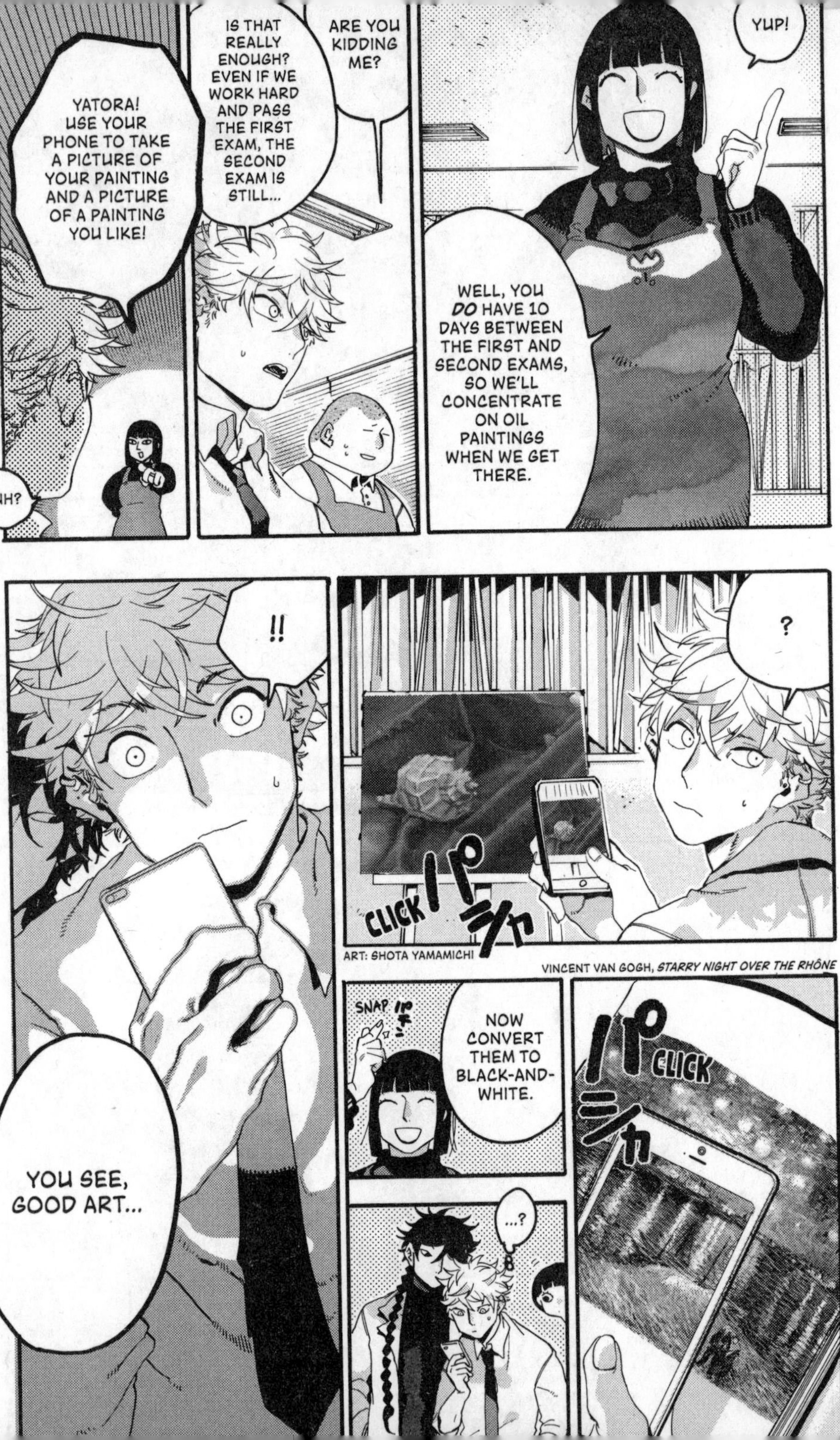
YUP!
WELL, YOU *DO* HAVE 10 DAYS BETWEEN THE FIRST AND SECOND EXAMS, SO WE'LL CONCENTRATE ON OIL PAINTINGS WHEN WE GET THERE.
ARE YOU KIDDING ME?
IS THAT REALLY ENOUGH? EVEN IF WE WORK HARD AND PASS THE FIRST EXAM, THE SECOND EXAM IS STILL...
YATORA! USE YOUR PHONE TO TAKE A PICTURE OF YOUR PAINTING AND A PICTURE OF A PAINTING YOU LIKE!
HUH?
?
CLICK パシャ
ART: SHOTA YAMAMICHI
VINCENT VAN GOGH, *STARRY NIGHT OVER THE RHÔNE*
パシャ CLICK
SNAP パチ
NOW CONVERT THEM TO BLACK-AND-WHITE.
...?
!!
YOU SEE, GOOD ART...

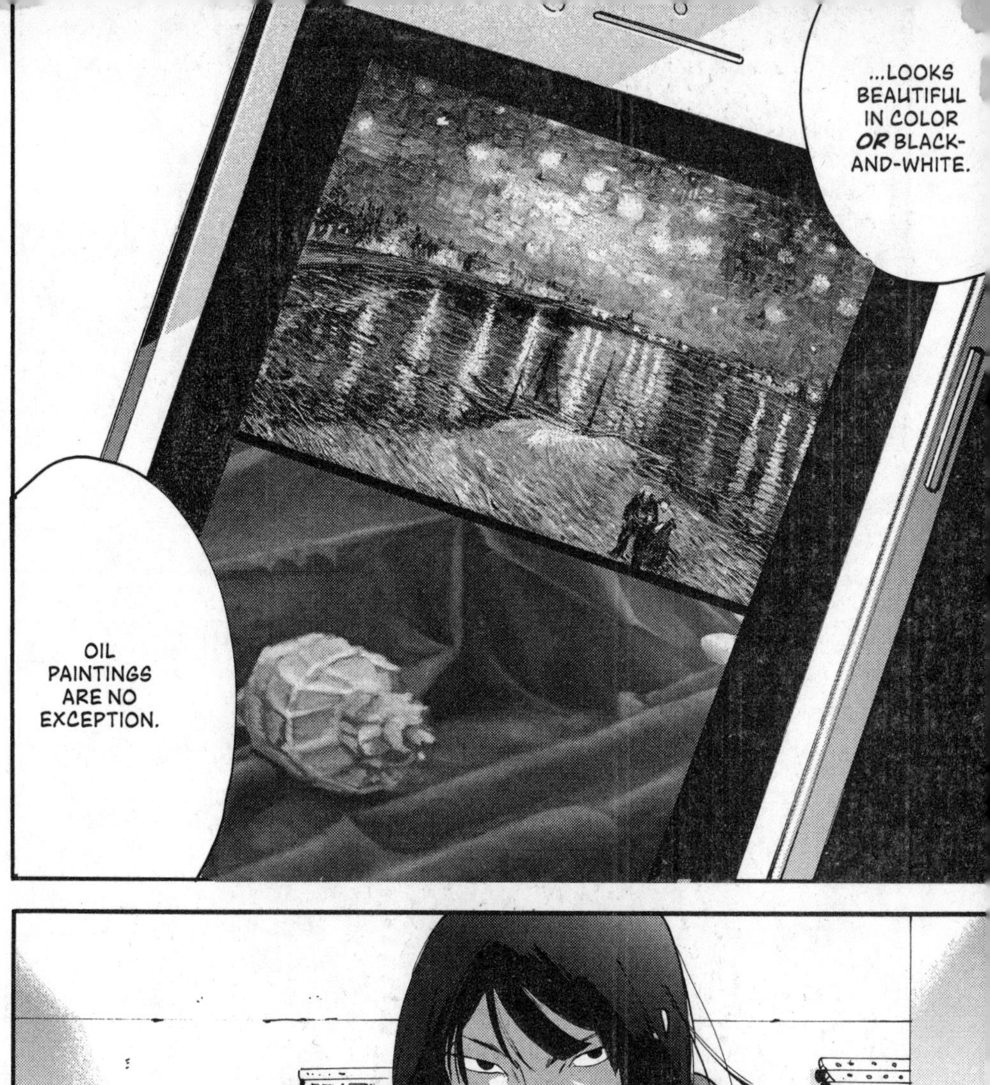
...LOOKS BEAUTIFUL IN COLOR OR BLACK-AND-WHITE.
OIL PAINTINGS ARE NO EXCEPTION.
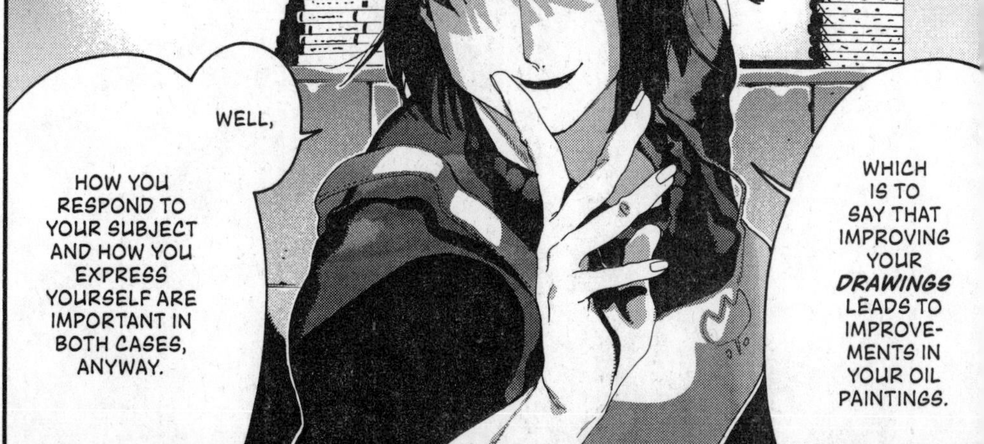
WHICH IS TO SAY THAT IMPROVING YOUR DRAWINGS LEADS TO IMPROVEMENTS IN YOUR OIL PAINTINGS.
WELL,
HOW YOU RESPOND TO YOUR SUBJECT AND HOW YOU EXPRESS YOURSELF ARE IMPORTANT IN BOTH CASES, ANYWAY.

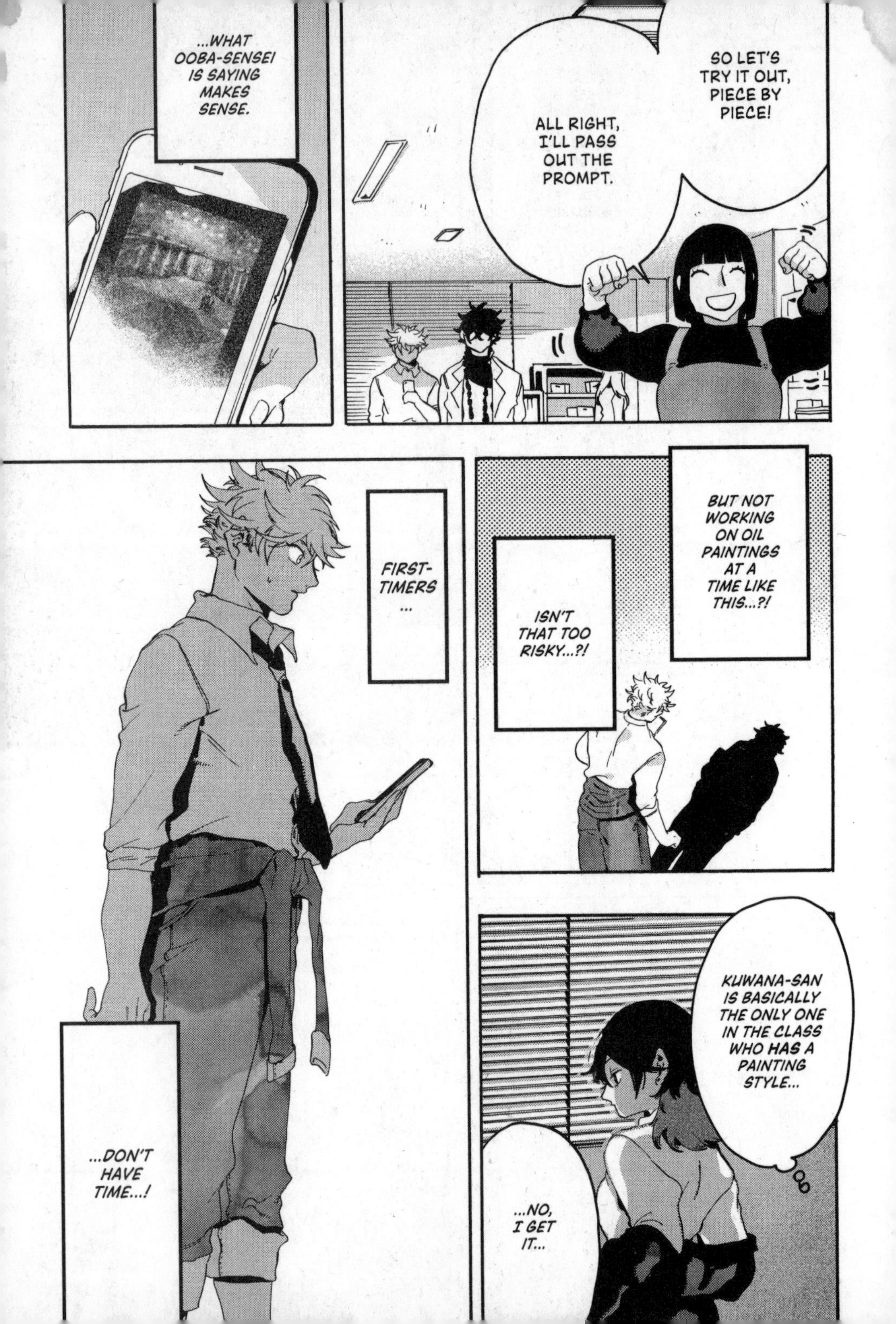
SO LET'S TRY IT OUT, PIECE BY PIECE!
ALL RIGHT, I'LL PASS OUT THE PROMPT.
...WHAT OOBA-SENSEI IS SAYING MAKES SENSE.
BUT NOT WORKING ON OIL PAINTINGS AT A TIME LIKE THIS...?!
ISN'T THAT TOO RISKY...?!
KUWANA-SAN IS BASICALLY THE ONLY ONE IN THE CLASS WHO HAS A PAINTING STYLE...
...NO, I GET IT...
FIRST-TIMERS ...
...DON'T HAVE TIME...!

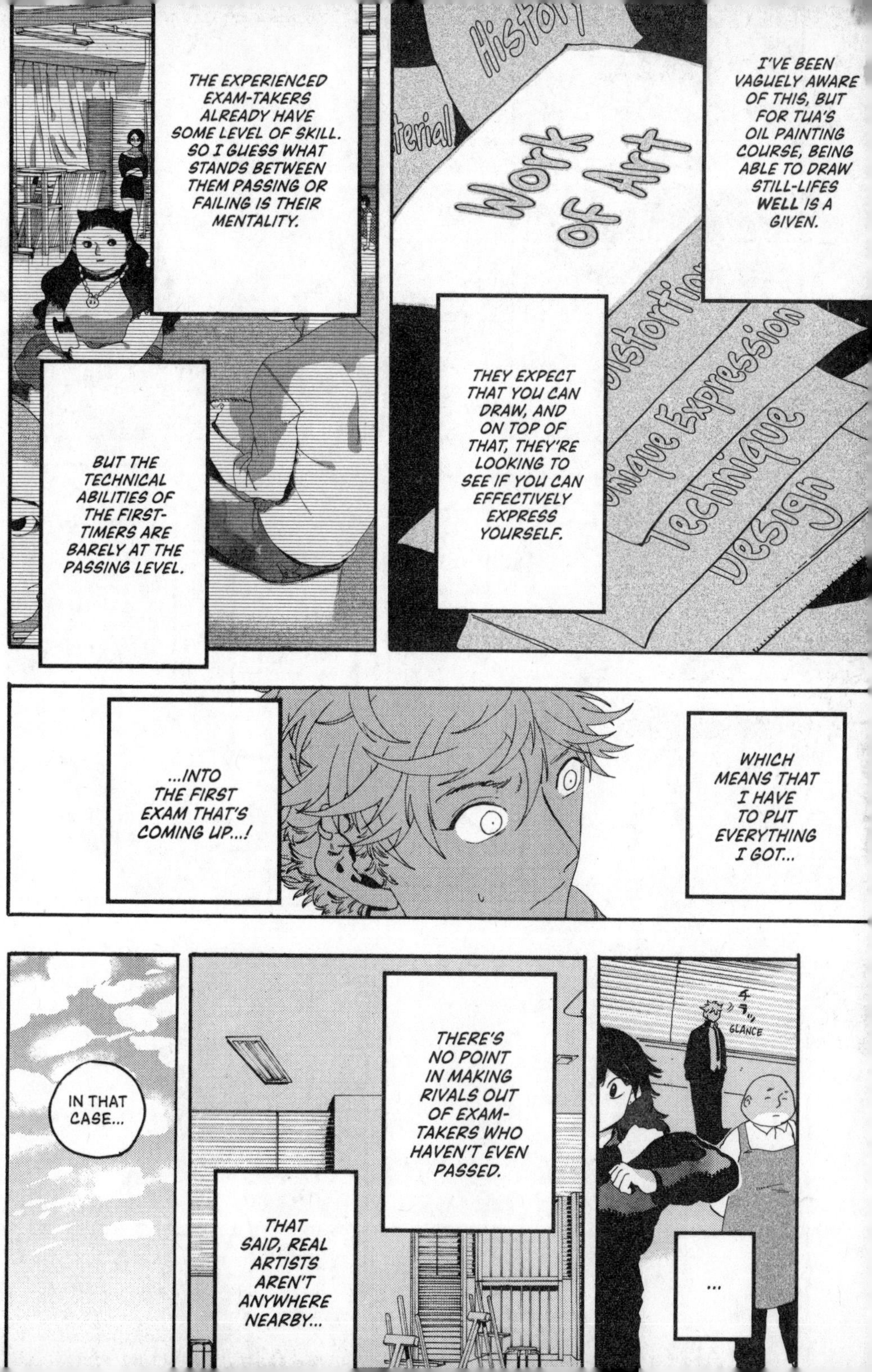
I'VE BEEN VAGUELY AWARE OF THIS, BUT FOR TUA'S OIL PAINTING COURSE, BEING ABLE TO DRAW STILL-LIFES WELL IS A GIVEN.
Work of Art
THEY EXPECT THAT YOU CAN DRAW, AND ON TOP OF THAT, THEY'RE LOOKING TO SEE IF YOU CAN EFFECTIVELY EXPRESS YOURSELF.
Technique
Design
THE EXPERIENCED EXAM-TAKERS ALREADY HAVE SOME LEVEL OF SKILL. SO I GUESS WHAT STANDS BETWEEN THEM PASSING OR FAILING IS THEIR MENTALITY.
BUT THE TECHNICAL ABILITIES OF THE FIRST-TIMERS ARE BARELY AT THE PASSING LEVEL.
WHICH MEANS THAT I HAVE TO PUT EVERYTHING I GOT...
...INTO THE FIRST EXAM THAT'S COMING UP...!
GLANCE
...
THERE'S NO POINT IN MAKING RIVALS OUT OF EXAM-TAKERS WHO HAVEN'T EVEN PASSED.
THAT SAID, REAL ARTISTS AREN'T ANYWHERE NEARBY...
IN THAT CASE...

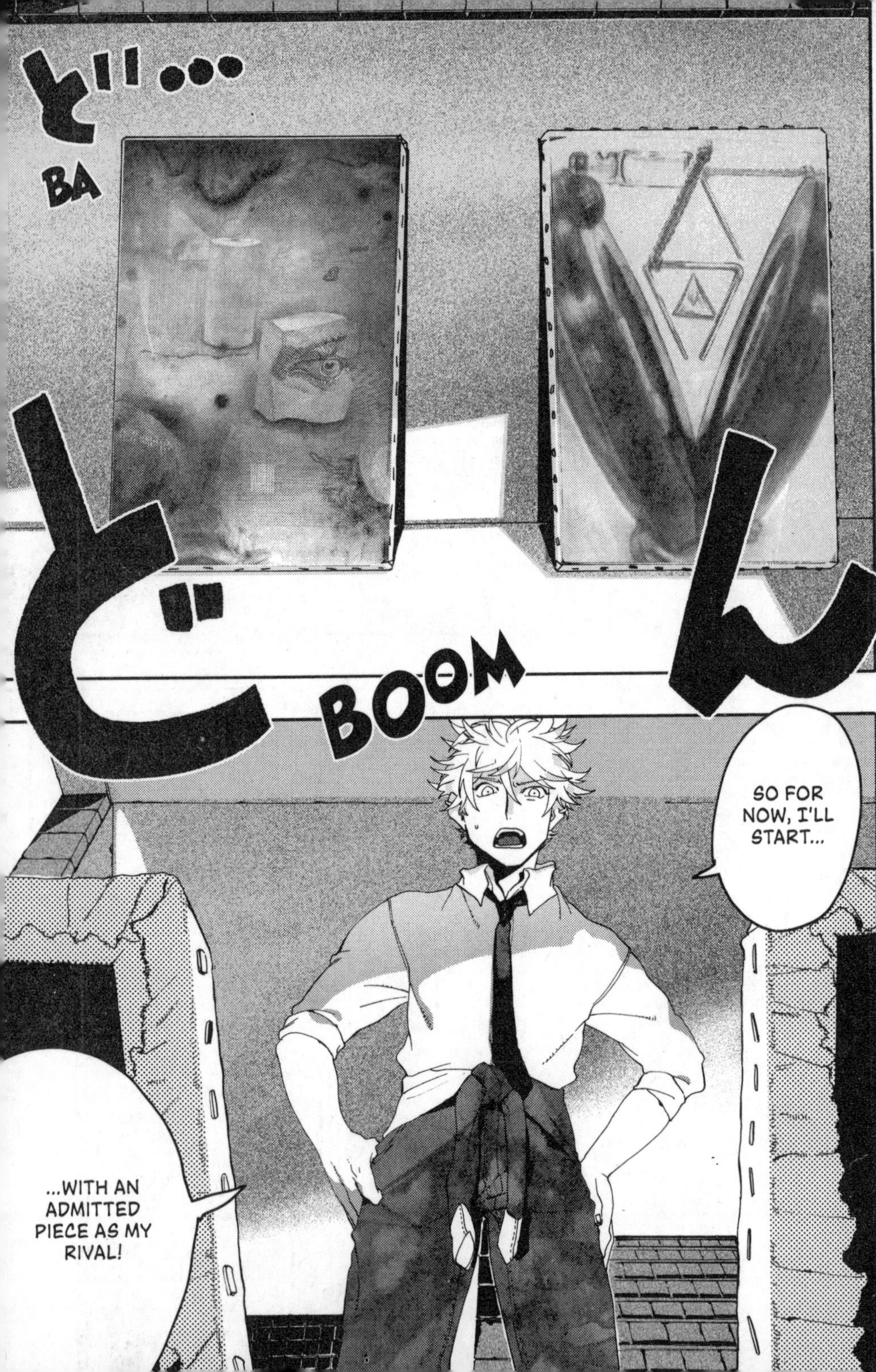

ど…
BA
どん
BOOM
SO FOR NOW, I'LL START...
...WITH AN ADMITTED PIECE AS MY RIVAL!

ART: (L) MATSUBA YACHIGUSA, (R) SHOTA YAMAMICHI

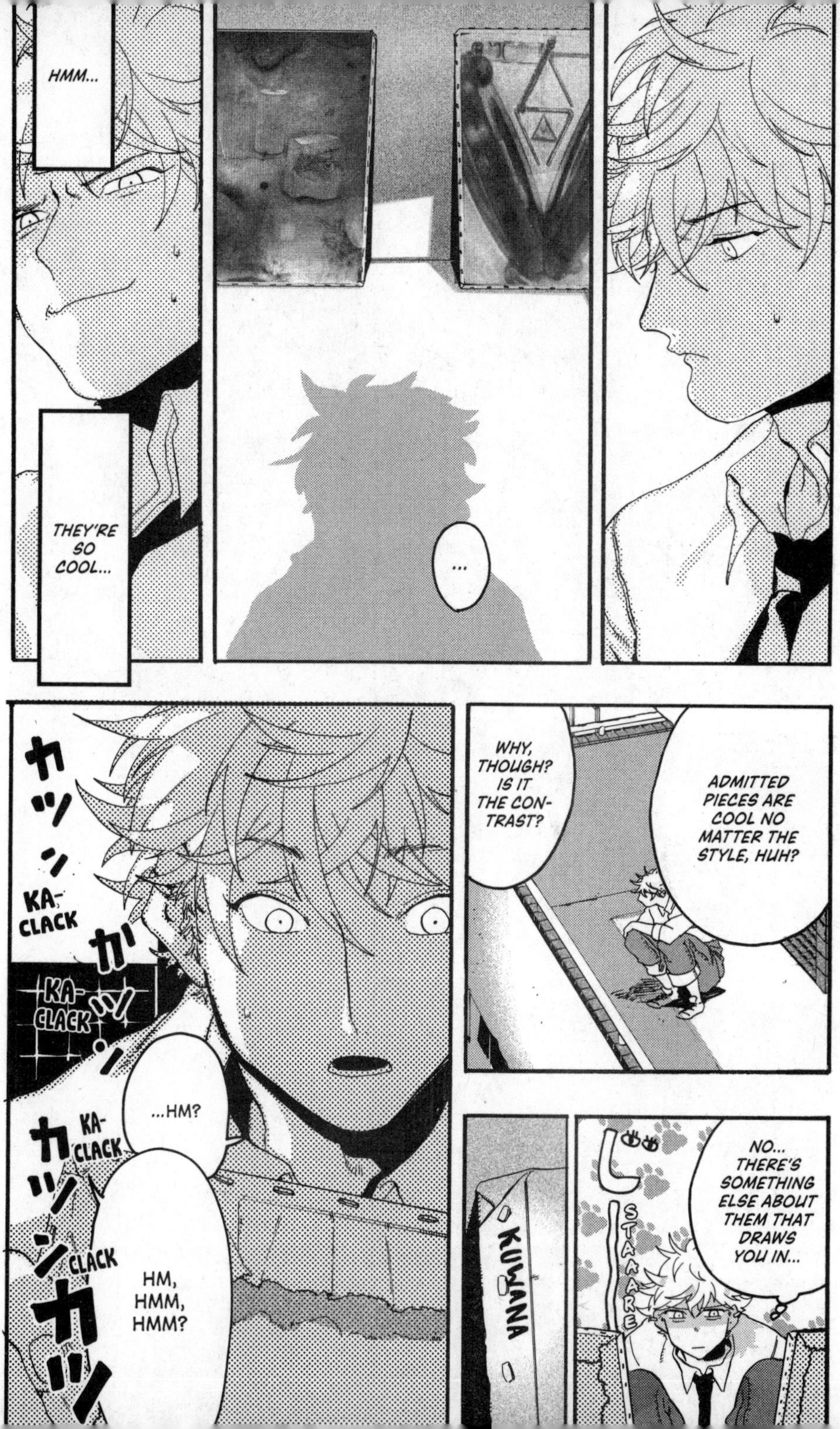
...
HMM...
THEY'RE SO COOL...
ADMITTED PIECES ARE COOL NO MATTER THE STYLE, HUH?
WHY, THOUGH? IS IT THE CON-TRAST?
NO... THERE'S SOMETHING ELSE ABOUT THEM THAT DRAWS YOU IN...
STAARE
KUWANA
KA-CLACK
KA-CLACK
...HM?
KA-CLACK
CLACK
HM, HMM, HMM?

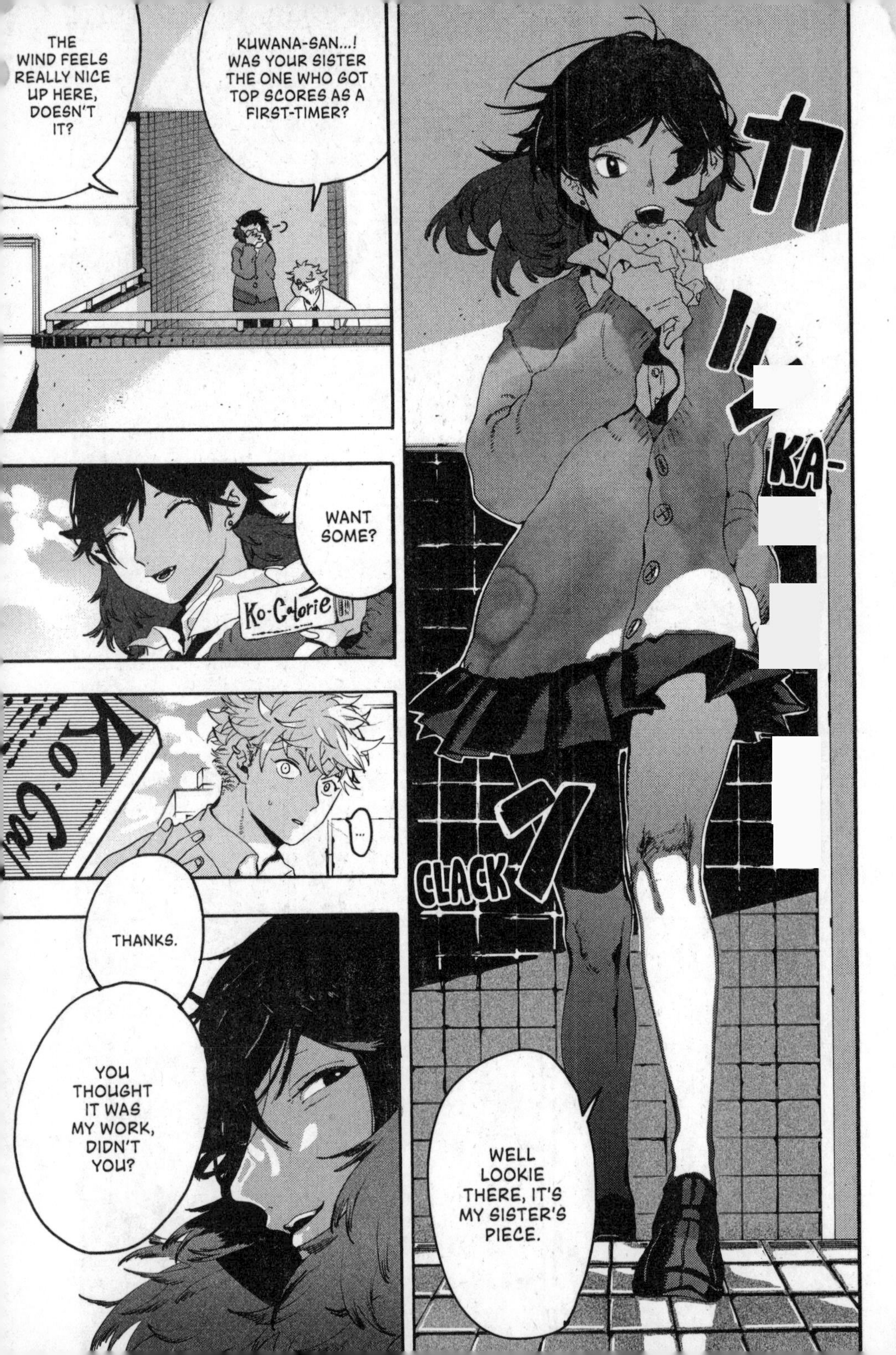
カ
KA-
CLACK
WELL LOOKIE THERE, IT'S MY SISTER'S PIECE.
KUWANA-SAN...! WAS YOUR SISTER THE ONE WHO GOT TOP SCORES AS A FIRST-TIMER?
THE WIND FEELS REALLY NICE UP HERE, DOESN'T IT?
WANT SOME?
Ko-Calorie
...
THANKS.
YOU THOUGHT IT WAS MY WORK, DIDN'T YOU?

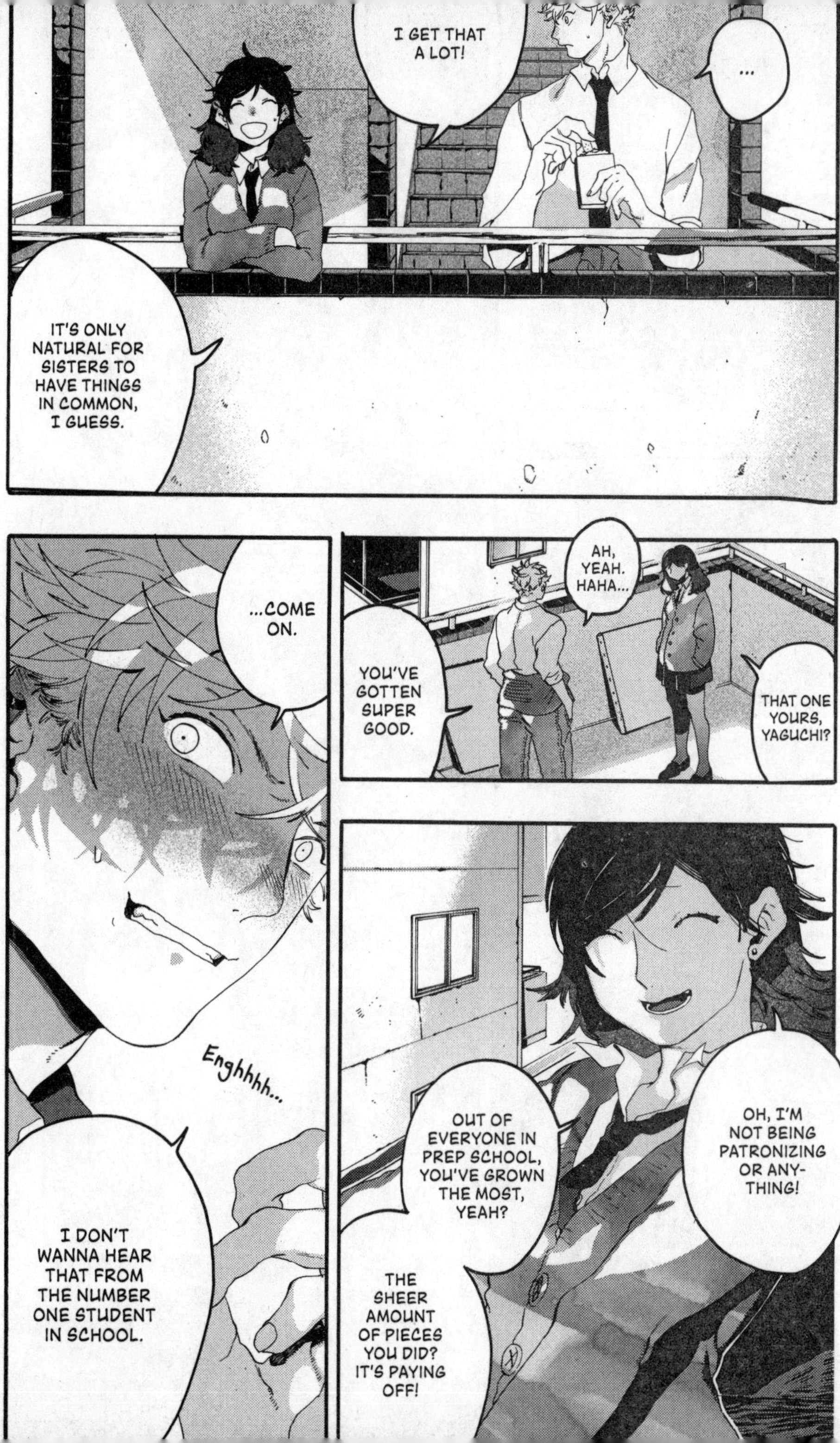
I GET THAT A LOT!
...
IT'S ONLY NATURAL FOR SISTERS TO HAVE THINGS IN COMMON, I GUESS.
THAT ONE YOURS, YAGUCHI?
AH, YEAH. HAHA...
YOU'VE GOTTEN SUPER GOOD.
OH, I'M NOT BEING PATRONIZING OR ANY-THING!
OUT OF EVERYONE IN PREP SCHOOL, YOU'VE GROWN THE MOST, YEAH?
THE SHEER AMOUNT OF PIECES YOU DID? IT'S PAYING OFF!
...COME ON.
Enghhhh...
I DON'T WANNA HEAR THAT FROM THE NUMBER ONE STUDENT IN SCHOOL.

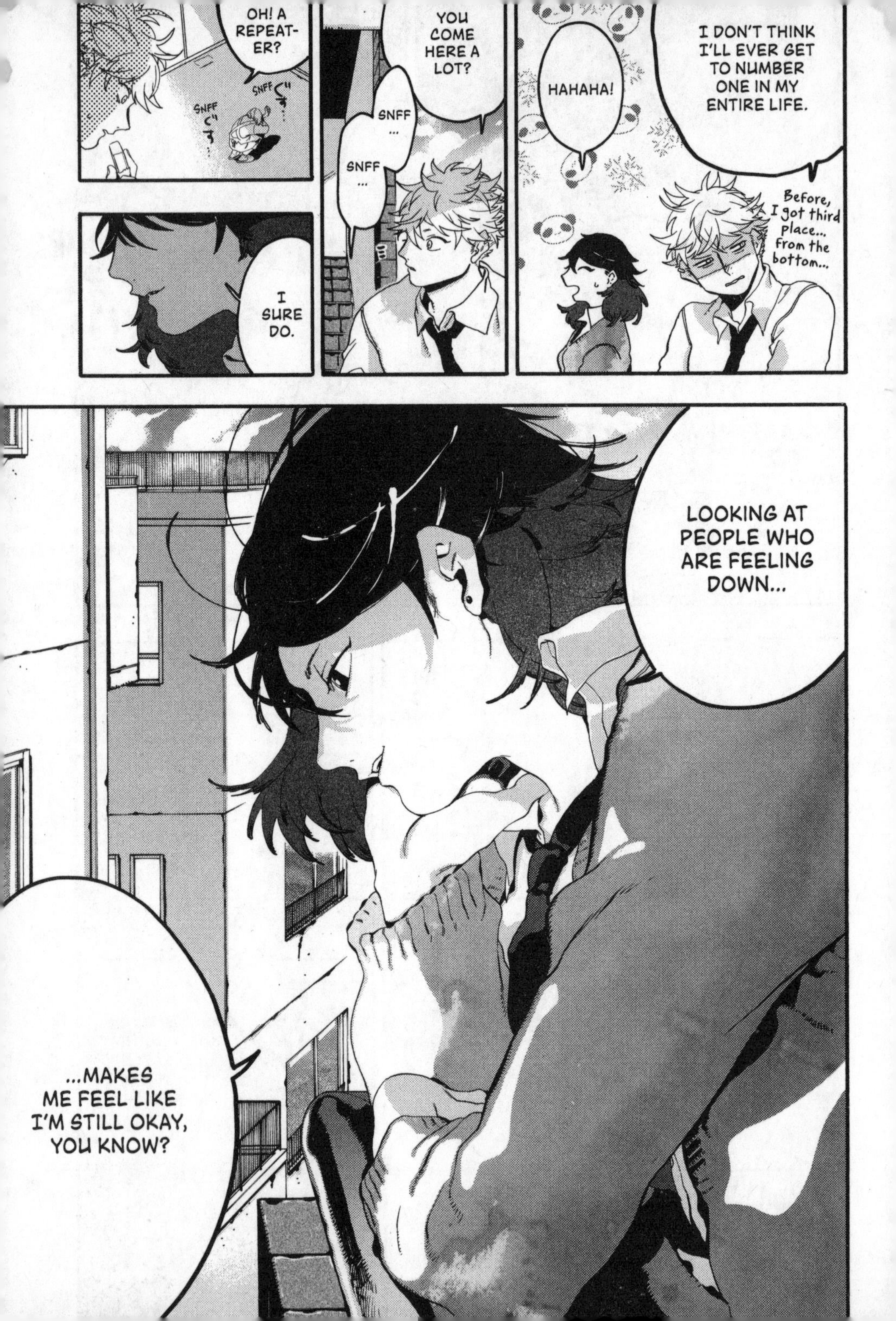
I DON'T THINK I'LL EVER GET TO NUMBER ONE IN MY ENTIRE LIFE.
HAHAHA!
Before, I got third place... from the bottom...
YOU COME HERE A LOT?
SNFF ...
SNFF ...
OH! A REPEATER?
SNFF
SNFF
I SURE DO.
LOOKING AT PEOPLE WHO ARE FEELING DOWN...
...MAKES ME FEEL LIKE I'M STILL OKAY, YOU KNOW?

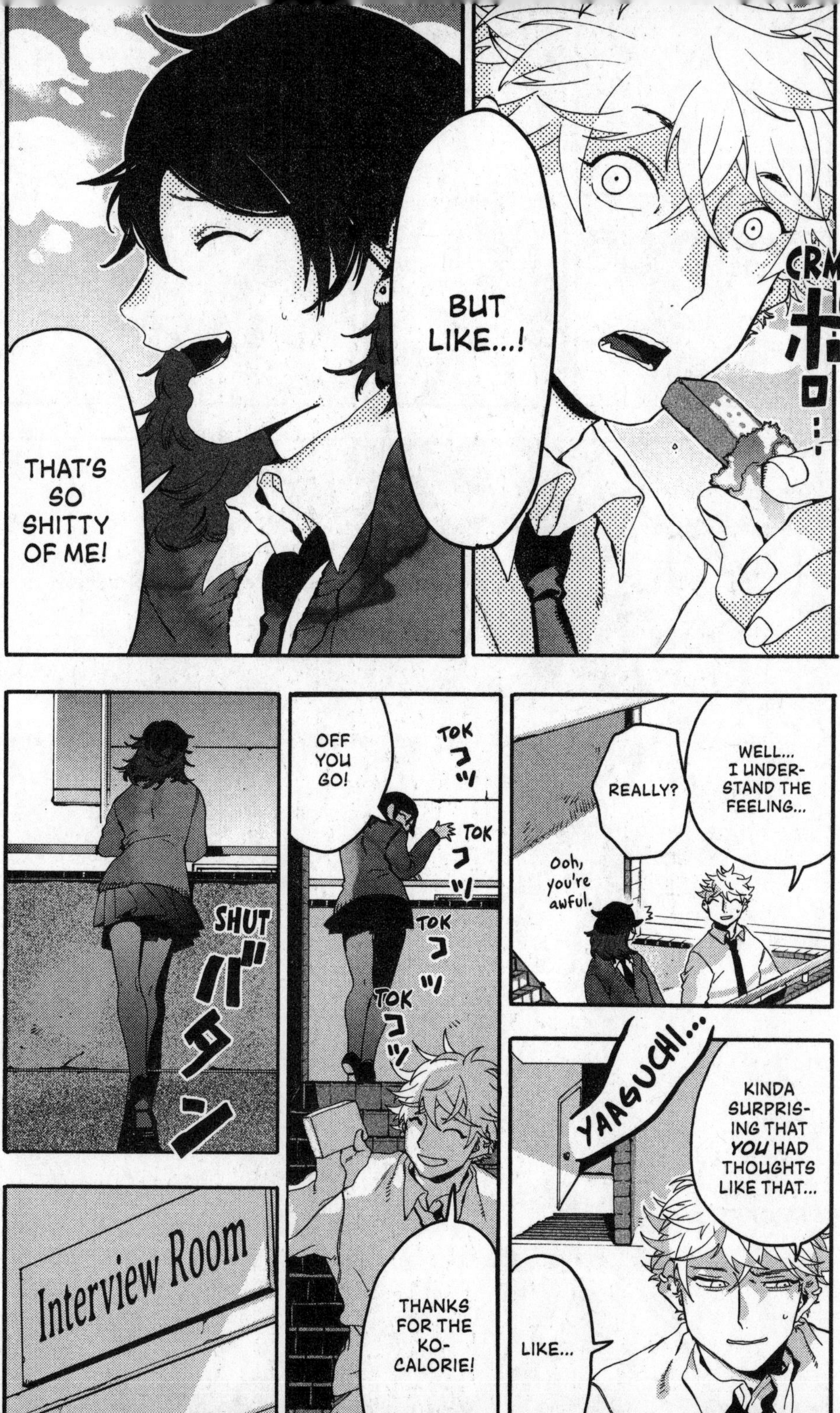
CRMBL
ポロ…
BUT LIKE...!
THAT'S SO SHITTY OF ME!
WELL... I UNDER-STAND THE FEELING...
REALLY?
Ooh, you're awful.
YAAGUCHI...
KINDA SURPRIS-ING THAT *YOU* HAD THOUGHTS LIKE THAT...
LIKE...
OFF YOU GO!
TOK
コッ
TOK
コッ
TOK
コッ
TOK
コッ
THANKS FOR THE KO-CALORIE!
SHUT
バタン
Interview Room

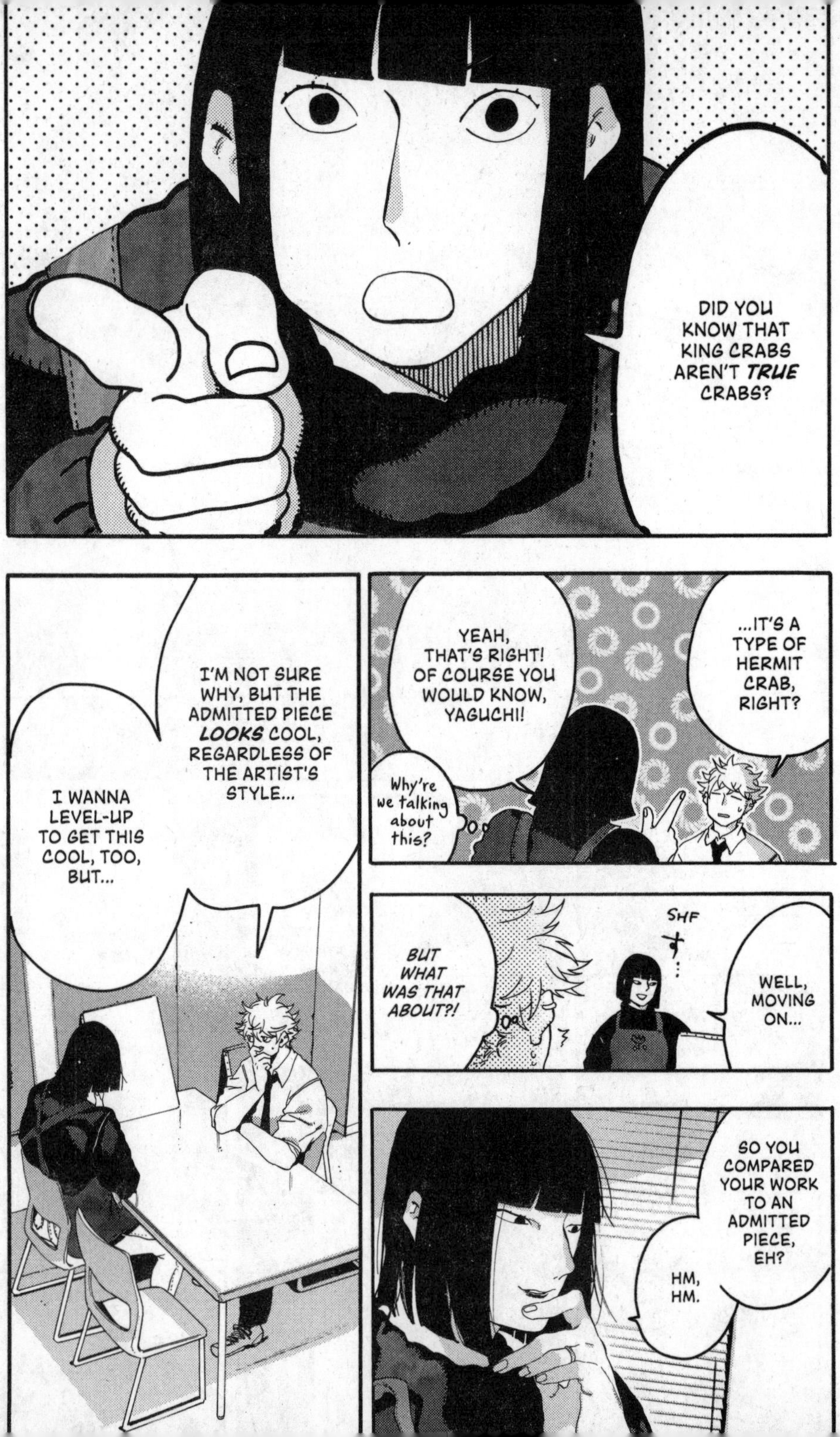
DID YOU KNOW THAT KING CRABS AREN'T *TRUE* CRABS?
...IT'S A TYPE OF HERMIT CRAB, RIGHT?
YEAH, THAT'S RIGHT! OF COURSE YOU WOULD KNOW, YAGUCHI!
Why're we talking about this?
SHF
WELL, MOVING ON...
BUT WHAT WAS THAT ABOUT?!
SO YOU COMPARED YOUR WORK TO AN ADMITTED PIECE, EH?
HM, HM.
I'M NOT SURE WHY, BUT THE ADMITTED PIECE *LOOKS* COOL, REGARDLESS OF THE ARTIST'S STYLE...
I WANNA LEVEL-UP TO GET THIS COOL, TOO, BUT...

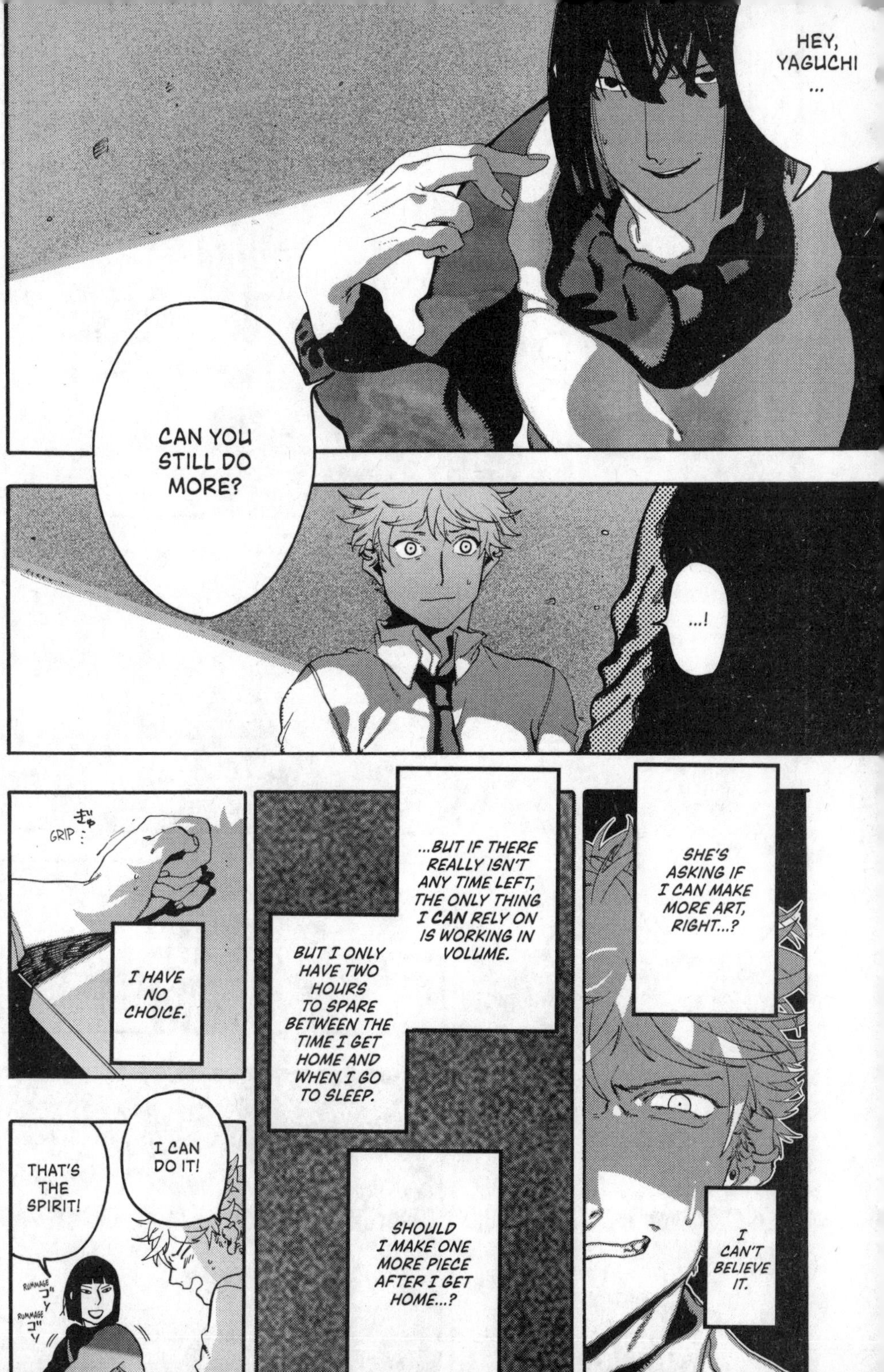
HEY, YAGUCHI ...
CAN YOU STILL DO MORE?
...!
SHE'S ASKING IF I CAN MAKE MORE ART, RIGHT...?
I CAN'T BELIEVE IT.
...BUT IF THERE REALLY ISN'T ANY TIME LEFT, THE ONLY THING I CAN RELY ON IS WORKING IN VOLUME.
BUT I ONLY HAVE TWO HOURS TO SPARE BETWEEN THE TIME I GET HOME AND WHEN I GO TO SLEEP.
SHOULD I MAKE ONE MORE PIECE AFTER I GET HOME...?
ぎゅ
GRIP
I HAVE NO CHOICE.
I CAN DO IT!
THAT'S THE SPIRIT!
ゴソ
RUMMAGE
ゴソ
RUMMAGE

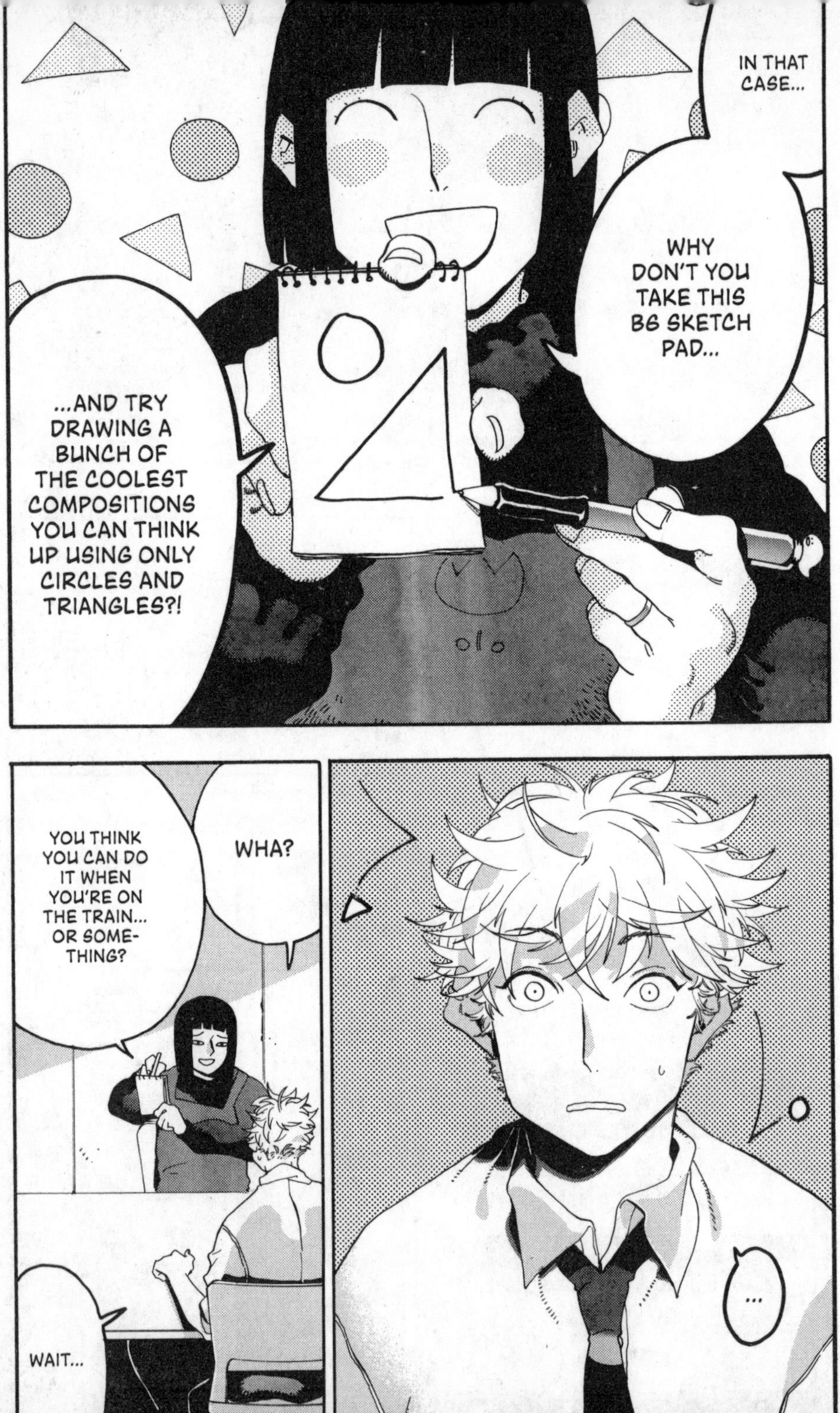
IN THAT CASE...
WHY DON'T YOU TAKE THIS B6 SKETCH PAD...
...AND TRY DRAWING A BUNCH OF THE COOLEST COMPOSITIONS YOU CAN THINK UP USING ONLY CIRCLES AND TRIANGLES?!
...
WHA?
YOU THINK YOU CAN DO IT WHEN YOU'RE ON THE TRAIN... OR SOME-THING?
WAIT...

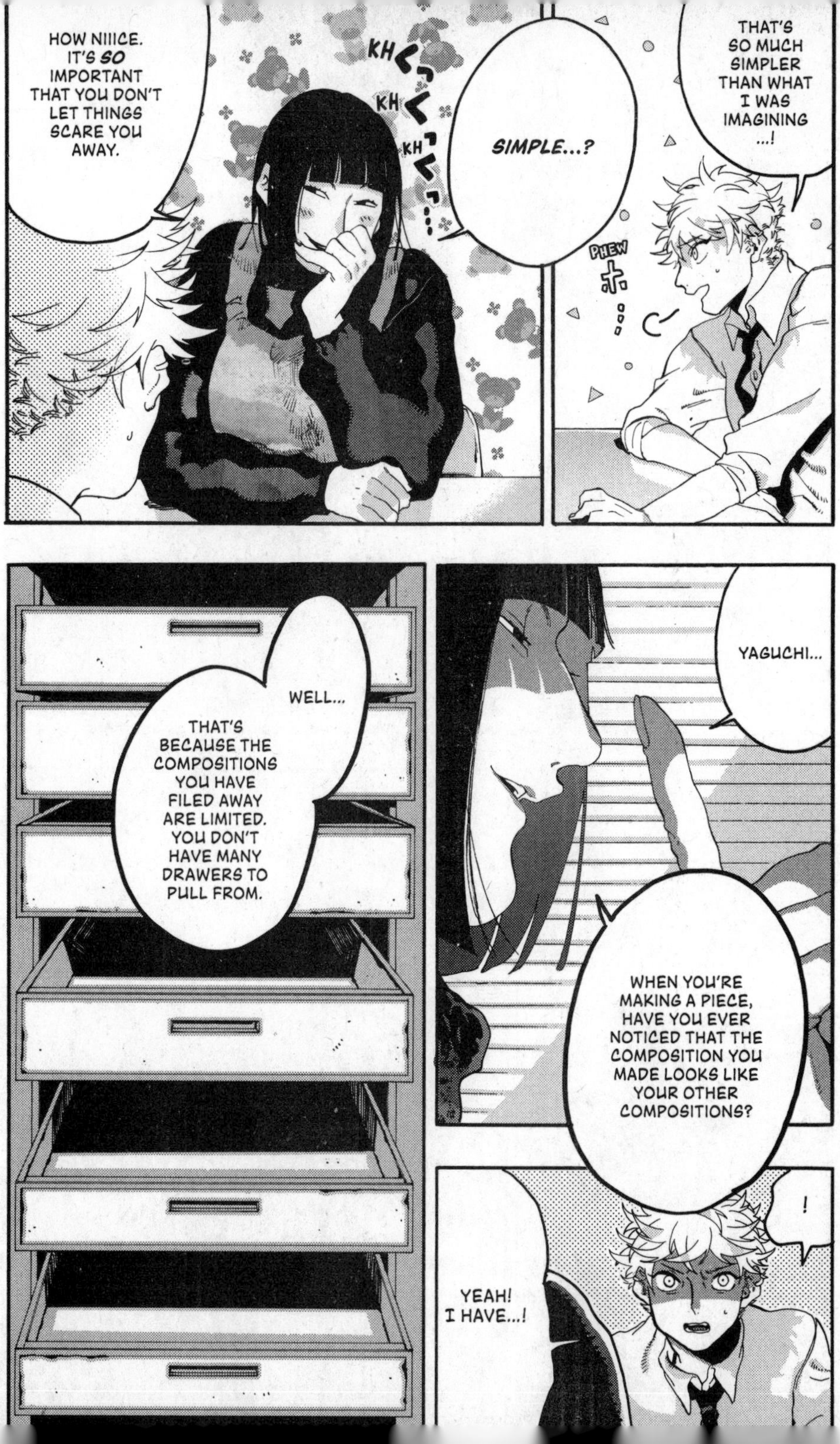
THAT'S SO MUCH SIMPLER THAN WHAT I WAS IMAGINING ...!
PHEW
SIMPLE...?
KH KH KH
HOW NIIICE. IT'S *SO* IMPORTANT THAT YOU DON'T LET THINGS SCARE YOU AWAY.
YAGUCHI...
WHEN YOU'RE MAKING A PIECE, HAVE YOU EVER NOTICED THAT THE COMPOSITION YOU MADE LOOKS LIKE YOUR OTHER COMPOSITIONS?
!
YEAH! I HAVE...!
WELL...
THAT'S BECAUSE THE COMPOSITIONS YOU HAVE FILED AWAY ARE LIMITED. YOU DON'T HAVE MANY DRAWERS TO PULL FROM.

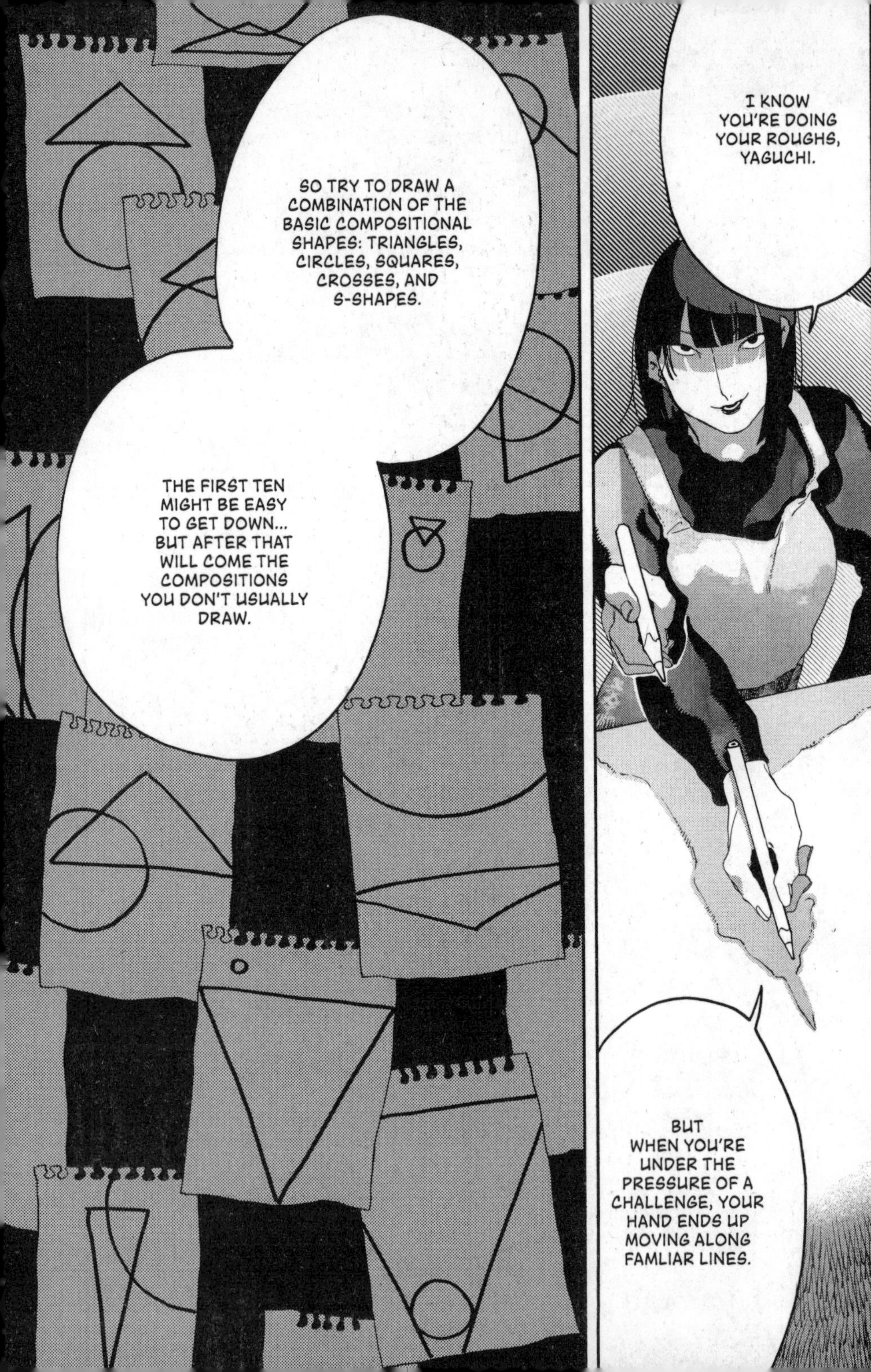
I KNOW YOU'RE DOING YOUR ROUGHS, YAGUCHI.
BUT WHEN YOU'RE UNDER THE PRESSURE OF A CHALLENGE, YOUR HAND ENDS UP MOVING ALONG FAMLIAR LINES.
SO TRY TO DRAW A COMBINATION OF THE BASIC COMPOSITIONAL SHAPES: TRIANGLES, CIRCLES, SQUARES, CROSSES, AND S-SHAPES.
THE FIRST TEN MIGHT BE EASY TO GET DOWN... BUT AFTER THAT WILL COME THE COMPOSITIONS YOU DON'T USUALLY DRAW.

*A ROUGH DRAWING OR PAINTING THAT IS MADE BEFORE MOVING ONTO A FULL PIECE.

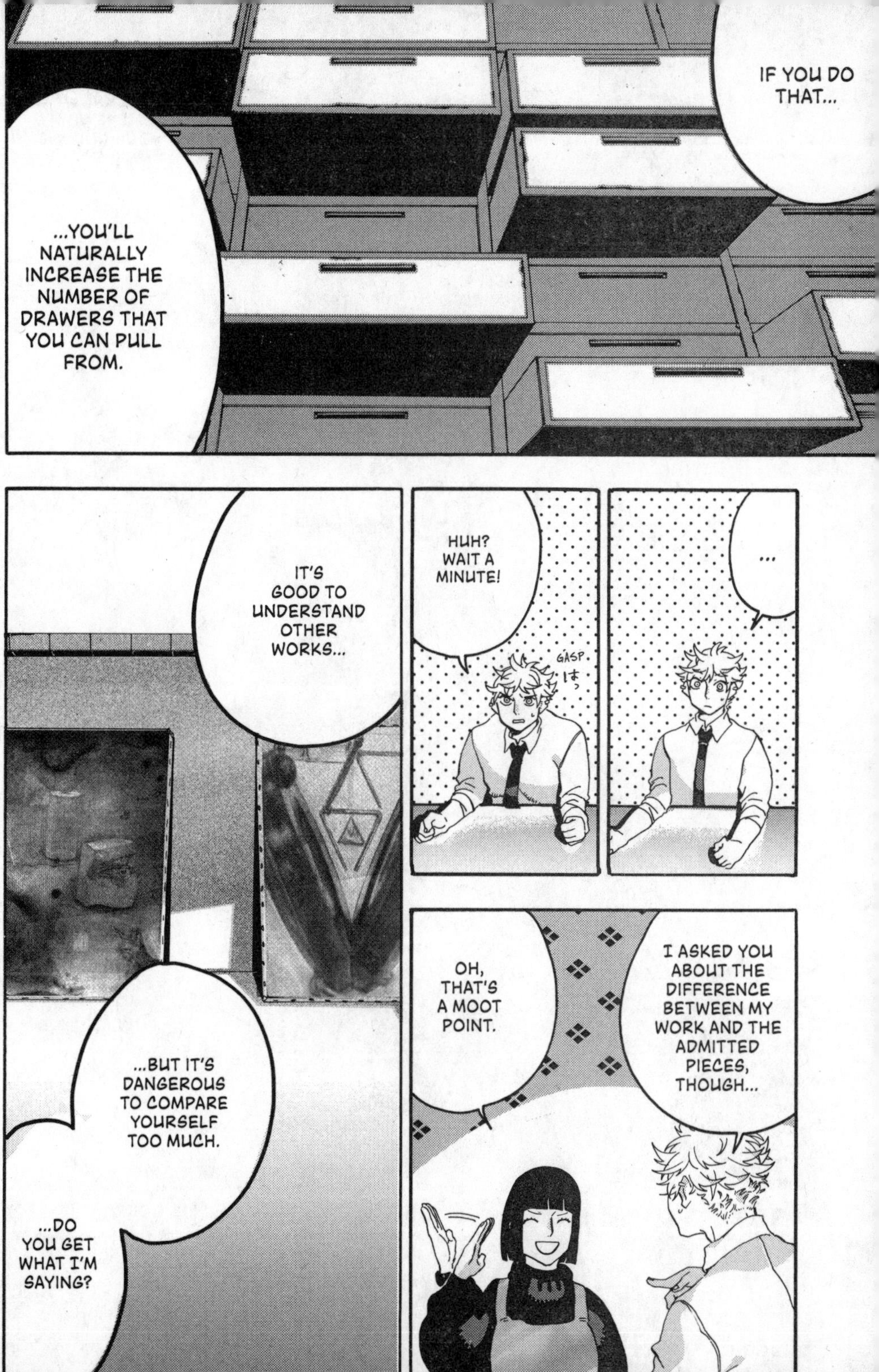
IF YOU DO THAT...
...YOU'LL NATURALLY INCREASE THE NUMBER OF DRAWERS THAT YOU CAN PULL FROM.
...
HUH? WAIT A MINUTE!
GASP
は
I ASKED YOU ABOUT THE DIFFERENCE BETWEEN MY WORK AND THE ADMITTED PIECES, THOUGH...
OH, THAT'S A MOOT POINT.
IT'S GOOD TO UNDERSTAND OTHER WORKS...
...BUT IT'S DANGEROUS TO COMPARE YOURSELF TOO MUCH.
...DO YOU GET WHAT I'M SAYING?

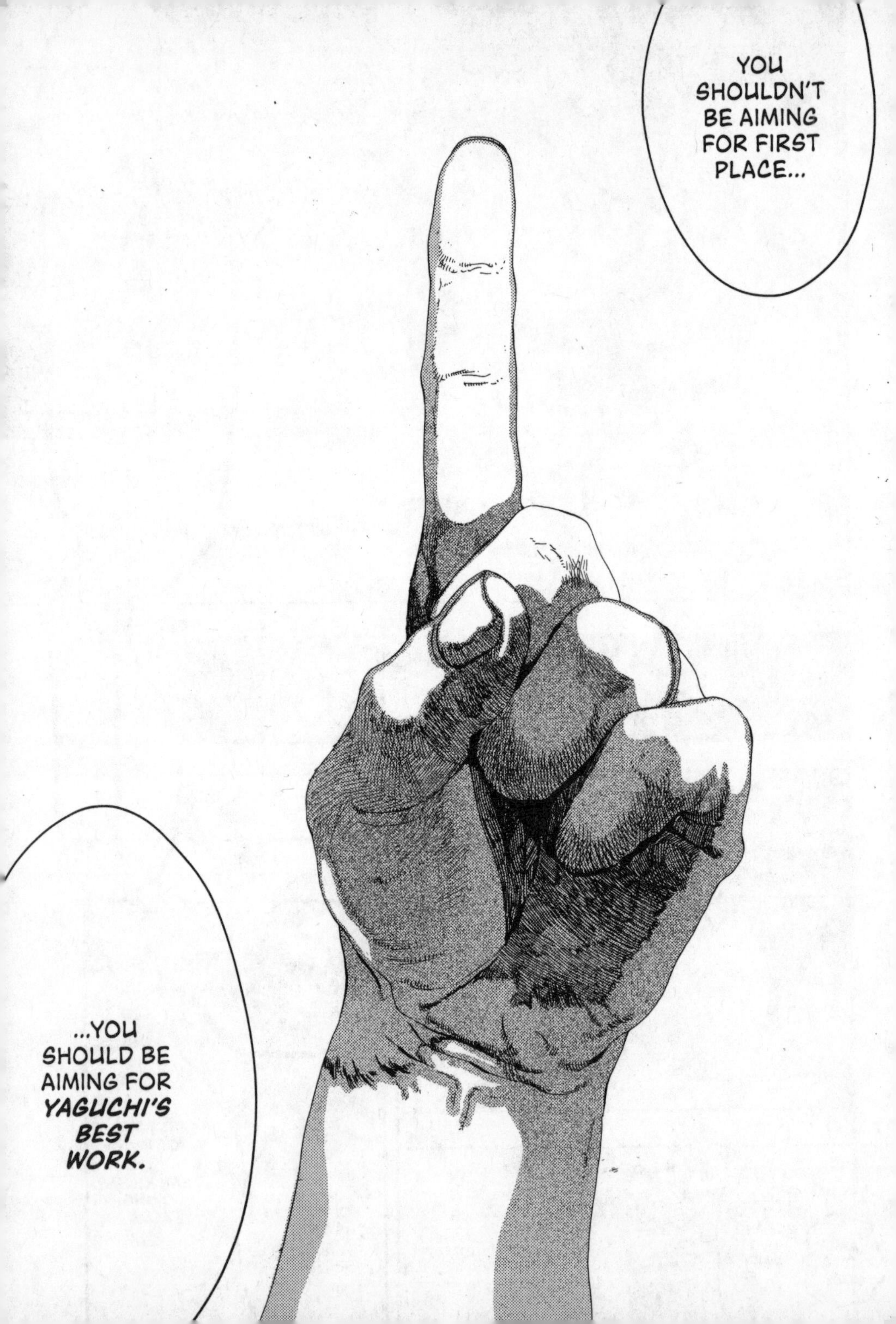
YOU SHOULDN'T BE AIMING FOR FIRST PLACE...
...YOU SHOULD BE AIMING FOR *YAGUCHI'S BEST WORK.*

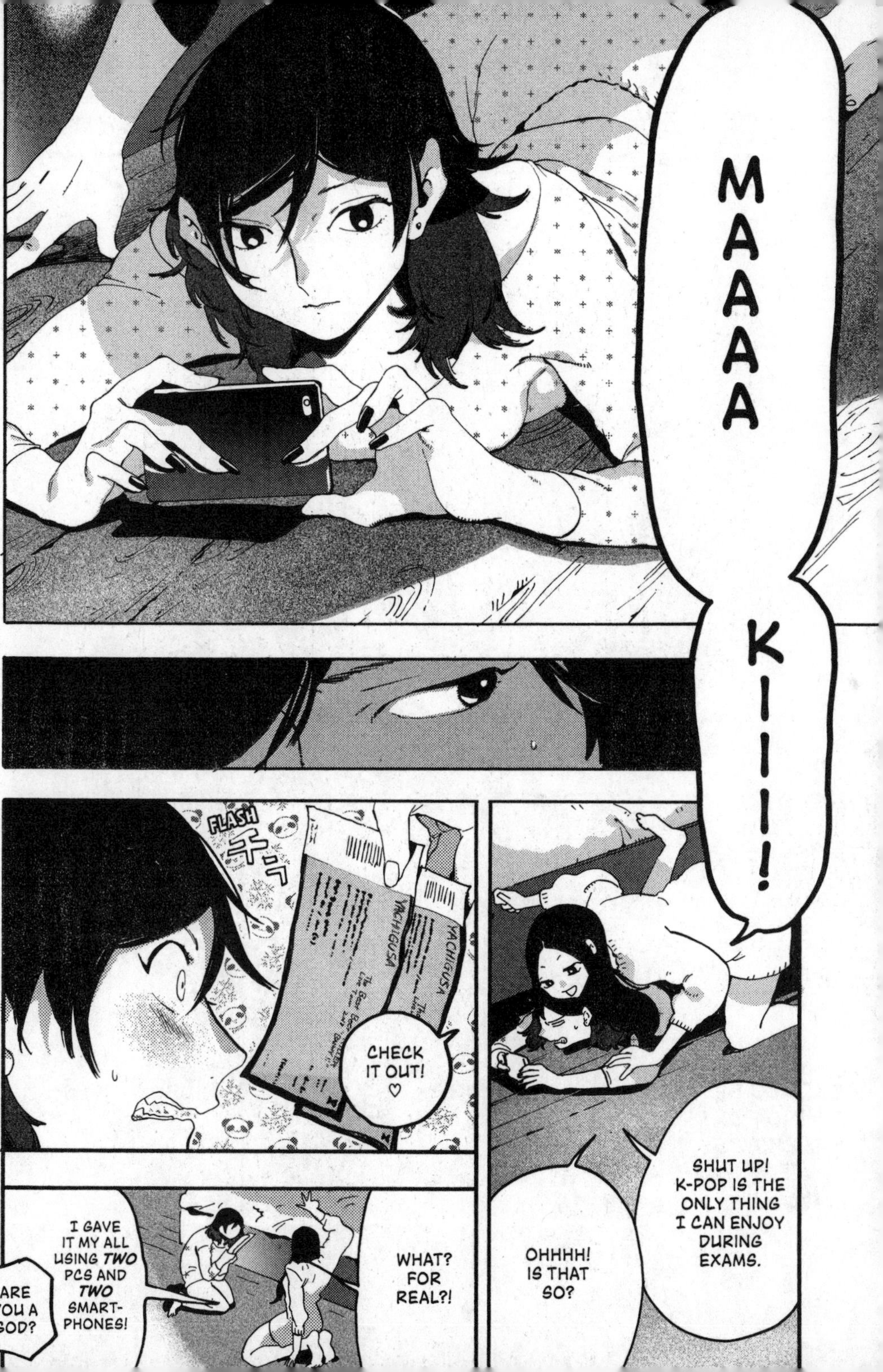

MAAAA KIIII!
FLASH
チッ
YACHIGUSA
YACHIGUSA
CHECK IT OUT! ♡
SHUT UP! K-POP IS THE ONLY THING I CAN ENJOY DURING EXAMS.
OHHHH! IS THAT SO?
WHAT? FOR REAL?!
I GAVE IT MY ALL USING *TWO* PCS AND *TWO* SMART-PHONES!
ARE YOU A GOD?

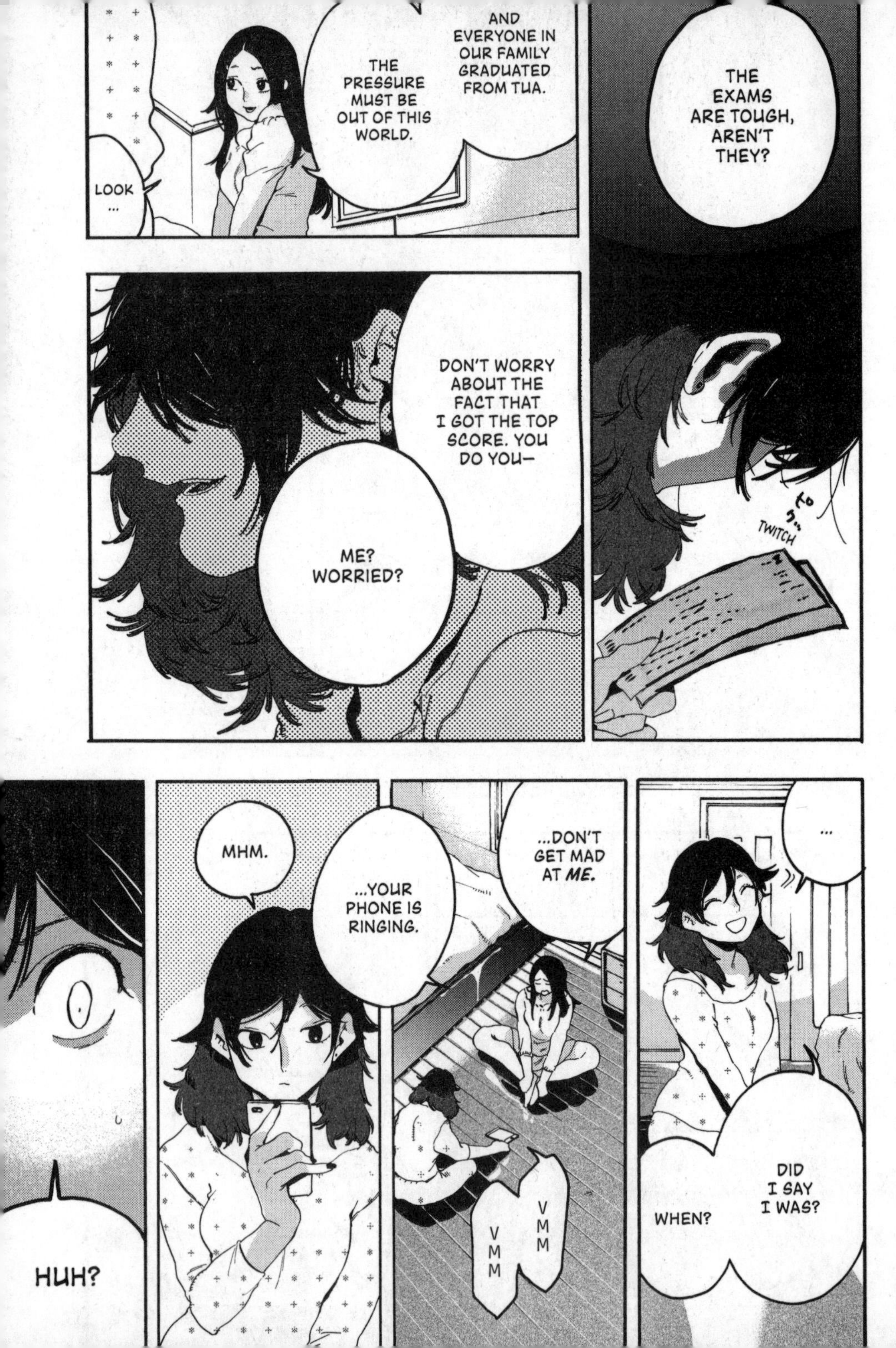
THE EXAMS ARE TOUGH, AREN'T THEY?
AND EVERYONE IN OUR FAMILY GRADUATED FROM TUA.
THE PRESSURE MUST BE OUT OF THIS WORLD.
LOOK ...
TWITCH
DON'T WORRY ABOUT THE FACT THAT I GOT THE TOP SCORE. YOU DO YOU—
ME? WORRIED?
...
DID I SAY I WAS?
WHEN?
...DON'T GET MAD AT *ME.*
VMM
VMM
...YOUR PHONE IS RINGING.
MHM.
HUH?

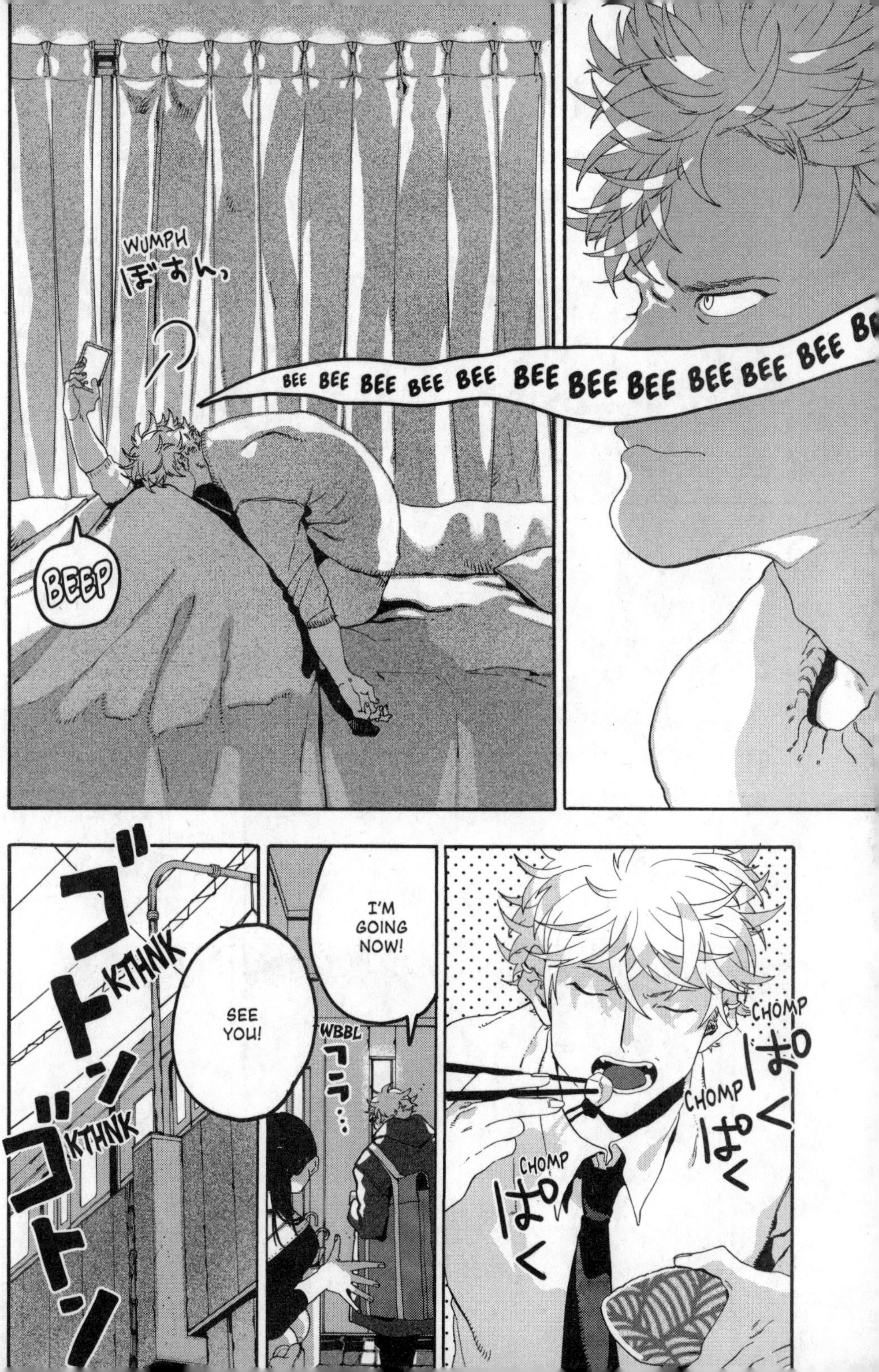
BEE BEE BEE BEE BEE BEE BEE BEE BEE BEE BEE BEE
WUMPH
ぼすん,
BEEP
CHOMP
ぱく
CHOMP
ぱく
CHOMP
ぱく
I'M GOING NOW!
SEE YOU!
WBBL
ゴトン
KTHNK
ゴトン
KTHNK

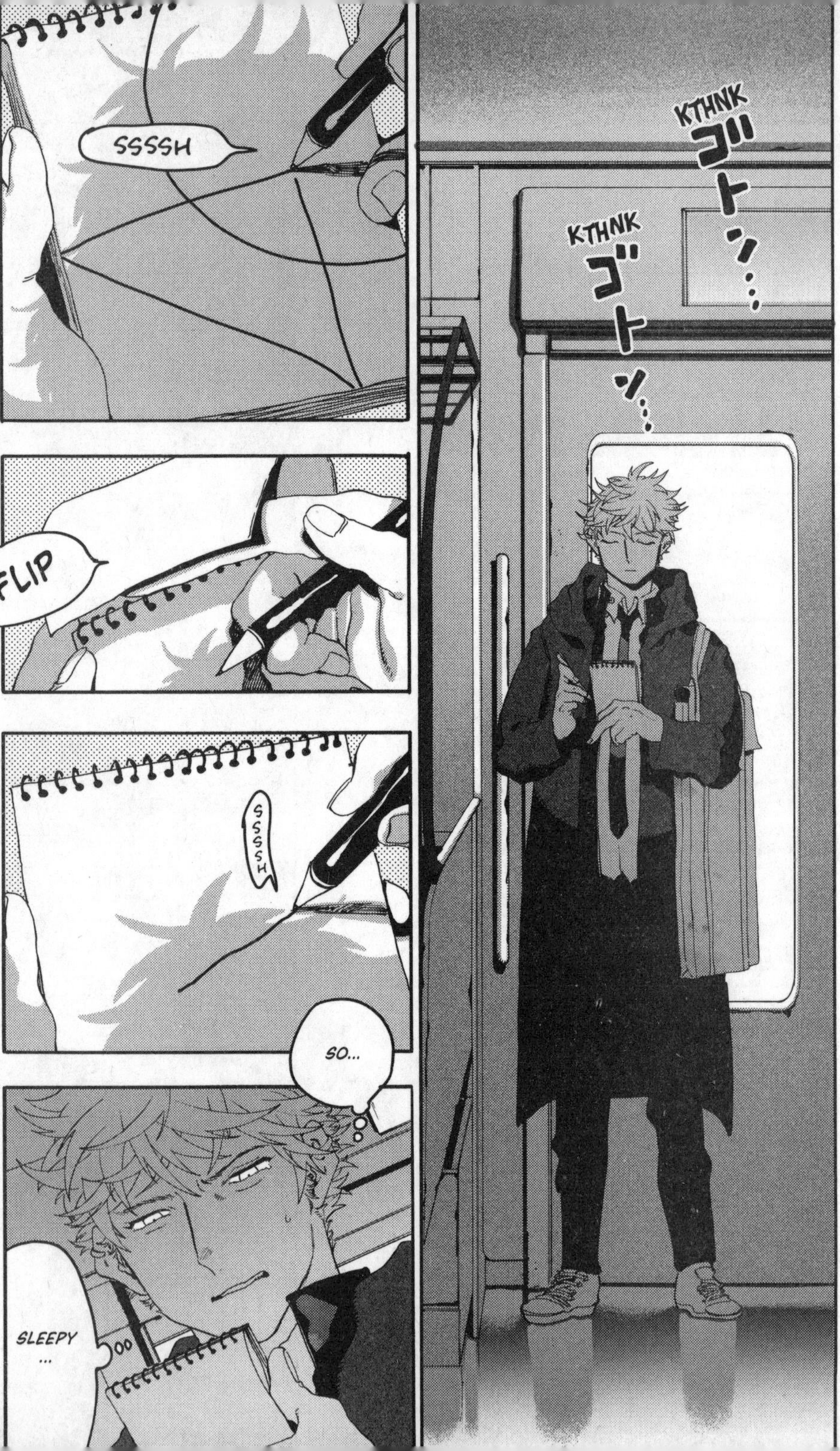
KTHNK
ゴトン…
KTHNK
ゴトン…
SSSSH
FLIP
SSSSH
SO...
SLEEPY
...

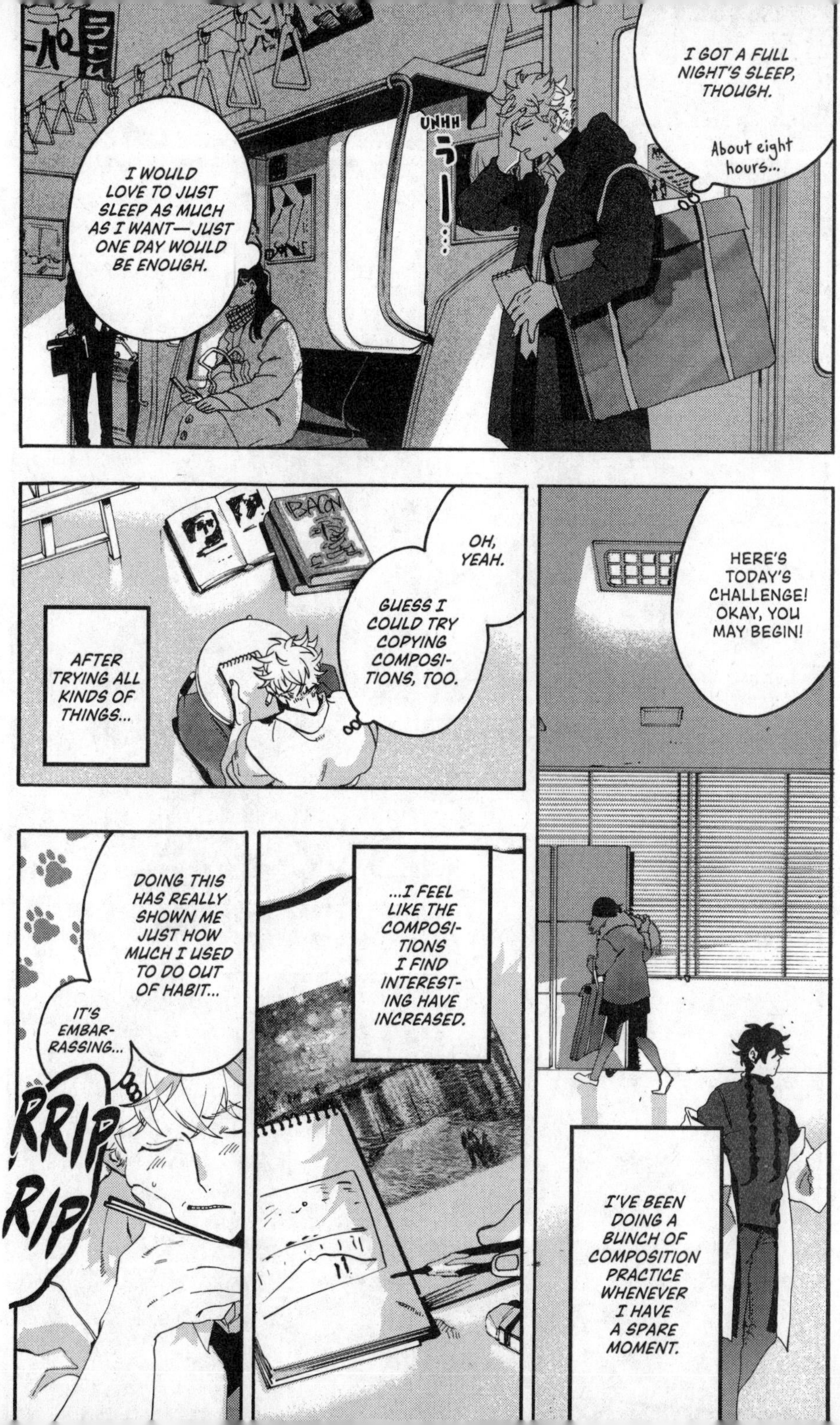
I GOT A FULL NIGHT'S SLEEP, THOUGH.
About eight hours...
UNHH
I WOULD LOVE TO JUST SLEEP AS MUCH AS I WANT—JUST ONE DAY WOULD BE ENOUGH.
HERE'S TODAY'S CHALLENGE! OKAY, YOU MAY BEGIN!
I'VE BEEN DOING A BUNCH OF COMPOSITION PRACTICE WHENEVER I HAVE A SPARE MOMENT.
OH, YEAH.
GUESS I COULD TRY COPYING COMPOSITIONS, TOO.
AFTER TRYING ALL KINDS OF THINGS...
...I FEEL LIKE THE COMPOSITIONS I FIND INTERESTING HAVE INCREASED.
DOING THIS HAS REALLY SHOWN ME JUST HOW MUCH I USED TO DO OUT OF HABIT...
IT'S EMBARRASSING...
RRIP
RIP

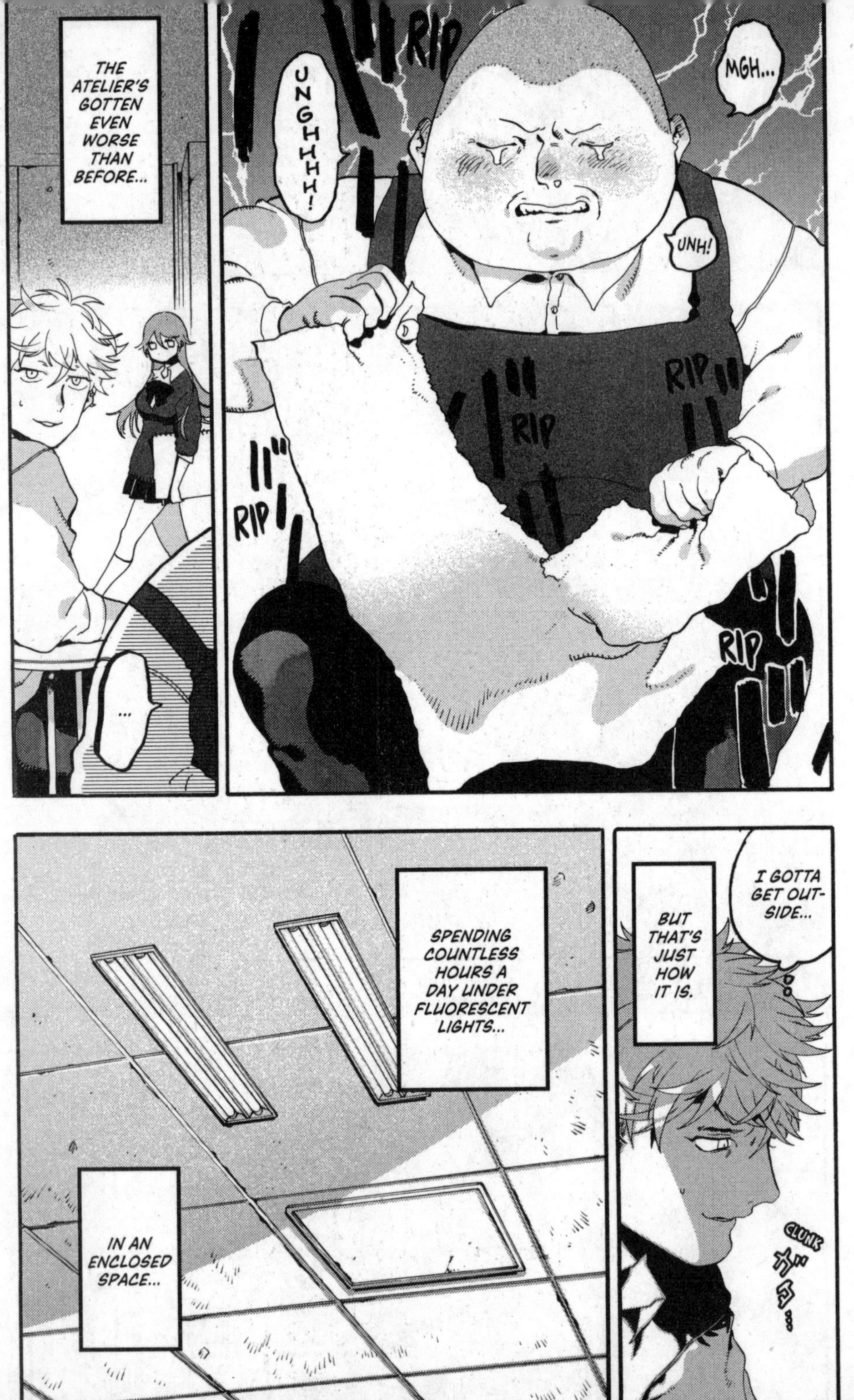
MGH...
RIP
UNGHHHH!
UNH!
RIP
RIP
RIP
RIP
THE ATELIER'S GOTTEN EVEN WORSE THAN BEFORE...
...
I GOTTA GET OUT-SIDE...
BUT THAT'S JUST HOW IT IS.
CLUNK
SPENDING COUNTLESS HOURS A DAY UNDER FLUORESCENT LIGHTS...
IN AN ENCLOSED SPACE...

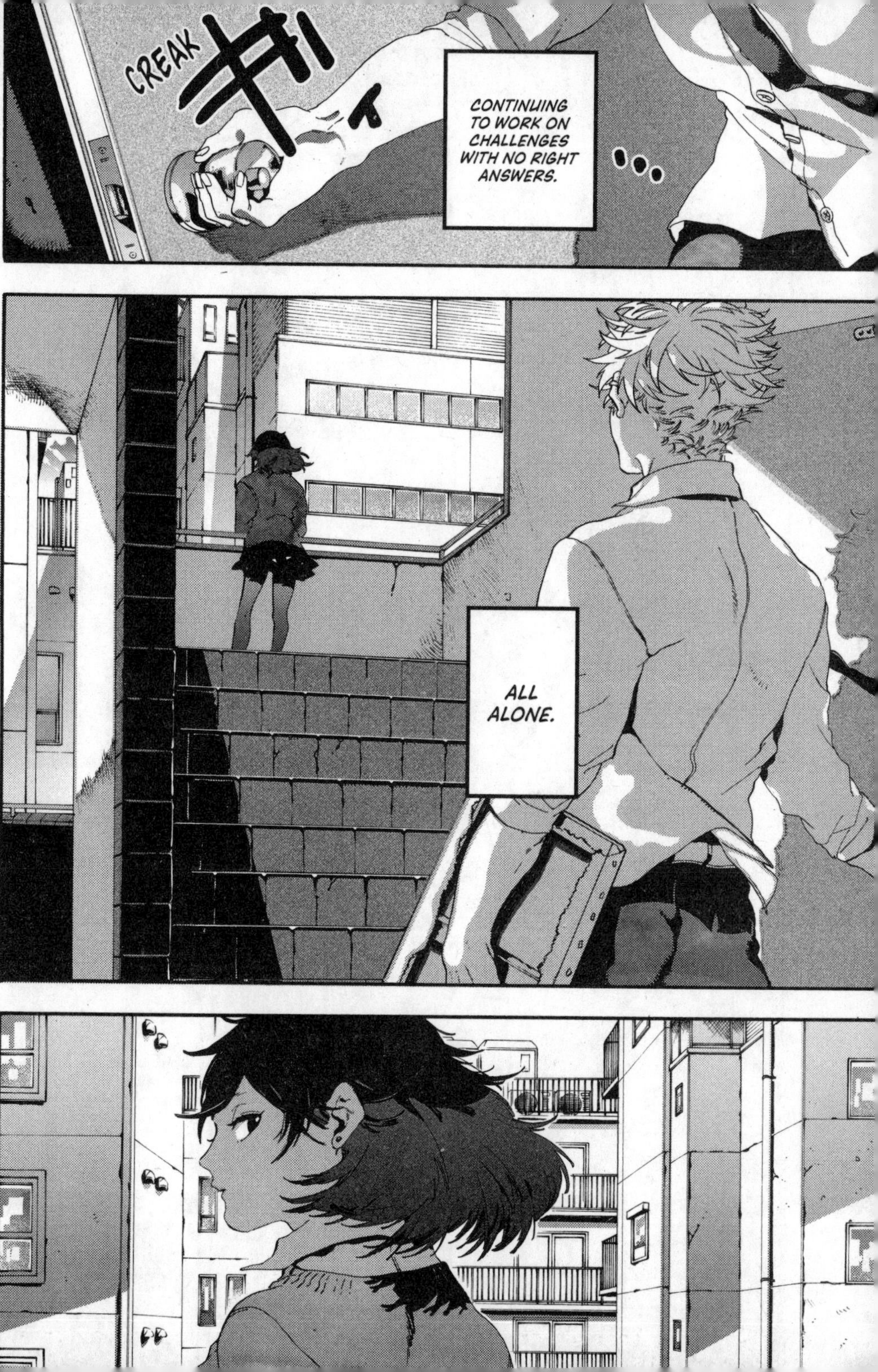
CONTINUING TO WORK ON CHALLENGES WITH NO RIGHT ANSWERS.
...
CREAK
ALL ALONE.

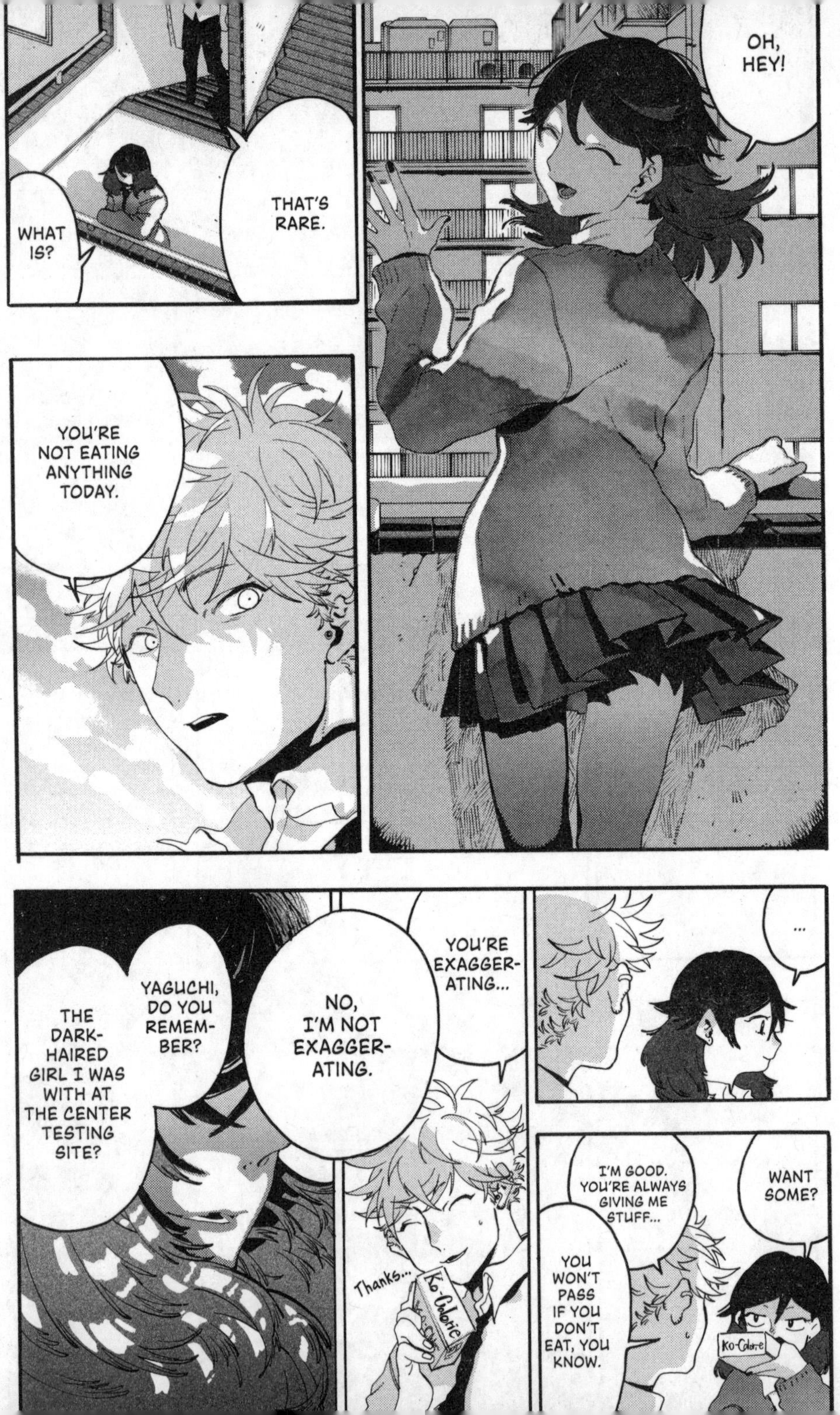
OH, HEY!
THAT'S RARE.
WHAT IS?
YOU'RE NOT EATING ANYTHING TODAY.
...
WANT SOME?
I'M GOOD. YOU'RE ALWAYS GIVING ME STUFF...
YOU WON'T PASS IF YOU DON'T EAT, YOU KNOW.
Ko-Calorie
YOU'RE EXAGGER-ATING...
NO, I'M NOT EXAGGER-ATING.
Thanks...
Ko-Calorie
YAGUCHI, DO YOU REMEM-BER?
THE DARK-HAIRED GIRL I WAS WITH AT THE CENTER TESTING SITE?

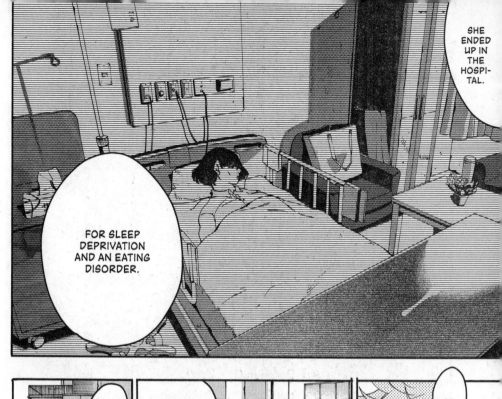

SHE ENDED UP IN THE HOSPITAL.

FOR SLEEP DEPRIVATION AND AN EATING DISORDER.

...

SHE SAID SHE CAN'T TAKE THE EXAMS THIS YEAR...

...

WHAT...?

I'M THE WORST.

I WONDER WHY...

SHE WAS WORKING SO HARD... NO, MAYBE IT'S BECAUSE SHE WAS WORKING *TOO* HARD.

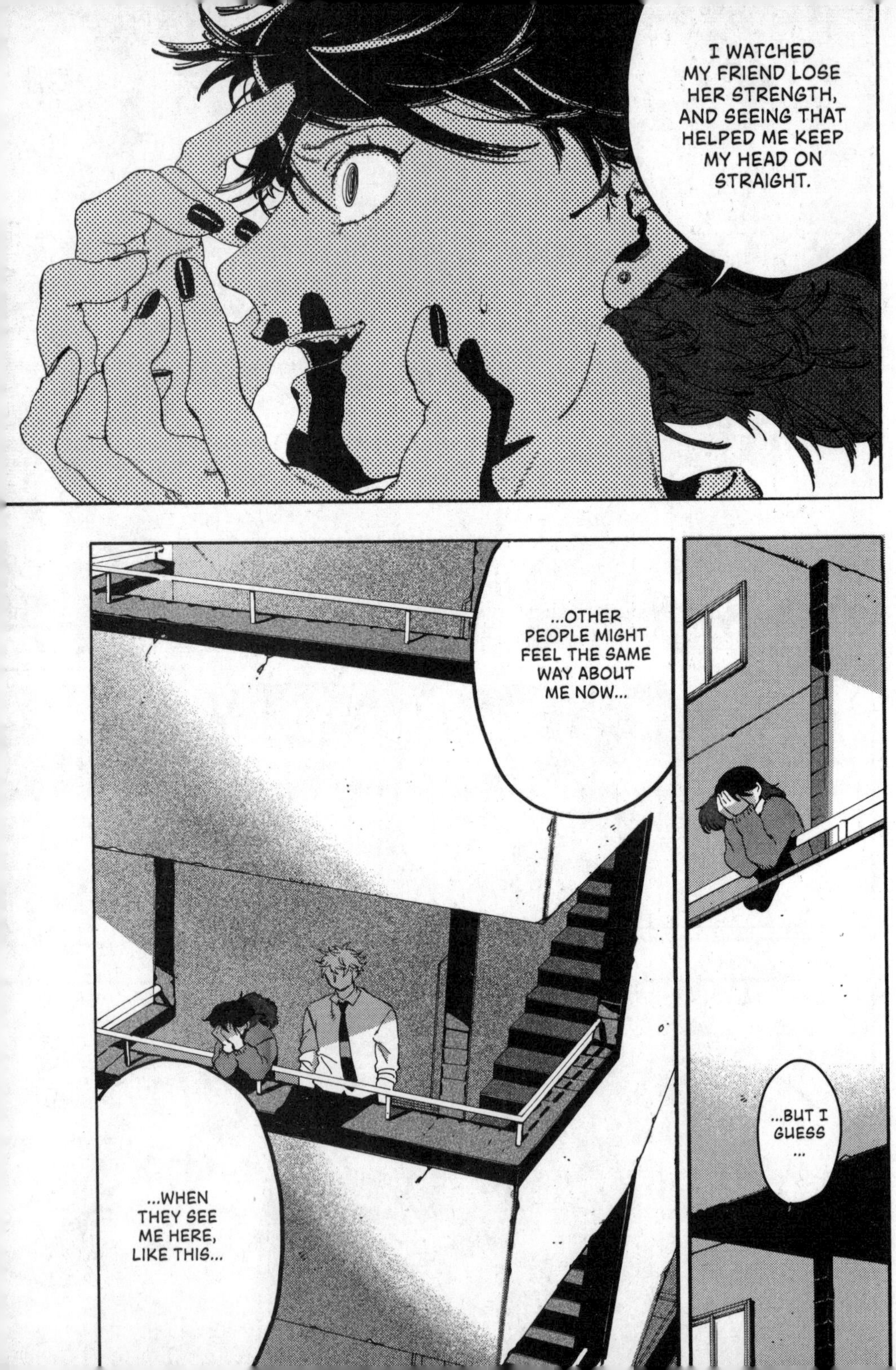
I WATCHED MY FRIEND LOSE HER STRENGTH, AND SEEING THAT HELPED ME KEEP MY HEAD ON STRAIGHT.
...BUT I GUESS ...
...OTHER PEOPLE MIGHT FEEL THE SAME WAY ABOUT ME NOW...
...WHEN THEY SEE ME HERE, LIKE THIS...

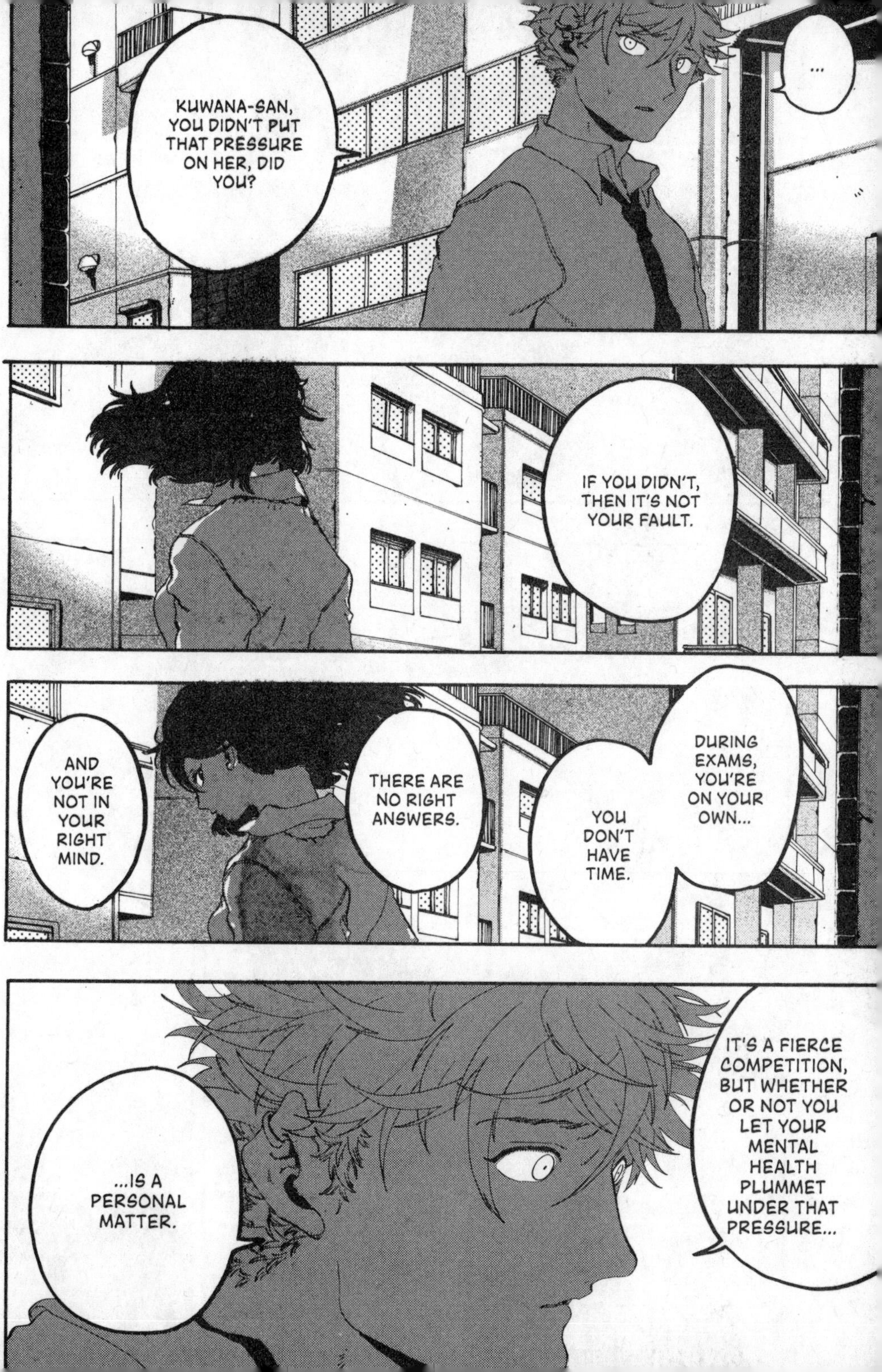
...
KUWANA-SAN, YOU DIDN'T PUT THAT PRESSURE ON HER, DID YOU?
IF YOU DIDN'T, THEN IT'S NOT YOUR FAULT.
DURING EXAMS, YOU'RE ON YOUR OWN...
YOU DON'T HAVE TIME.
THERE ARE NO RIGHT ANSWERS.
AND YOU'RE NOT IN YOUR RIGHT MIND.
IT'S A FIERCE COMPETITION, BUT WHETHER OR NOT YOU LET YOUR MENTAL HEALTH PLUMMET UNDER THAT PRESSURE...
...IS A PERSONAL MATTER.

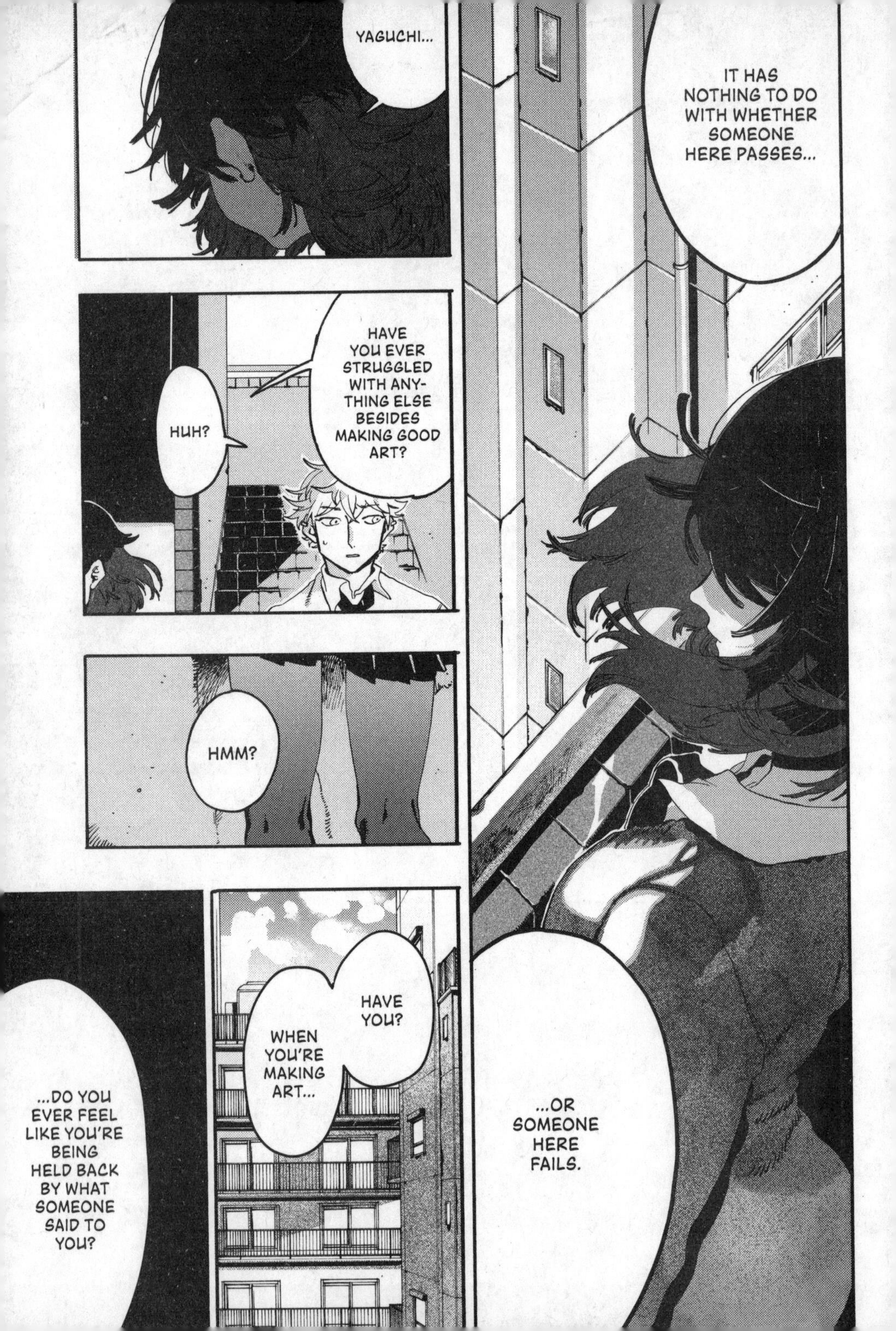
IT HAS NOTHING TO DO WITH WHETHER SOMEONE HERE PASSES...
...OR SOMEONE HERE FAILS.
YAGUCHI...
HAVE YOU EVER STRUGGLED WITH ANY-THING ELSE BESIDES MAKING GOOD ART?
HUH?
HMM?
HAVE YOU?
WHEN YOU'RE MAKING ART...
...DO YOU EVER FEEL LIKE YOU'RE BEING HELD BACK BY WHAT SOMEONE SAID TO YOU?

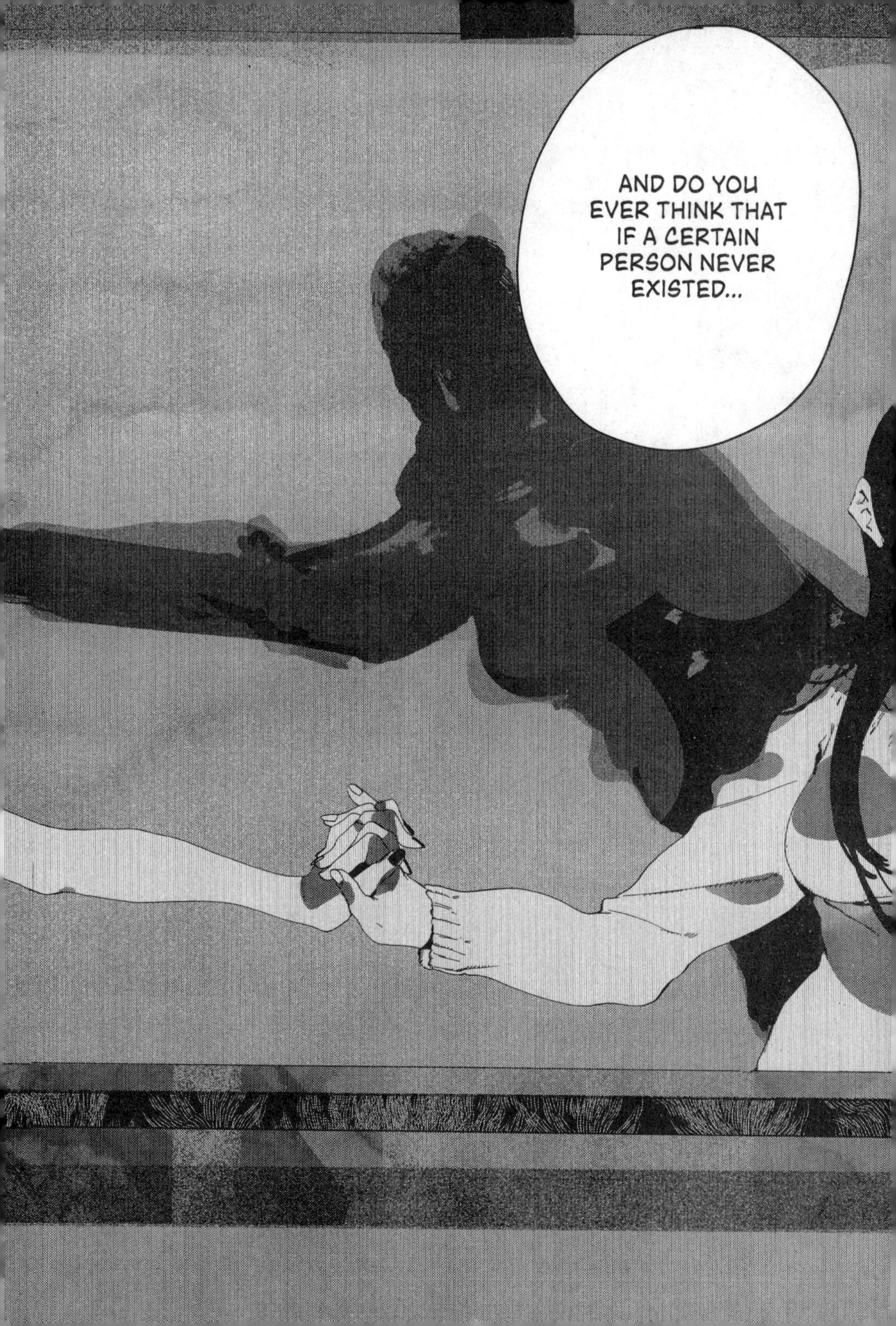
AND DO YOU EVER THINK THAT IF A CERTAIN PERSON NEVER EXISTED...

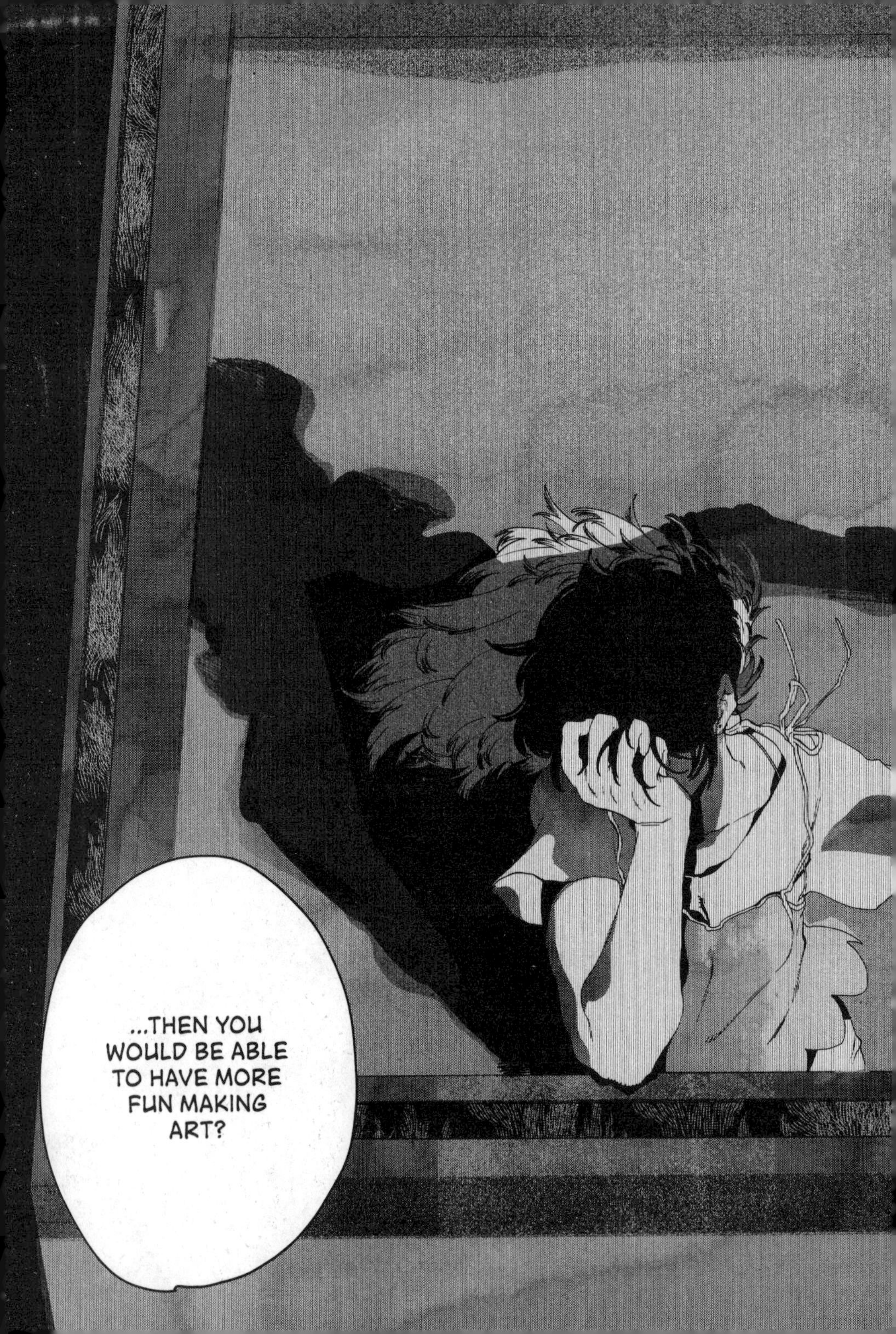
...THEN YOU WOULD BE ABLE TO HAVE MORE FUN MAKING ART?

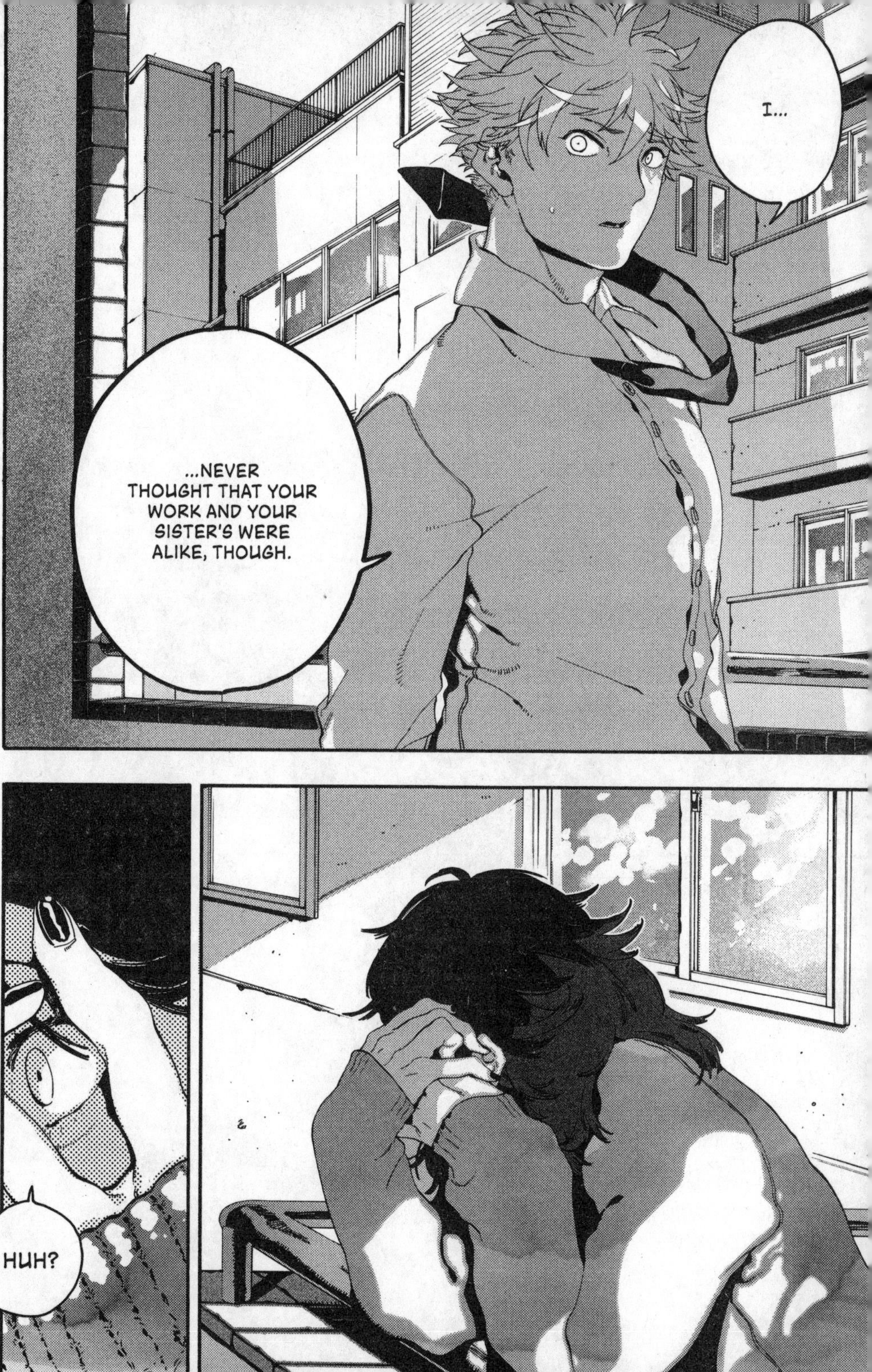
I...
...NEVER THOUGHT THAT YOUR WORK AND YOUR SISTER'S WERE ALIKE, THOUGH.
HUH?

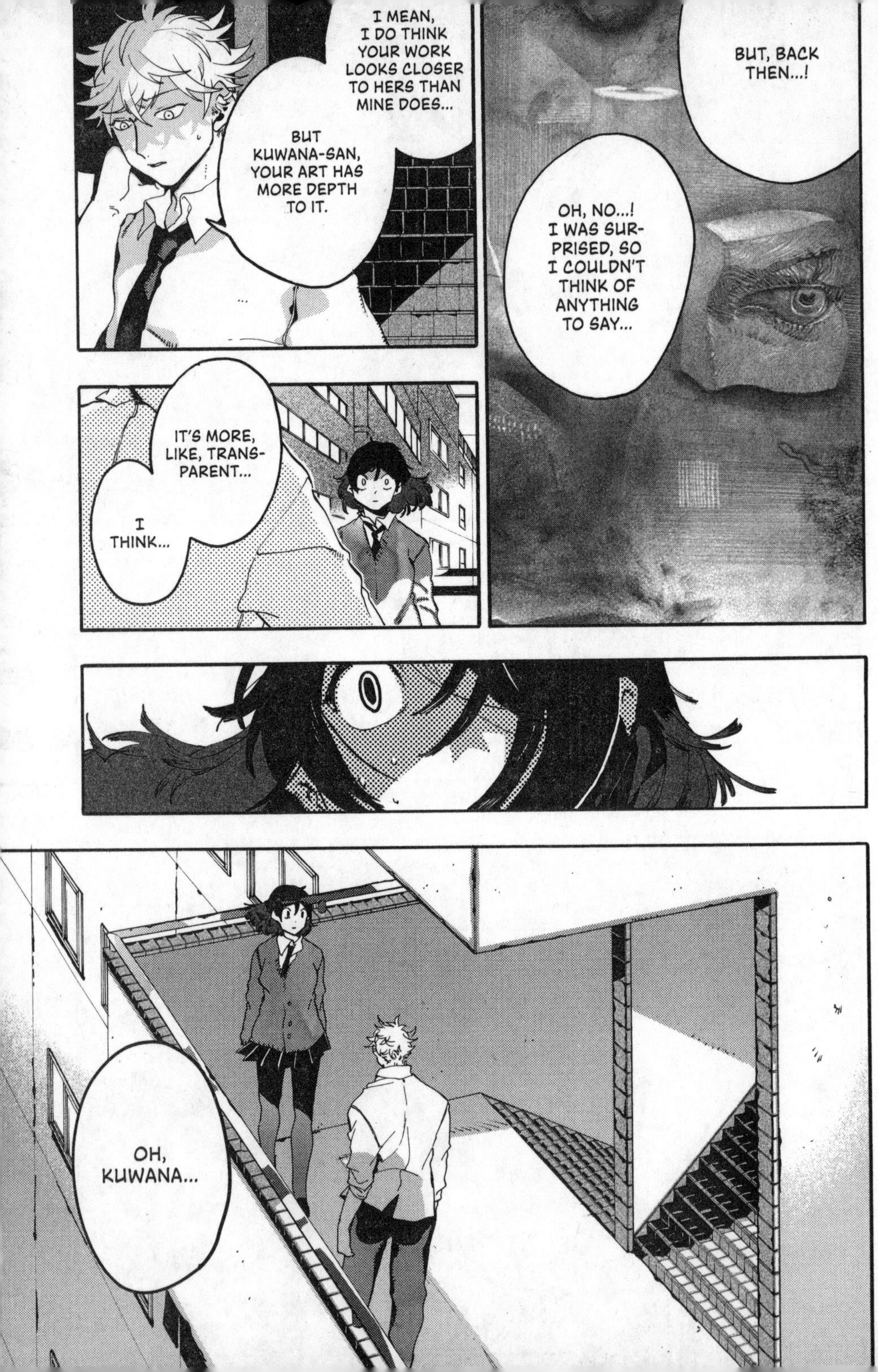
BUT, BACK THEN...!
OH, NO...! I WAS SUR-PRISED, SO I COULDN'T THINK OF ANYTHING TO SAY...
I MEAN, I DO THINK YOUR WORK LOOKS CLOSER TO HERS THAN MINE DOES...
BUT KUWANA-SAN, YOUR ART HAS MORE DEPTH TO IT.
...
IT'S MORE, LIKE, TRANS-PARENT...
I THINK...
OH, KUWANA...

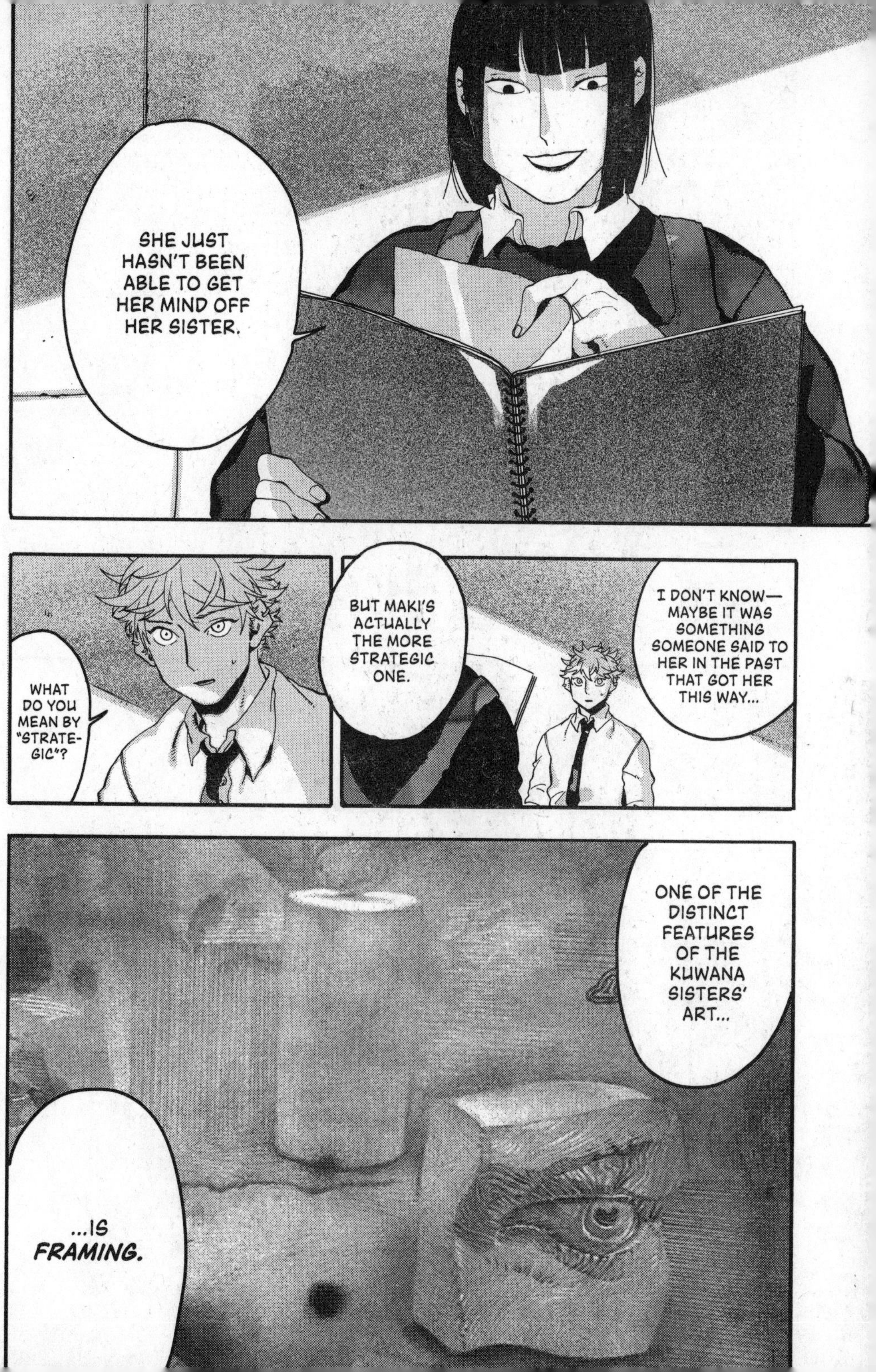
SHE JUST HASN'T BEEN ABLE TO GET HER MIND OFF HER SISTER.
I DON'T KNOW— MAYBE IT WAS SOMETHING SOMEONE SAID TO HER IN THE PAST THAT GOT HER THIS WAY...
BUT MAKI'S ACTUALLY THE MORE STRATEGIC ONE.
WHAT DO YOU MEAN BY "STRATE-GIC"?
ONE OF THE DISTINCT FEATURES OF THE KUWANA SISTERS' ART...
...IS *FRAMING.*

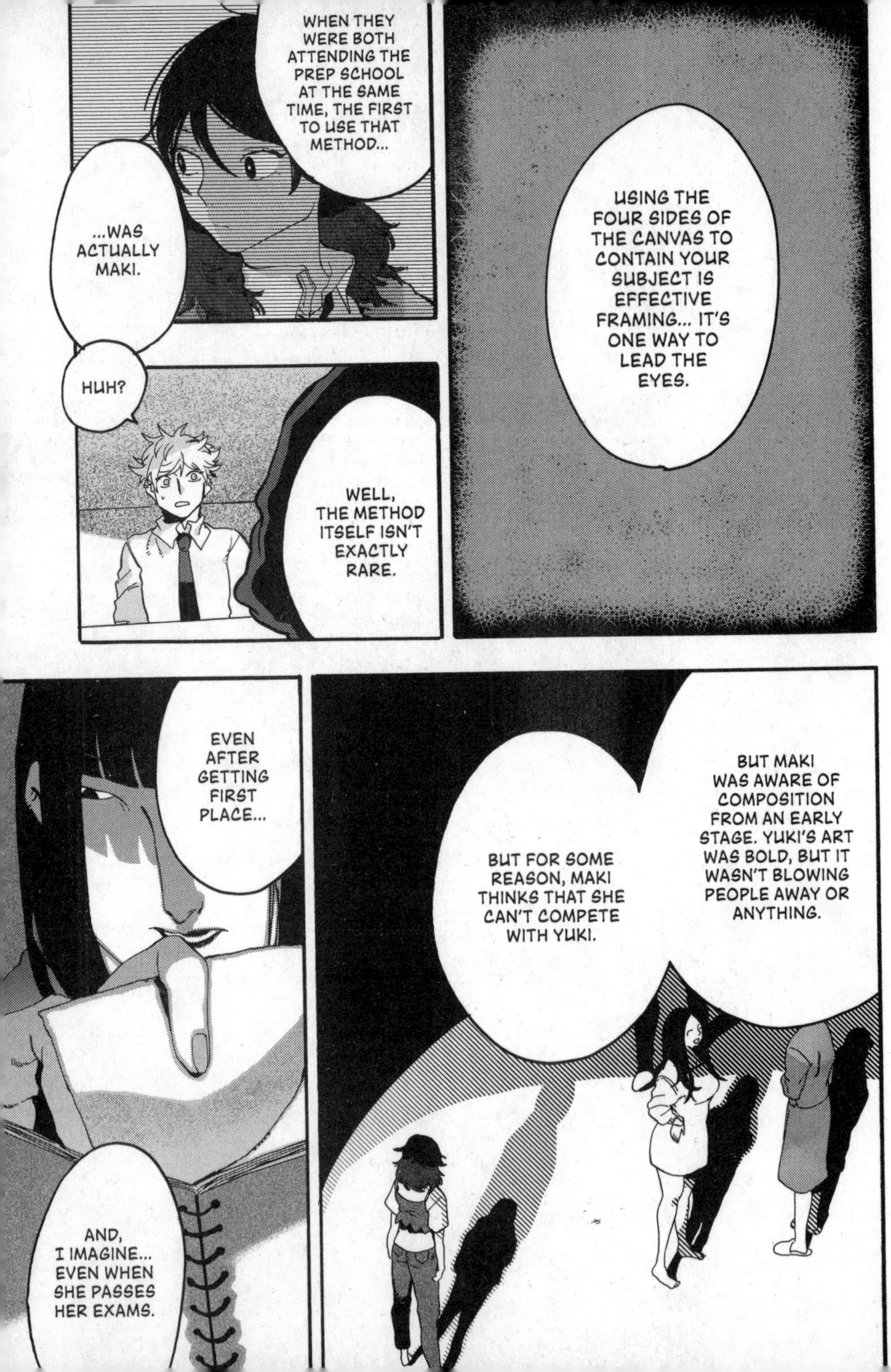
USING THE FOUR SIDES OF THE CANVAS TO CONTAIN YOUR SUBJECT IS EFFECTIVE FRAMING... IT'S ONE WAY TO LEAD THE EYES.
WHEN THEY WERE BOTH ATTENDING THE PREP SCHOOL AT THE SAME TIME, THE FIRST TO USE THAT METHOD...
...WAS ACTUALLY MAKI.
HUH?
WELL, THE METHOD ITSELF ISN'T EXACTLY RARE.
BUT MAKI WAS AWARE OF COMPOSITION FROM AN EARLY STAGE. YUKI'S ART WAS BOLD, BUT IT WASN'T BLOWING PEOPLE AWAY OR ANYTHING.
BUT FOR SOME REASON, MAKI THINKS THAT SHE CAN'T COMPETE WITH YUKI.
EVEN AFTER GETTING FIRST PLACE...
AND, I IMAGINE... EVEN WHEN SHE PASSES HER EXAMS.

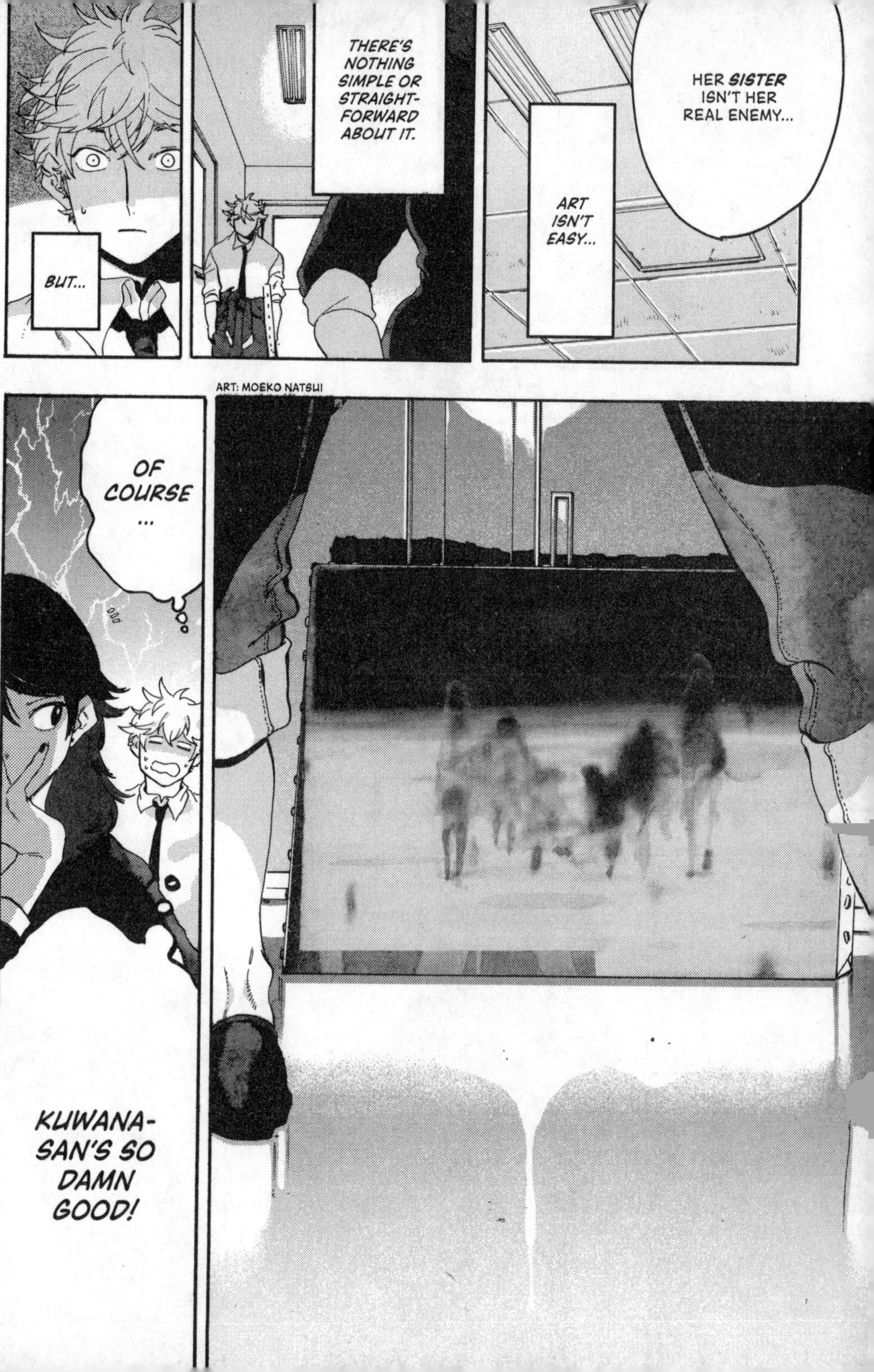
HER SISTER ISN'T HER REAL ENEMY...
ART ISN'T EASY...
THERE'S NOTHING SIMPLE OR STRAIGHT-FORWARD ABOUT IT.
BUT...
ART: MOEKO NATSUI
OF COURSE ...
KUWANA-SAN'S SO DAMN GOOD!

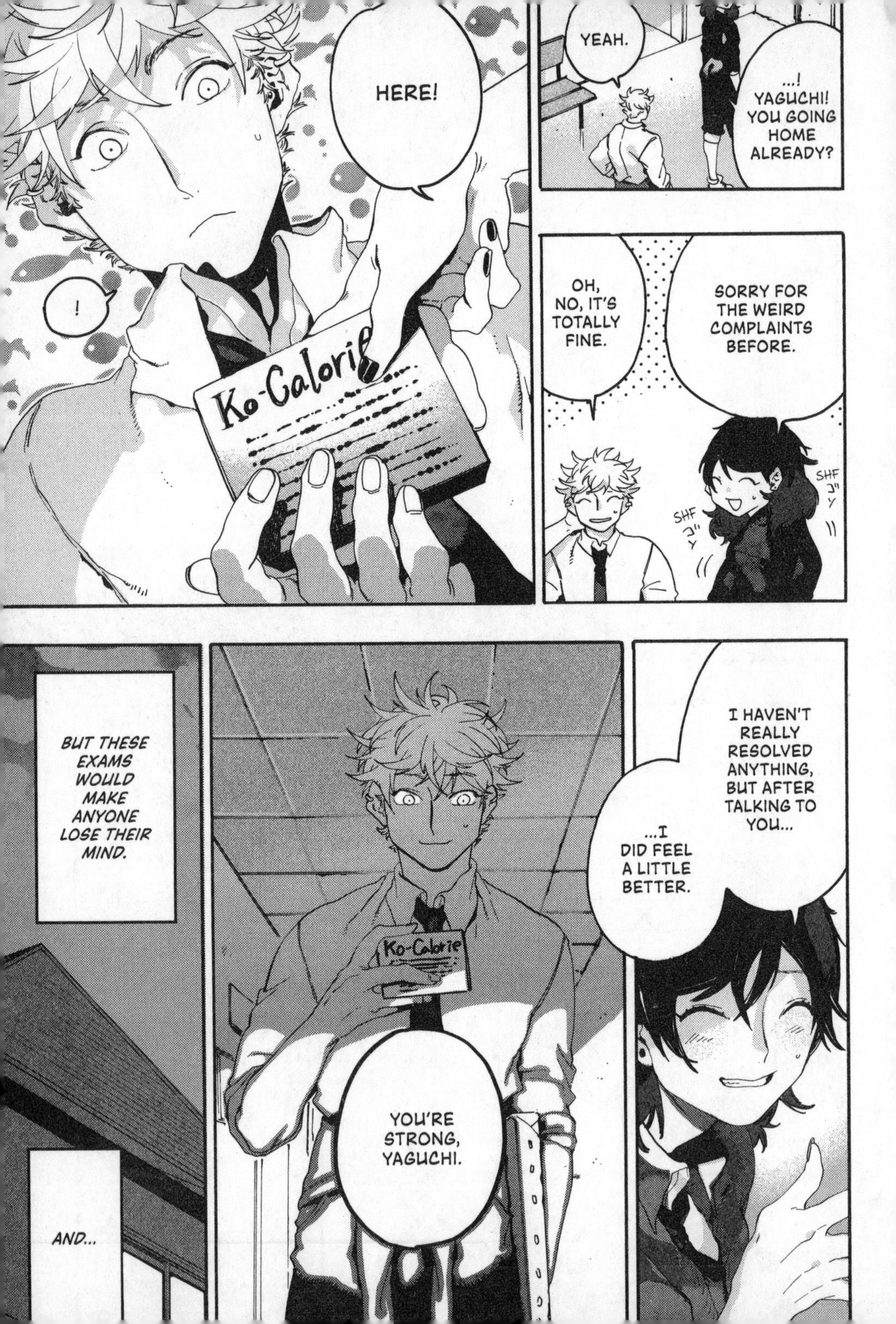
...! YAGUCHI! YOU GOING HOME ALREADY?
YEAH.
SORRY FOR THE WEIRD COMPLAINTS BEFORE.
OH, NO, IT'S TOTALLY FINE.
SHF ゴソ
SHF ゴソ
HERE!
!
Ko-Calorie
I HAVEN'T REALLY RESOLVED ANYTHING, BUT AFTER TALKING TO YOU...
...I DID FEEL A LITTLE BETTER.
Ko-Calorie
YOU'RE STRONG, YAGUCHI.
BUT THESE EXAMS WOULD MAKE ANYONE LOSE THEIR MIND.
AND...

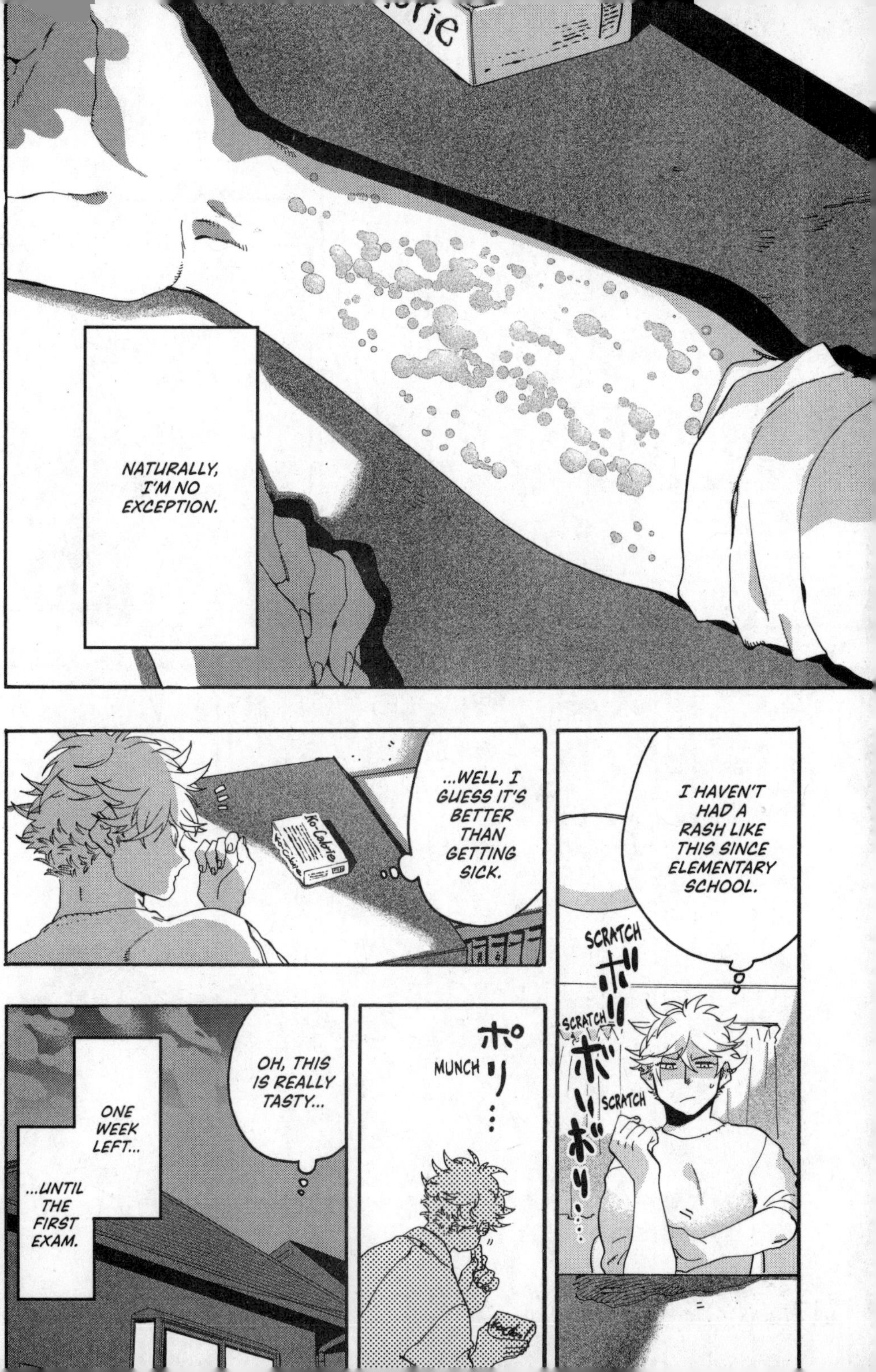
NATURALLY, I'M NO EXCEPTION.
I HAVEN'T HAD A RASH LIKE THIS SINCE ELEMENTARY SCHOOL.
SCRATCH
ボリ!!
SCRATCH
ボリ!
SCRATCH
ボリボリ…
...WELL, I GUESS IT'S BETTER THAN GETTING SICK.
MUNCH
ポリ…
OH, THIS IS REALLY TASTY...
ONE WEEK LEFT...
...UNTIL THE FIRST EXAM.

STROKE 13 END

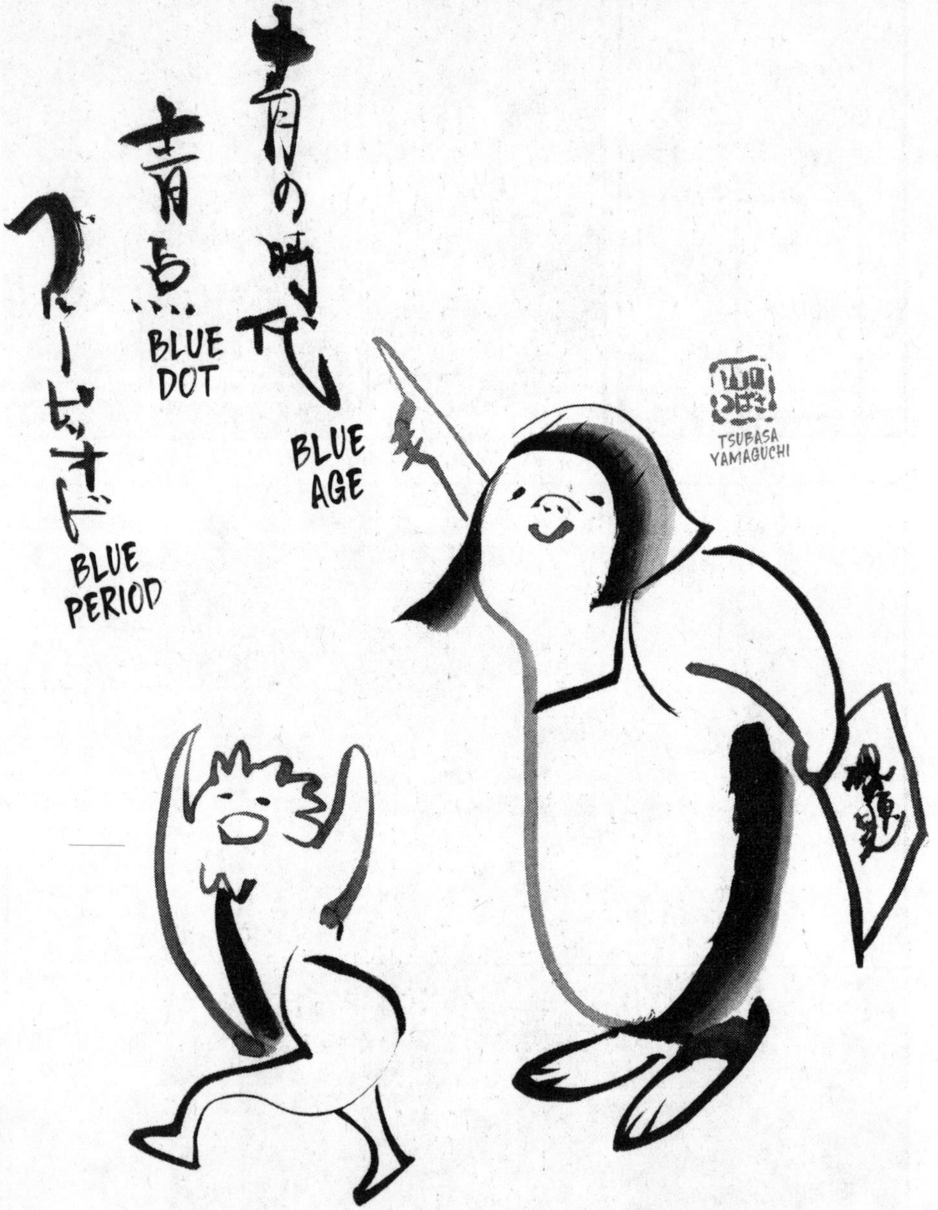

青の時代
BLUE AGE
青点
BLUE DOT
ブルーピリオド
BLUE PERIOD
TSUBASA YAMAGUCHI

STROKE 14 THE ABILITY TO HAVE FUN

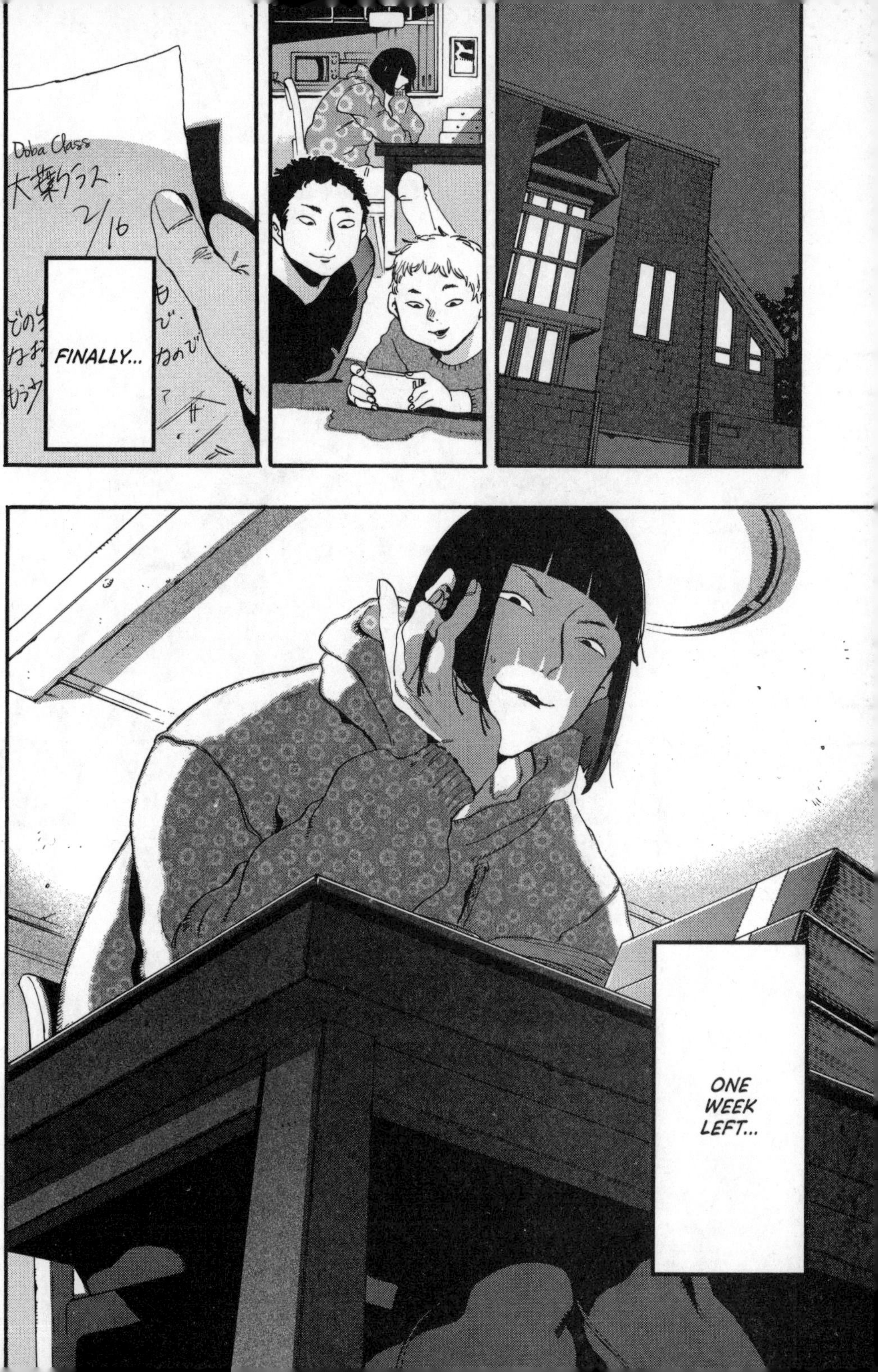
Doba Class
大葉クラス
2/16
FINALLY...
ONE WEEK LEFT...

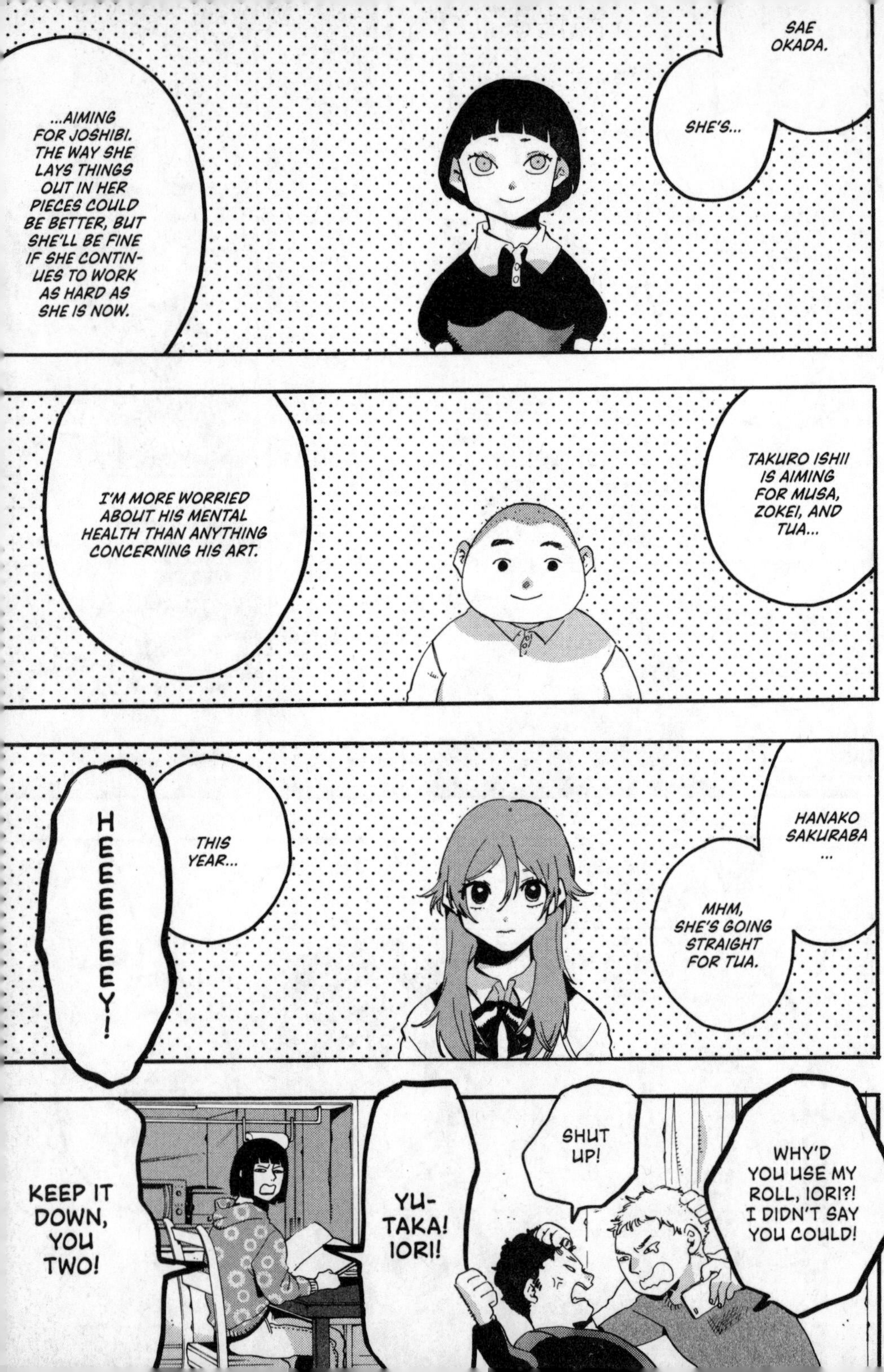
SAE OKADA.
SHE'S...
...AIMING FOR JOSHIBI. THE WAY SHE LAYS THINGS OUT IN HER PIECES COULD BE BETTER, BUT SHE'LL BE FINE IF SHE CONTINUES TO WORK AS HARD AS SHE IS NOW.
TAKURO ISHII IS AIMING FOR MUSA, ZOKEI, AND TUA...
I'M MORE WORRIED ABOUT HIS MENTAL HEALTH THAN ANYTHING CONCERNING HIS ART.
HANAKO SAKURABA ...
MHM, SHE'S GOING STRAIGHT FOR TUA.
THIS YEAR...
HEEEEEEEY!
WHY'D YOU USE MY ROLL, IORI?! I DIDN'T SAY YOU COULD!
SHUT UP!
YU-TAKA! IORI!
KEEP IT DOWN, YOU TWO!

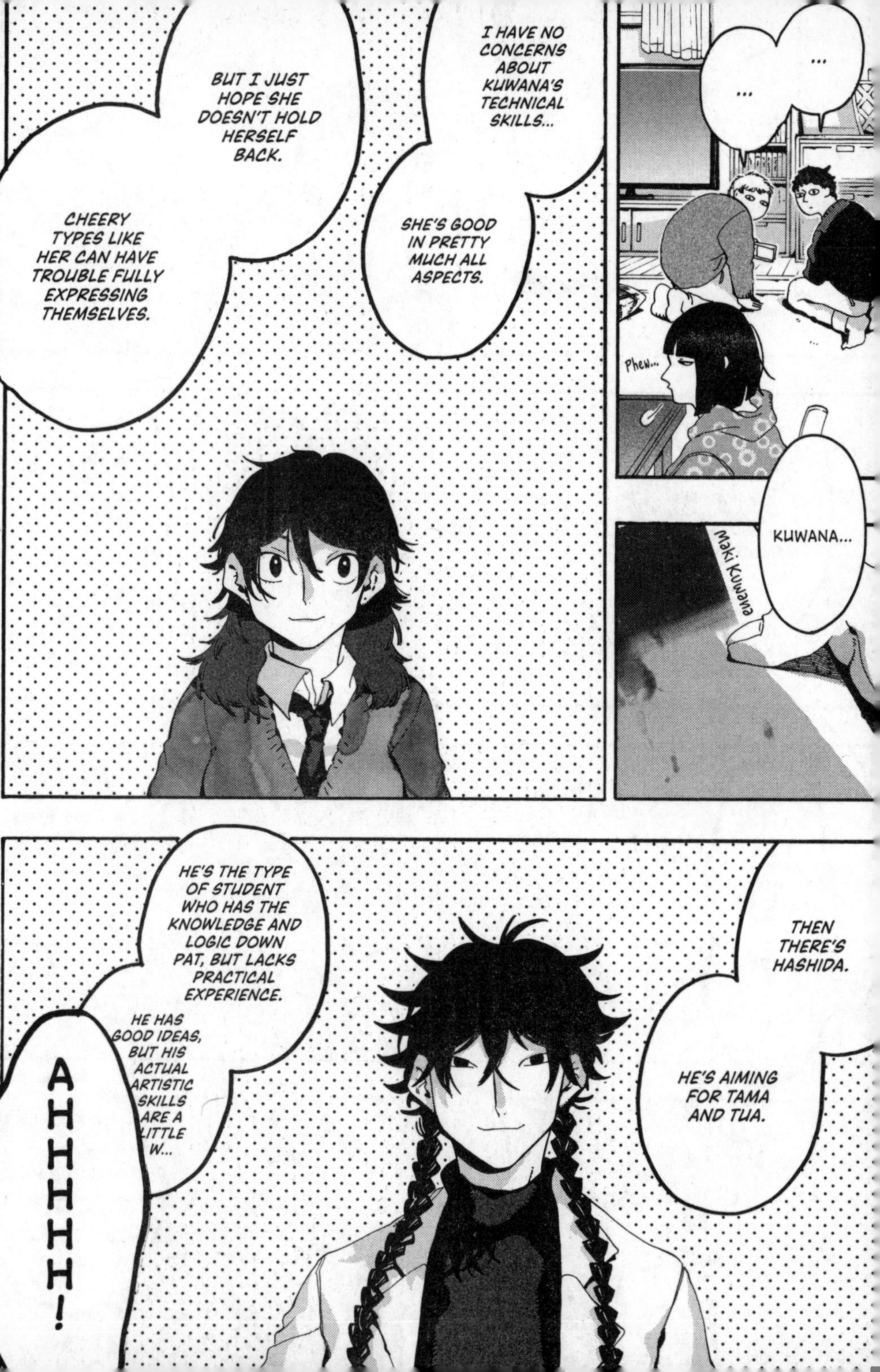
...
...
Phew...
...
KUWANA...
Maki Kuwana
I HAVE NO CONCERNS ABOUT KUWANA'S TECHNICAL SKILLS...
SHE'S GOOD IN PRETTY MUCH ALL ASPECTS.
BUT I JUST HOPE SHE DOESN'T HOLD HERSELF BACK.
CHEERY TYPES LIKE HER CAN HAVE TROUBLE FULLY EXPRESSING THEMSELVES.
THEN THERE'S HASHIDA.
HE'S AIMING FOR TAMA AND TUA.
HE'S THE TYPE OF STUDENT WHO HAS THE KNOWLEDGE AND LOGIC DOWN PAT, BUT LACKS PRACTICAL EXPERIENCE.
HE HAS GOOD IDEAS, BUT HIS ACTUAL ARTISTIC SKILLS ARE A LITTLE W...
AHHHHH!

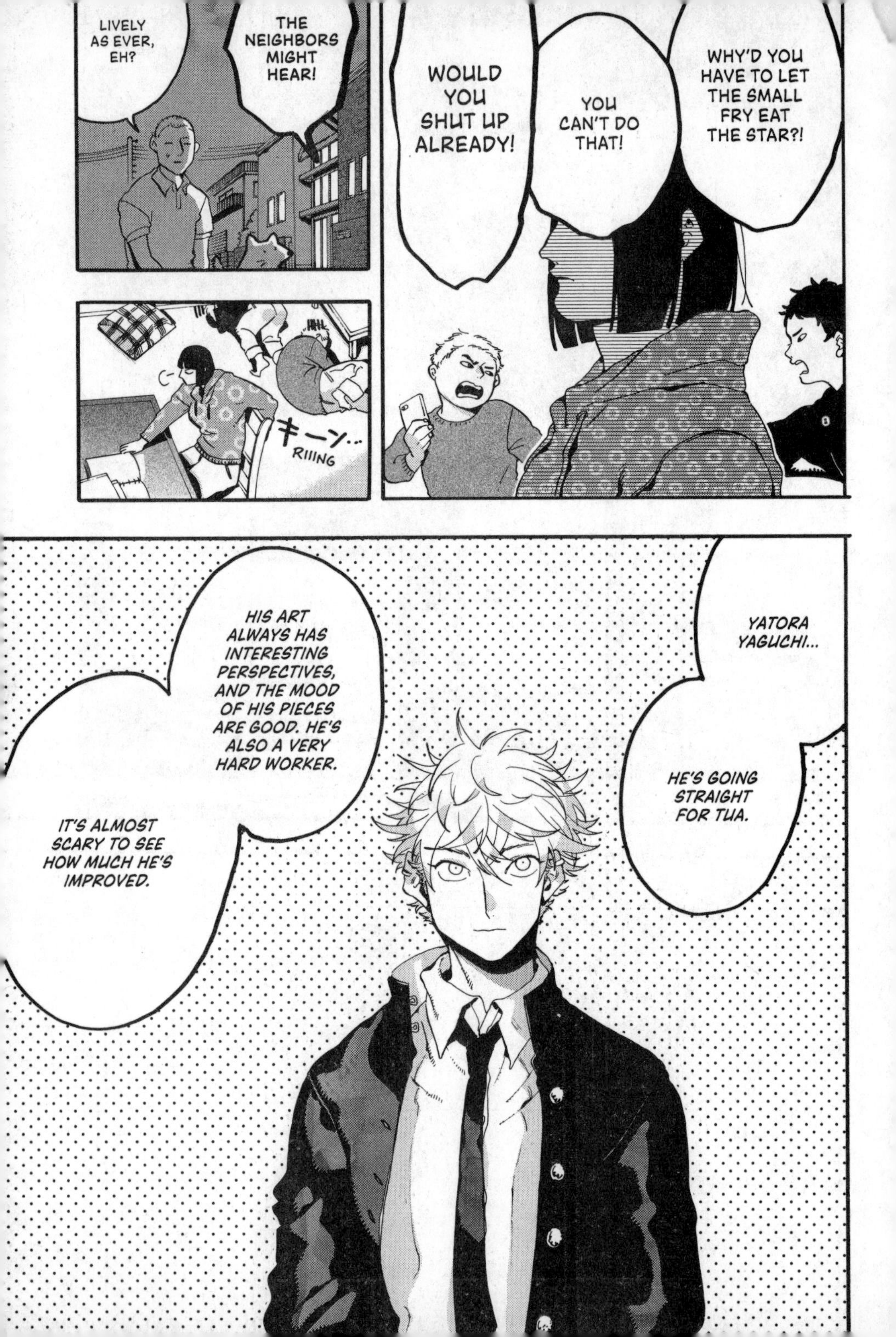
WHY'D YOU HAVE TO LET THE SMALL FRY EAT THE STAR?!
YOU CAN'T DO THAT!
WOULD YOU SHUT UP ALREADY!
THE NEIGHBORS MIGHT HEAR!
LIVELY AS EVER, EH?
キーン…
RIIING
YATORA YAGUCHI...
HE'S GOING STRAIGHT FOR TUA.
HIS ART ALWAYS HAS INTERESTING PERSPECTIVES, AND THE MOOD OF HIS PIECES ARE GOOD. HE'S ALSO A VERY HARD WORKER.
IT'S ALMOST SCARY TO SEE HOW MUCH HE'S IMPROVED.

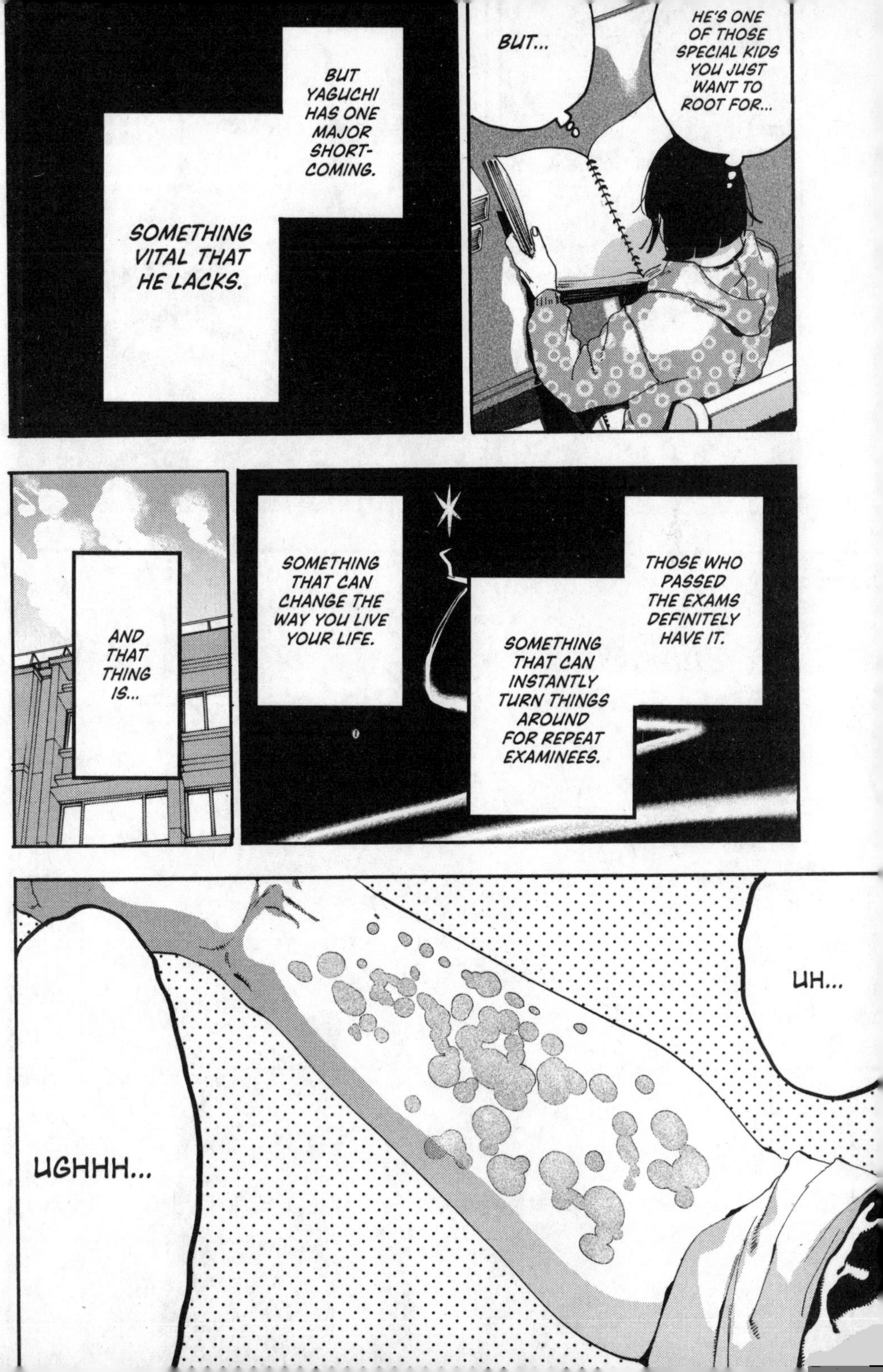
HE'S ONE OF THOSE SPECIAL KIDS YOU JUST WANT TO ROOT FOR...
BUT...
BUT YAGUCHI HAS ONE MAJOR SHORT-COMING.
SOMETHING VITAL THAT HE LACKS.
THOSE WHO PASSED THE EXAMS DEFINITELY HAVE IT.
SOMETHING THAT CAN INSTANTLY TURN THINGS AROUND FOR REPEAT EXAMINEES.
SOMETHING THAT CAN CHANGE THE WAY YOU LIVE YOUR LIFE.
AND THAT THING IS...
UH...
UGHHH...

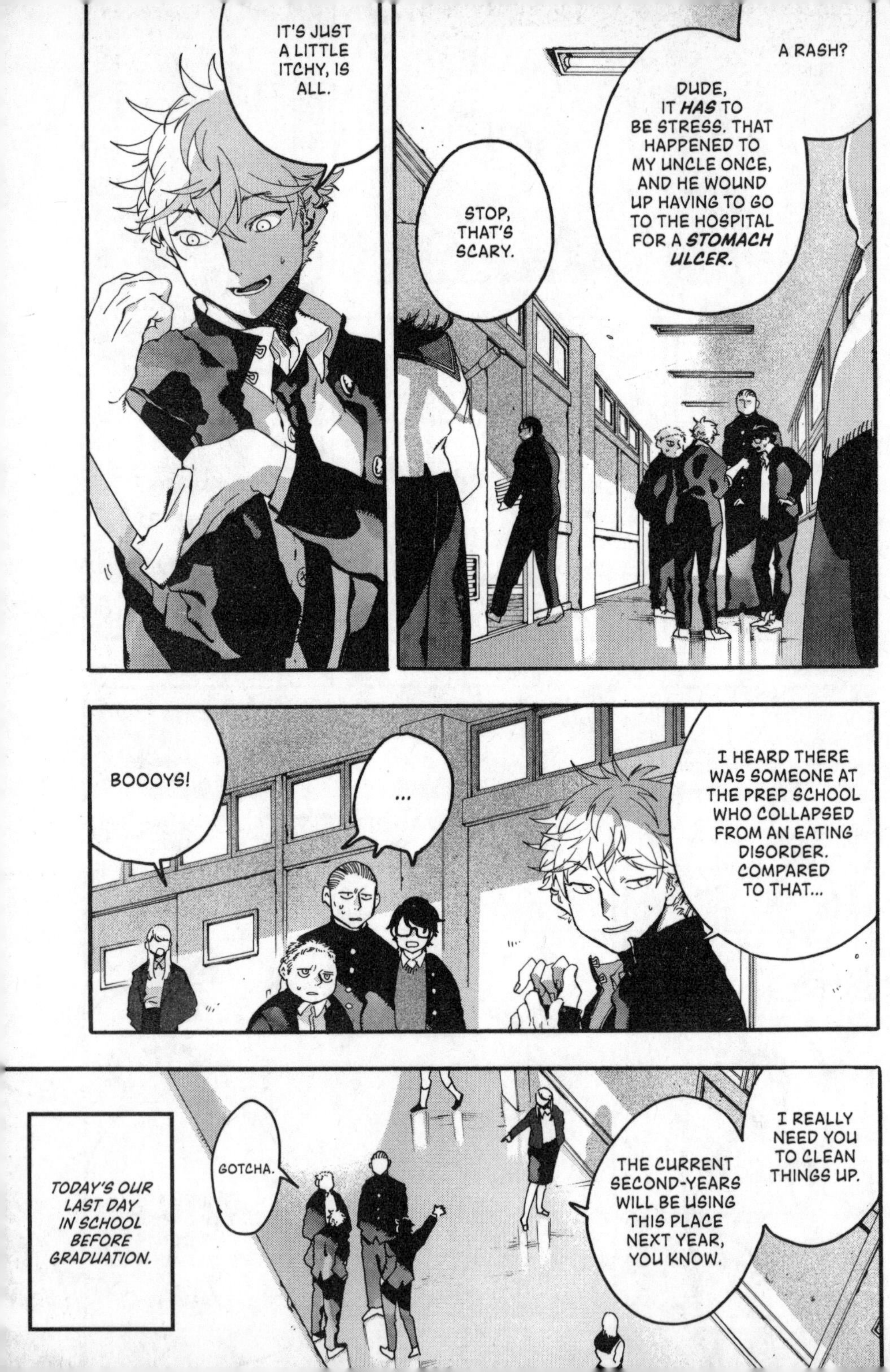
A RASH?
DUDE, IT **HAS** TO BE STRESS. THAT HAPPENED TO MY UNCLE ONCE, AND HE WOUND UP HAVING TO GO TO THE HOSPITAL FOR A ***STOMACH ULCER.***
STOP, THAT'S SCARY.
IT'S JUST A LITTLE ITCHY, IS ALL.
I HEARD THERE WAS SOMEONE AT THE PREP SCHOOL WHO COLLAPSED FROM AN EATING DISORDER. COMPARED TO THAT...
...
BOOOYS!
I REALLY NEED YOU TO CLEAN THINGS UP.
THE CURRENT SECOND-YEARS WILL BE USING THIS PLACE NEXT YEAR, YOU KNOW.
GOTCHA.
TODAY'S OUR LAST DAY IN SCHOOL BEFORE GRADUATION.

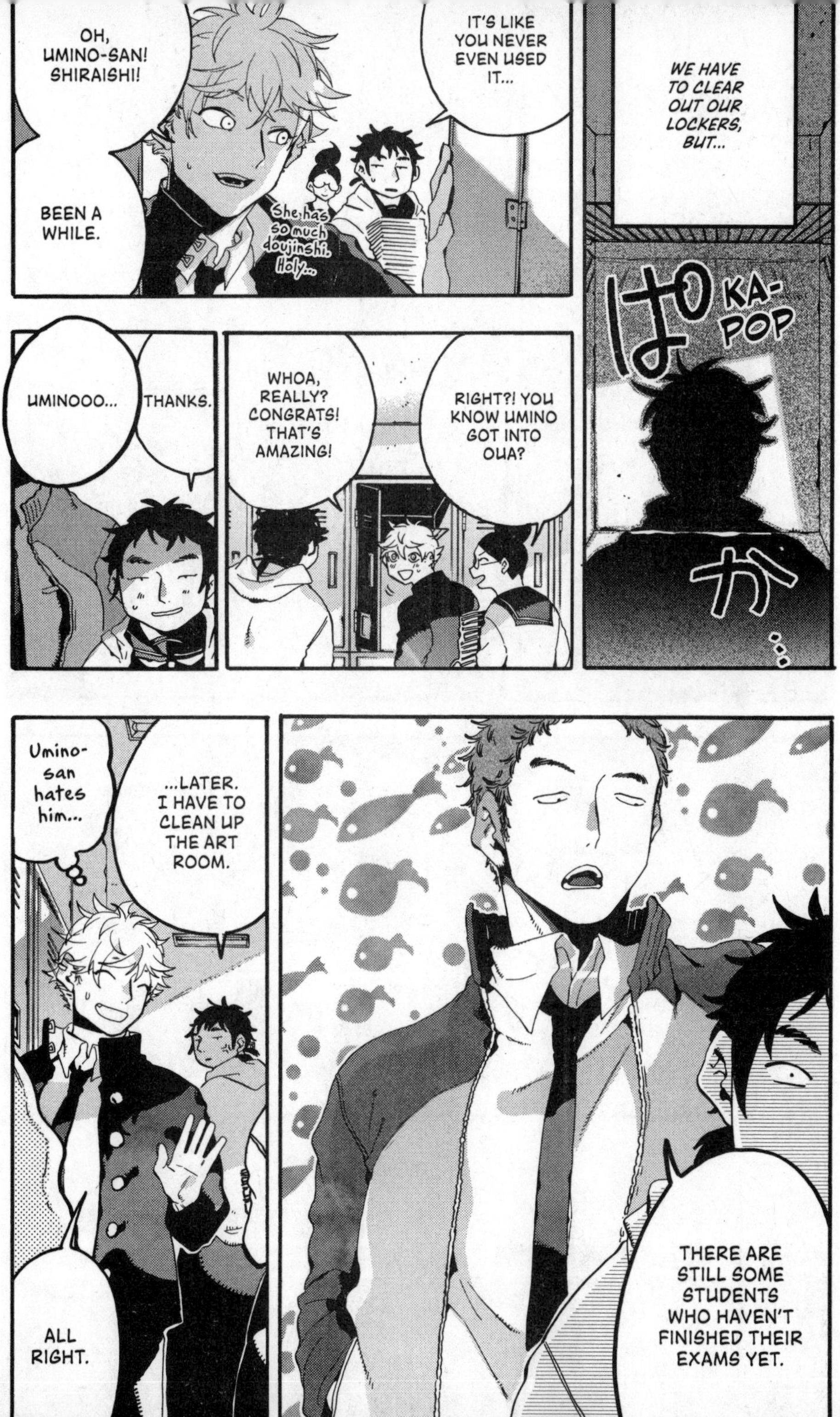
WE HAVE TO CLEAR OUT OUR LOCKERS, BUT...
ぱか
KA-POP
...
IT'S LIKE YOU NEVER EVEN USED IT...
OH, UMINO-SAN! SHIRAISHI!
She has so much doujinshi. Holy...
BEEN A WHILE.
RIGHT?! YOU KNOW UMINO GOT INTO OUA?
WHOA, REALLY? CONGRATS! THAT'S AMAZING!
THANKS.
UMINOOO...
THERE ARE STILL SOME STUDENTS WHO HAVEN'T FINISHED THEIR EXAMS YET.
...LATER. I HAVE TO CLEAN UP THE ART ROOM.
Umino-san hates him...
ALL RIGHT.

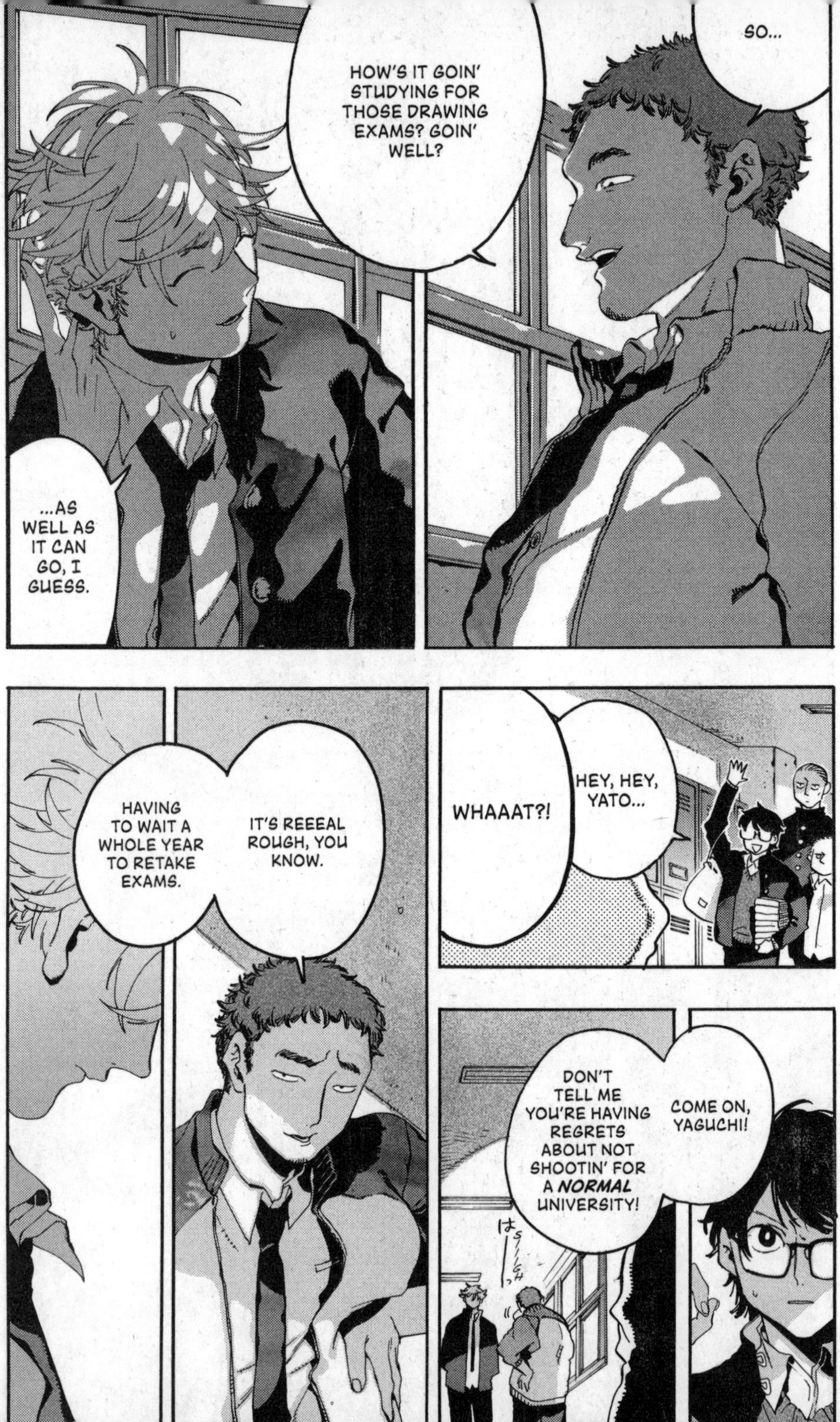
SO...
HOW'S IT GOIN' STUDYING FOR THOSE DRAWING EXAMS? GOIN' WELL?
...AS WELL AS IT CAN GO, I GUESS.
HEY, HEY, YATO...
WHAAAT?!
COME ON, YAGUCHI!
DON'T TELL ME YOU'RE HAVING REGRETS ABOUT NOT SHOOTIN' FOR A *NORMAL* UNIVERSITY!
SIIIGH
IT'S REEEAL ROUGH, YOU KNOW.
HAVING TO WAIT A WHOLE YEAR TO RETAKE EXAMS.

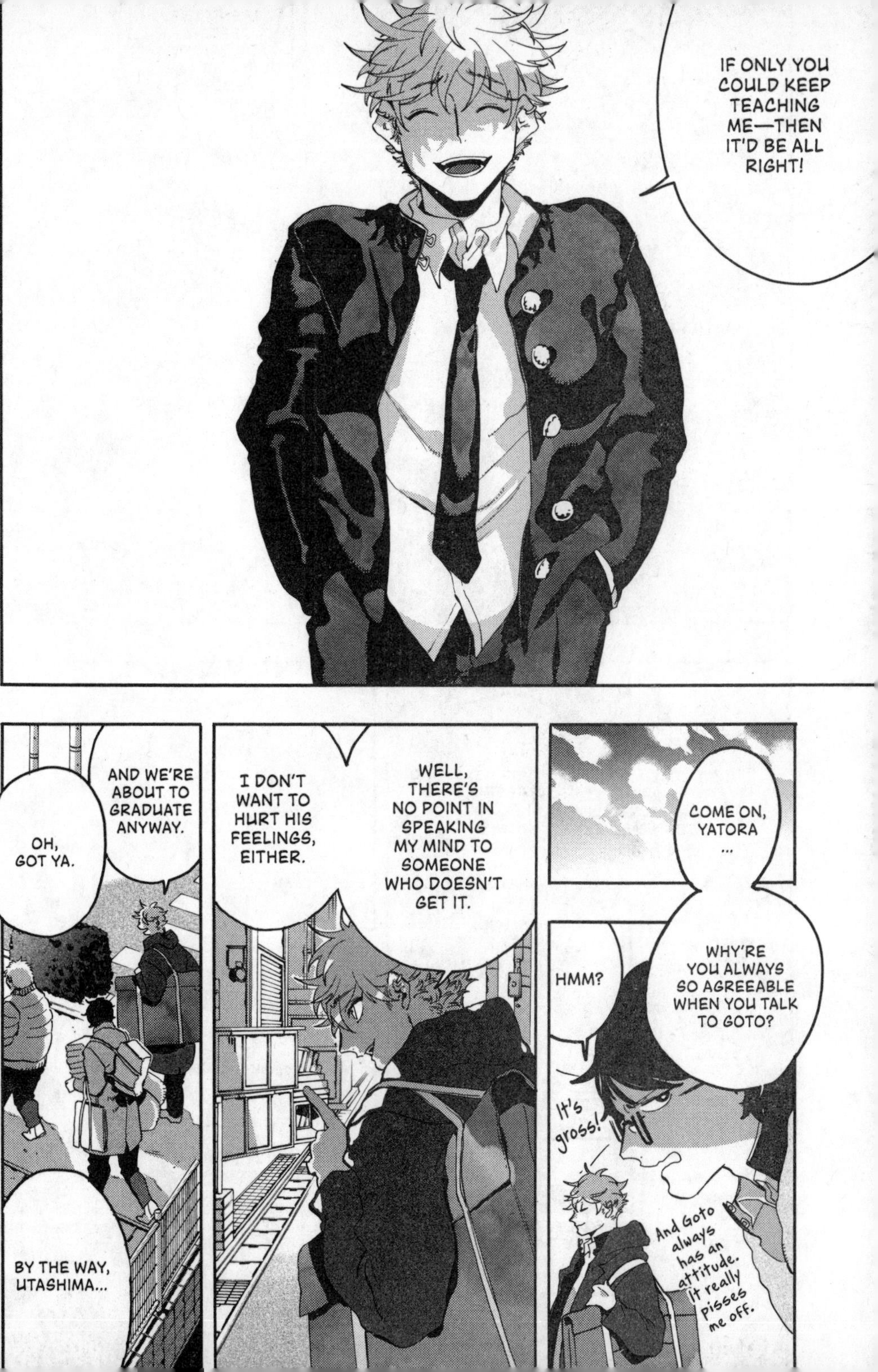
IF ONLY YOU COULD KEEP TEACHING ME—THEN IT'D BE ALL RIGHT!
COME ON, YATORA ...
WHY'RE YOU ALWAYS SO AGREEABLE WHEN YOU TALK TO GOTO?
HMM?
It's gross!
And Goto always has an attitude. It really pisses me off.
WELL, THERE'S NO POINT IN SPEAKING MY MIND TO SOMEONE WHO DOESN'T GET IT.
I DON'T WANT TO HURT HIS FEELINGS, EITHER.
AND WE'RE ABOUT TO GRADUATE ANYWAY.
OH, GOT YA.
BY THE WAY, UTASHIMA...

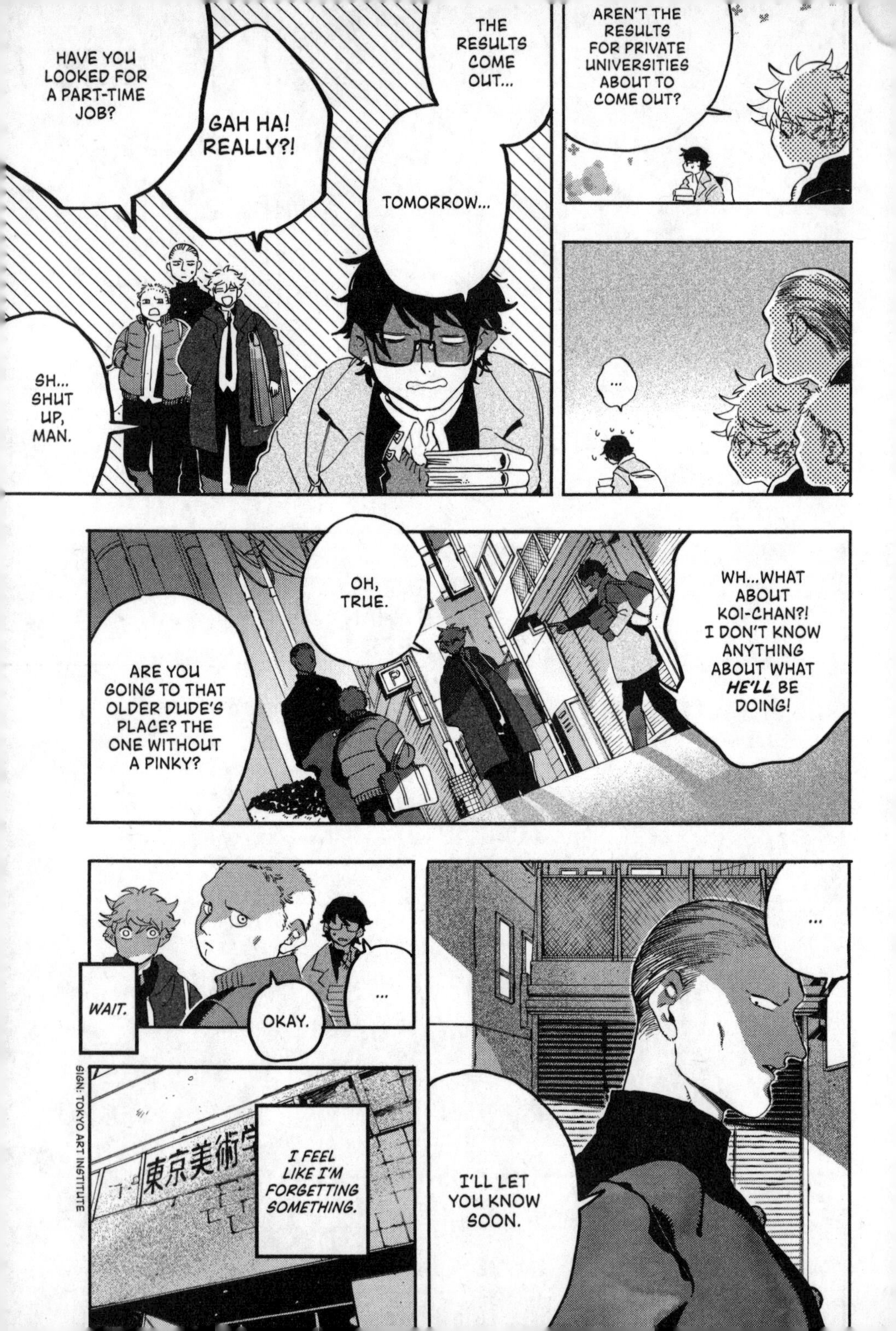
AREN'T THE RESULTS FOR PRIVATE UNIVERSITIES ABOUT TO COME OUT?
...
THE RESULTS COME OUT...
TOMORROW...
GAH HA! REALLY?!
HAVE YOU LOOKED FOR A PART-TIME JOB?
SH... SHUT UP, MAN.
WH...WHAT ABOUT KOI-CHAN?! I DON'T KNOW ANYTHING ABOUT WHAT *HE'LL* BE DOING!
OH, TRUE.
ARE YOU GOING TO THAT OLDER DUDE'S PLACE? THE ONE WITHOUT A PINKY?
...
I'LL LET YOU KNOW SOON.
...
OKAY.
WAIT.
I FEEL LIKE I'M FORGETTING SOMETHING.
東京美術学
SIGN: TOKYO ART INSTITUTE

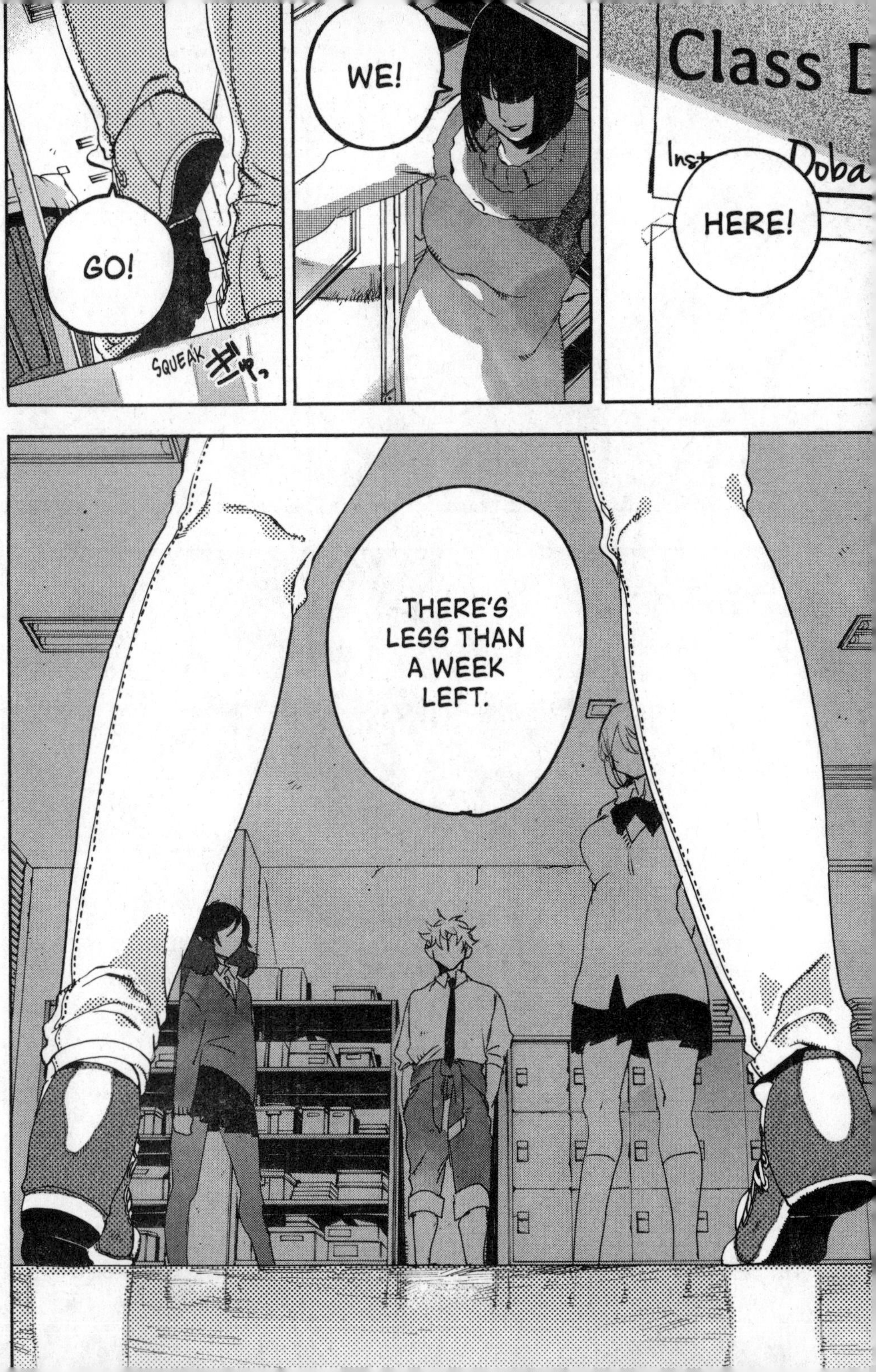
HERE!
WE!
GO!
SQUEAK
THERE'S LESS THAN A WEEK LEFT.

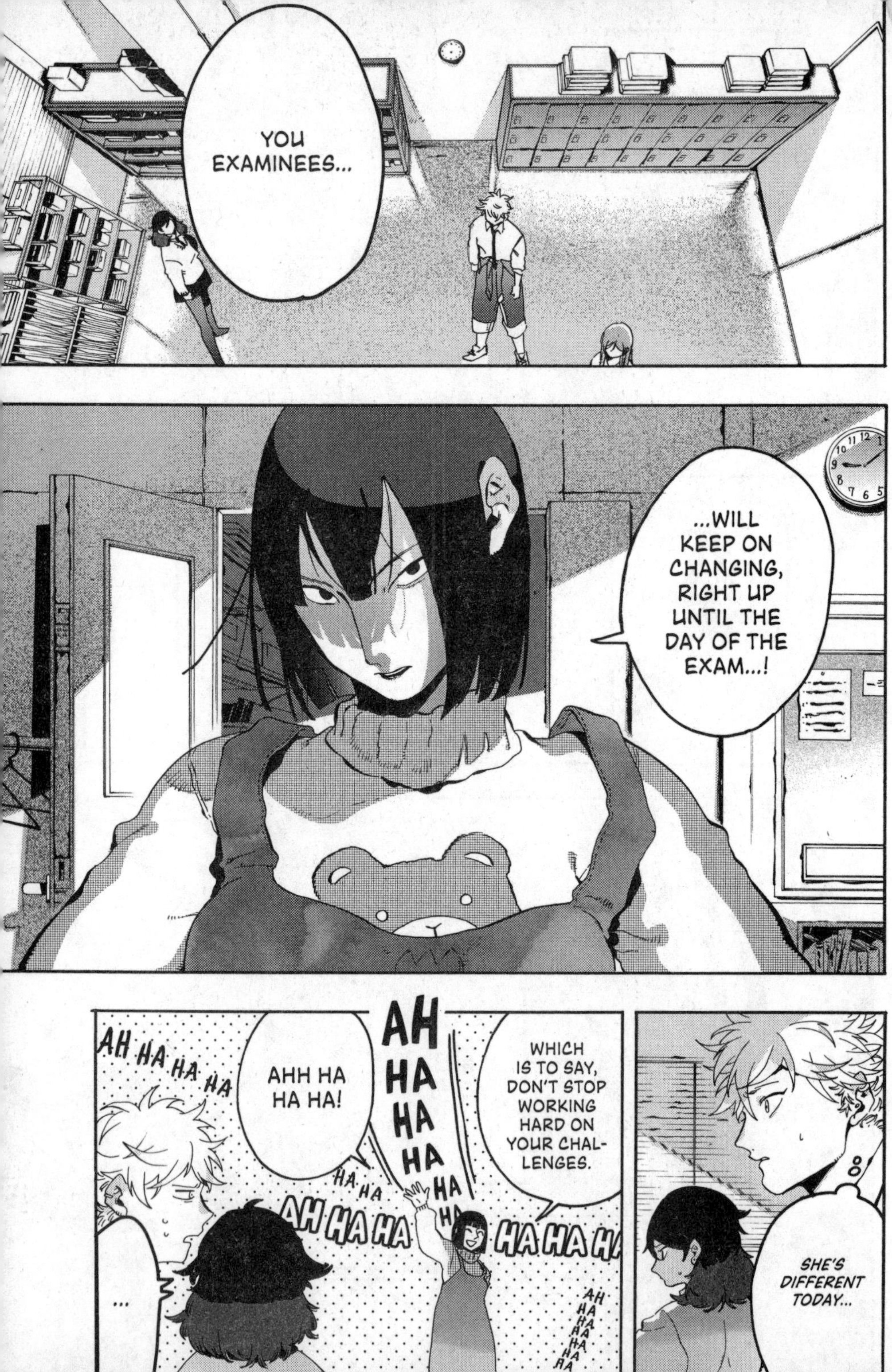
YOU EXAMINEES...
...WILL KEEP ON CHANGING, RIGHT UP UNTIL THE DAY OF THE EXAM...!
SHE'S DIFFERENT TODAY...
WHICH IS TO SAY, DON'T STOP WORKING HARD ON YOUR CHAL-LENGES.
AH HA HA HA HA HA HA
AHH HA HA HA!
AH HA HA HA
HA HA
AH HA HA
HA HA HA
AH HA HA HA HA HA HA
...

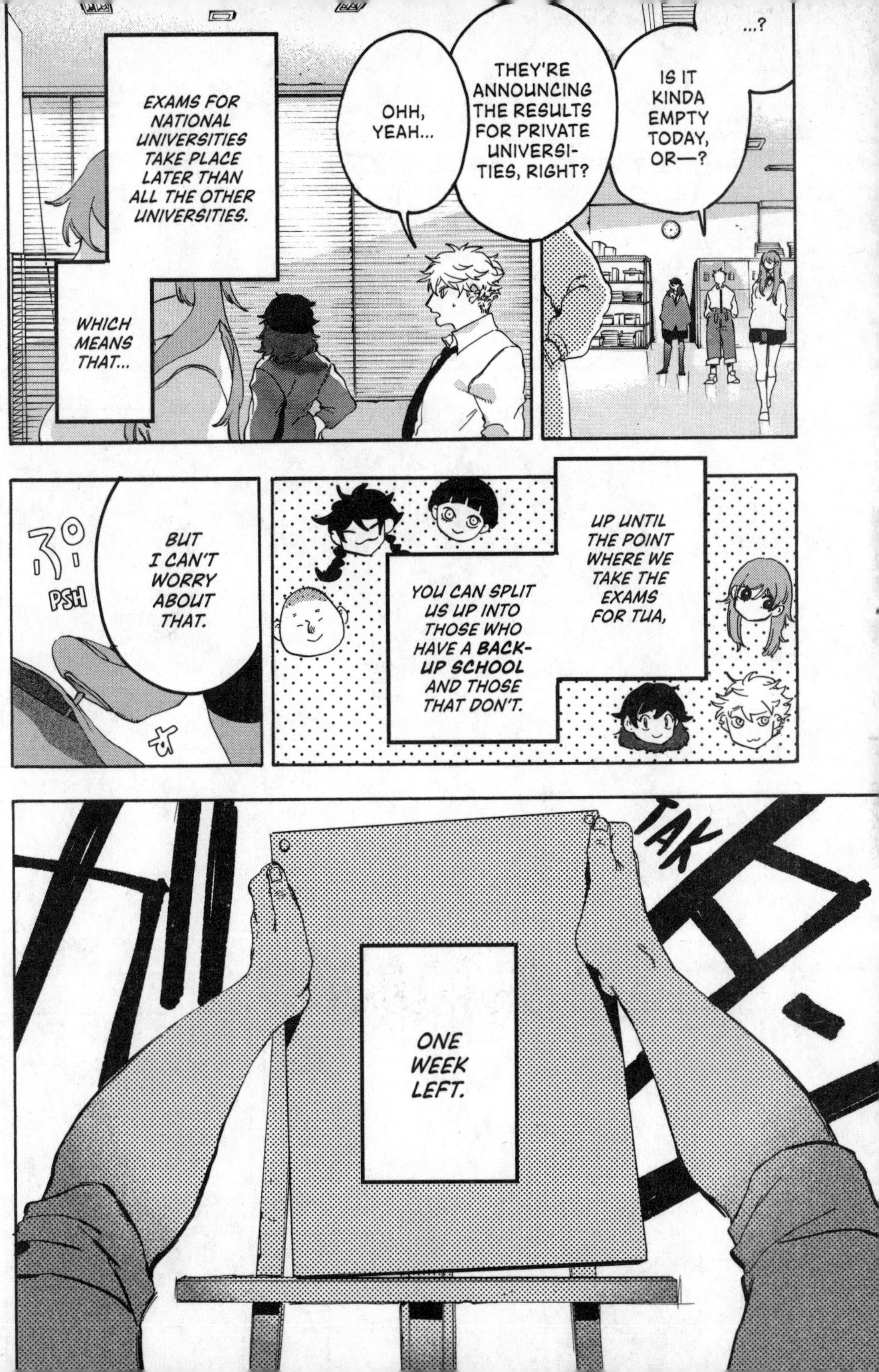
...?
IS IT KINDA EMPTY TODAY, OR—?
THEY'RE ANNOUNCING THE RESULTS FOR PRIVATE UNIVERSI-TIES, RIGHT?
OHH, YEAH...
EXAMS FOR NATIONAL UNIVERSITIES TAKE PLACE LATER THAN ALL THE OTHER UNIVERSITIES.
WHICH MEANS THAT...
UP UNTIL THE POINT WHERE WE TAKE THE EXAMS FOR TUA,
YOU CAN SPLIT US UP INTO THOSE WHO HAVE A BACK-UP SCHOOL AND THOSE THAT DON'T.
BUT I CAN'T WORRY ABOUT THAT.
PSH
TAK
ONE WEEK LEFT.

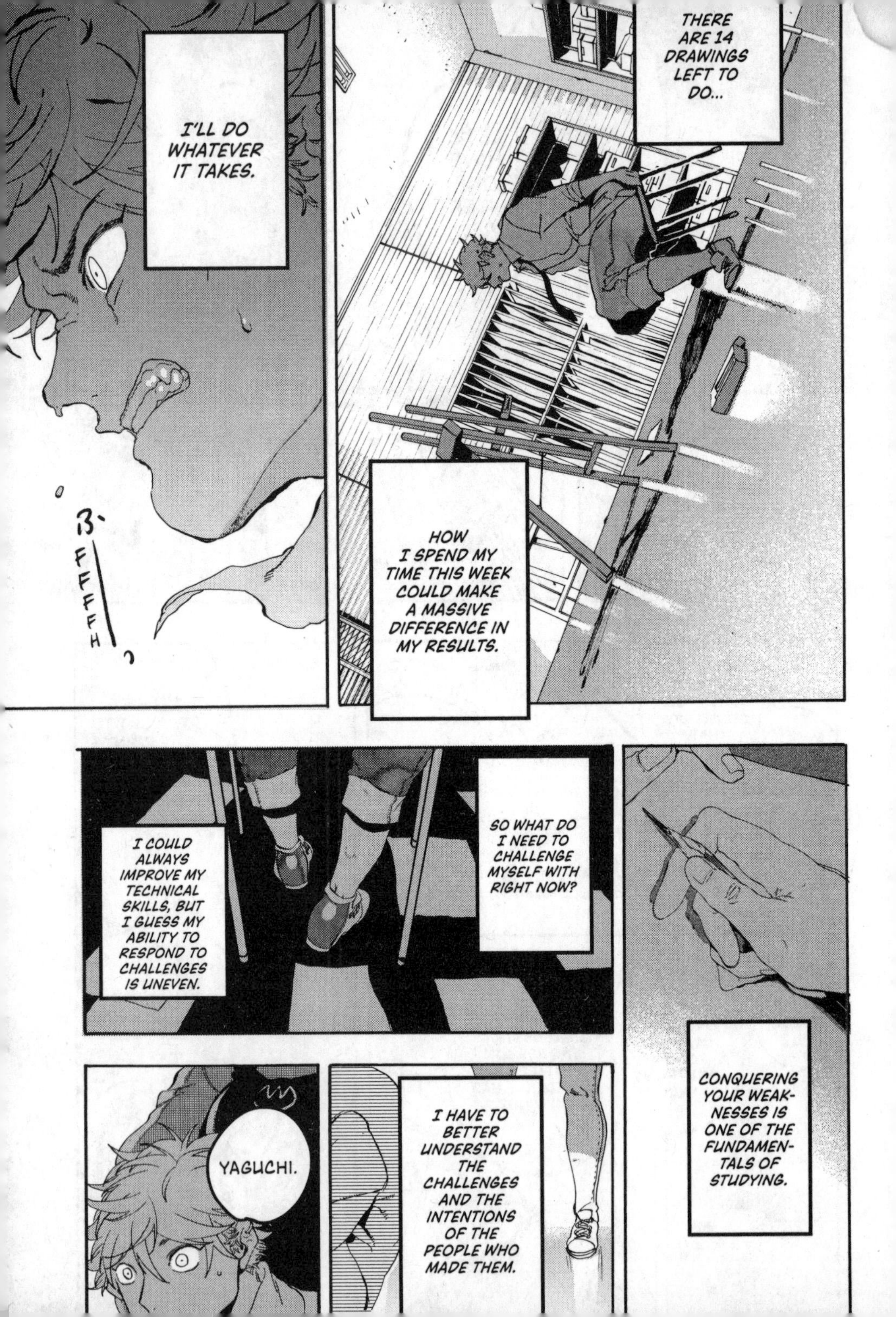
THERE ARE 14 DRAWINGS LEFT TO DO...
HOW I SPEND MY TIME THIS WEEK COULD MAKE A MASSIVE DIFFERENCE IN MY RESULTS.
I'LL DO WHATEVER IT TAKES.
FFFFH
CONQUERING YOUR WEAKNESSES IS ONE OF THE FUNDAMENTALS OF STUDYING.
SO WHAT DO I NEED TO CHALLENGE MYSELF WITH RIGHT NOW?
I COULD ALWAYS IMPROVE MY TECHNICAL SKILLS, BUT I GUESS MY ABILITY TO RESPOND TO CHALLENGES IS UNEVEN.
I HAVE TO BETTER UNDERSTAND THE CHALLENGES AND THE INTENTIONS OF THE PEOPLE WHO MADE THEM.
YAGUCHI.

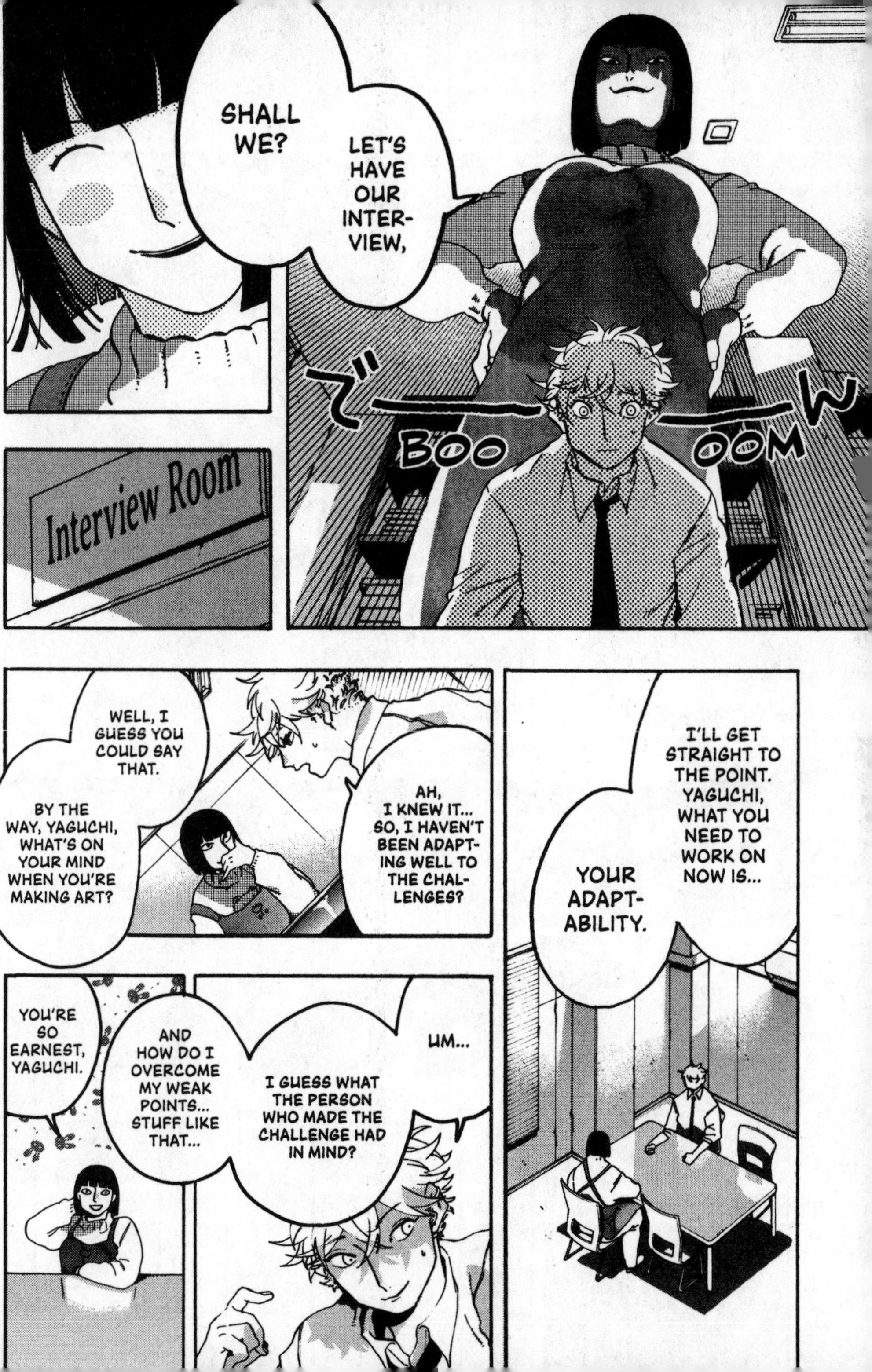
BOO——OOM
LET'S HAVE OUR INTER-VIEW,
SHALL WE?
Interview Room
I'LL GET STRAIGHT TO THE POINT. YAGUCHI, WHAT YOU NEED TO WORK ON NOW IS...
YOUR ADAPT-ABILITY.
AH, I KNEW IT... SO, I HAVEN'T BEEN ADAPT-ING WELL TO THE CHAL-LENGES?
WELL, I GUESS YOU COULD SAY THAT.
BY THE WAY, YAGUCHI, WHAT'S ON YOUR MIND WHEN YOU'RE MAKING ART?
UM...
I GUESS WHAT THE PERSON WHO MADE THE CHALLENGE HAD IN MIND?
AND HOW DO I OVERCOME MY WEAK POINTS... STUFF LIKE THAT...
YOU'RE SO EARNEST, YAGUCHI.

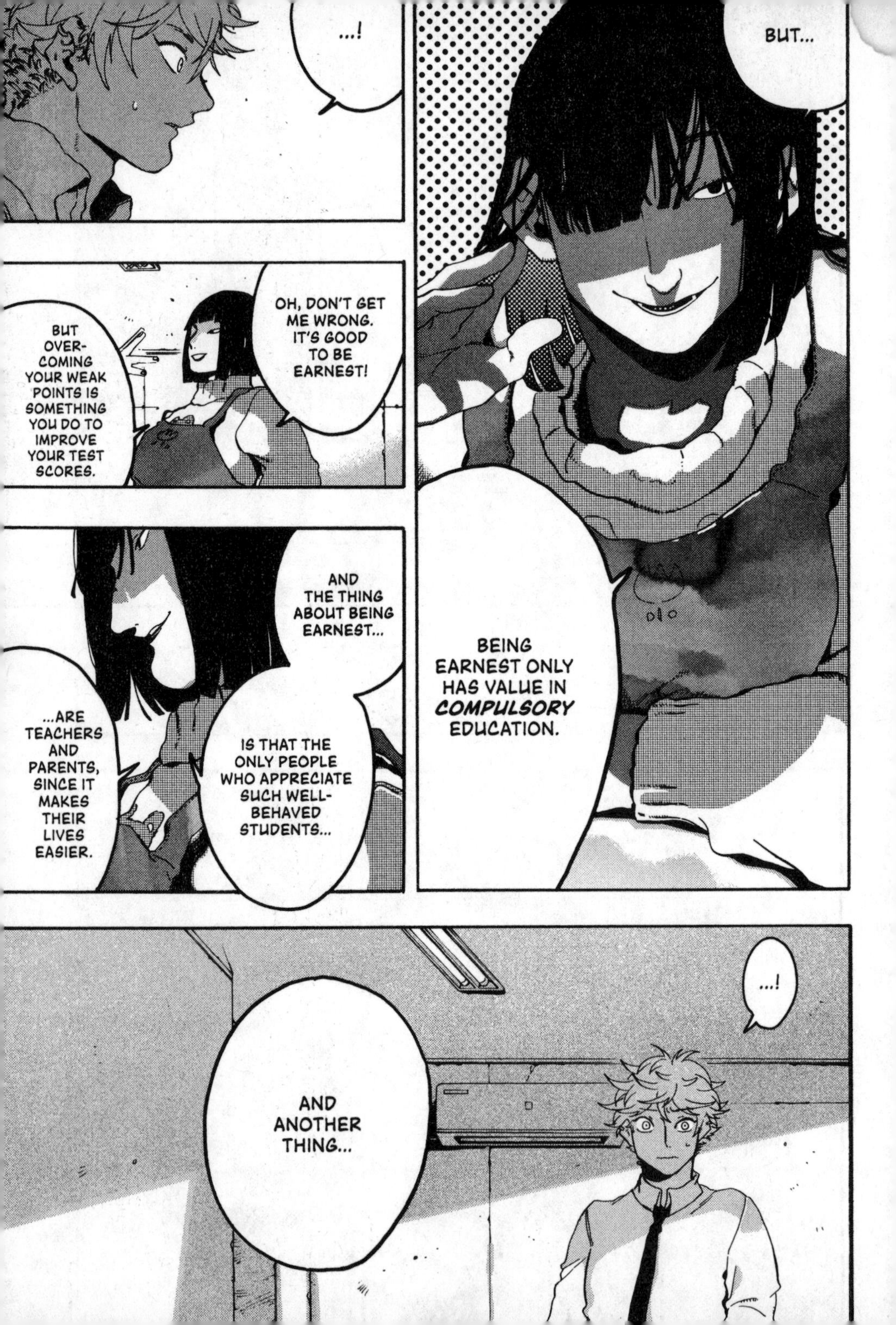
BUT...
BEING EARNEST ONLY HAS VALUE IN *COMPULSORY* EDUCATION.
...!
OH, DON'T GET ME WRONG. IT'S GOOD TO BE EARNEST!
BUT OVER-COMING YOUR WEAK POINTS IS SOMETHING YOU DO TO IMPROVE YOUR TEST SCORES.
AND THE THING ABOUT BEING EARNEST...
IS THAT THE ONLY PEOPLE WHO APPRECIATE SUCH WELL-BEHAVED STUDENTS...
...ARE TEACHERS AND PARENTS, SINCE IT MAKES THEIR LIVES EASIER.
...!
AND ANOTHER THING...

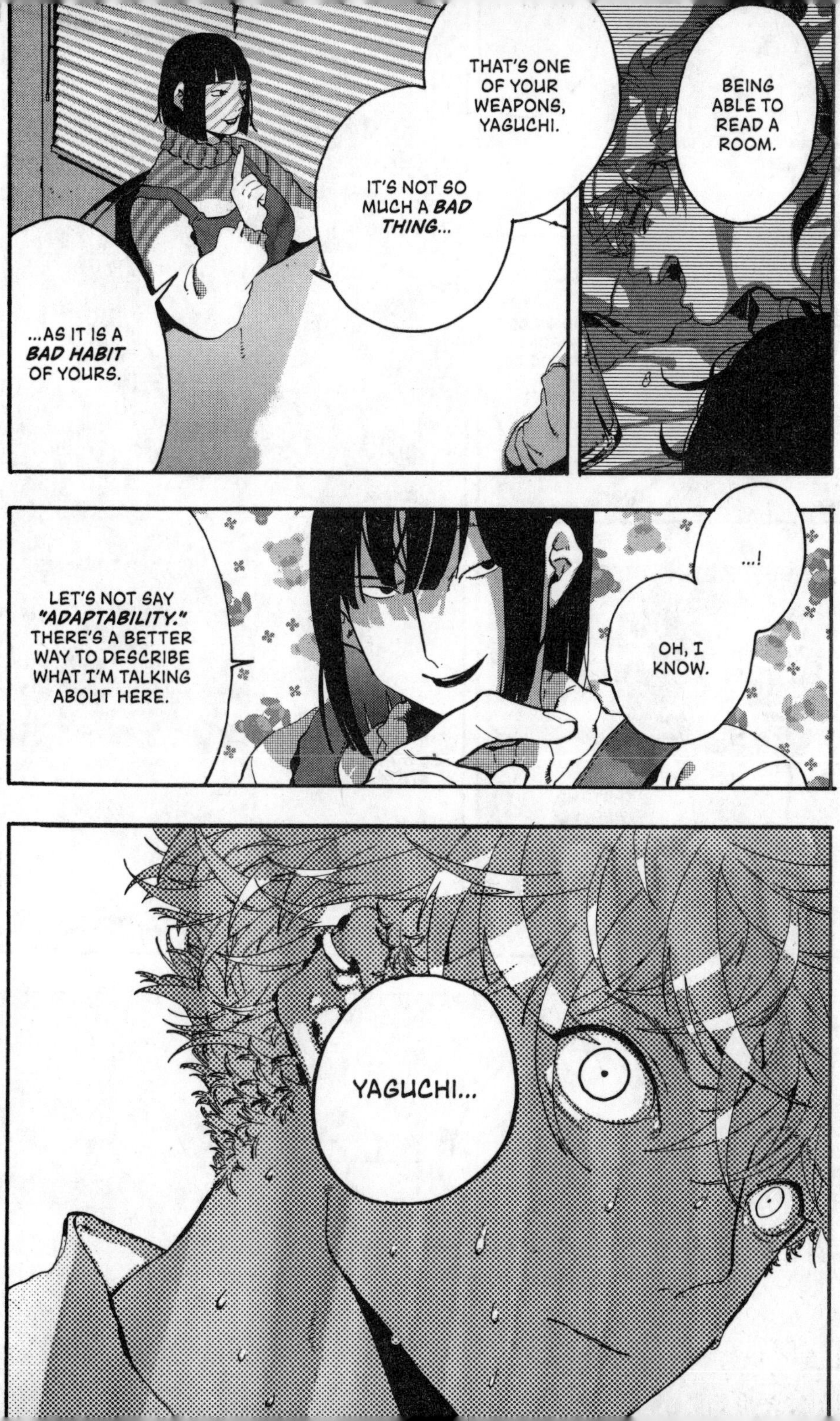
BEING ABLE TO READ A ROOM.
THAT'S ONE OF YOUR WEAPONS, YAGUCHI.
IT'S NOT SO MUCH A *BAD THING*...
...AS IT IS A *BAD HABIT* OF YOURS.
...!
OH, I KNOW.
LET'S NOT SAY *"ADAPTABILITY."* THERE'S A BETTER WAY TO DESCRIBE WHAT I'M TALKING ABOUT HERE.
YAGUCHI...

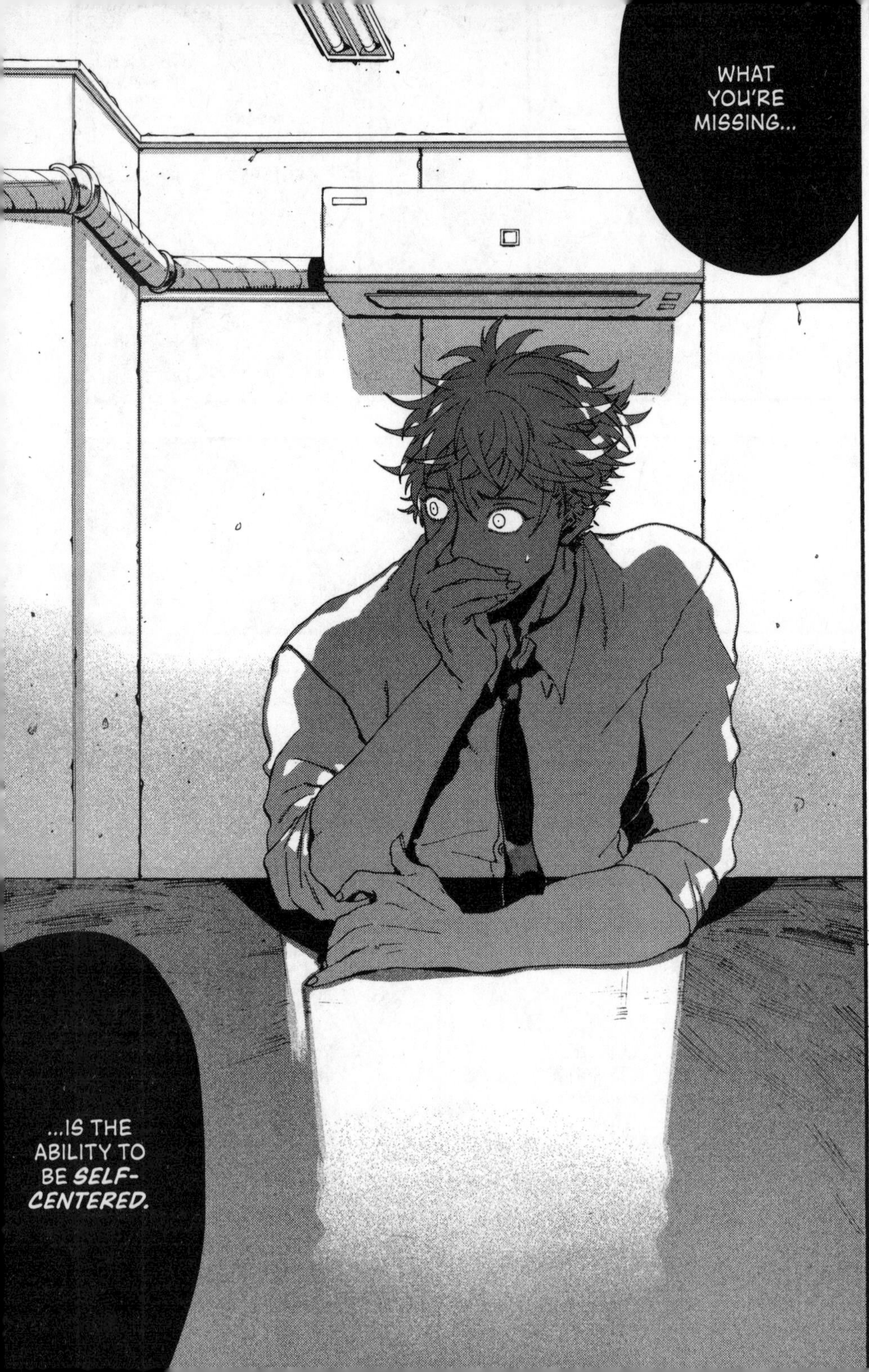
WHAT YOU'RE MISSING...
...IS THE ABILITY TO BE *SELF-CENTERED.*

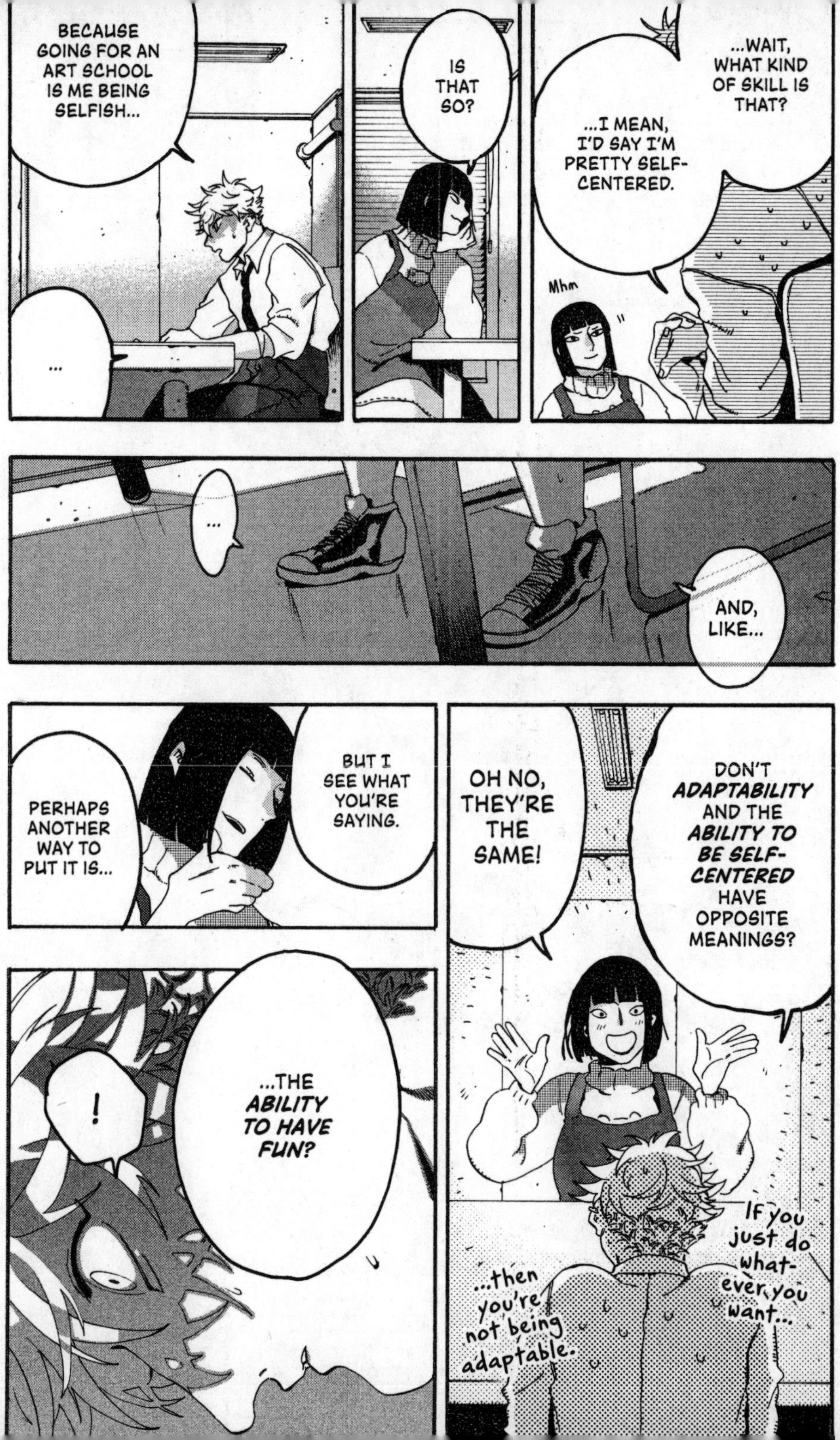
...WAIT, WHAT KIND OF SKILL IS THAT?
...I MEAN, I'D SAY I'M PRETTY SELF-CENTERED.
Mhm
IS THAT SO?
BECAUSE GOING FOR AN ART SCHOOL IS ME BEING SELFISH...
...
AND, LIKE...
...
DON'T ADAPTABILITY AND THE ABILITY TO BE SELF-CENTERED HAVE OPPOSITE MEANINGS?
OH NO, THEY'RE THE SAME!
If you just do whatever you want...
...then you're not being adaptable.
BUT I SEE WHAT YOU'RE SAYING.
PERHAPS ANOTHER WAY TO PUT IT IS...
...THE ABILITY TO HAVE FUN?
!

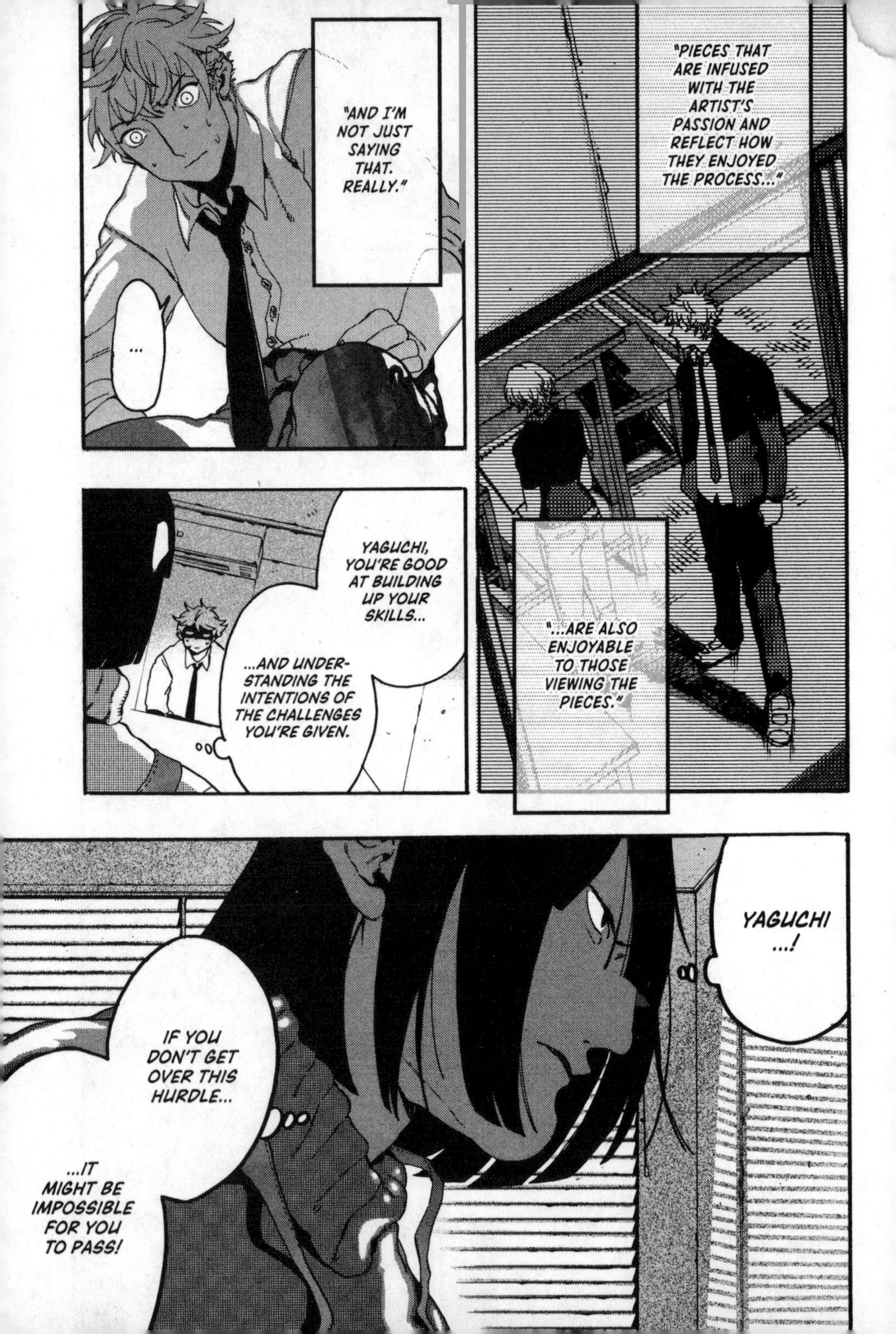
"PIECES THAT ARE INFUSED WITH THE ARTIST'S PASSION AND REFLECT HOW THEY ENJOYED THE PROCESS..."
"...ARE ALSO ENJOYABLE TO THOSE VIEWING THE PIECES."
"AND I'M NOT JUST SAYING THAT. REALLY."
...
YAGUCHI, YOU'RE GOOD AT BUILDING UP YOUR SKILLS...
...AND UNDER-STANDING THE INTENTIONS OF THE CHALLENGES YOU'RE GIVEN.
YAGUCHI ...!
IF YOU DON'T GET OVER THIS HURDLE...
...IT MIGHT BE IMPOSSIBLE FOR YOU TO PASS!

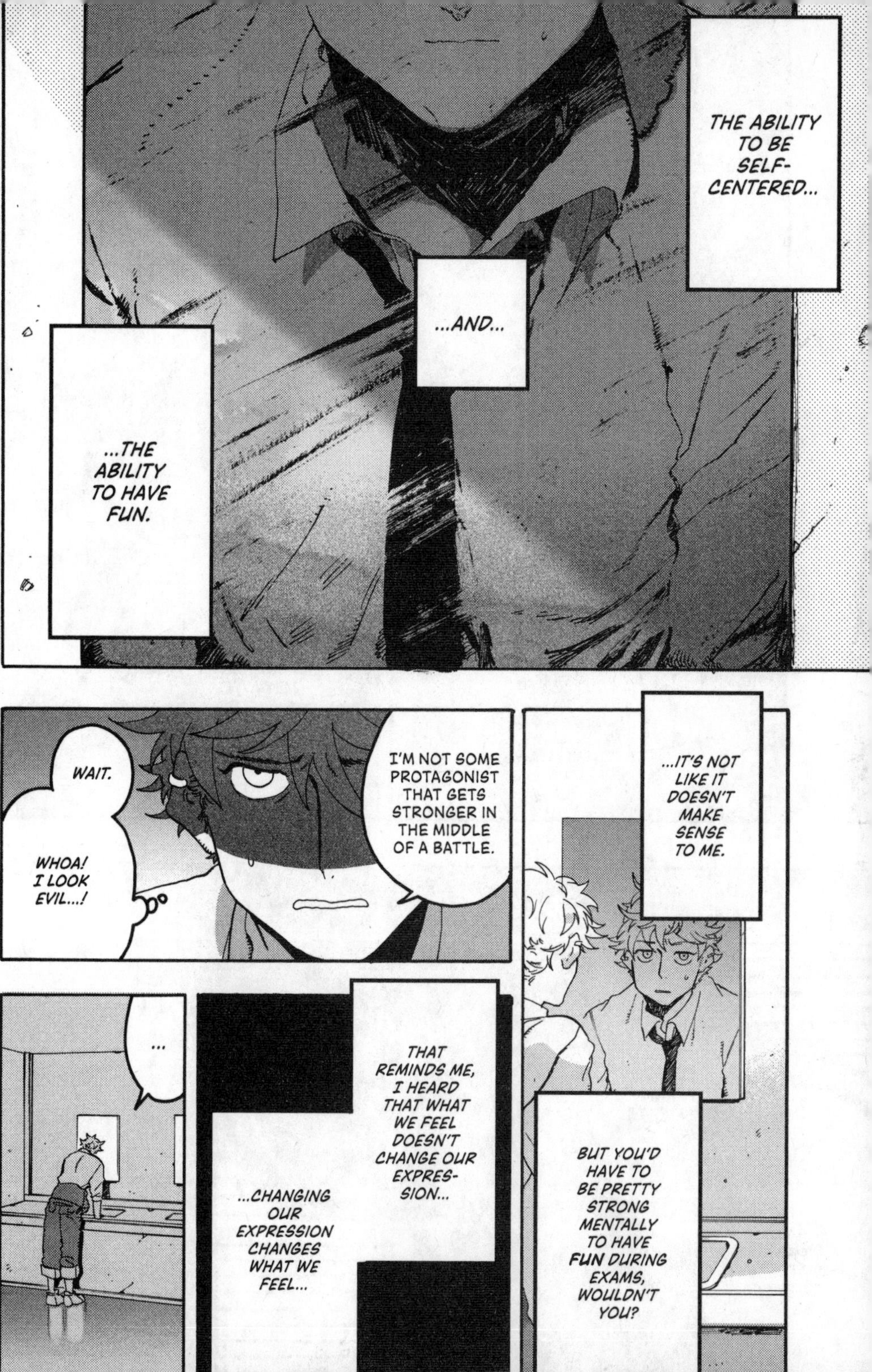
THE ABILITY TO BE SELF-CENTERED...
...AND...
...THE ABILITY TO HAVE FUN.
...IT'S NOT LIKE IT DOESN'T MAKE SENSE TO ME.
BUT YOU'D HAVE TO BE PRETTY STRONG MENTALLY TO HAVE FUN DURING EXAMS, WOULDN'T YOU?
I'M NOT SOME PROTAGONIST THAT GETS STRONGER IN THE MIDDLE OF A BATTLE.
WAIT.
WHOA! I LOOK EVIL...!
THAT REMINDS ME, I HEARD THAT WHAT WE FEEL DOESN'T CHANGE OUR EXPRES-SION...
...CHANGING OUR EXPRESSION CHANGES WHAT WE FEEL...
...

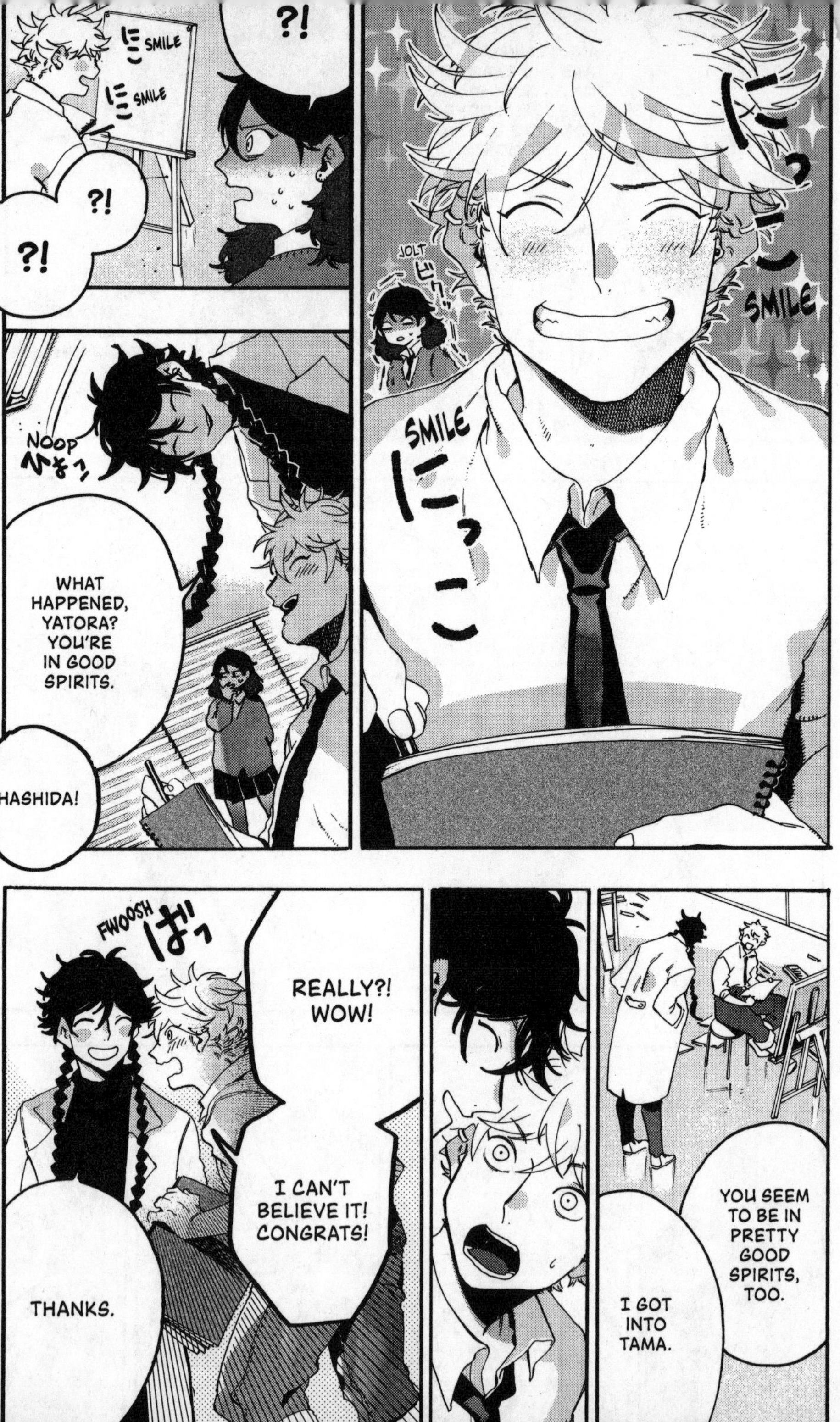

にっこー
SMILE
JOLT
ビクッ
SMILE
にっこー
?!
ニコ SMILE
ニコ SMILE
?!
?!
NOOP
ひょっ
WHAT HAPPENED, YATORA? YOU'RE IN GOOD SPIRITS.
HASHIDA!
YOU SEEM TO BE IN PRETTY GOOD SPIRITS, TOO.
I GOT INTO TAMA.
FWOOSH
ぱっ
REALLY?! WOW!
I CAN'T BELIEVE IT! CONGRATS!
THANKS.

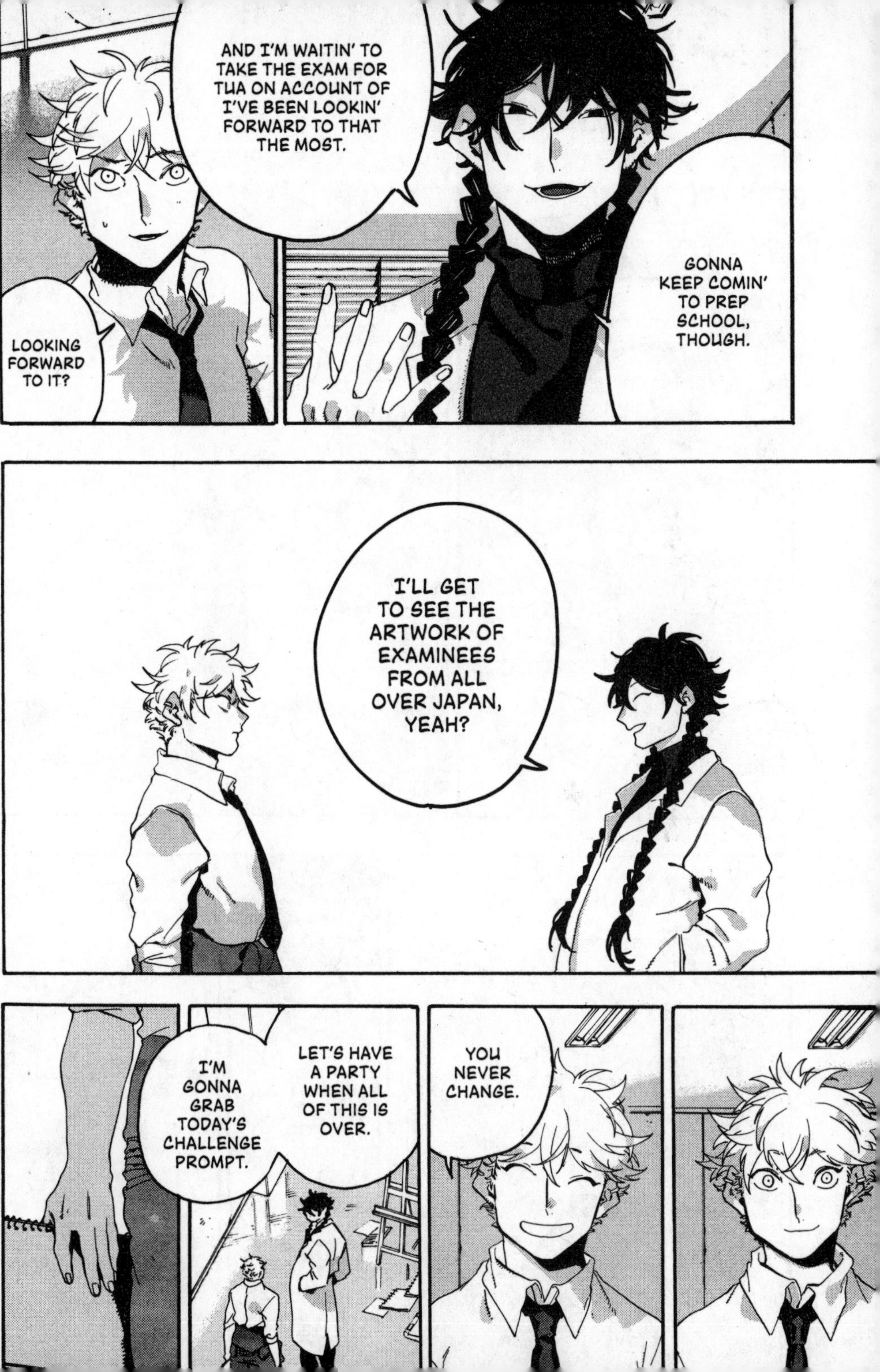
AND I'M WAITIN' TO TAKE THE EXAM FOR TUA ON ACCOUNT OF I'VE BEEN LOOKIN' FORWARD TO THAT THE MOST.
GONNA KEEP COMIN' TO PREP SCHOOL, THOUGH.
LOOKING FORWARD TO IT?
I'LL GET TO SEE THE ARTWORK OF EXAMINEES FROM ALL OVER JAPAN, YEAH?
YOU NEVER CHANGE.
LET'S HAVE A PARTY WHEN ALL OF THIS IS OVER.
I'M GONNA GRAB TODAY'S CHALLENGE PROMPT.

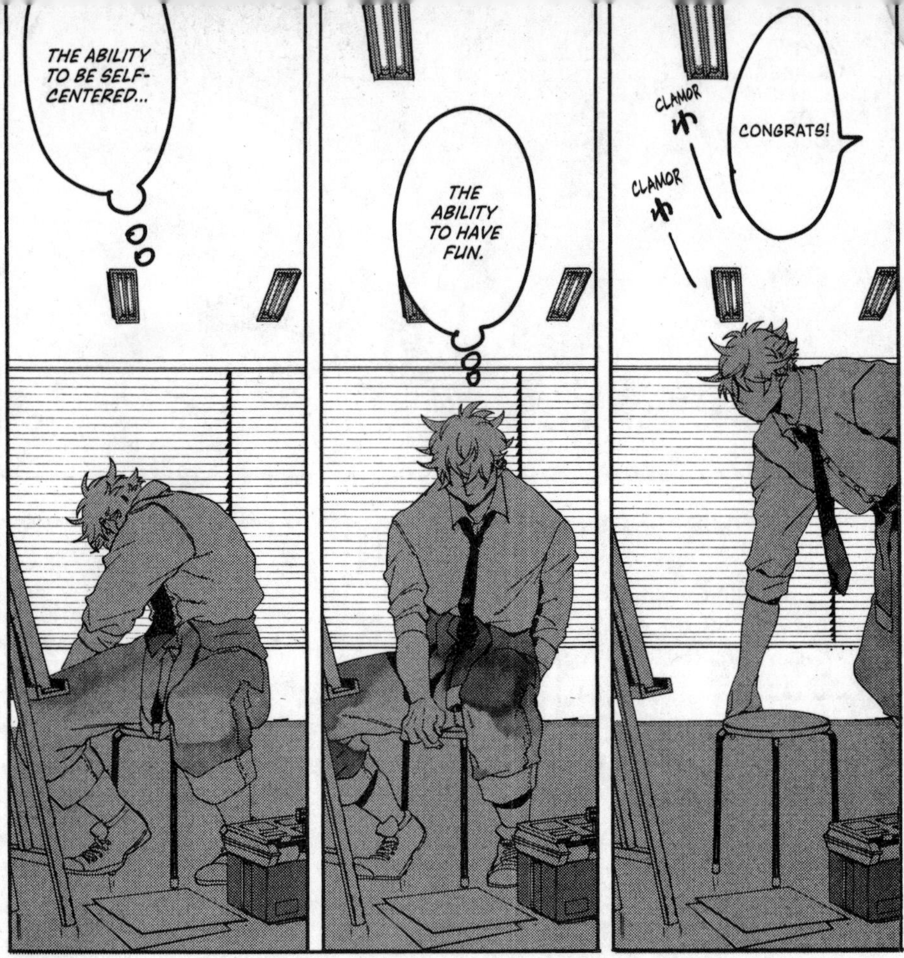
CLAMOR
CLAMOR
CONGRATS!
THE ABILITY TO HAVE FUN.
THE ABILITY TO BE SELF-CENTERED...

ART: SHOTA YAMAMICHI

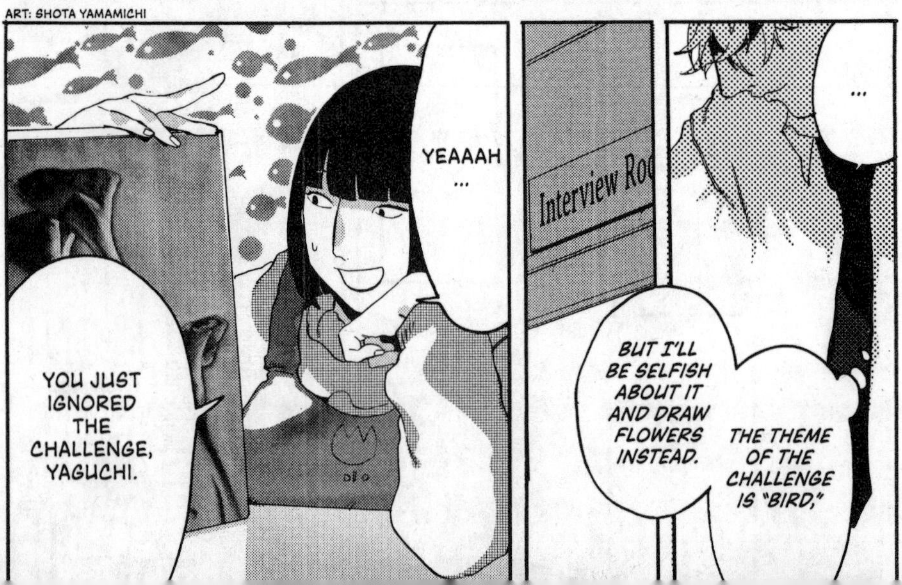
...
THE THEME OF THE CHALLENGE IS "BIRD,"
BUT I'LL BE SELFISH ABOUT IT AND DRAW FLOWERS INSTEAD.
YEAAAH ...
YOU JUST IGNORED THE CHALLENGE, YAGUCHI.

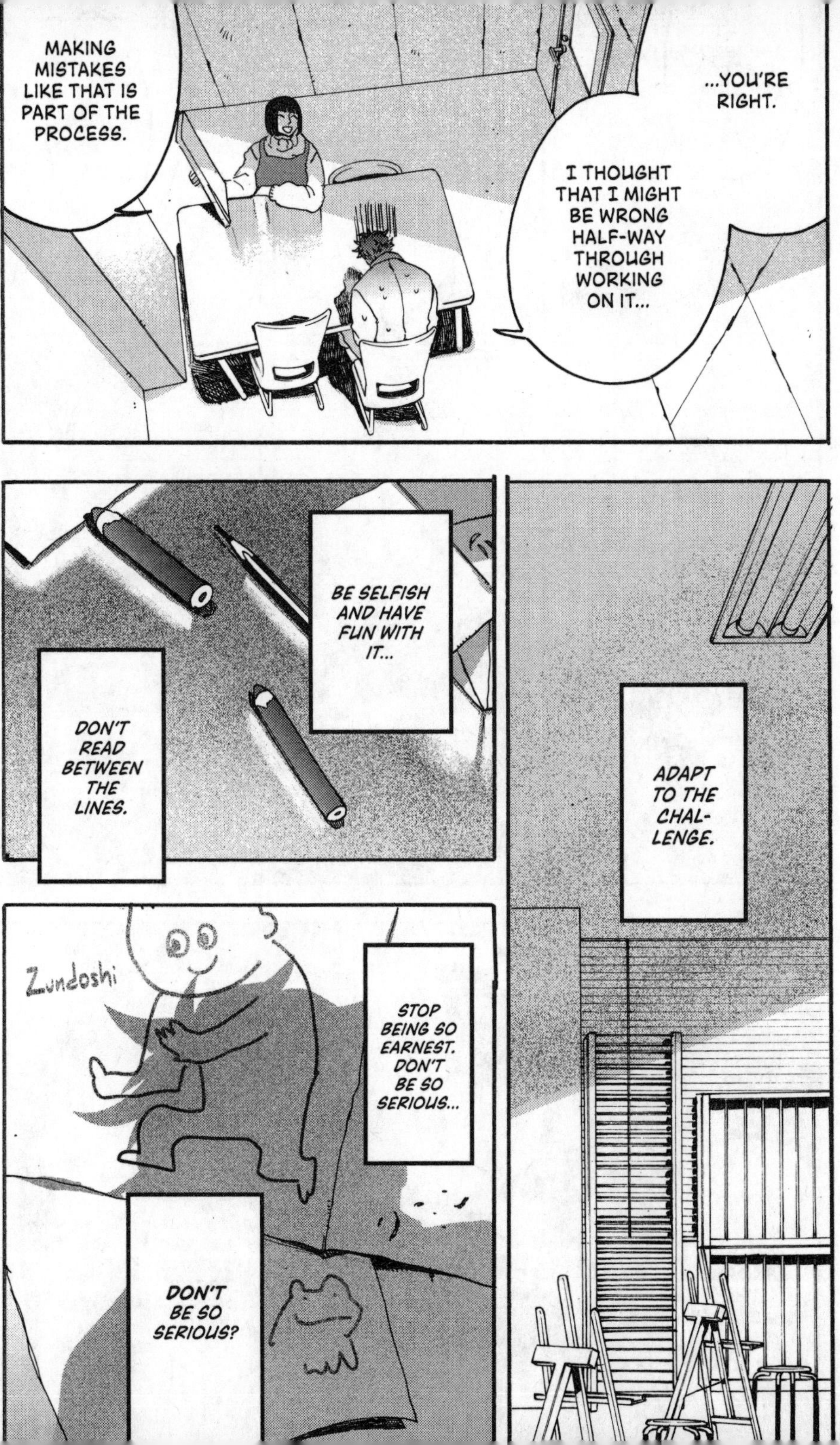
...YOU'RE RIGHT.
I THOUGHT THAT I MIGHT BE WRONG HALF-WAY THROUGH WORKING ON IT...
MAKING MISTAKES LIKE THAT IS PART OF THE PROCESS.
ADAPT TO THE CHAL-LENGE.
BE SELFISH AND HAVE FUN WITH IT...
DON'T READ BETWEEN THE LINES.
STOP BEING SO EARNEST. DON'T BE SO SERIOUS...
Zundoshi
DON'T BE SO SERIOUS?

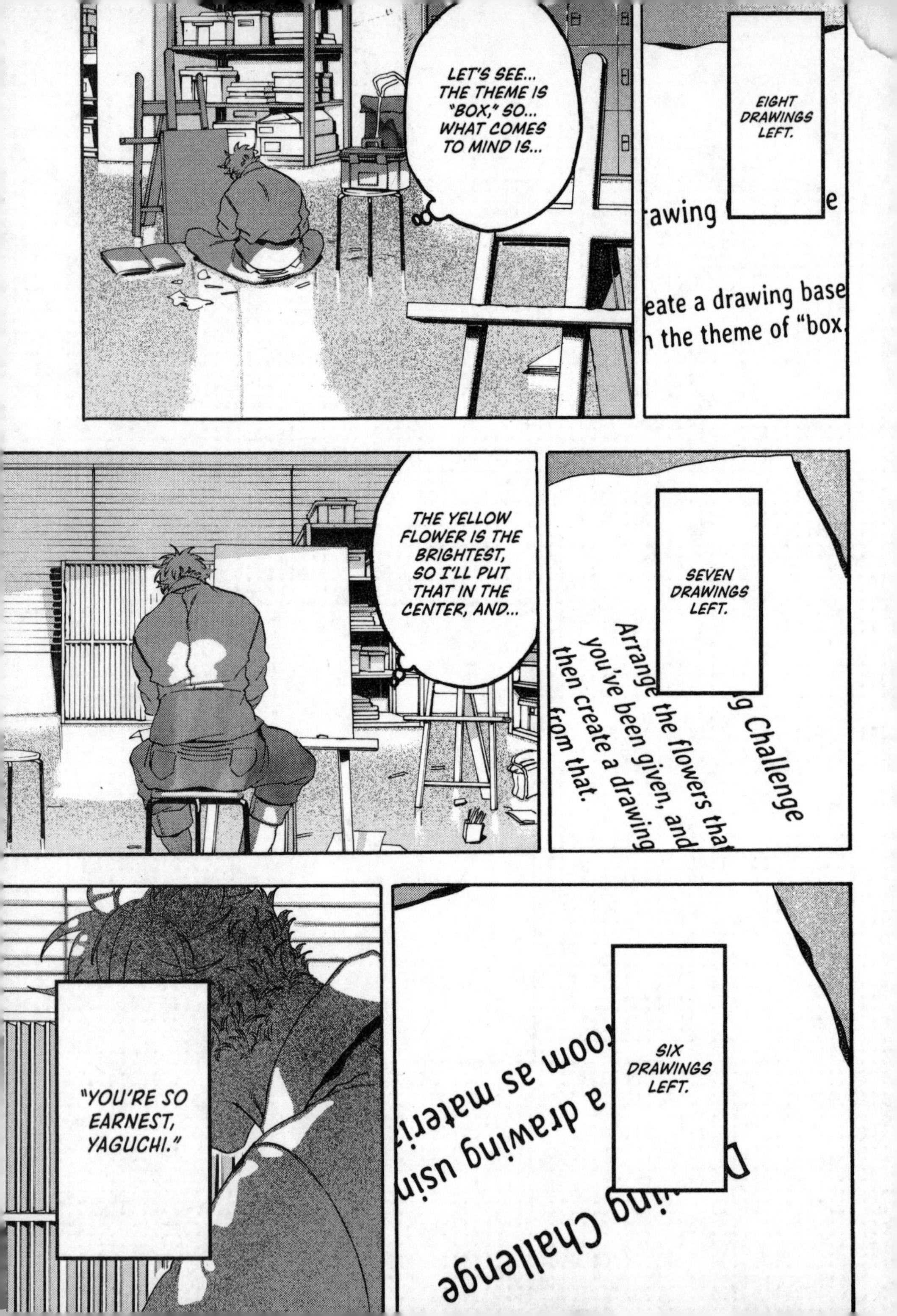
EIGHT DRAWINGS LEFT.
rawing
eate a drawing base
n the theme of "box.
LET'S SEE... THE THEME IS "BOX," SO... WHAT COMES TO MIND IS...
SEVEN DRAWINGS LEFT.
g Challenge
Arrange the flowers tha
you've been given, and
then create a drawing
from that.
THE YELLOW FLOWER IS THE BRIGHTEST, SO I'LL PUT THAT IN THE CENTER, AND...
SIX DRAWINGS LEFT.
ing Challenge
a drawing usin
room as materi
"YOU'RE SO EARNEST, YAGUCHI."

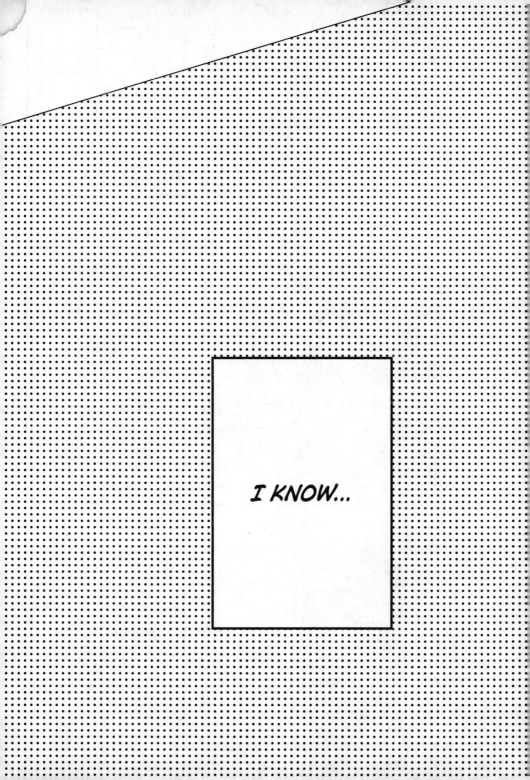

I KNOW...

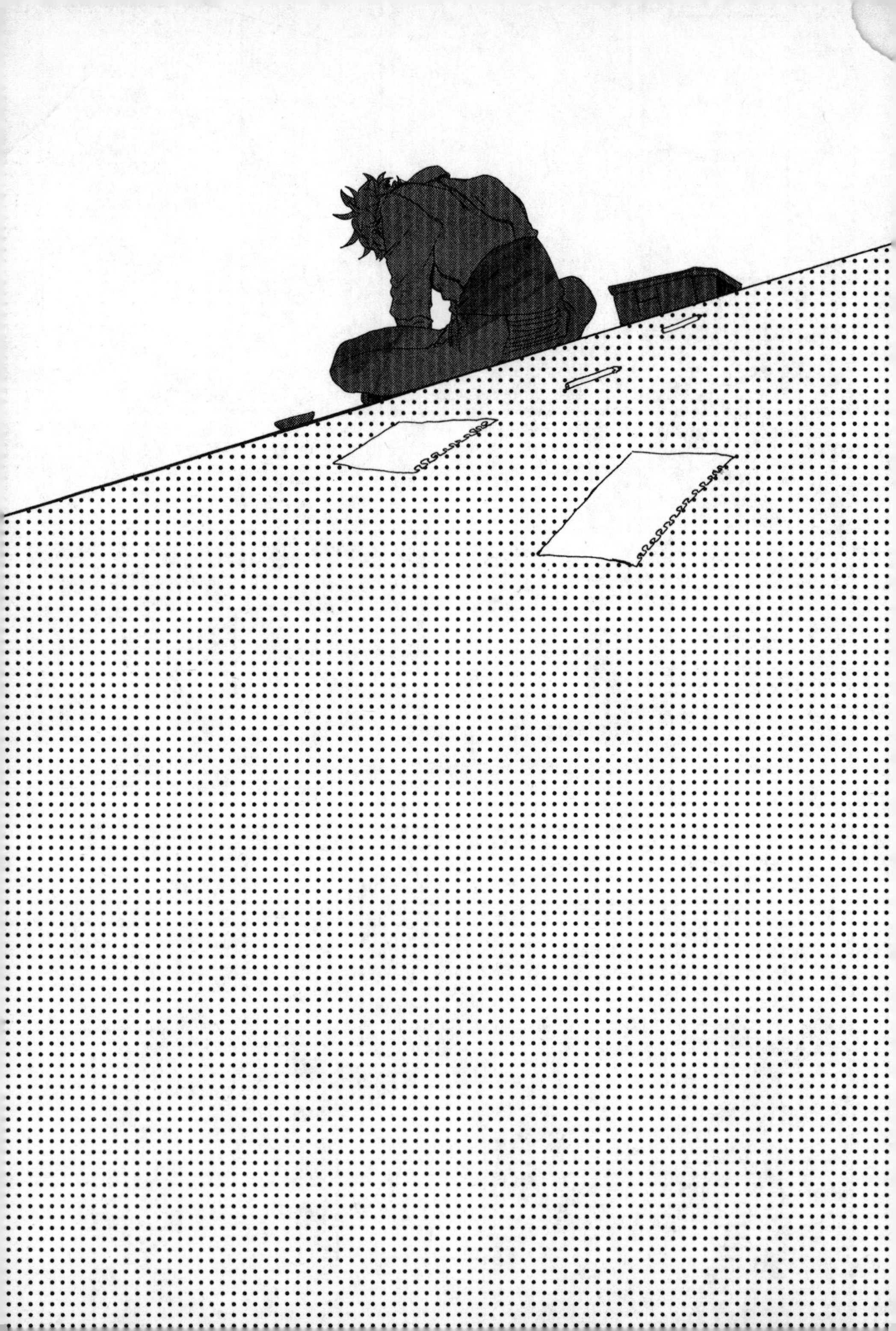

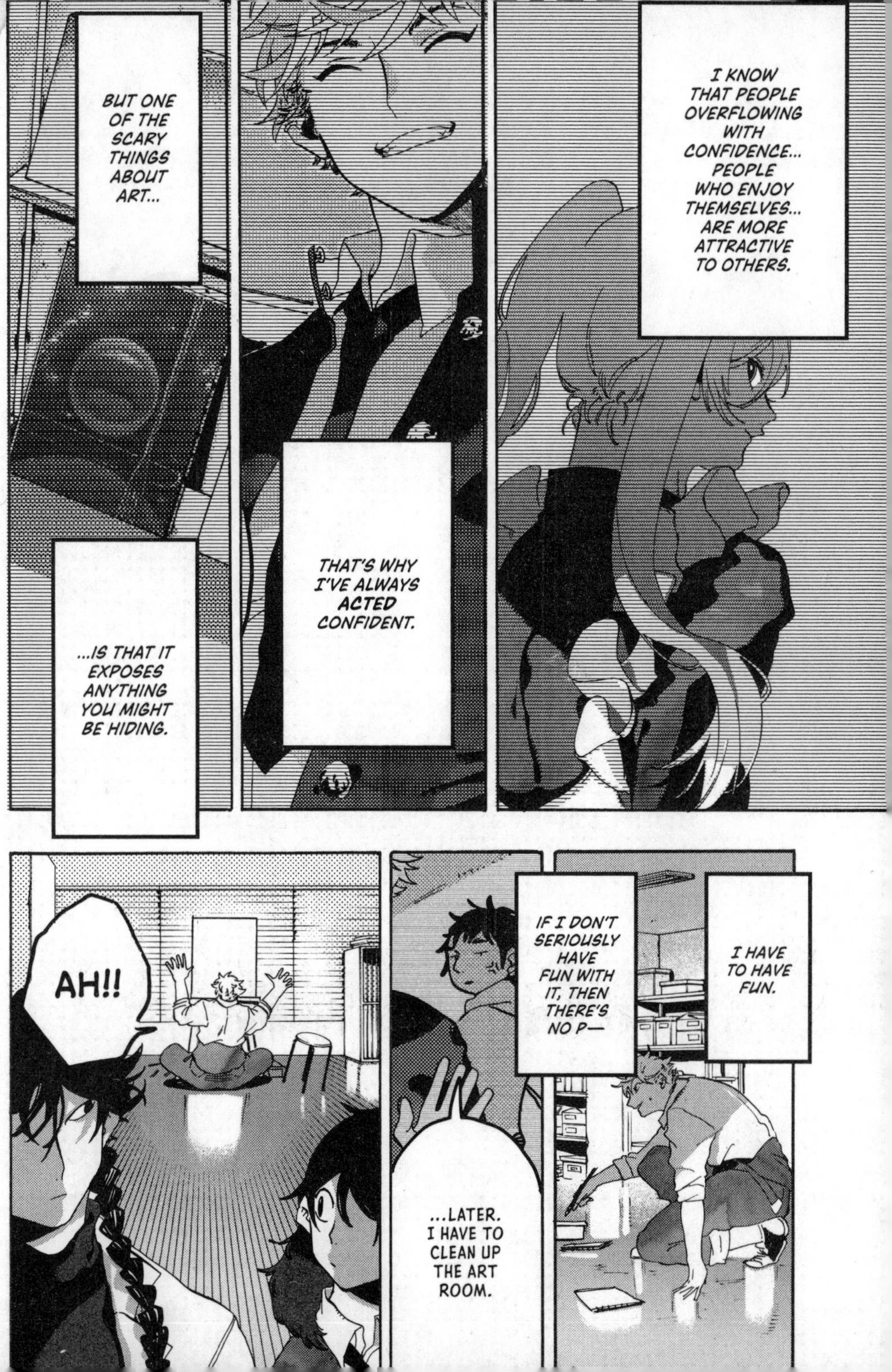
I KNOW THAT PEOPLE OVERFLOWING WITH CONFIDENCE... PEOPLE WHO ENJOY THEMSELVES... ARE MORE ATTRACTIVE TO OTHERS.
THAT'S WHY I'VE ALWAYS ACTED CONFIDENT.
BUT ONE OF THE SCARY THINGS ABOUT ART...
...IS THAT IT EXPOSES ANYTHING YOU MIGHT BE HIDING.
I HAVE TO HAVE FUN.
IF I DON'T SERIOUSLY HAVE FUN WITH IT, THEN THERE'S NO P—
...LATER. I HAVE TO CLEAN UP THE ART ROOM.
AH!!

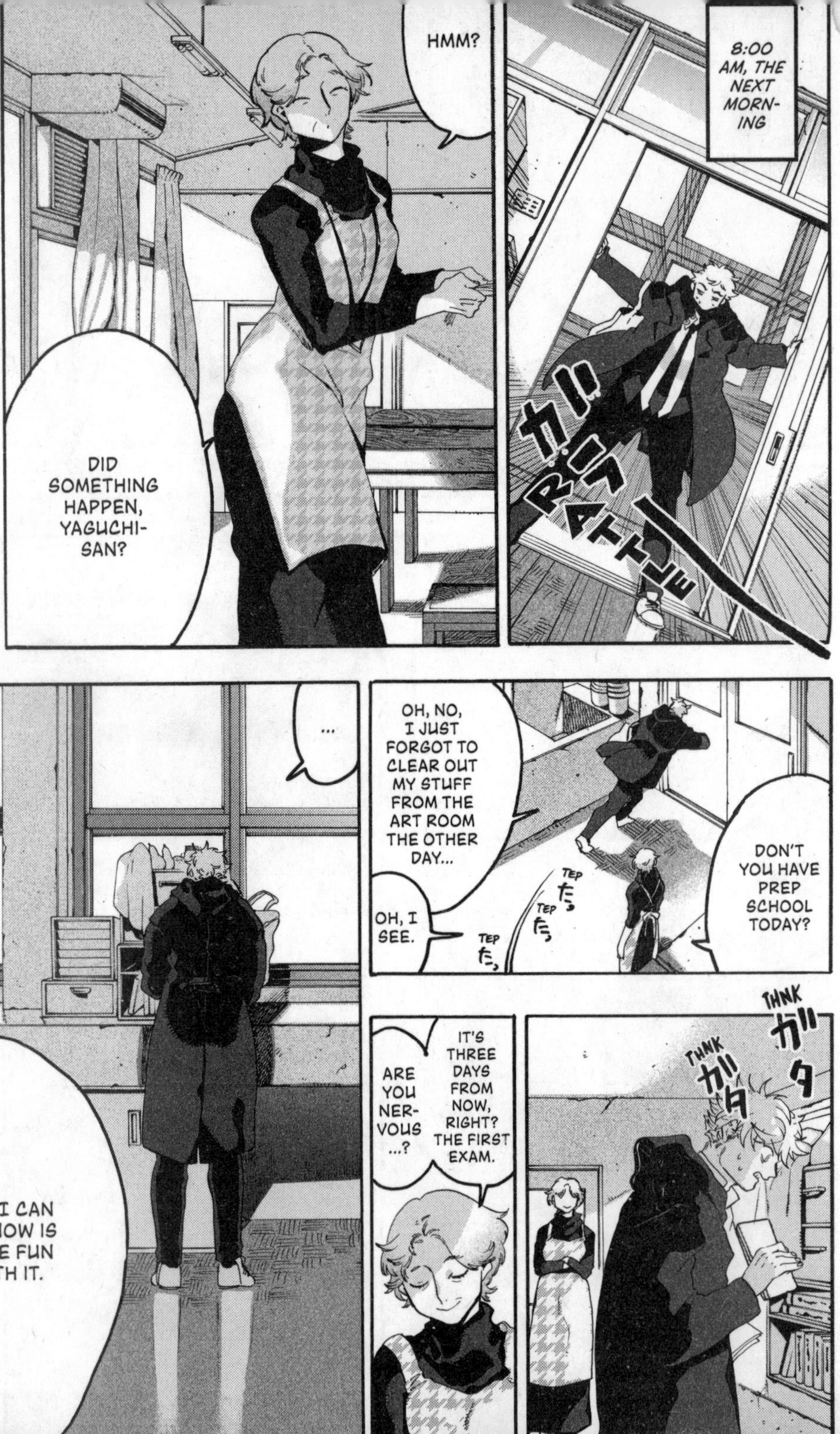

8:00 AM, THE NEXT MORNING-ING
RATTLE
HMM?
DID SOMETHING HAPPEN, YAGUCHI-SAN?
DON'T YOU HAVE PREP SCHOOL TODAY?
OH, NO, I JUST FORGOT TO CLEAR OUT MY STUFF FROM THE ART ROOM THE OTHER DAY...
OH, I SEE.
TEP
TEP
TEP
THNK
THNK
IT'S THREE DAYS FROM NOW, RIGHT? THE FIRST EXAM.
ARE YOU NER-VOUS ...?
...
ALL I CAN DO NOW IS HAVE FUN WITH IT.

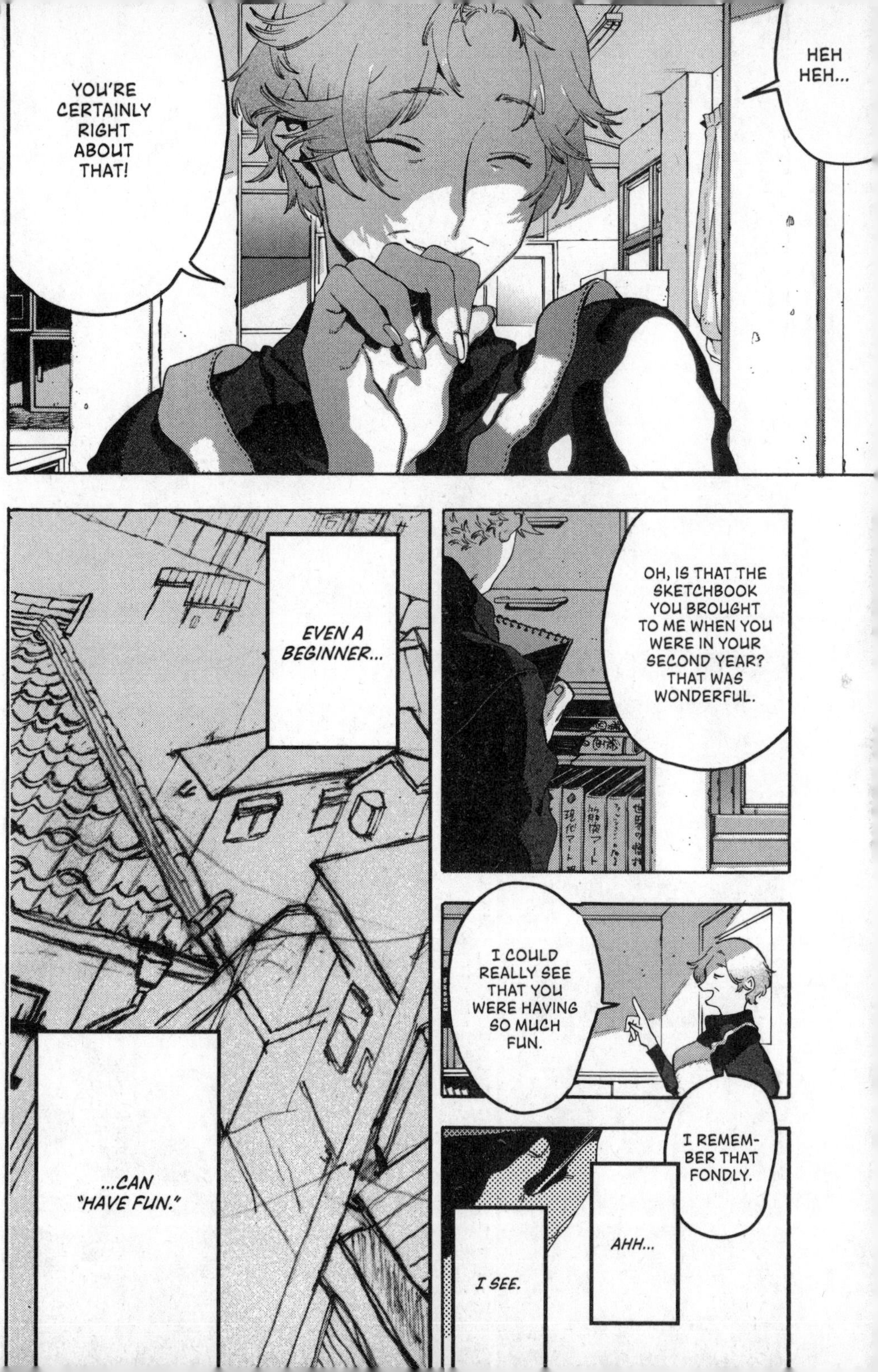
HEH HEH...
YOU'RE CERTAINLY RIGHT ABOUT THAT!
OH, IS THAT THE SKETCHBOOK YOU BROUGHT TO ME WHEN YOU WERE IN YOUR SECOND YEAR? THAT WAS WONDERFUL.
I COULD REALLY SEE THAT YOU WERE HAVING SO MUCH FUN.
I REMEMBER THAT FONDLY.
AHH...
I SEE.
EVEN A BEGINNER...
...CAN "HAVE FUN."

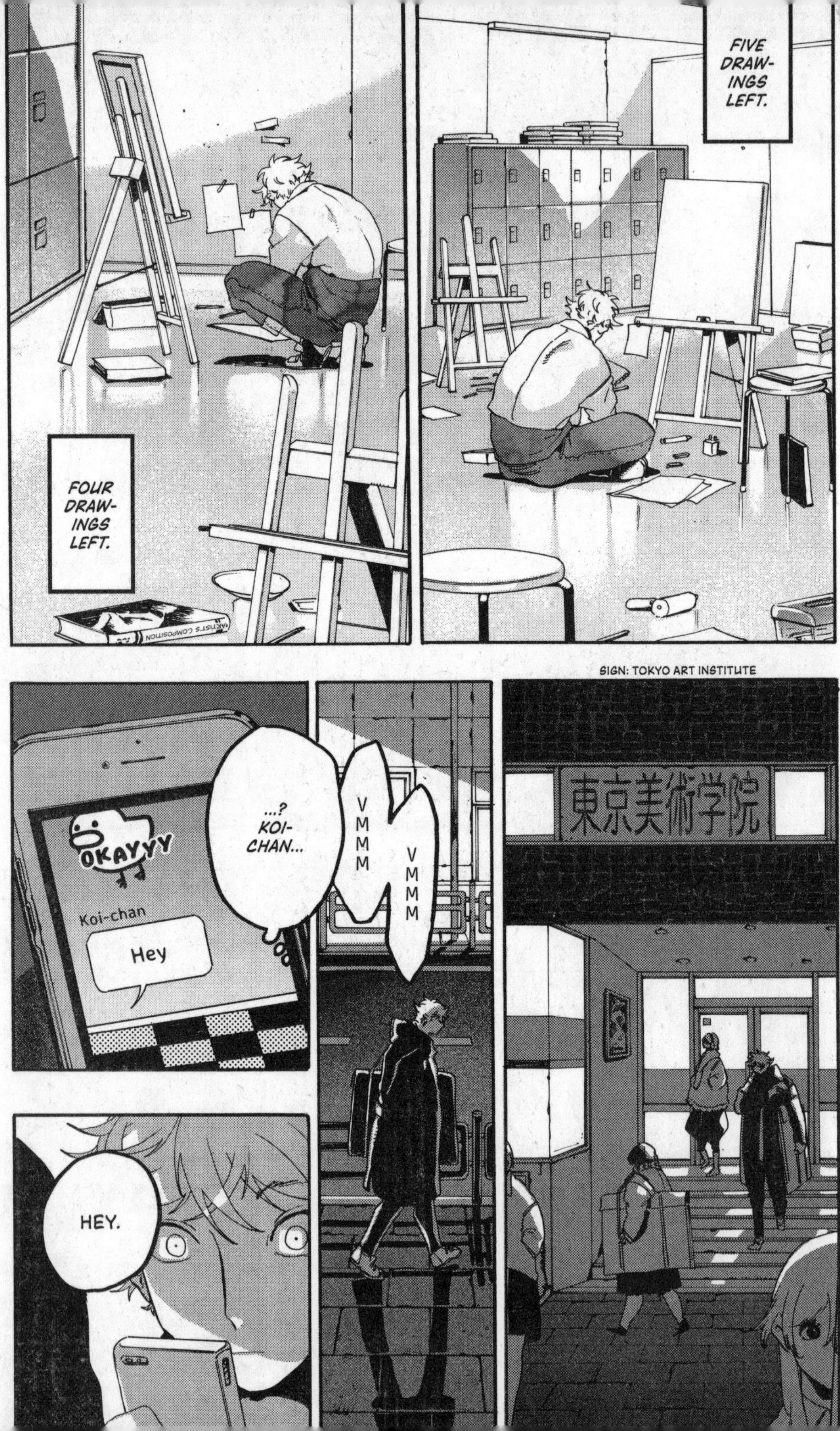
FIVE DRAWINGS LEFT.
FOUR DRAWINGS LEFT.
SIGN: TOKYO ART INSTITUTE
東京美術学院
VMMM
VMMM
...? KOI-CHAN...
OKAYYY
Koi-chan
Hey
HEY.

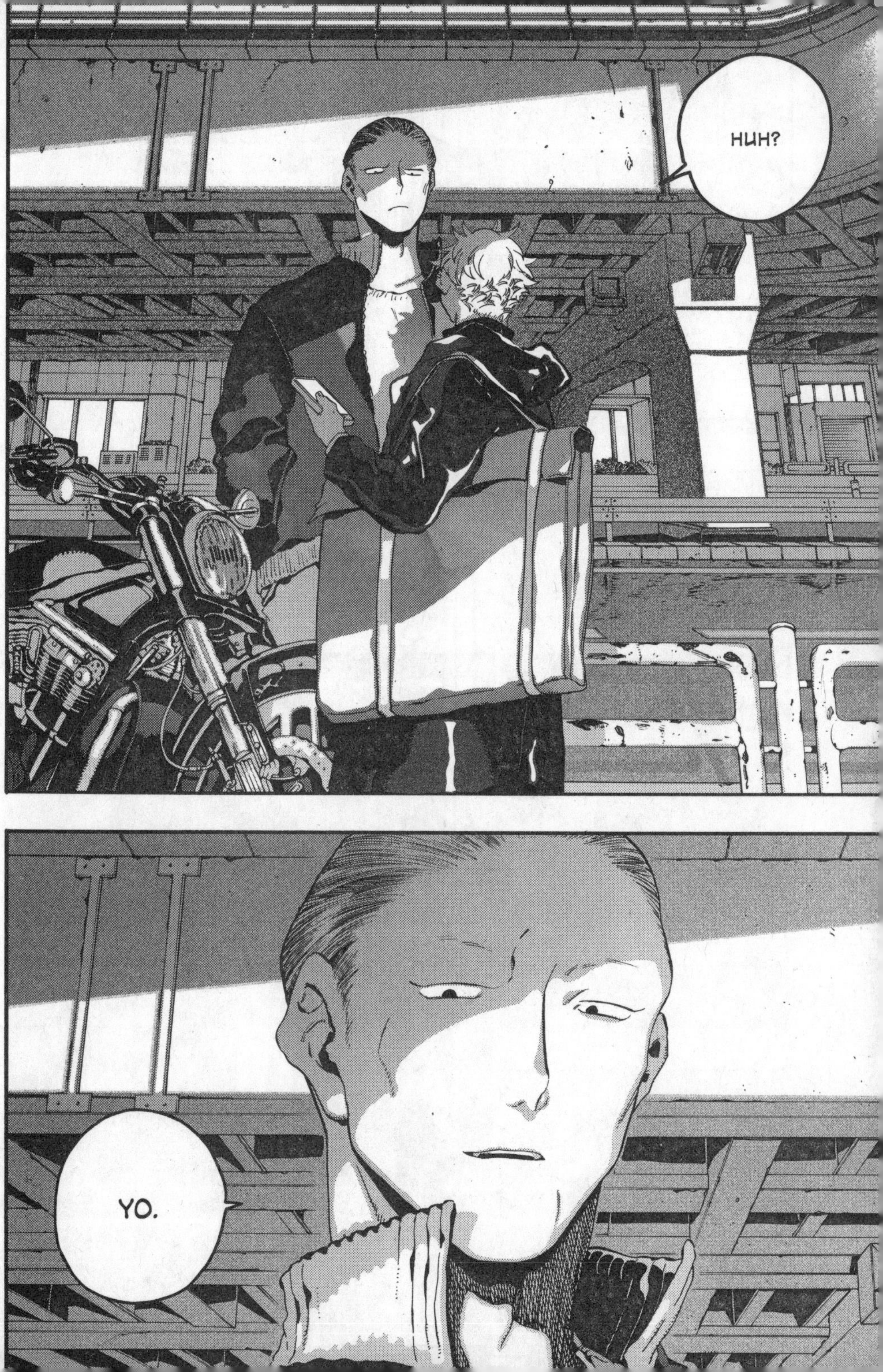
HUH?
YO.

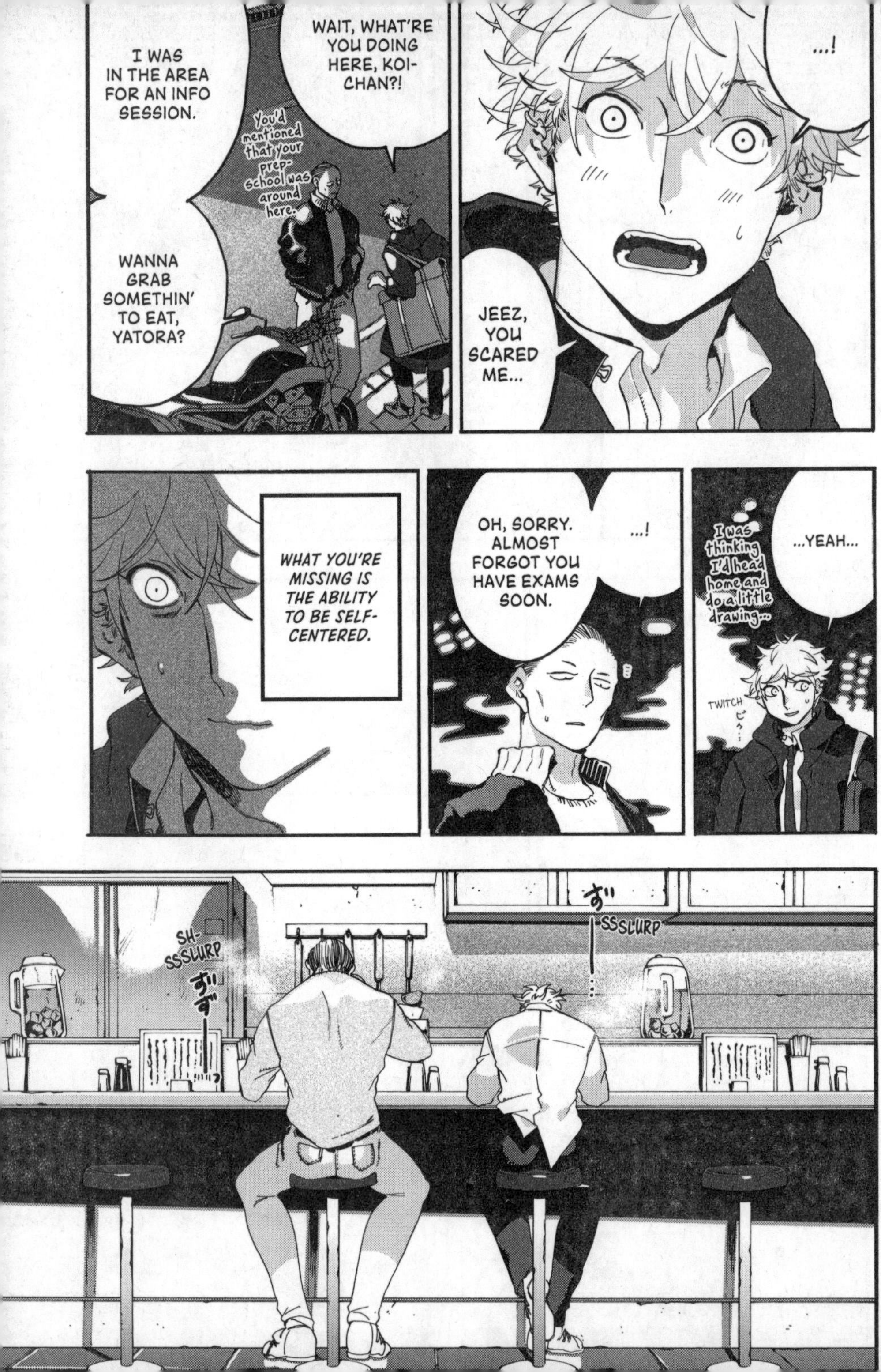
...!
JEEZ, YOU SCARED ME...
WAIT, WHAT'RE YOU DOING HERE, KOI-CHAN?!
I WAS IN THE AREA FOR AN INFO SESSION.
You'd mentioned that your prep-school was around here.
WANNA GRAB SOMETHIN' TO EAT, YATORA?
...YEAH...
I was thinking I'd head home and do a little drawing...
TWITCH
ピク…
...!
OH, SORRY. ALMOST FORGOT YOU HAVE EXAMS SOON.
WHAT YOU'RE MISSING IS THE ABILITY TO BE SELF-CENTERED.
ずー
SSSLURP
SH-SSSLURP
ずずー

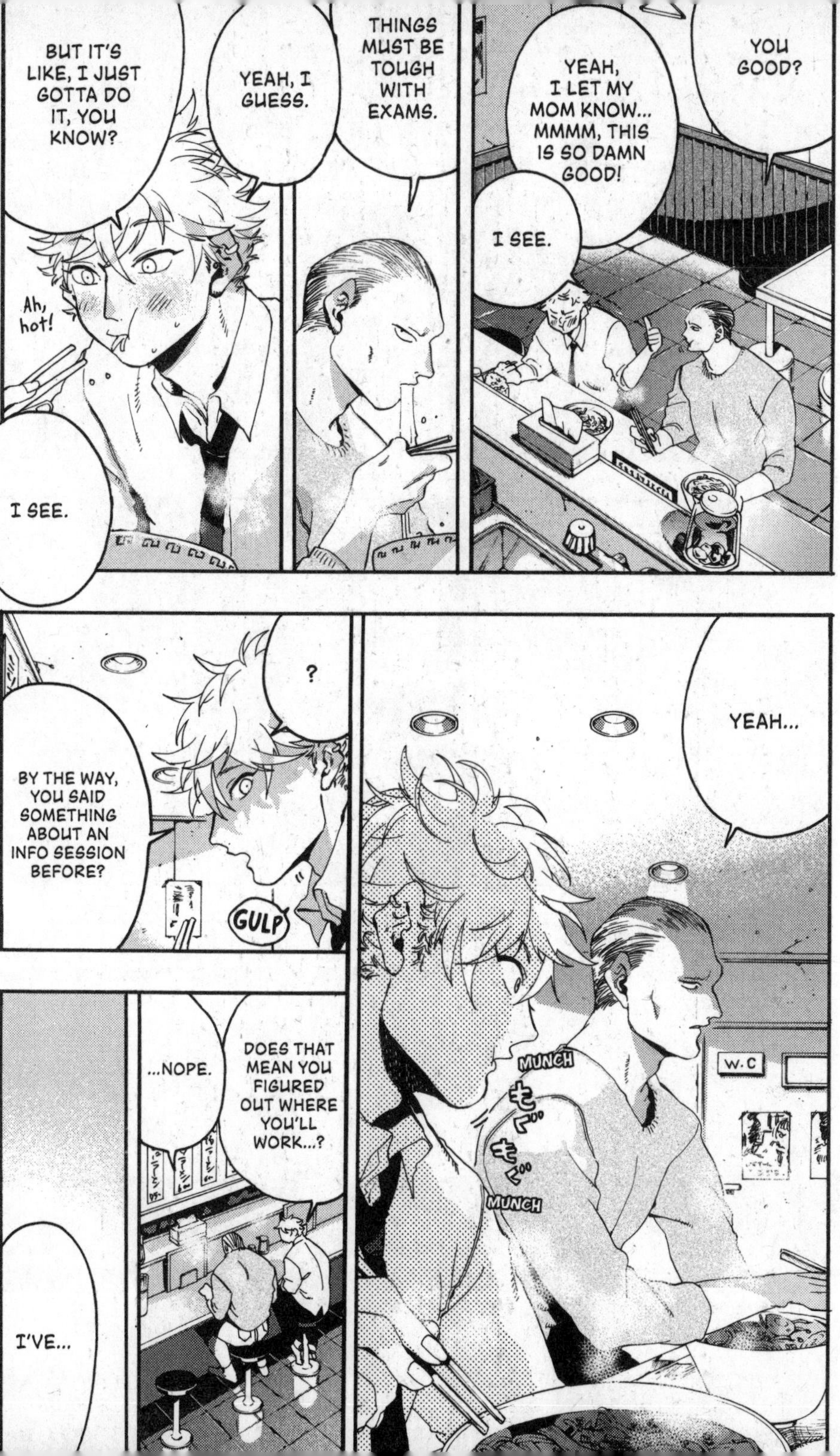
YOU GOOD?
YEAH, I LET MY MOM KNOW... MMMM, THIS IS SO DAMN GOOD!
I SEE.
THINGS MUST BE TOUGH WITH EXAMS.
YEAH, I GUESS.
BUT IT'S LIKE, I JUST GOTTA DO IT, YOU KNOW?
Ah, hot!
I SEE.
YEAH...
MUNCH
もぐ
もぐ
MUNCH
?
BY THE WAY, YOU SAID SOMETHING ABOUT AN INFO SESSION BEFORE?
GULP
DOES THAT MEAN YOU FIGURED OUT WHERE YOU'LL WORK...?
...NOPE.
I'VE...

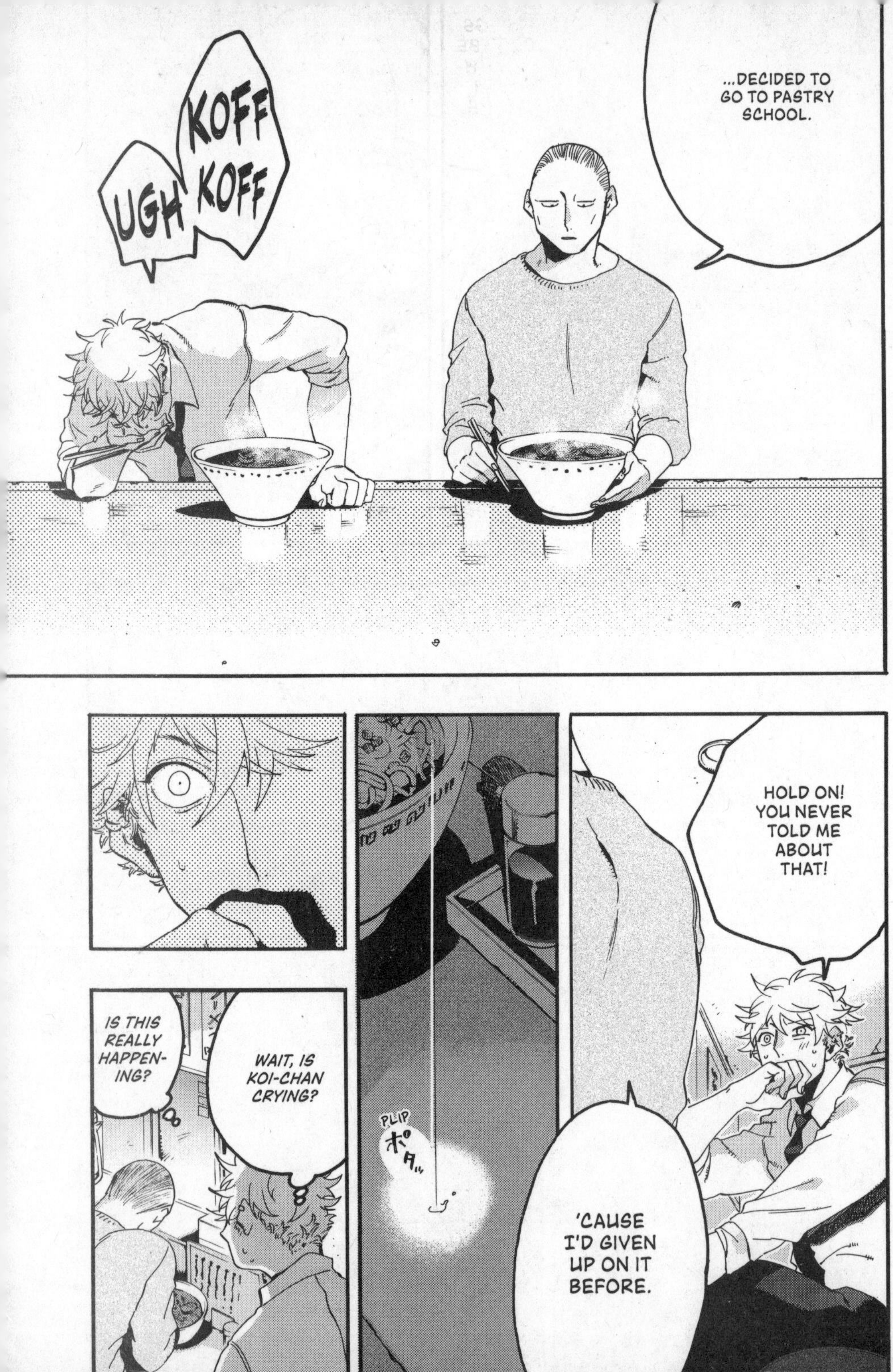
...DECIDED TO GO TO PASTRY SCHOOL.
KOFF KOFF
UGH
HOLD ON! YOU NEVER TOLD ME ABOUT THAT!
'CAUSE I'D GIVEN UP ON IT BEFORE.
PLIP
ポタ
WAIT, IS KOI-CHAN CRYING?
IS THIS REALLY HAPPEN-ING?

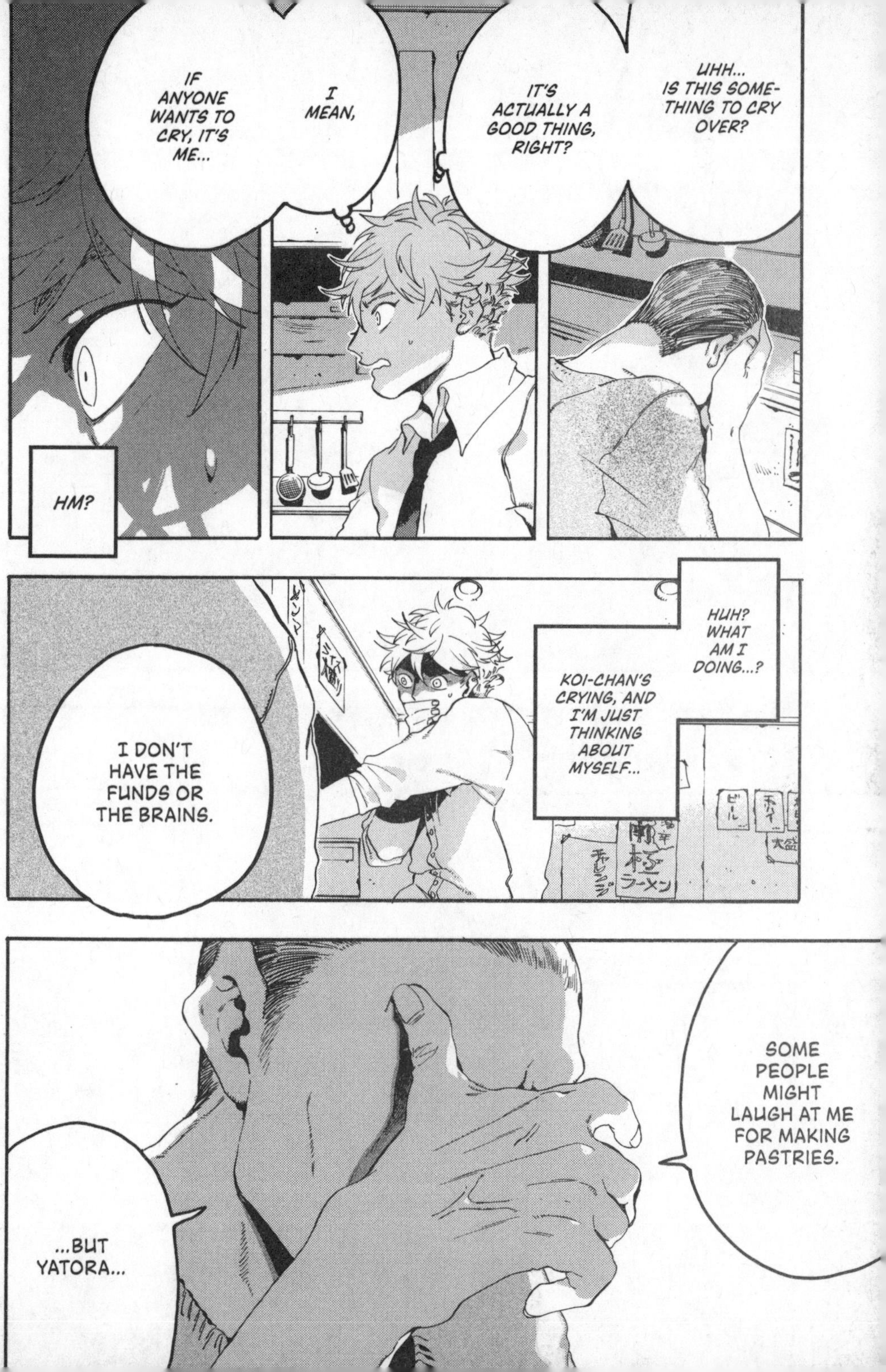
UHH... IS THIS SOME-THING TO CRY OVER?
IT'S ACTUALLY A GOOD THING, RIGHT?
I MEAN,
IF ANYONE WANTS TO CRY, IT'S ME...
HM?
HUH? WHAT AM I DOING...?
KOI-CHAN'S CRYING, AND I'M JUST THINKING ABOUT MYSELF...
I DON'T HAVE THE FUNDS OR THE BRAINS.
SOME PEOPLE MIGHT LAUGH AT ME FOR MAKING PASTRIES.
...BUT YATORA...

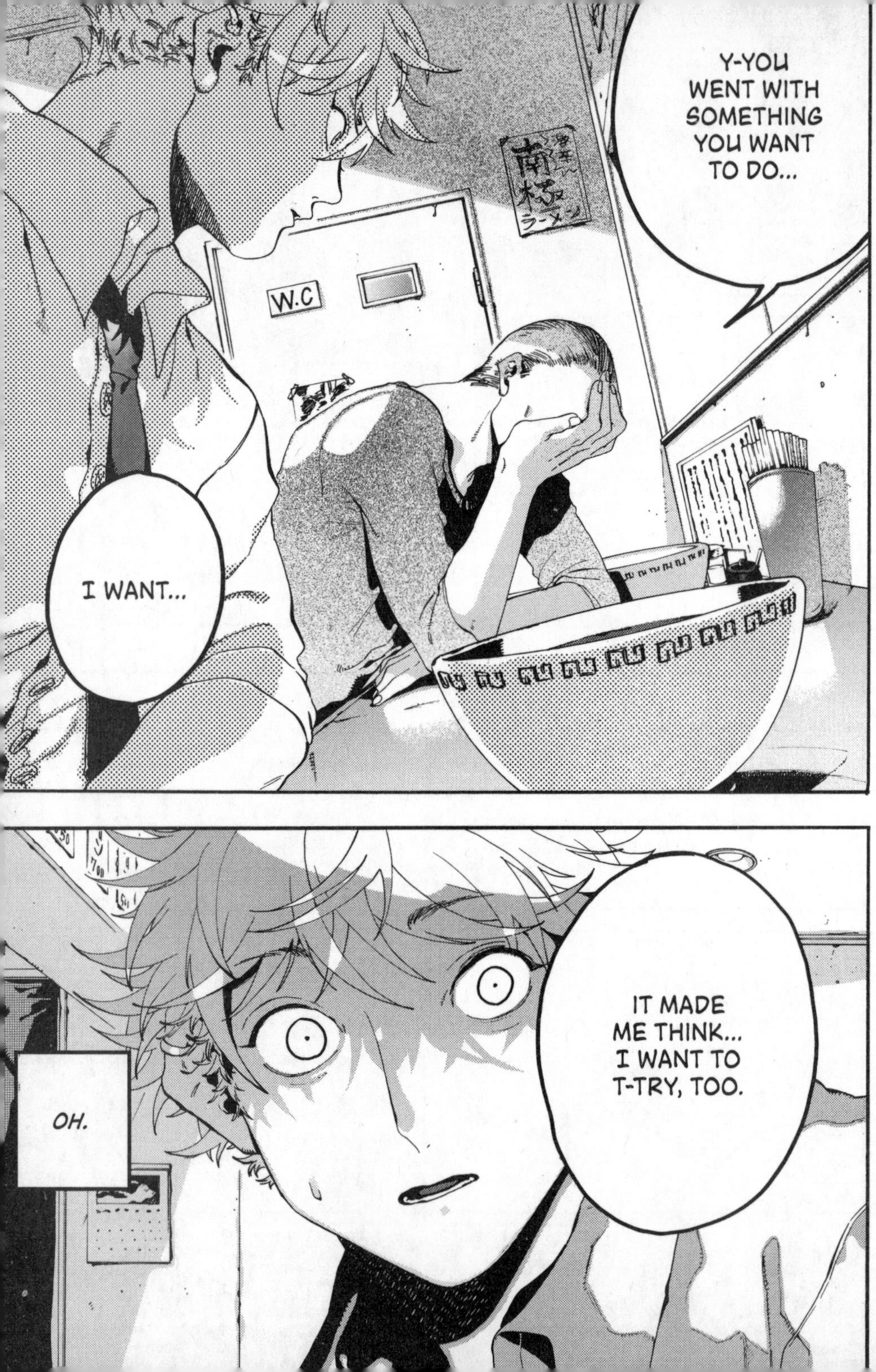
Y-YOU WENT WITH SOMETHING YOU WANT TO DO...
南極
ラーメン
W.C
I WANT...
IT MADE ME THINK... I WANT TO T-TRY, TOO.
OH.

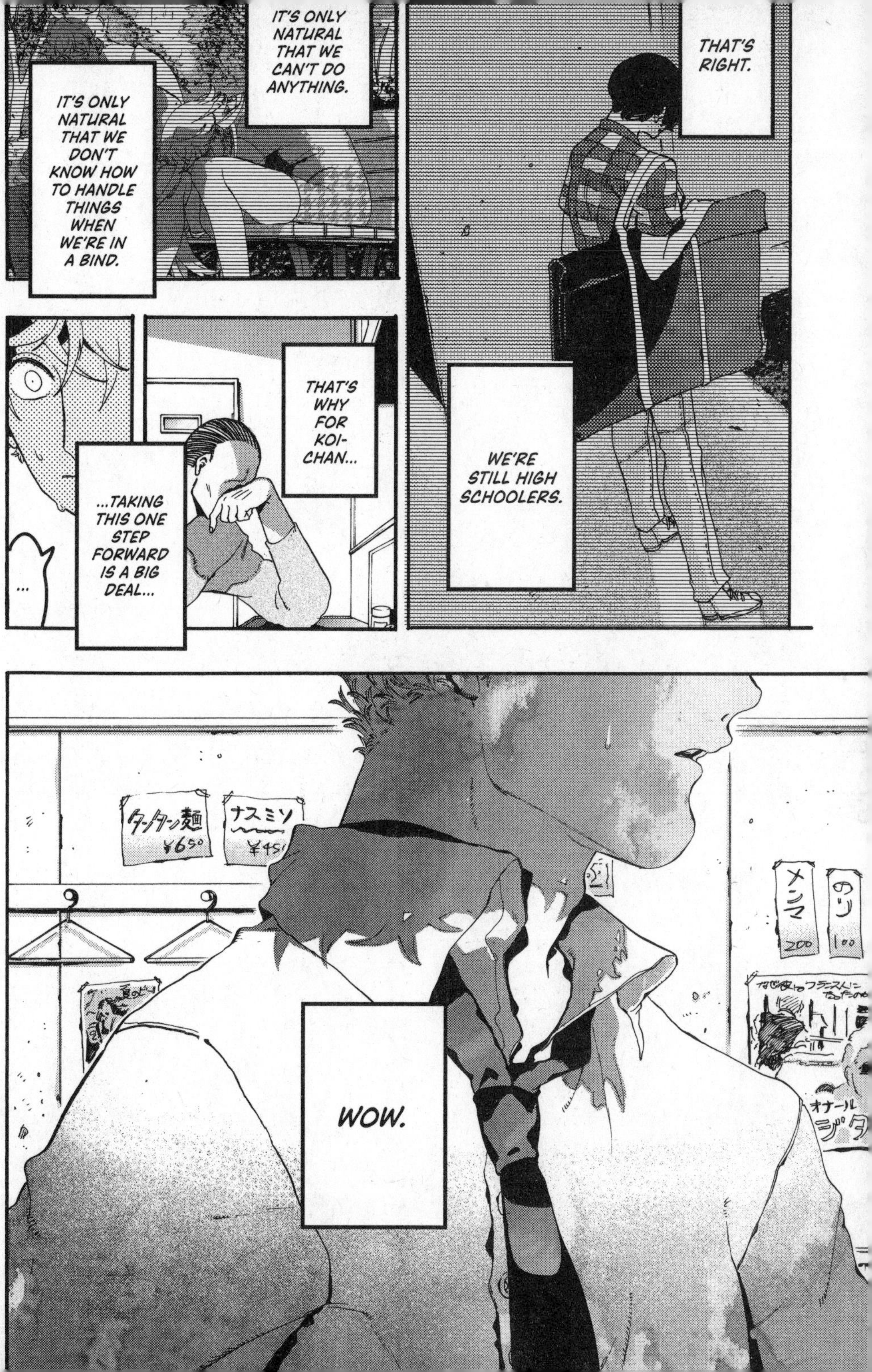
THAT'S RIGHT.
WE'RE STILL HIGH SCHOOLERS.
IT'S ONLY NATURAL THAT WE CAN'T DO ANYTHING.
IT'S ONLY NATURAL THAT WE DON'T KNOW HOW TO HANDLE THINGS WHEN WE'RE IN A BIND.
THAT'S WHY FOR KOI-CHAN...
...TAKING THIS ONE STEP FORWARD IS A BIG DEAL...
...
メンマ 200
のり 100
ナスミソ
WOW.

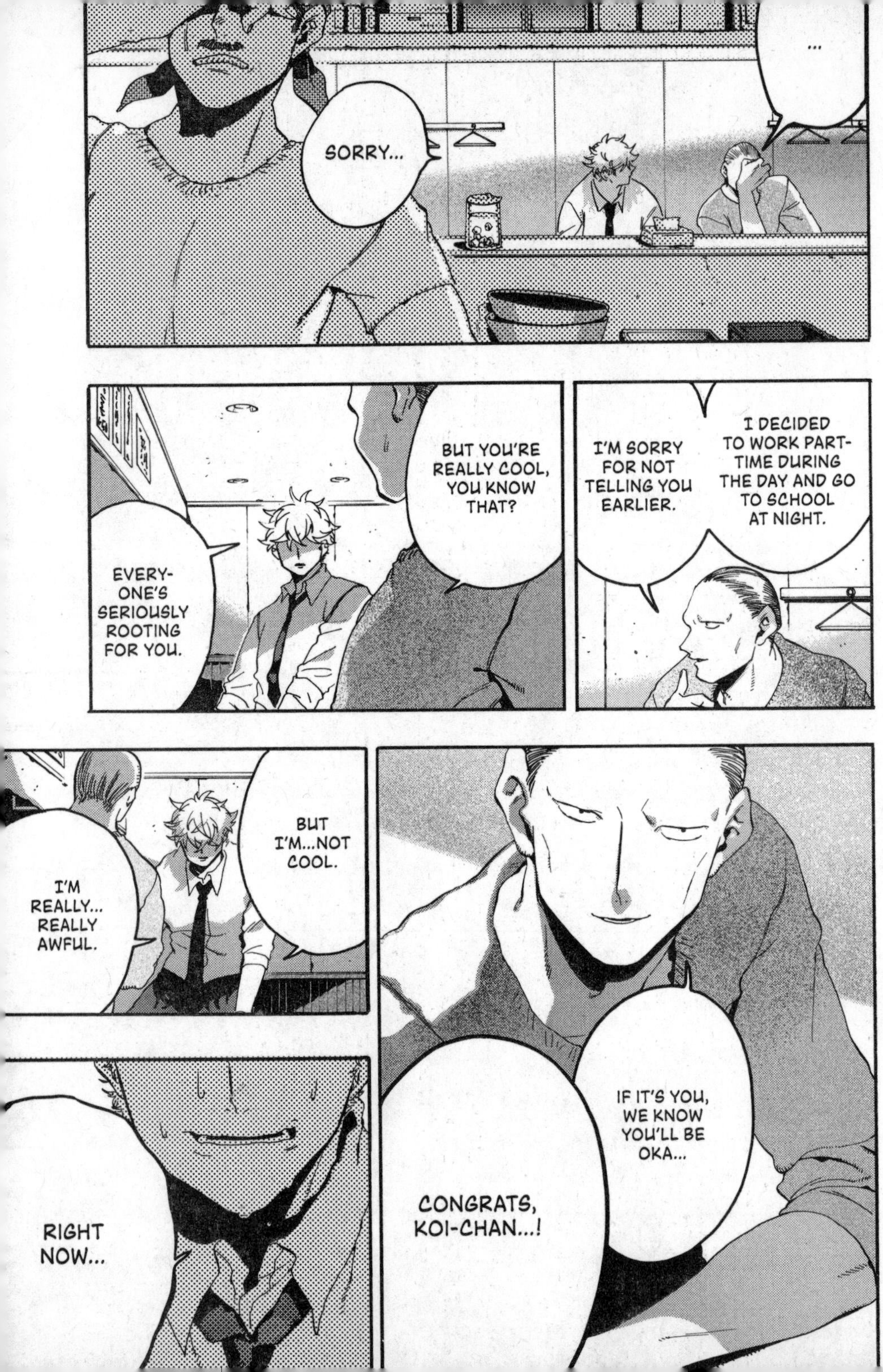
...
SORRY...
I DECIDED TO WORK PART-TIME DURING THE DAY AND GO TO SCHOOL AT NIGHT.
I'M SORRY FOR NOT TELLING YOU EARLIER.
BUT YOU'RE REALLY COOL, YOU KNOW THAT?
EVERY-ONE'S SERIOUSLY ROOTING FOR YOU.
IF IT'S YOU, WE KNOW YOU'LL BE OKA...
CONGRATS, KOI-CHAN...!
BUT I'M...NOT COOL.
I'M REALLY... REALLY AWFUL.
RIGHT NOW...

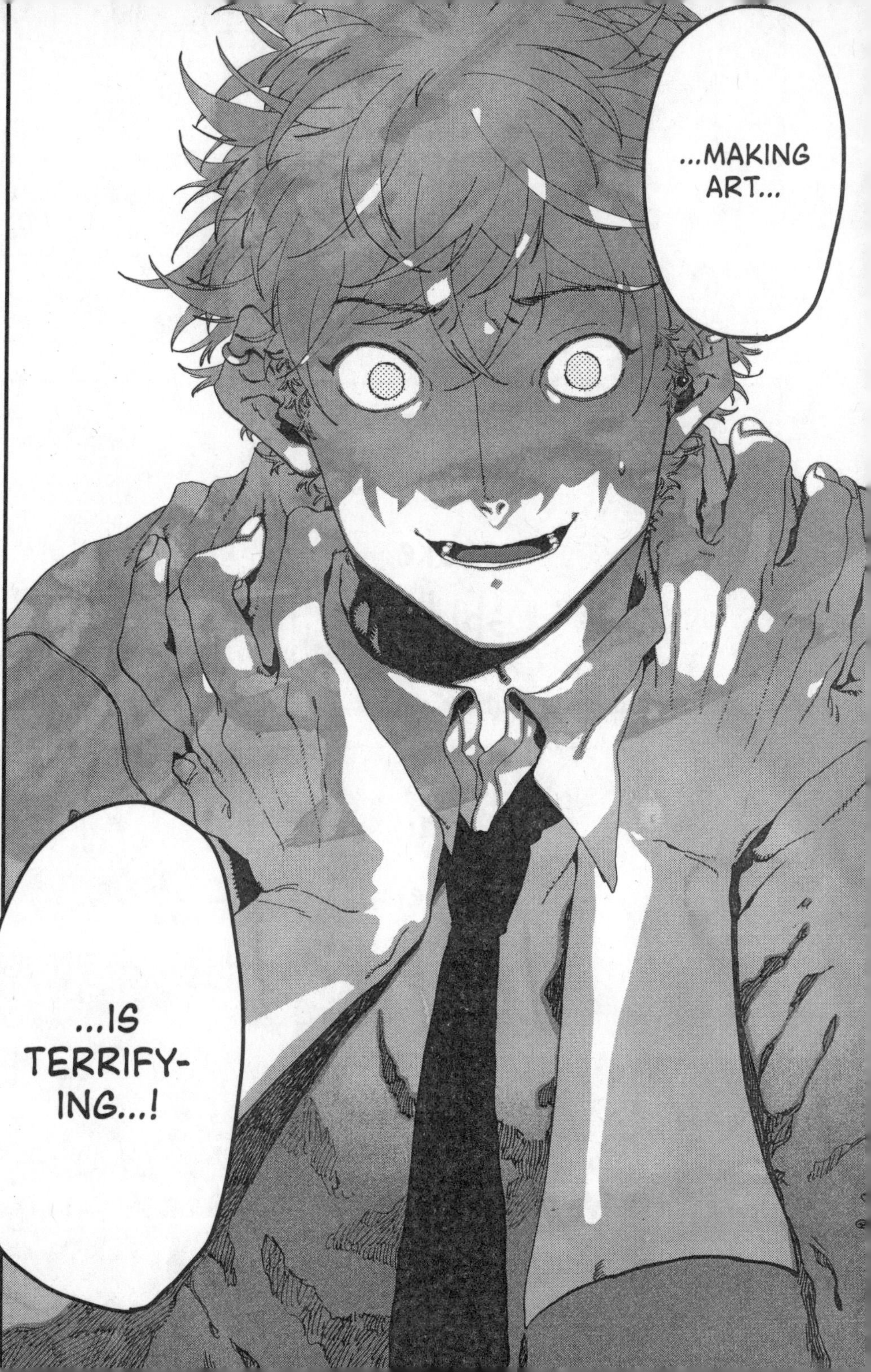
...MAKING ART...
...IS TERRIFY-ING...!
STROKE 14 END

Everyone's Birthdays

Yatora → 7/5

Yuka-chan → 10/18

Yotasuke → 9/19

Hashida → 2/5

Kuwana → 4/23

Mori-senpai → 12/31

Saeki-sensei → 6/7

Ooba-sensei → 12/30

Umino-san → 6/1

Utashima → 3/28

Koigakubo → 6/28

Sumida → 4/14

BLUE PERIOD

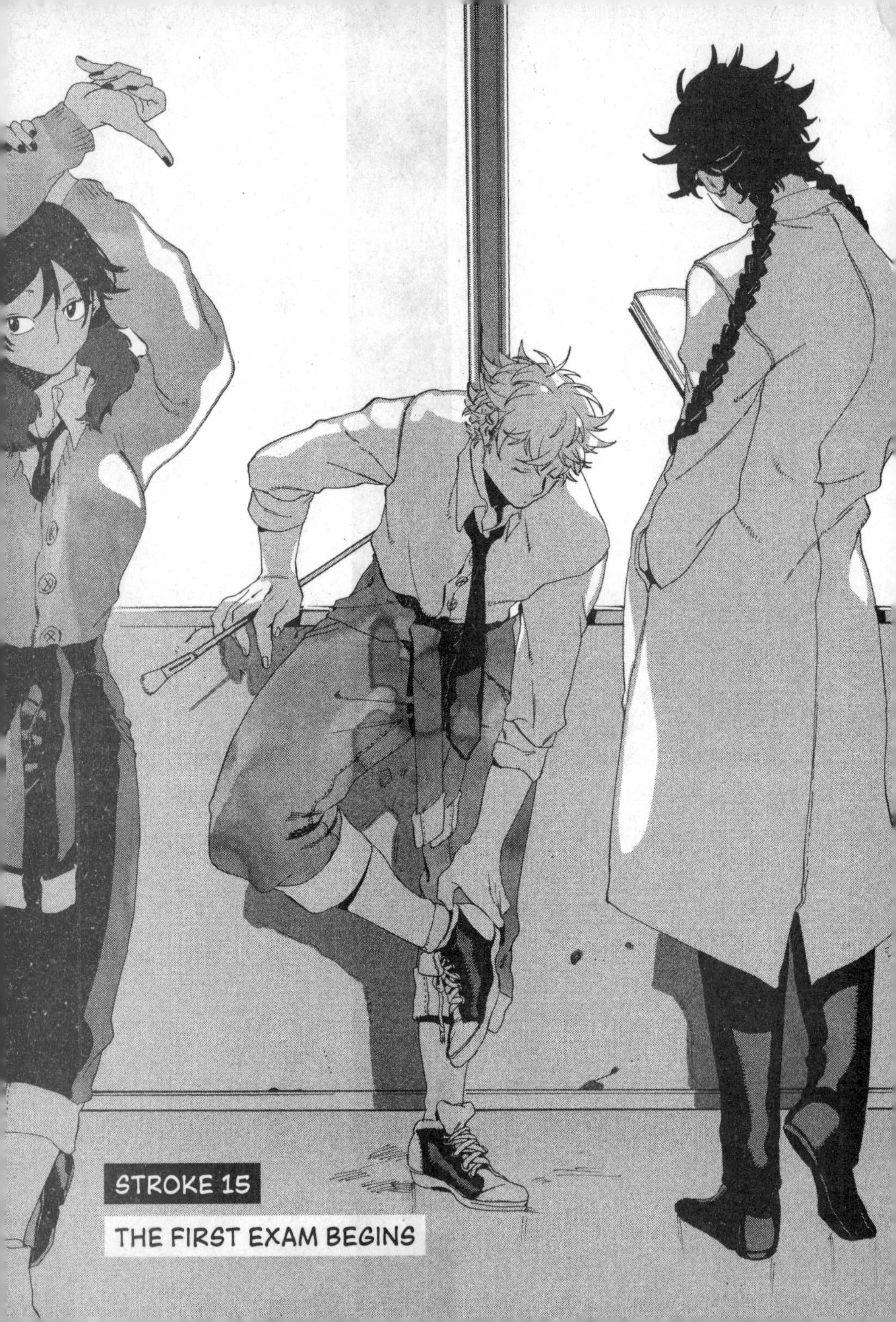
STROKE 15
THE FIRST EXAM BEGINS

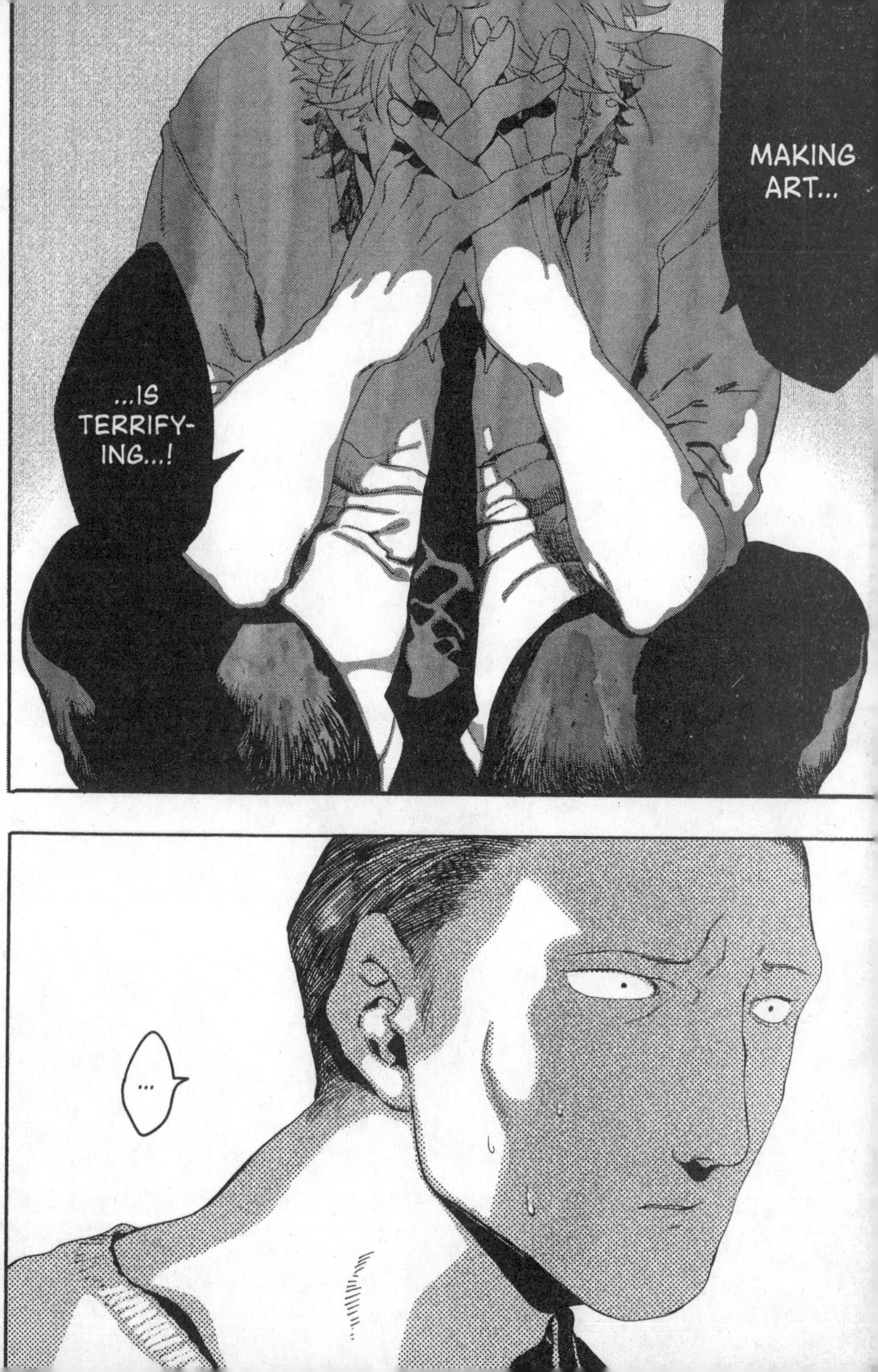
MAKING ART...
...IS TERRIFY-ING...!
...

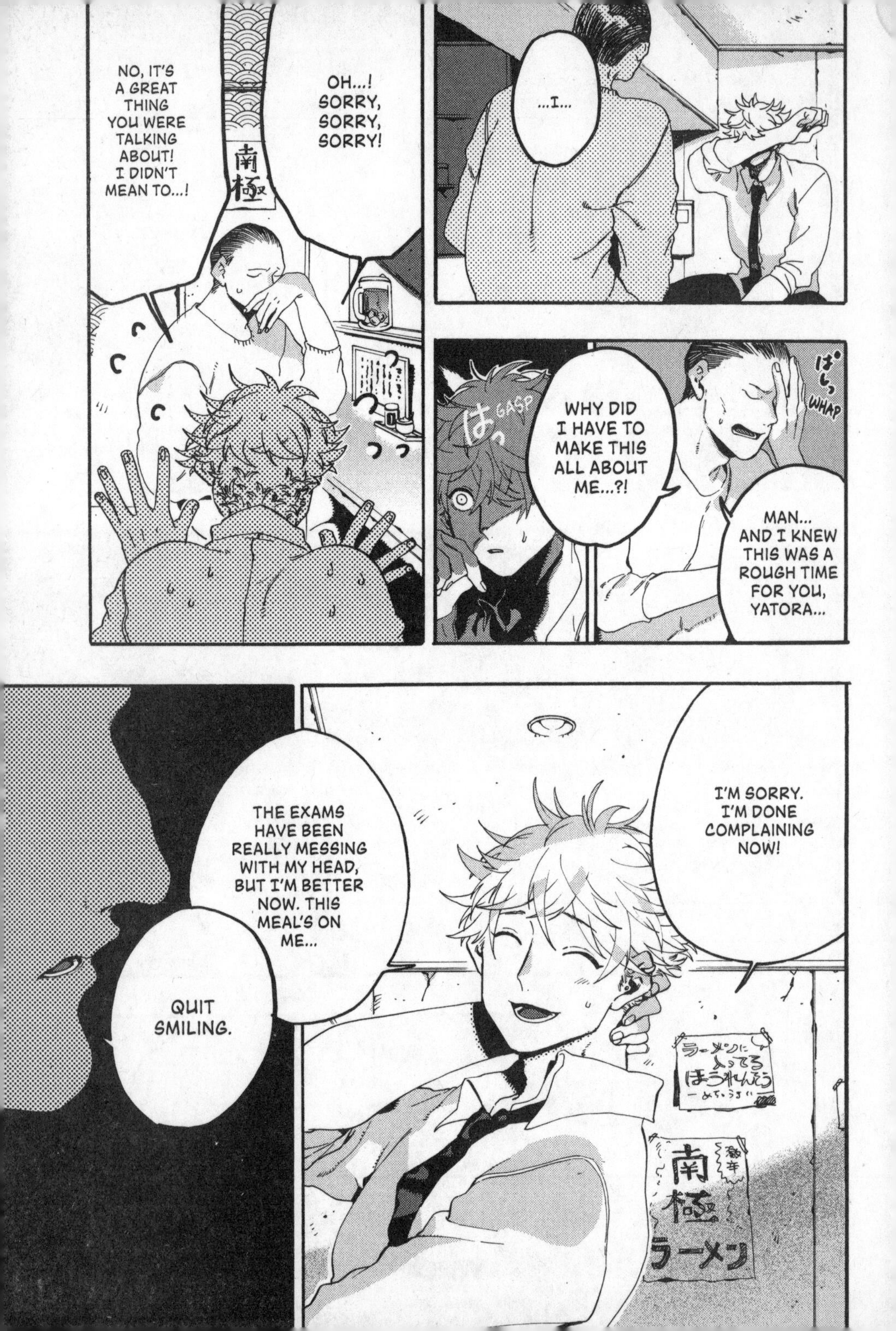
...I...
ぱしっ WHAP
WHY DID I HAVE TO MAKE THIS ALL ABOUT ME...?!
MAN... AND I KNEW THIS WAS A ROUGH TIME FOR YOU, YATORA...
はっ GASP
南極
OH...! SORRY, SORRY, SORRY!
NO, IT'S A GREAT THING YOU WERE TALKING ABOUT! I DIDN'T MEAN TO...!
I'M SORRY. I'M DONE COMPLAINING NOW!
THE EXAMS HAVE BEEN REALLY MESSING WITH MY HEAD, BUT I'M BETTER NOW. THIS MEAL'S ON ME...
QUIT SMILING.
ラーメンに入ってるほうれんそう
激辛 南極 ラーメン

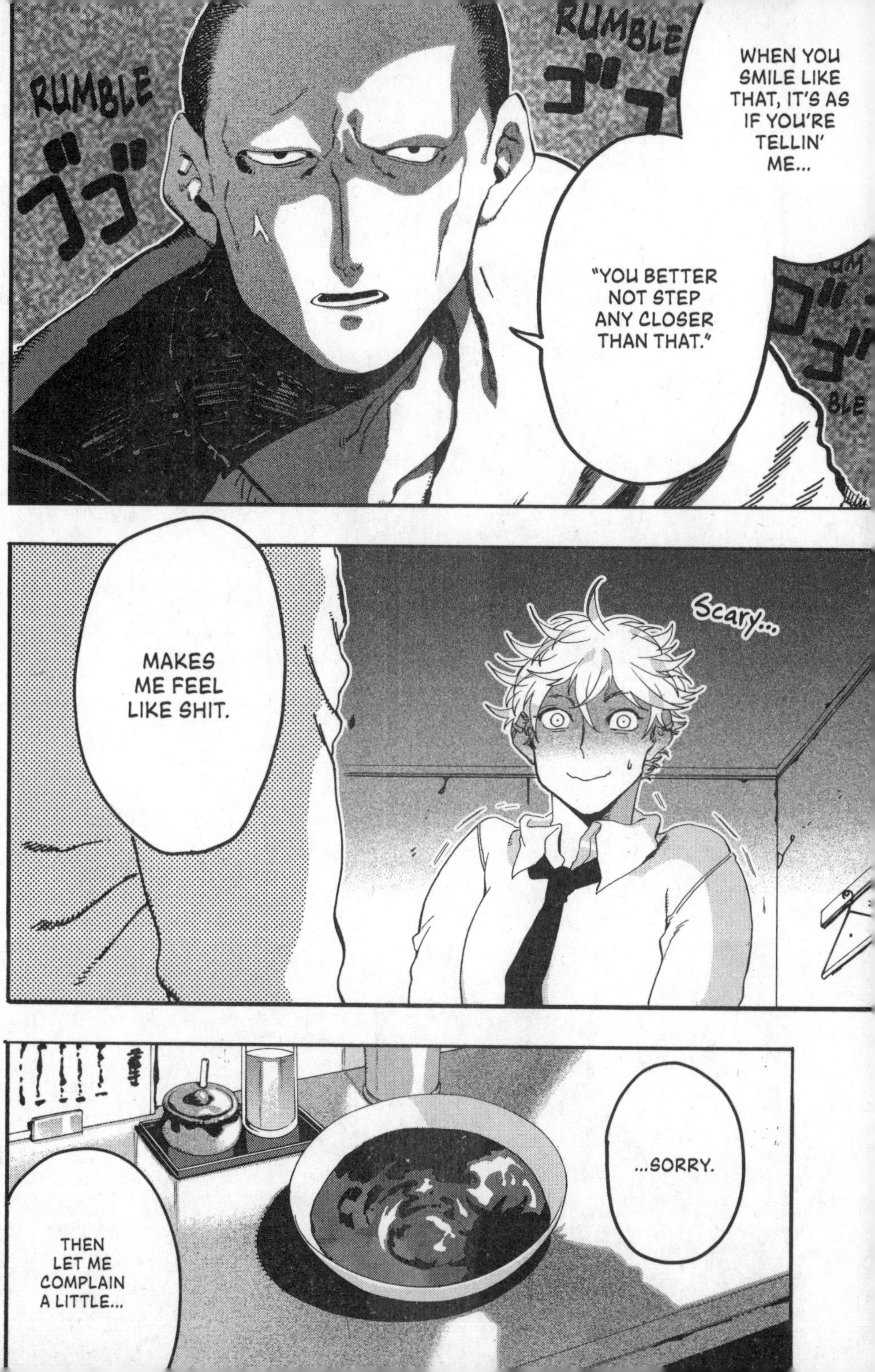
RUMBLE
ゴゴ
WHEN YOU SMILE LIKE THAT, IT'S AS IF YOU'RE TELLIN' ME...
"YOU BETTER NOT STEP ANY CLOSER THAN THAT."
RUMBLE
ゴゴ
Scary...
MAKES ME FEEL LIKE SHIT.
...SORRY.
THEN LET ME COMPLAIN A LITTLE...

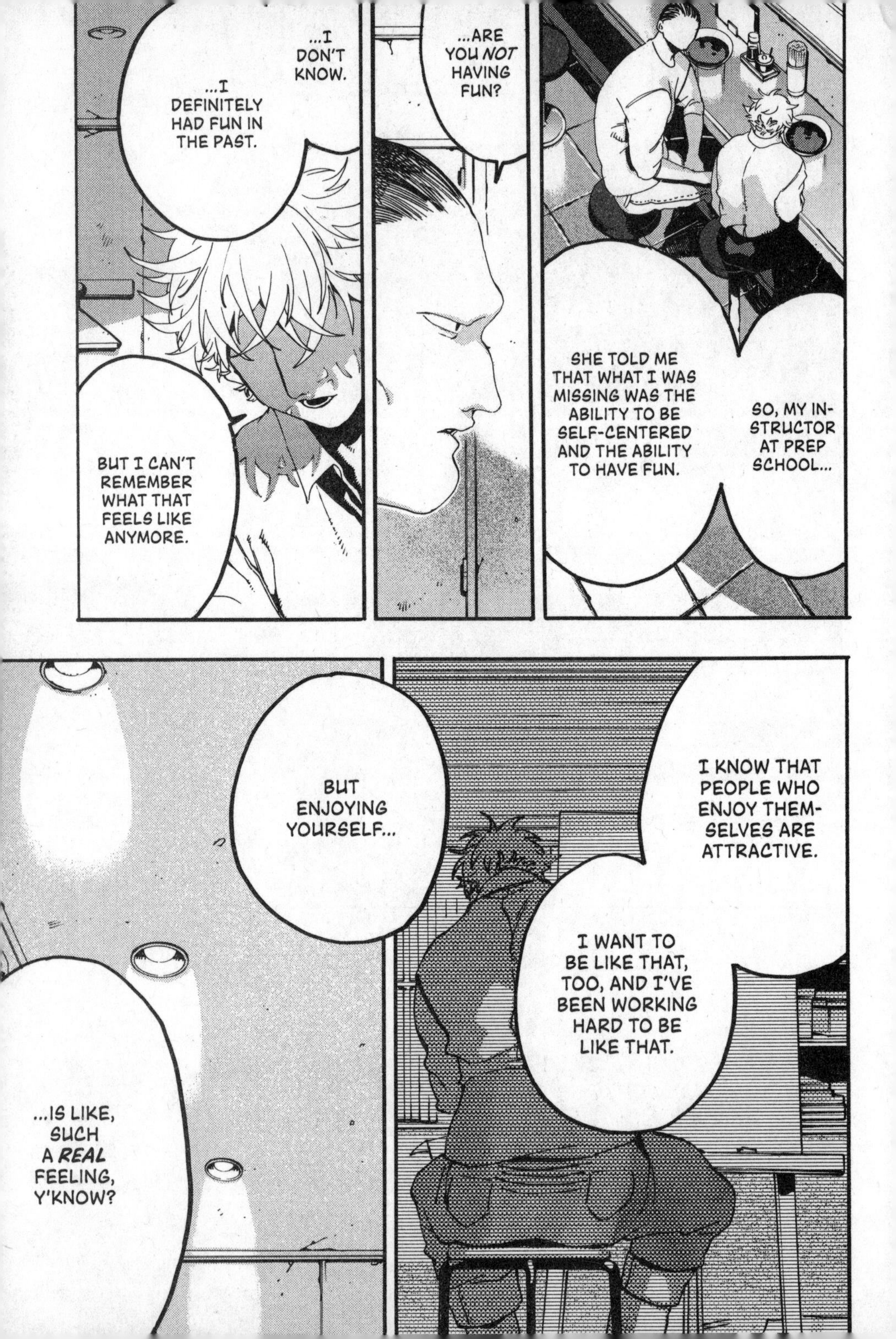
SO, MY INSTRUCTOR AT PREP SCHOOL...
SHE TOLD ME THAT WHAT I WAS MISSING WAS THE ABILITY TO BE SELF-CENTERED AND THE ABILITY TO HAVE FUN.
...ARE YOU *NOT* HAVING FUN?
...I DON'T KNOW.
...I DEFINITELY HAD FUN IN THE PAST.
BUT I CAN'T REMEMBER WHAT THAT FEELS LIKE ANYMORE.
I KNOW THAT PEOPLE WHO ENJOY THEMSELVES ARE ATTRACTIVE.
I WANT TO BE LIKE THAT, TOO, AND I'VE BEEN WORKING HARD TO BE LIKE THAT.
BUT ENJOYING YOURSELF...
...IS LIKE, SUCH A *REAL* FEELING, Y'KNOW?

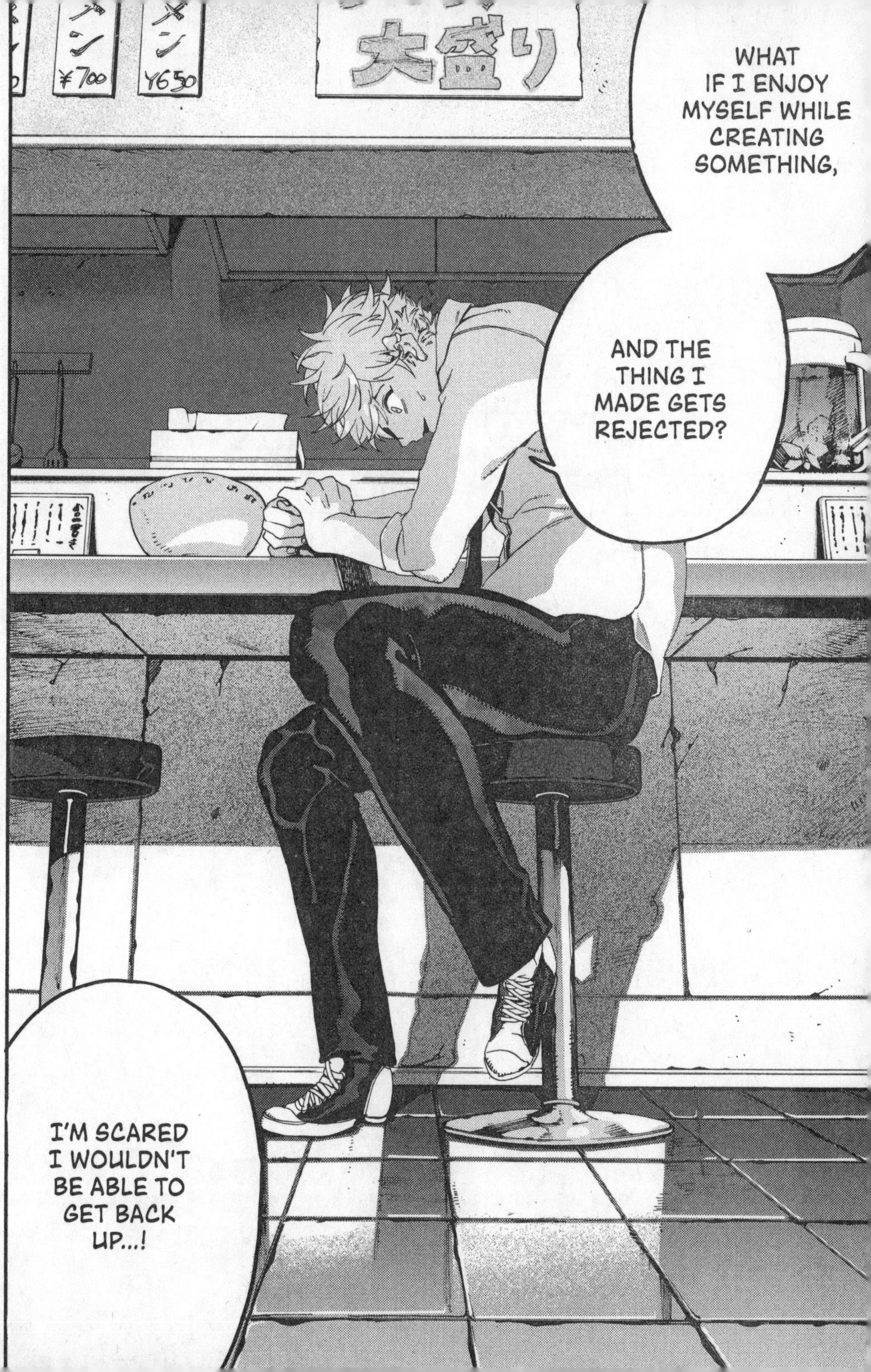
大盛り
¥700
¥650
WHAT IF I ENJOY MYSELF WHILE CREATING SOMETHING,
AND THE THING I MADE GETS REJECTED?
I'M SCARED I WOULDN'T BE ABLE TO GET BACK UP...!

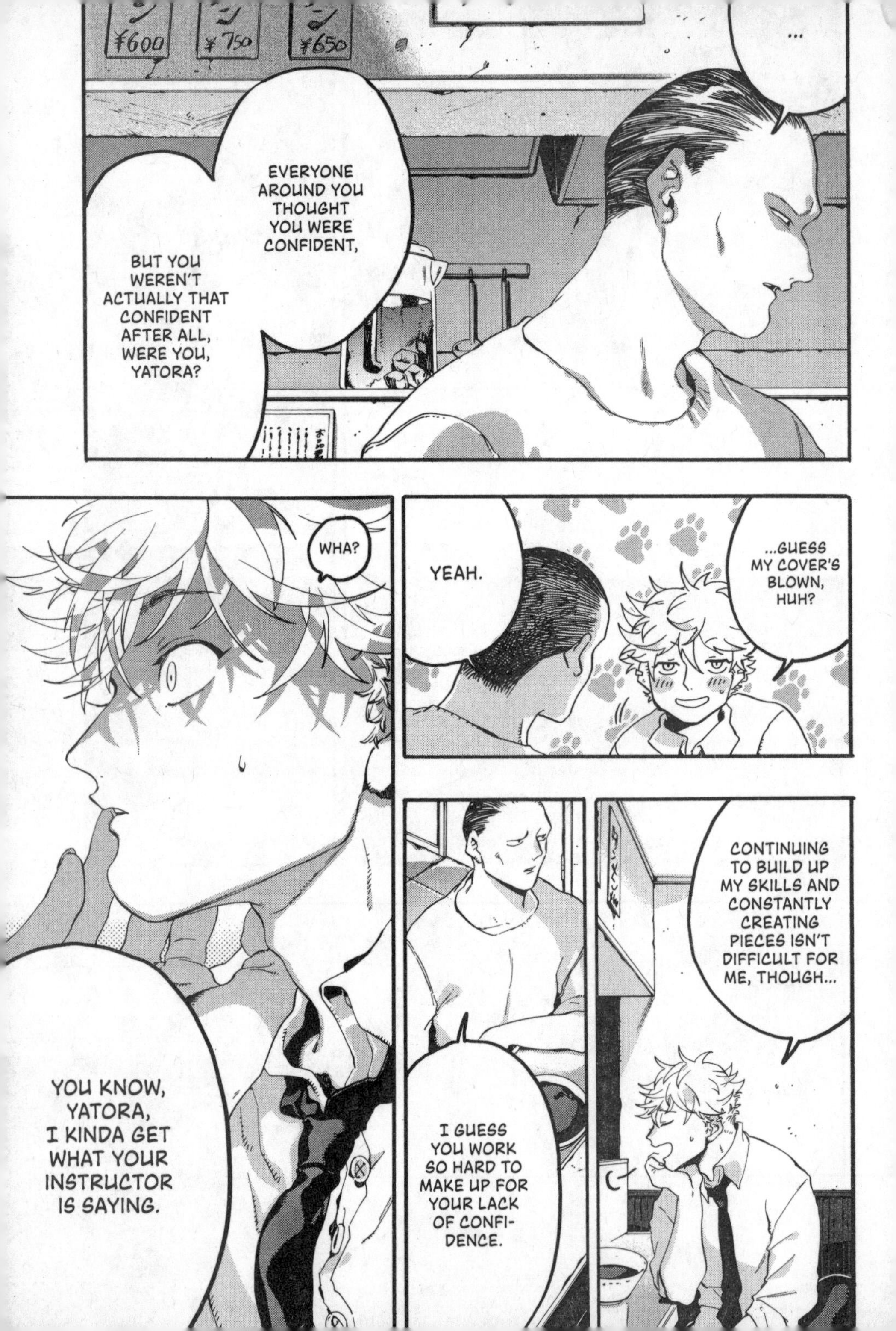
¥650
¥750
¥600
...
EVERYONE AROUND YOU THOUGHT YOU WERE CONFIDENT,
BUT YOU WEREN'T ACTUALLY THAT CONFIDENT AFTER ALL, WERE YOU, YATORA?
...GUESS MY COVER'S BLOWN, HUH?
YEAH.
CONTINUING TO BUILD UP MY SKILLS AND CONSTANTLY CREATING PIECES ISN'T DIFFICULT FOR ME, THOUGH...
I GUESS YOU WORK SO HARD TO MAKE UP FOR YOUR LACK OF CONFI-DENCE.
WHA?
YOU KNOW, YATORA, I KINDA GET WHAT YOUR INSTRUCTOR IS SAYING.

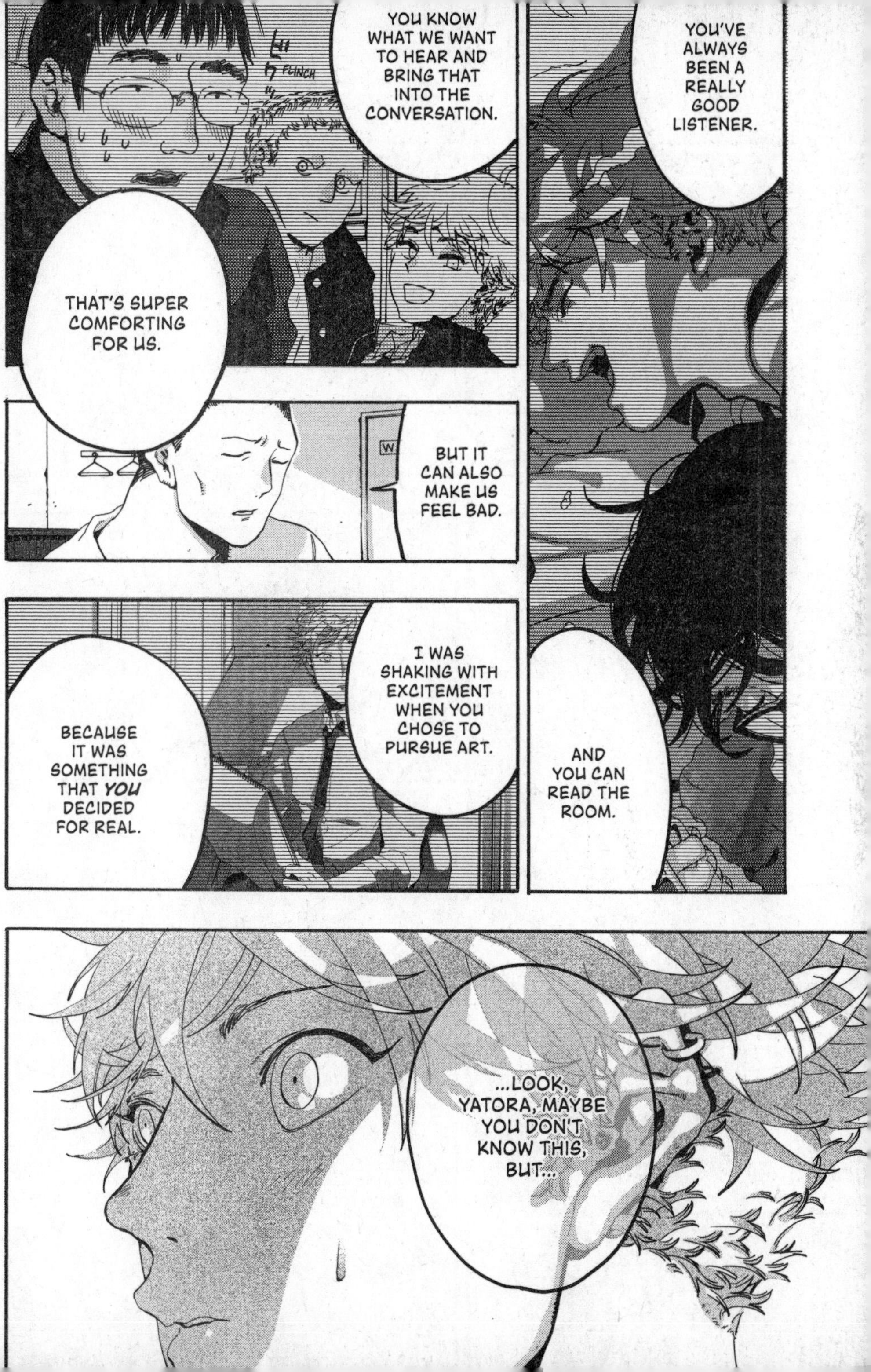
YOU'VE ALWAYS BEEN A REALLY GOOD LISTENER.
AND YOU CAN READ THE ROOM.
YOU KNOW WHAT WE WANT TO HEAR AND BRING THAT INTO THE CONVERSATION.
FLINCH
THAT'S SUPER COMFORTING FOR US.
BUT IT CAN ALSO MAKE US FEEL BAD.
I WAS SHAKING WITH EXCITEMENT WHEN YOU CHOSE TO PURSUE ART.
BECAUSE IT WAS SOMETHING THAT *YOU* DECIDED FOR REAL.
...LOOK, YATORA, MAYBE YOU DON'T KNOW THIS, BUT...

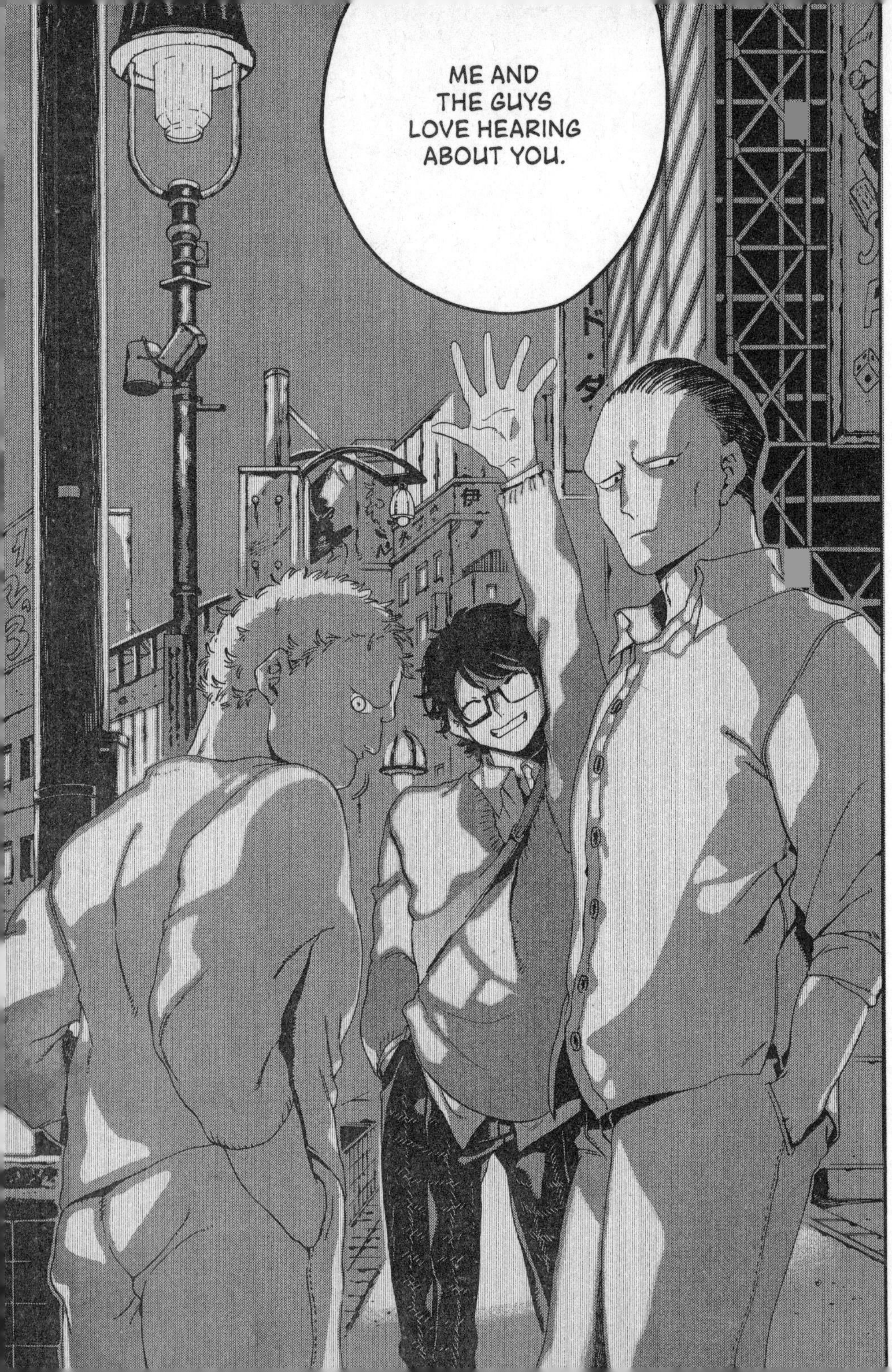
ME AND THE GUYS LOVE HEARING ABOUT YOU.

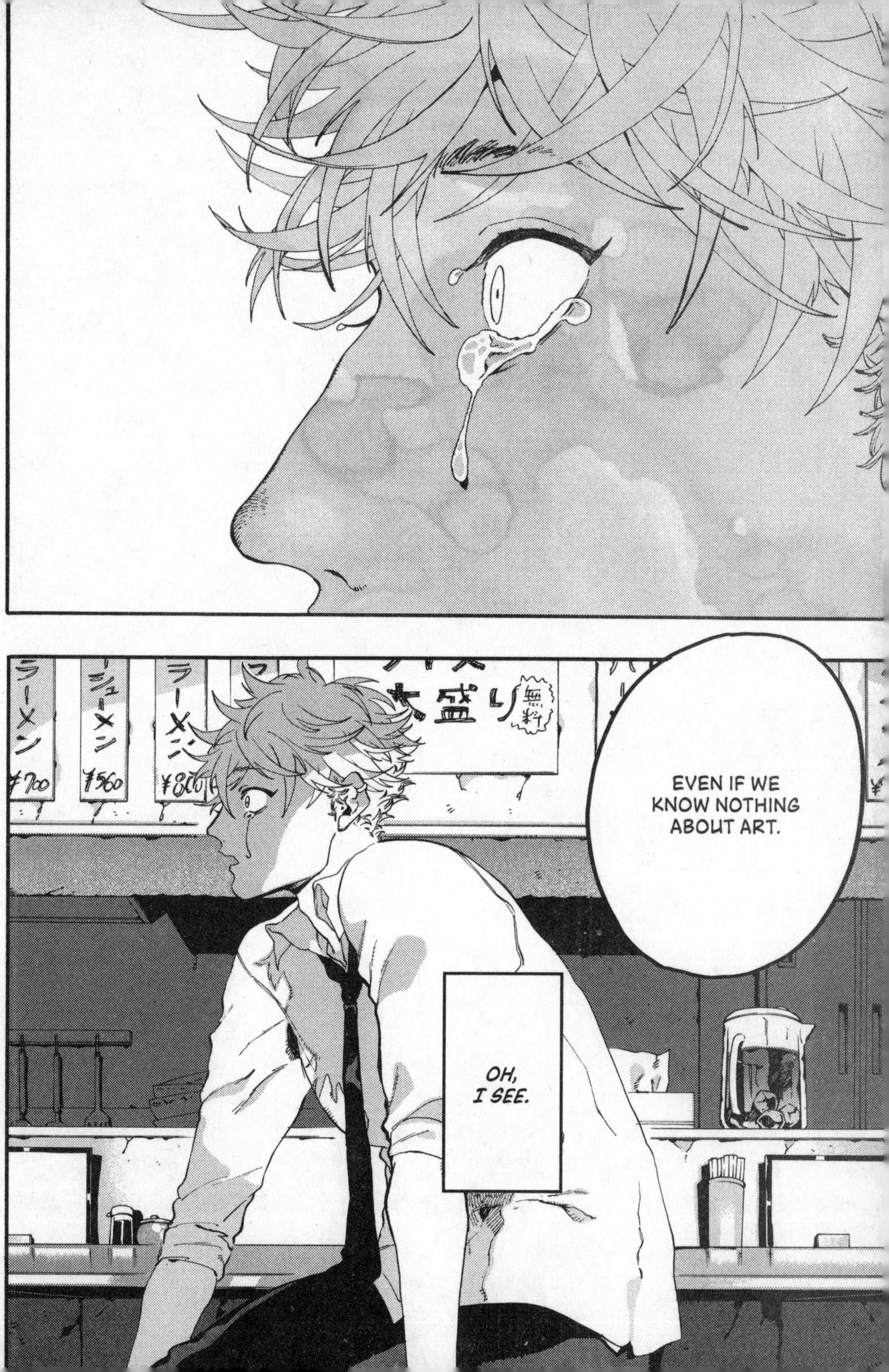
EVEN IF WE KNOW NOTHING ABOUT ART.
OH, I SEE.

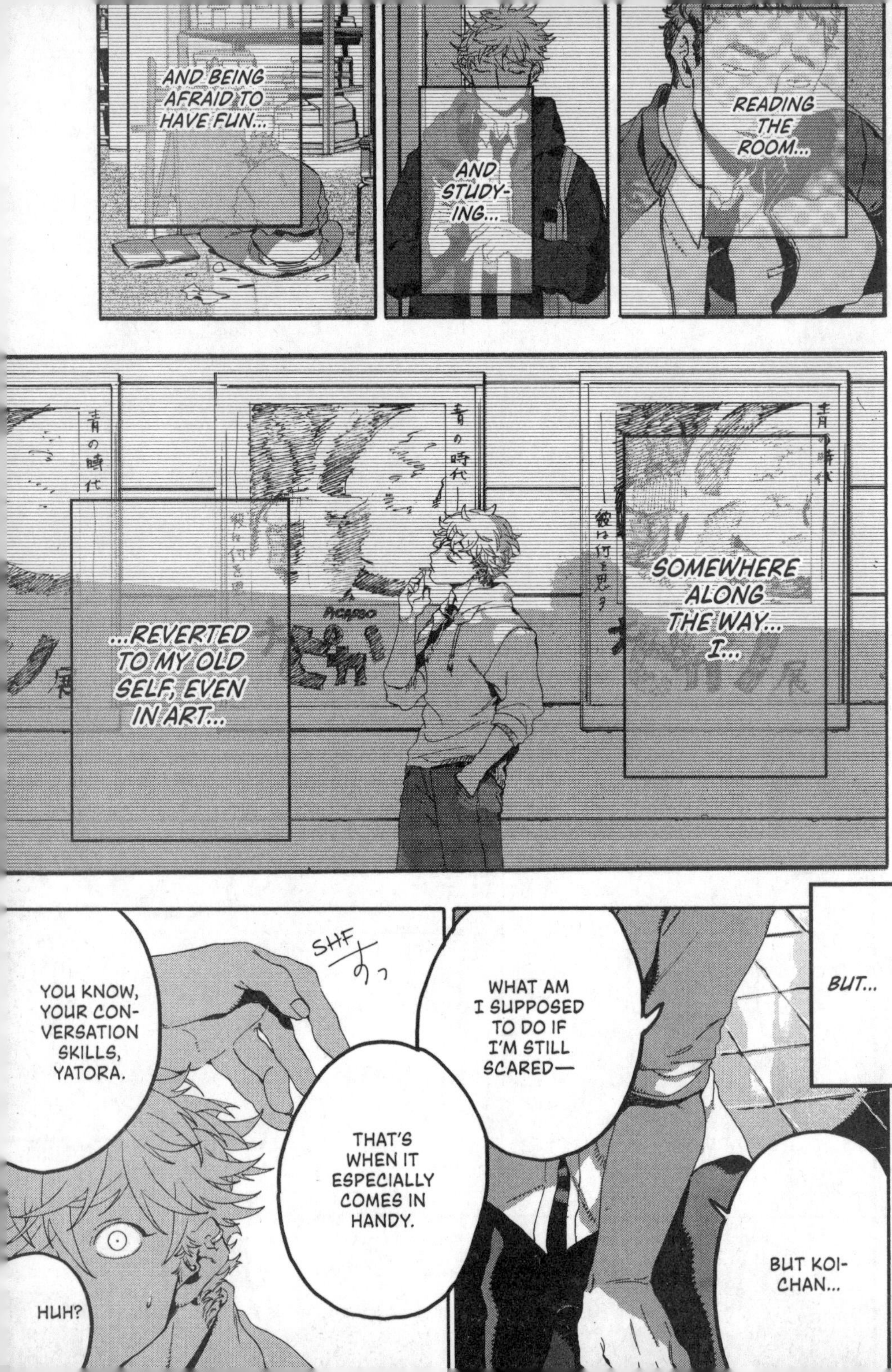
READING THE ROOM...
AND STUDYING...
AND BEING AFRAID TO HAVE FUN...
青の時代
SOMEWHERE ALONG THE WAY... I...
...REVERTED TO MY OLD SELF, EVEN IN ART...
BUT...
BUT KOI-CHAN...
WHAT AM I SUPPOSED TO DO IF I'M STILL SCARED—
SHF
YOU KNOW, YOUR CONVERSATION SKILLS, YATORA.
THAT'S WHEN IT ESPECIALLY COMES IN HANDY.
HUH?

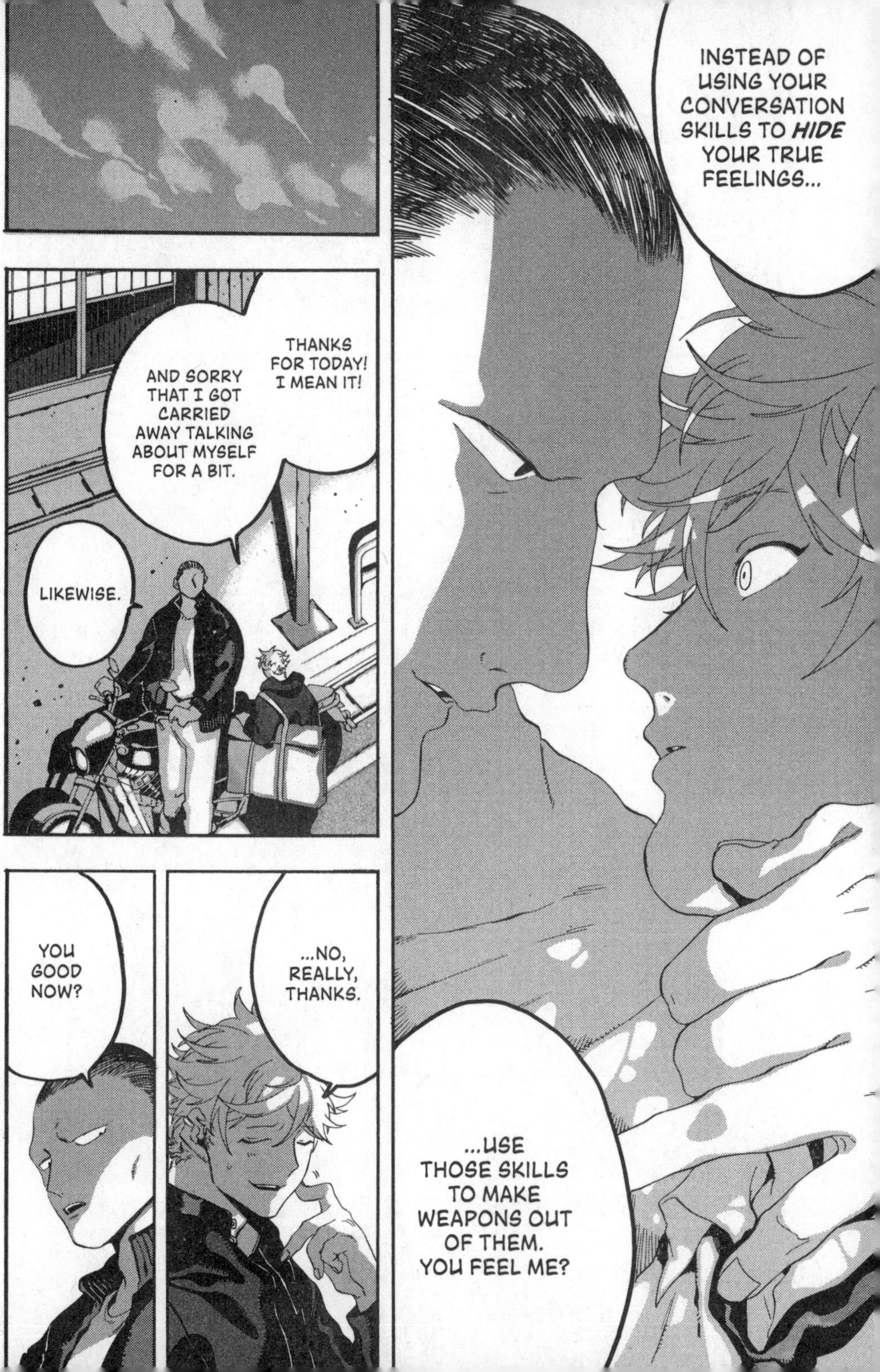
INSTEAD OF USING YOUR CONVERSATION SKILLS TO *HIDE* YOUR TRUE FEELINGS...
...USE THOSE SKILLS TO MAKE WEAPONS OUT OF THEM. YOU FEEL ME?
THANKS FOR TODAY! I MEAN IT!
AND SORRY THAT I GOT CARRIED AWAY TALKING ABOUT MYSELF FOR A BIT.
LIKEWISE.
...NO, REALLY, THANKS.
YOU GOOD NOW?

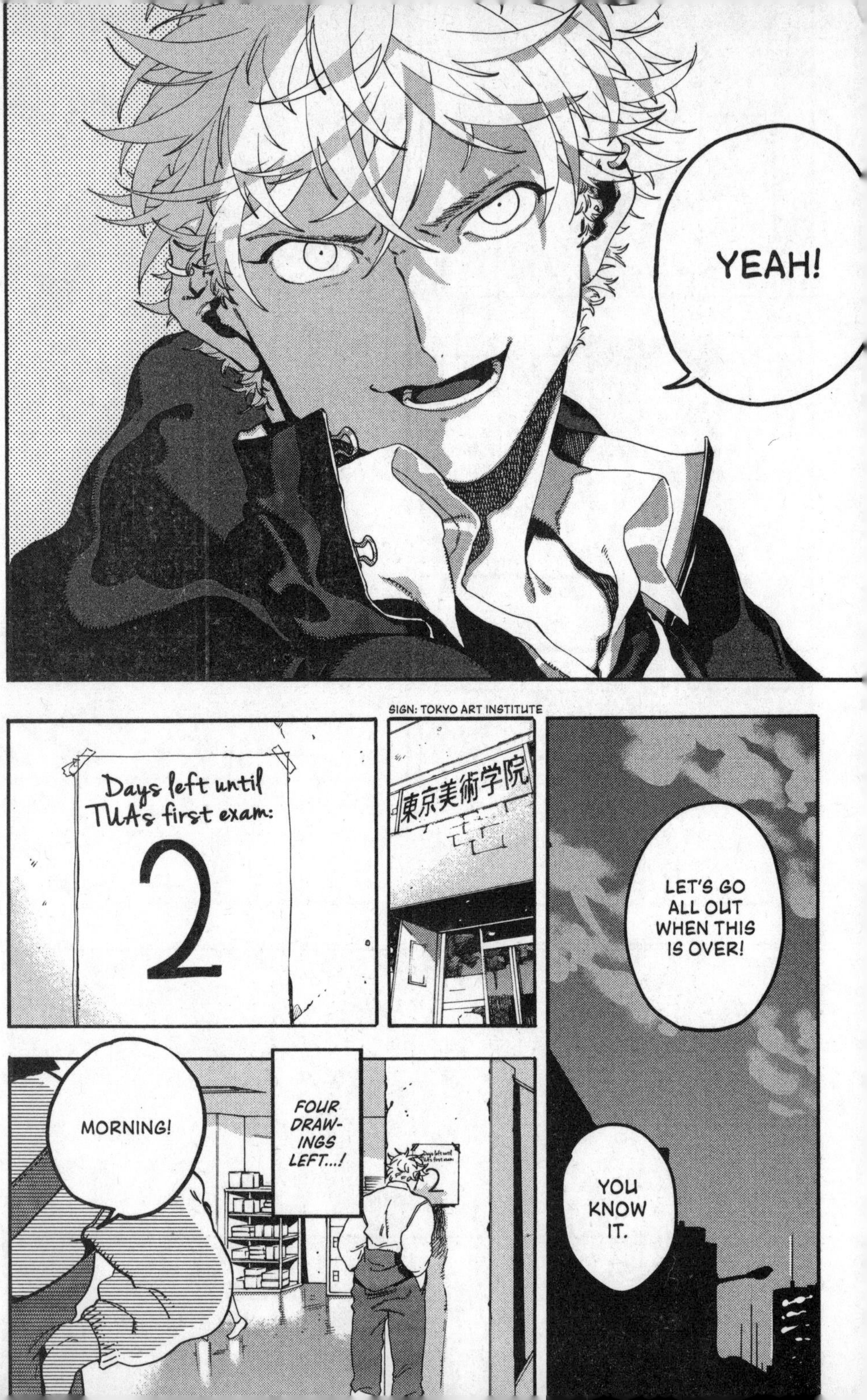
YEAH!
LET'S GO ALL OUT WHEN THIS IS OVER!
YOU KNOW IT.
SIGN: TOKYO ART INSTITUTE
東京美術学院
Days left until TUA's first exam:
2
FOUR DRAWINGS LEFT...!
MORNING!

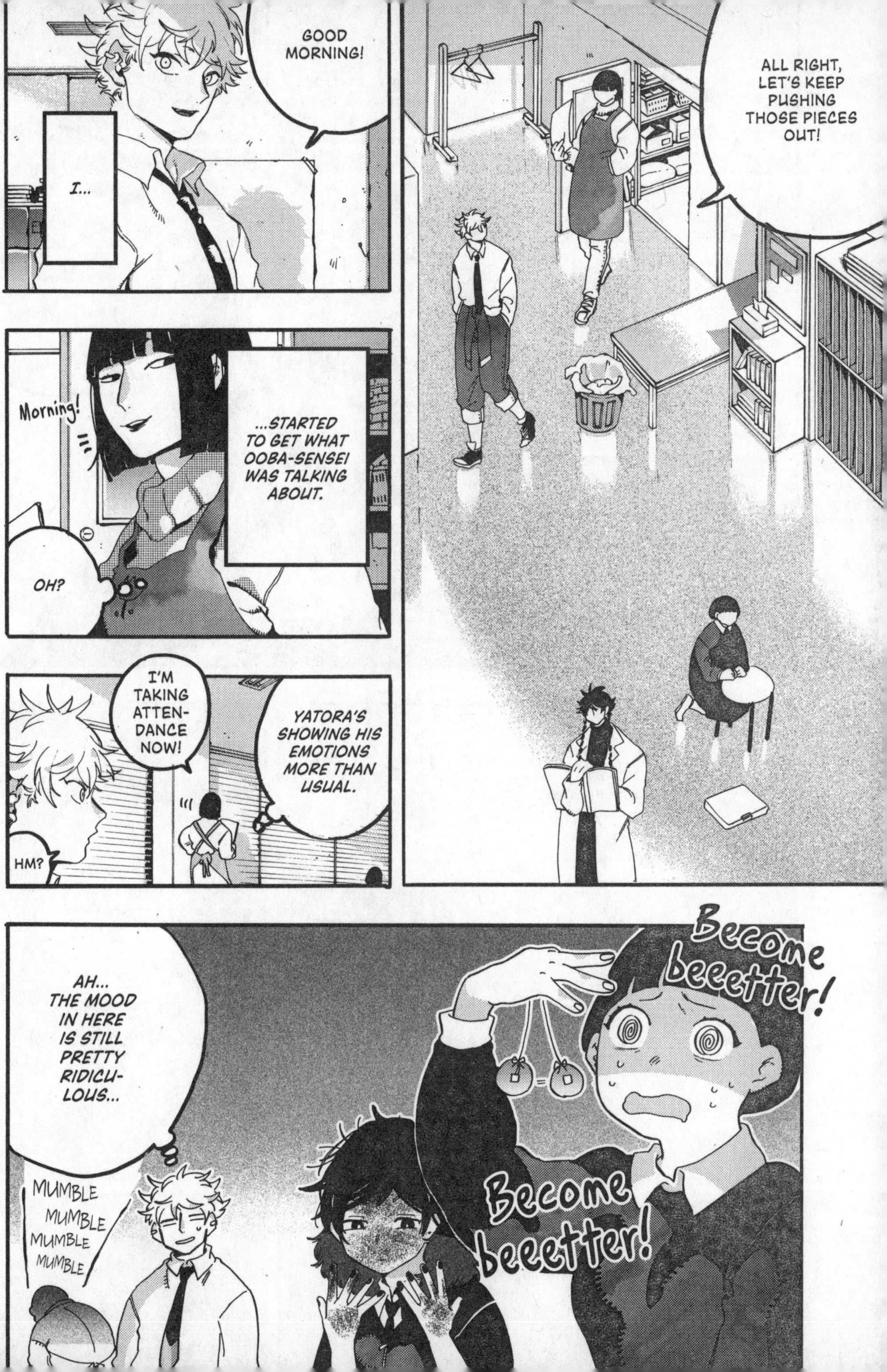
ALL RIGHT, LET'S KEEP PUSHING THOSE PIECES OUT!
GOOD MORNING!
I...
...STARTED TO GET WHAT OOBA-SENSEI WAS TALKING ABOUT.
Morning!
OH?
YATORA'S SHOWING HIS EMOTIONS MORE THAN USUAL.
I'M TAKING ATTEN-DANCE NOW!
HM?
Become beeetter!
AH... THE MOOD IN HERE IS STILL PRETTY RIDICU-LOUS...
Become beeetter!
MUMBLE MUMBLE MUMBLE MUMBLE

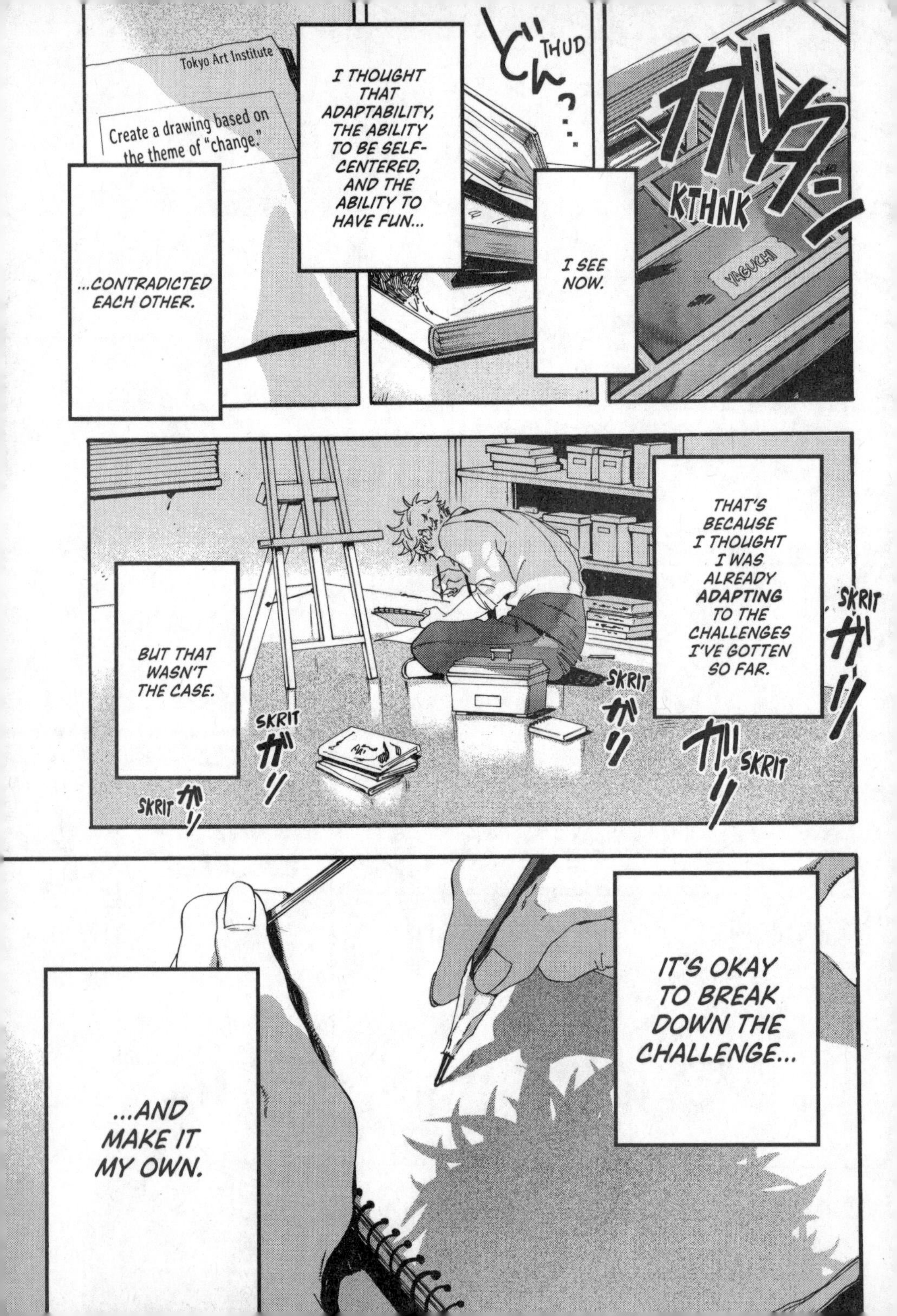
KTHNK
YAGUCHI
I SEE NOW.
THUD
I THOUGHT THAT ADAPTABILITY, THE ABILITY TO BE SELF-CENTERED, AND THE ABILITY TO HAVE FUN...
Tokyo Art Institute
Create a drawing based on the theme of "change."
...CONTRADICTED EACH OTHER.
SKRIT
THAT'S BECAUSE I THOUGHT I WAS ALREADY ADAPTING TO THE CHALLENGES I'VE GOTTEN SO FAR.
SKRIT
SKRIT
SKRIT
BUT THAT WASN'T THE CASE.
SKRIT
IT'S OKAY TO BREAK DOWN THE CHALLENGE...
...AND MAKE IT MY OWN.

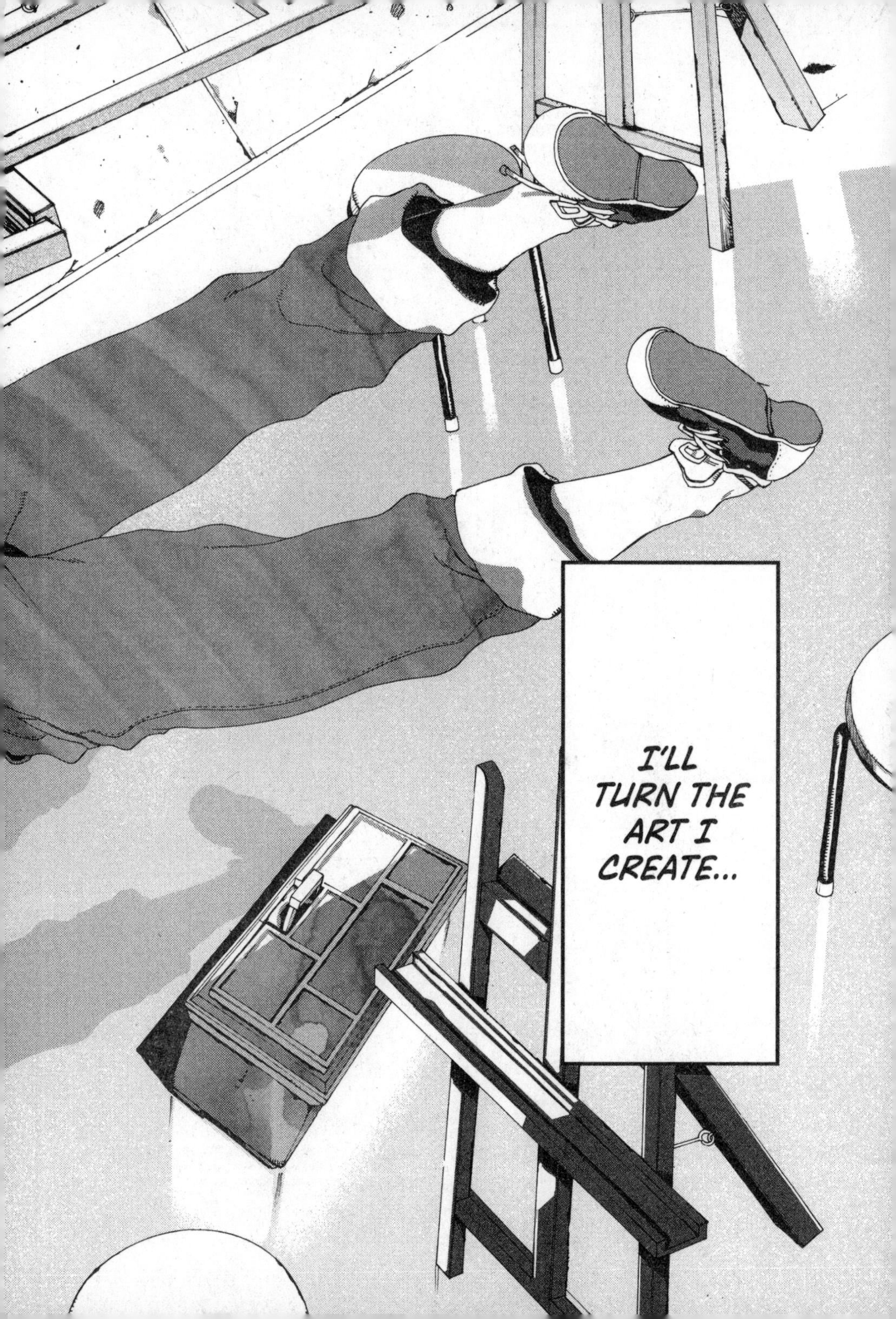
I'LL TURN THE ART I CREATE...

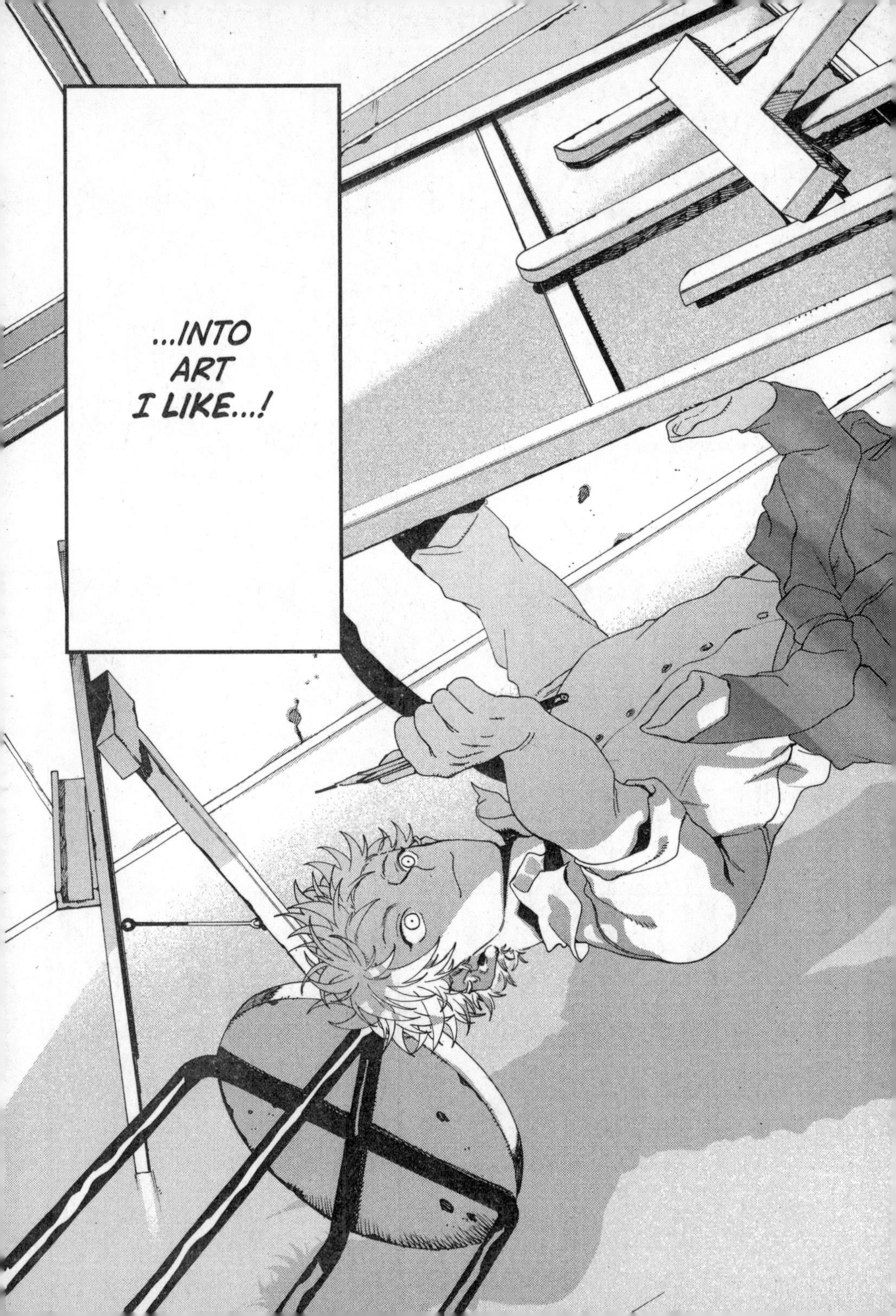
...INTO ART I LIKE...!

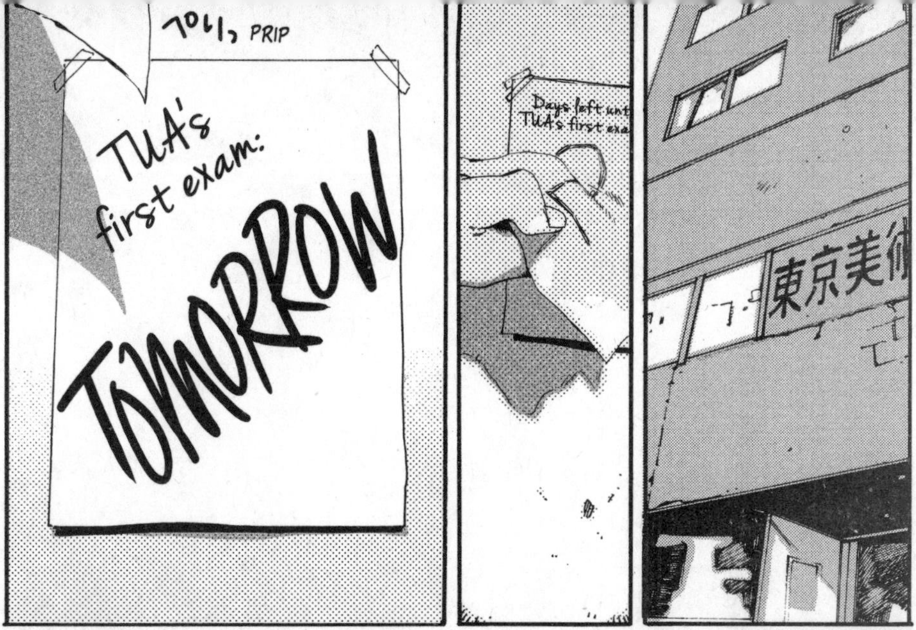
東京美術
Days left unt
TUA's first exa
プリッ PRIP
TUA's first exam:
TOMORROW

SIGN: TOKYO ART INSTITUTE

ART: SHOTA YAMAMICHI

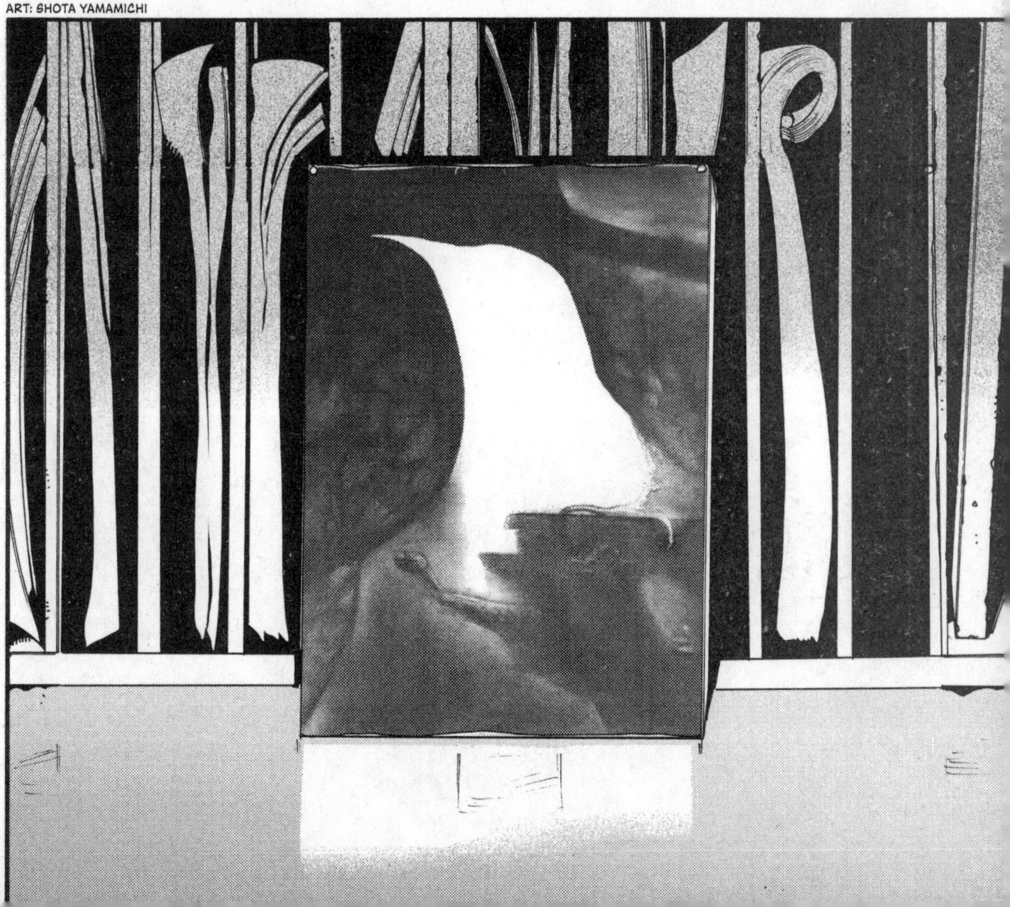

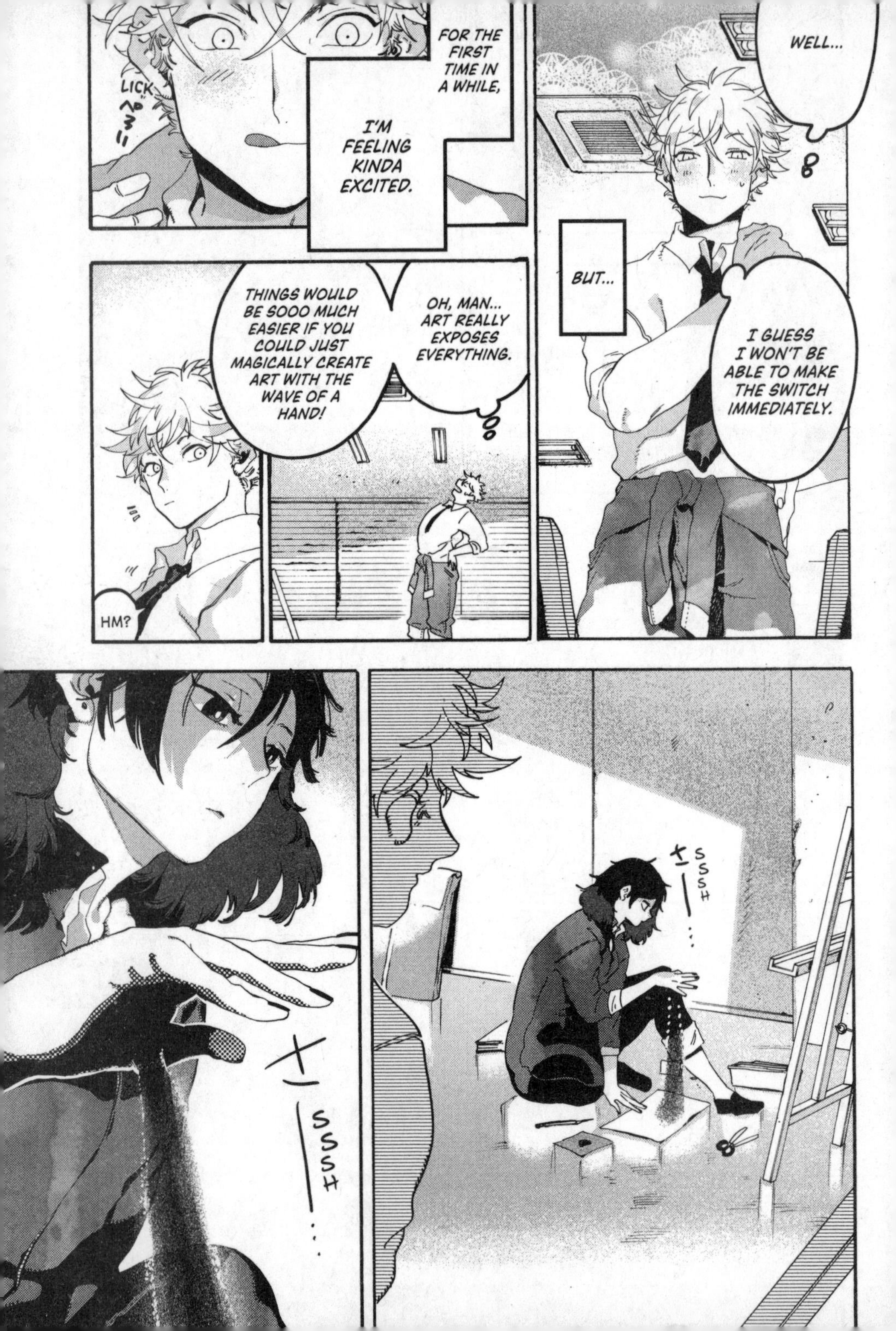
WELL...
BUT...
I GUESS I WON'T BE ABLE TO MAKE THE SWITCH IMMEDIATELY.
FOR THE FIRST TIME IN A WHILE,
I'M FEELING KINDA EXCITED.
LICK
OH, MAN... ART REALLY EXPOSES EVERYTHING.
THINGS WOULD BE SOOO MUCH EASIER IF YOU COULD JUST MAGICALLY CREATE ART WITH THE WAVE OF A HAND!
HM?
SSSH...
SSSH...

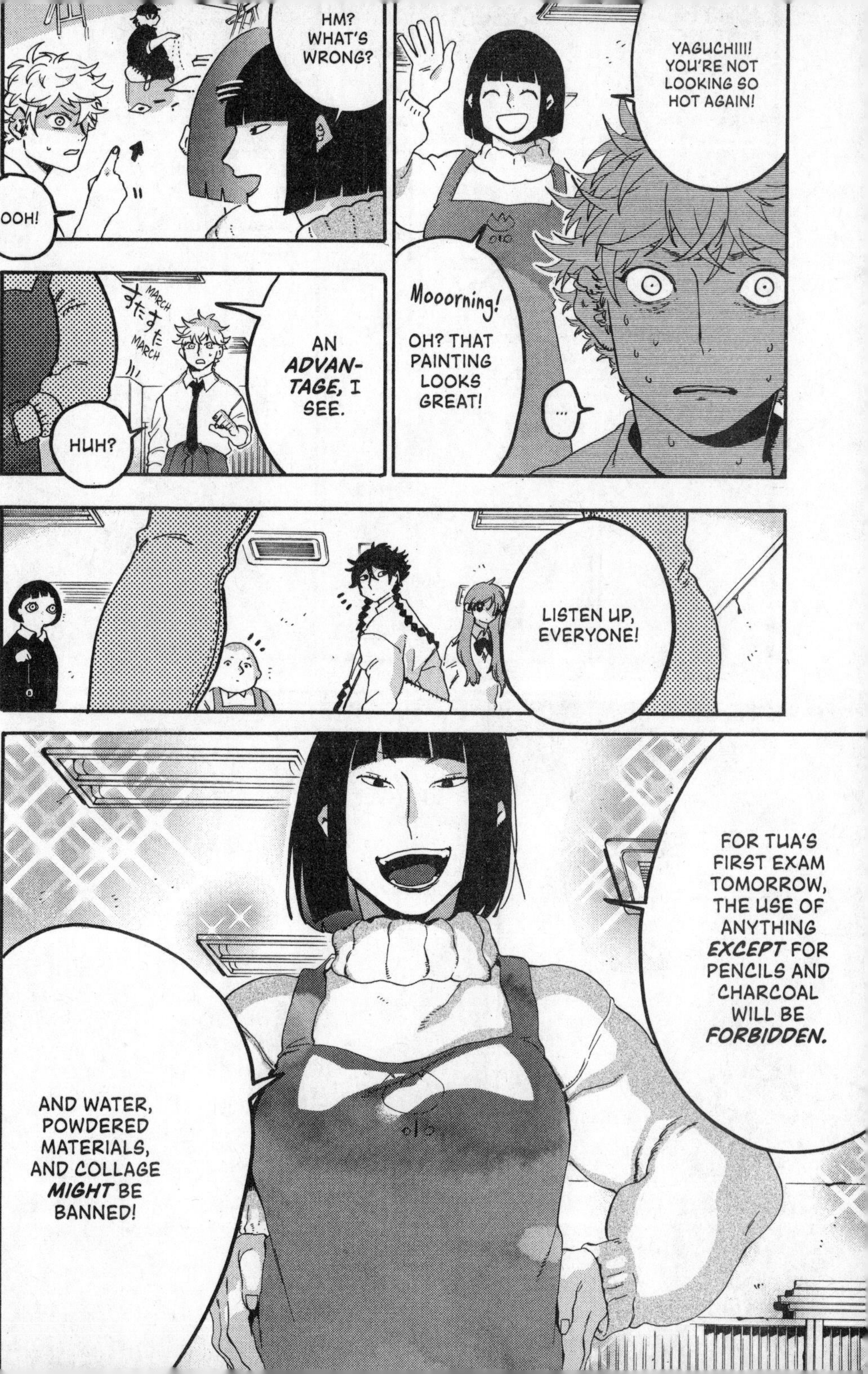

YAGUCHIIII! YOU'RE NOT LOOKING SO HOT AGAIN!
Mooorning!
OH? THAT PAINTING LOOKS GREAT!
...
HM? WHAT'S WRONG?
OOH!
AN *ADVANTAGE,* I SEE.
すたすた
MARCH MARCH
HUH?
LISTEN UP, EVERYONE!
FOR TUA'S FIRST EXAM TOMORROW, THE USE OF ANYTHING ***EXCEPT*** FOR PENCILS AND CHARCOAL WILL BE ***FORBIDDEN.***
AND WATER, POWDERED MATERIALS, AND COLLAGE ***MIGHT*** BE BANNED!

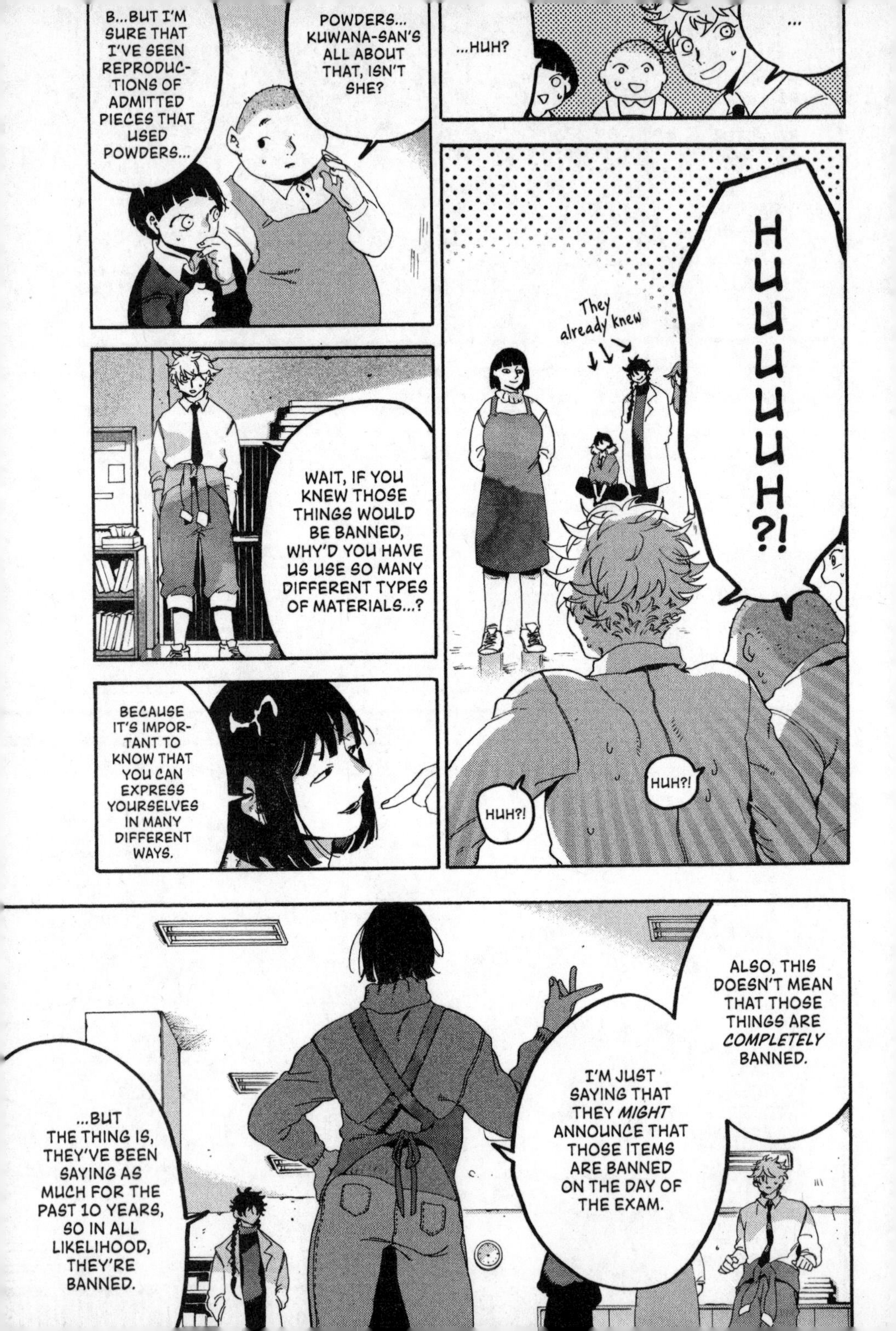
...
...HUH?
POWDERS... KUWANA-SAN'S ALL ABOUT THAT, ISN'T SHE?
B...BUT I'M SURE THAT I'VE SEEN REPRODUCTIONS OF ADMITTED PIECES THAT USED POWDERS...
HUUUUUUH?!
They already knew
HUH?!
HUH?!
WAIT, IF YOU KNEW THOSE THINGS WOULD BE BANNED, WHY'D YOU HAVE US USE SO MANY DIFFERENT TYPES OF MATERIALS...?
BECAUSE IT'S IMPORTANT TO KNOW THAT YOU CAN EXPRESS YOURSELVES IN MANY DIFFERENT WAYS.
ALSO, THIS DOESN'T MEAN THAT THOSE THINGS ARE *COMPLETELY* BANNED.
I'M JUST SAYING THAT THEY *MIGHT* ANNOUNCE THAT THOSE ITEMS ARE BANNED ON THE DAY OF THE EXAM.
...BUT THE THING IS, THEY'VE BEEN SAYING AS MUCH FOR THE PAST 10 YEARS, SO IN ALL LIKELIHOOD, THEY'RE BANNED.

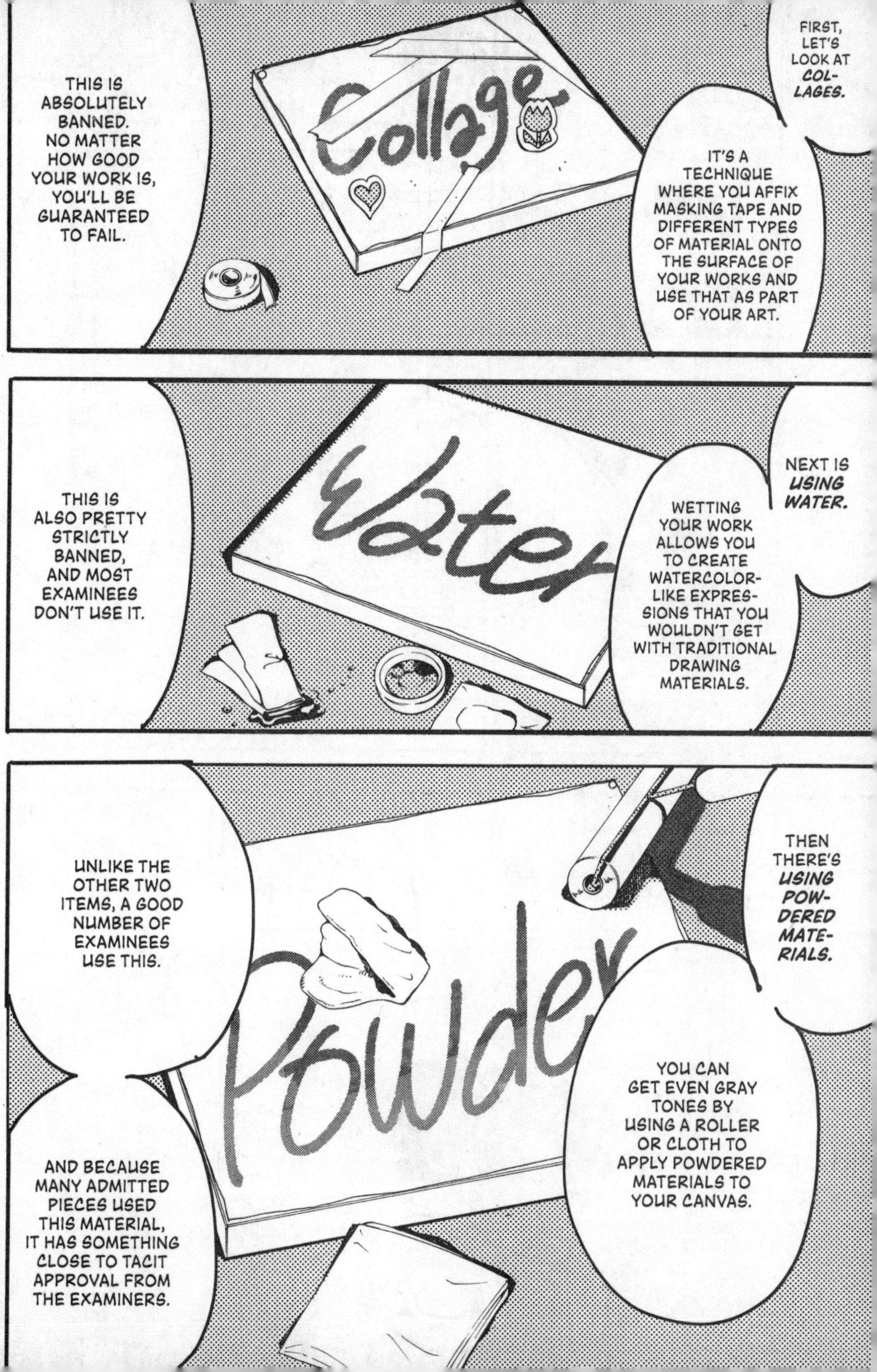
FIRST, LET'S LOOK AT *COLLAGES.*
IT'S A TECHNIQUE WHERE YOU AFFIX MASKING TAPE AND DIFFERENT TYPES OF MATERIAL ONTO THE SURFACE OF YOUR WORKS AND USE THAT AS PART OF YOUR ART.
Collage
THIS IS ABSOLUTELY BANNED. NO MATTER HOW GOOD YOUR WORK IS, YOU'LL BE GUARANTEED TO FAIL.
NEXT IS *USING WATER.*
WETTING YOUR WORK ALLOWS YOU TO CREATE WATERCOLOR-LIKE EXPRESSIONS THAT YOU WOULDN'T GET WITH TRADITIONAL DRAWING MATERIALS.
Water
THIS IS ALSO PRETTY STRICTLY BANNED, AND MOST EXAMINEES DON'T USE IT.
THEN THERE'S *USING POWDERED MATERIALS.*
YOU CAN GET EVEN GRAY TONES BY USING A ROLLER OR CLOTH TO APPLY POWDERED MATERIALS TO YOUR CANVAS.
Powder
UNLIKE THE OTHER TWO ITEMS, A GOOD NUMBER OF EXAMINEES USE THIS.
AND BECAUSE MANY ADMITTED PIECES USED THIS MATERIAL, IT HAS SOMETHING CLOSE TO TACIT APPROVAL FROM THE EXAMINERS.

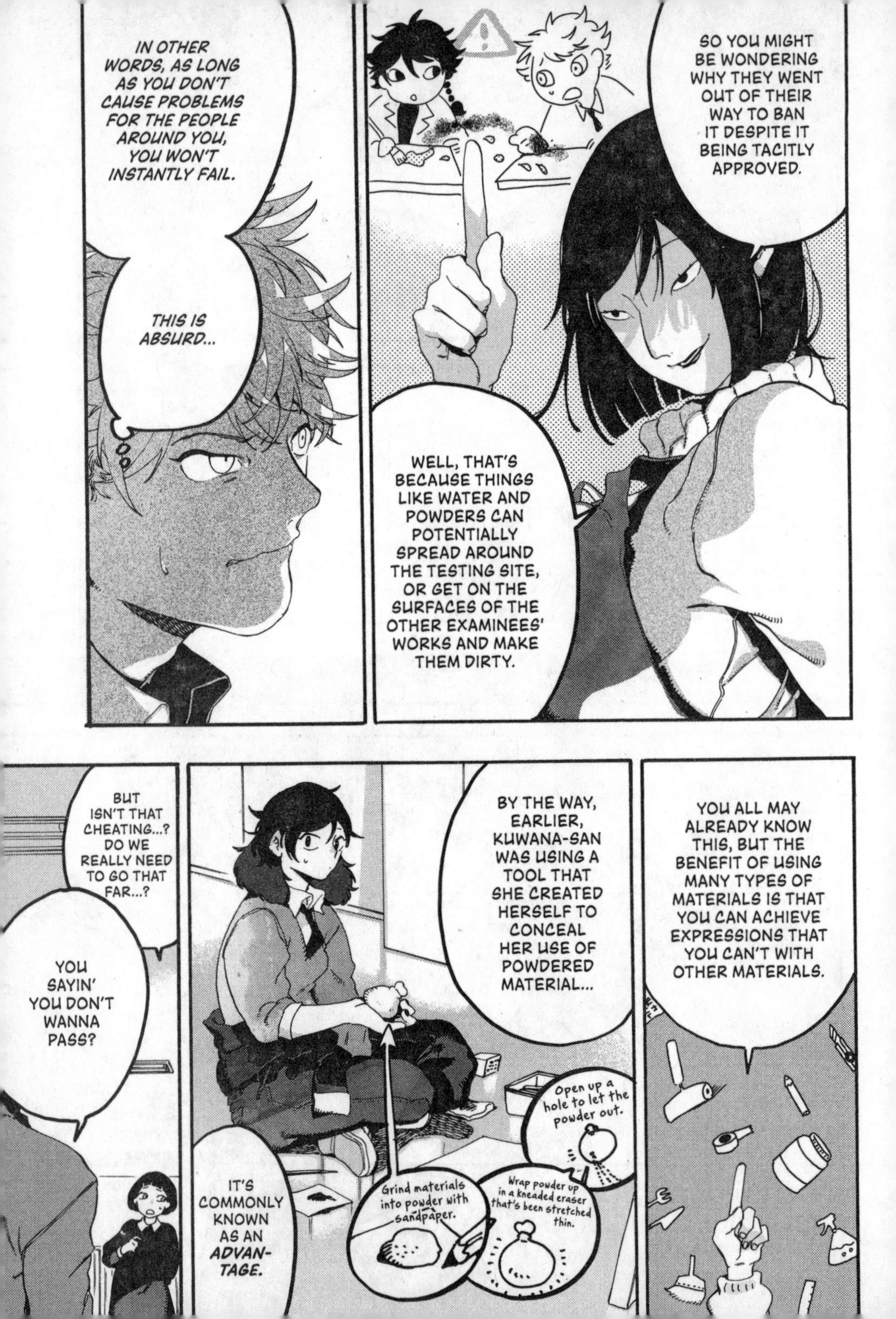
SO YOU MIGHT BE WONDERING WHY THEY WENT OUT OF THEIR WAY TO BAN IT DESPITE IT BEING TACITLY APPROVED.
WELL, THAT'S BECAUSE THINGS LIKE WATER AND POWDERS CAN POTENTIALLY SPREAD AROUND THE TESTING SITE, OR GET ON THE SURFACES OF THE OTHER EXAMINEES' WORKS AND MAKE THEM DIRTY.
IN OTHER WORDS, AS LONG AS YOU DON'T CAUSE PROBLEMS FOR THE PEOPLE AROUND YOU, YOU WON'T INSTANTLY FAIL.
THIS IS ABSURD...
YOU ALL MAY ALREADY KNOW THIS, BUT THE BENEFIT OF USING MANY TYPES OF MATERIALS IS THAT YOU CAN ACHIEVE EXPRESSIONS THAT YOU CAN'T WITH OTHER MATERIALS.
BY THE WAY, EARLIER, KUWANA-SAN WAS USING A TOOL THAT SHE CREATED HERSELF TO CONCEAL HER USE OF POWDERED MATERIAL...
Open up a hole to let the powder out.
Wrap powder up in a kneaded eraser that's been stretched thin.
Grind materials into powder with sandpaper.
IT'S COMMONLY KNOWN AS AN ADVANTAGE.
BUT ISN'T THAT CHEATING...? DO WE REALLY NEED TO GO THAT FAR...?
YOU SAYIN' YOU DON'T WANNA PASS?

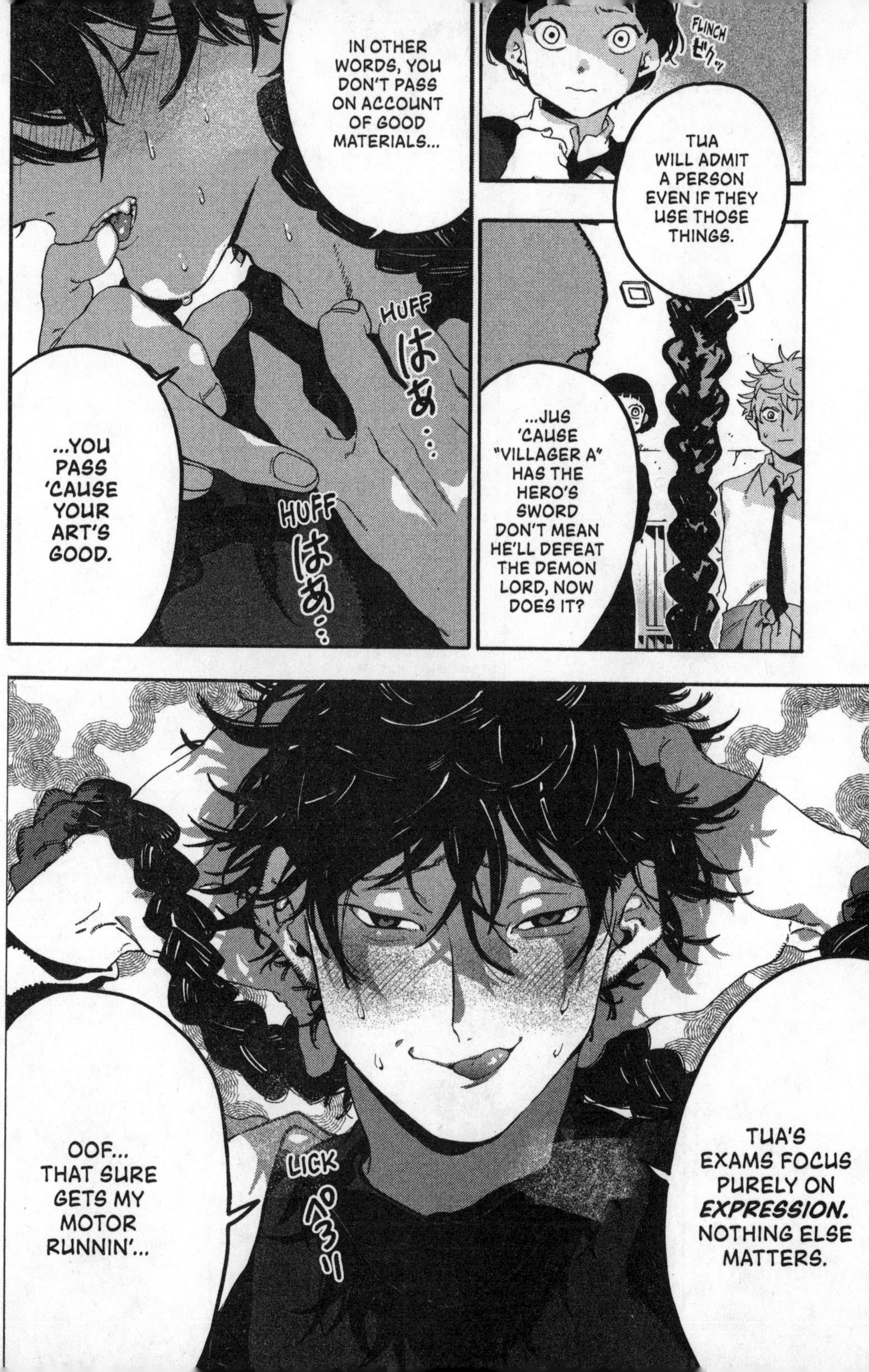
FLINCH
ビクッ
TUA WILL ADMIT A PERSON EVEN IF THEY USE THOSE THINGS.
...JUS 'CAUSE "VILLAGER A" HAS THE HERO'S SWORD DON'T MEAN HE'LL DEFEAT THE DEMON LORD, NOW DOES IT?
IN OTHER WORDS, YOU DON'T PASS ON ACCOUNT OF GOOD MATERIALS...
HUFF
はぁ...
HUFF
はぁ...
...YOU PASS 'CAUSE YOUR ART'S GOOD.
TUA'S EXAMS FOCUS PURELY ON *EXPRESSION.* NOTHING ELSE MATTERS.
LICK
ぺろ
OOF... THAT SURE GETS MY MOTOR RUNNIN'...

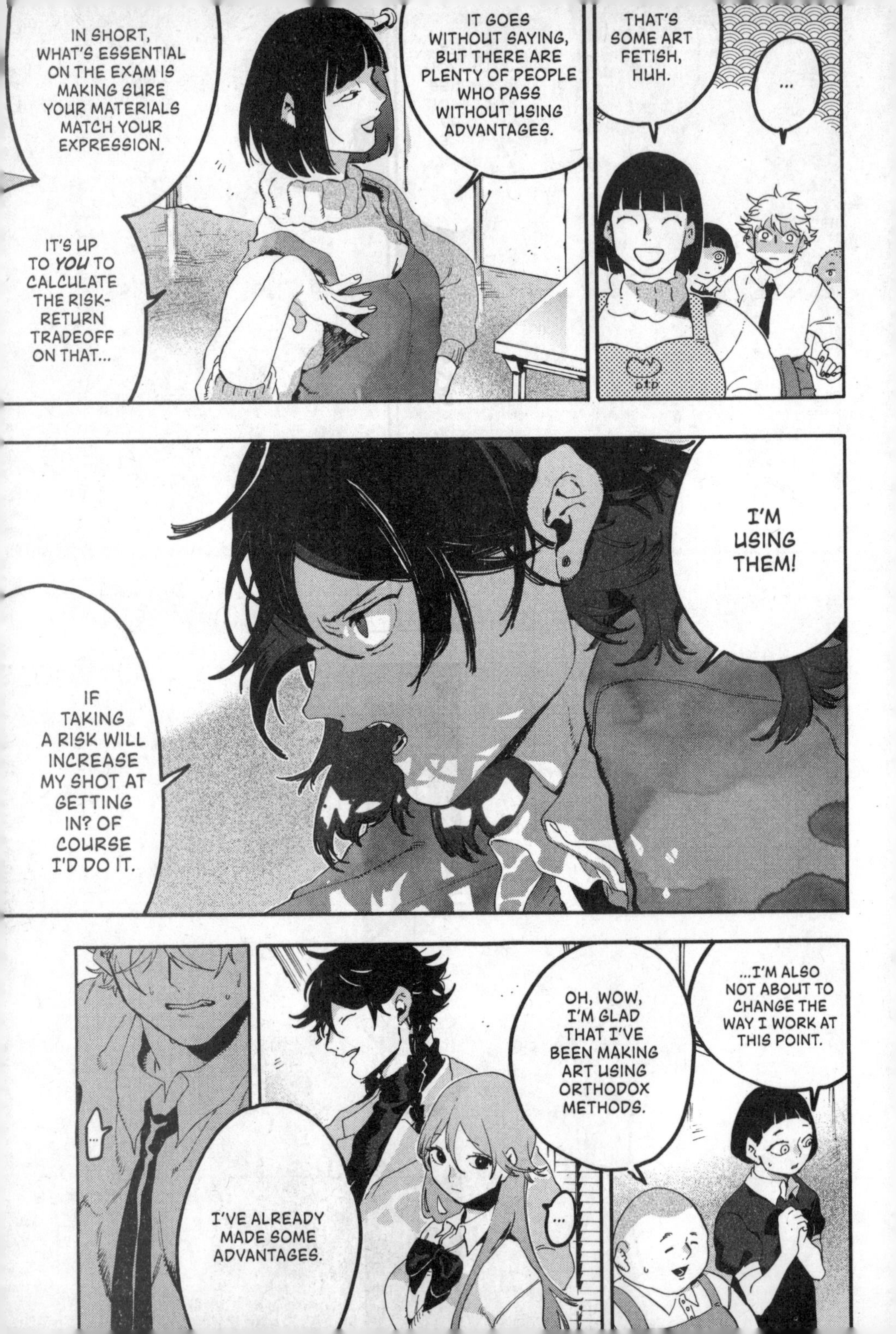
...
THAT'S SOME ART FETISH, HUH.
IT GOES WITHOUT SAYING, BUT THERE ARE PLENTY OF PEOPLE WHO PASS WITHOUT USING ADVANTAGES.
IN SHORT, WHAT'S ESSENTIAL ON THE EXAM IS MAKING SURE YOUR MATERIALS MATCH YOUR EXPRESSION.
IT'S UP TO *YOU* TO CALCULATE THE RISK-RETURN TRADEOFF ON THAT...
I'M USING THEM!
IF TAKING A RISK WILL INCREASE MY SHOT AT GETTING IN? OF COURSE I'D DO IT.
...I'M ALSO NOT ABOUT TO CHANGE THE WAY I WORK AT THIS POINT.
OH, WOW, I'M GLAD THAT I'VE BEEN MAKING ART USING ORTHODOX METHODS.
...
I'VE ALREADY MADE SOME ADVANTAGES.
...

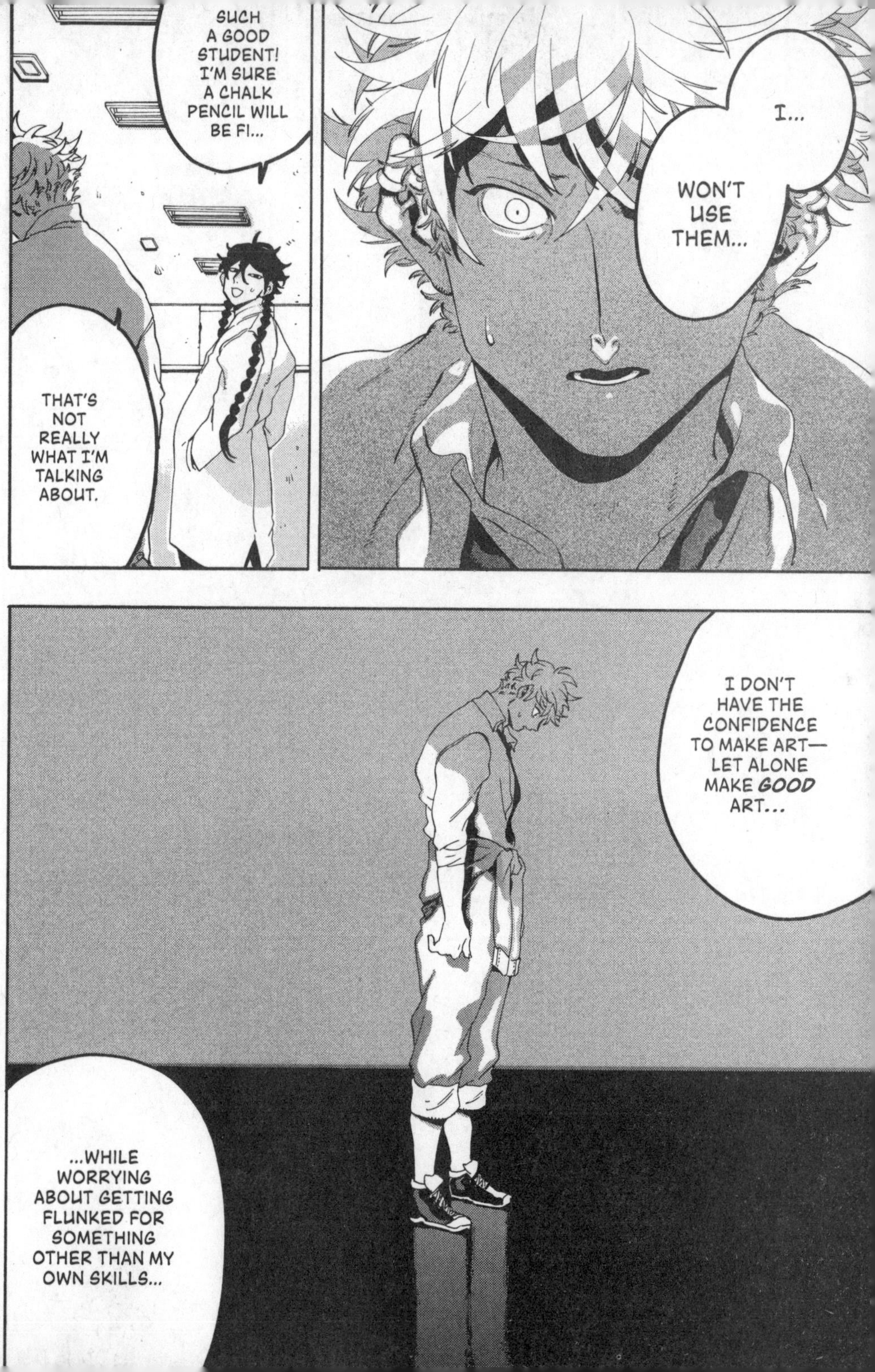
I... WON'T USE THEM...
SUCH A GOOD STUDENT! I'M SURE A CHALK PENCIL WILL BE FI...
THAT'S NOT REALLY WHAT I'M TALKING ABOUT.
I DON'T HAVE THE CONFIDENCE TO MAKE ART— LET ALONE MAKE *GOOD* ART...
...WHILE WORRYING ABOUT GETTING FLUNKED FOR SOMETHING OTHER THAN MY OWN SKILLS...

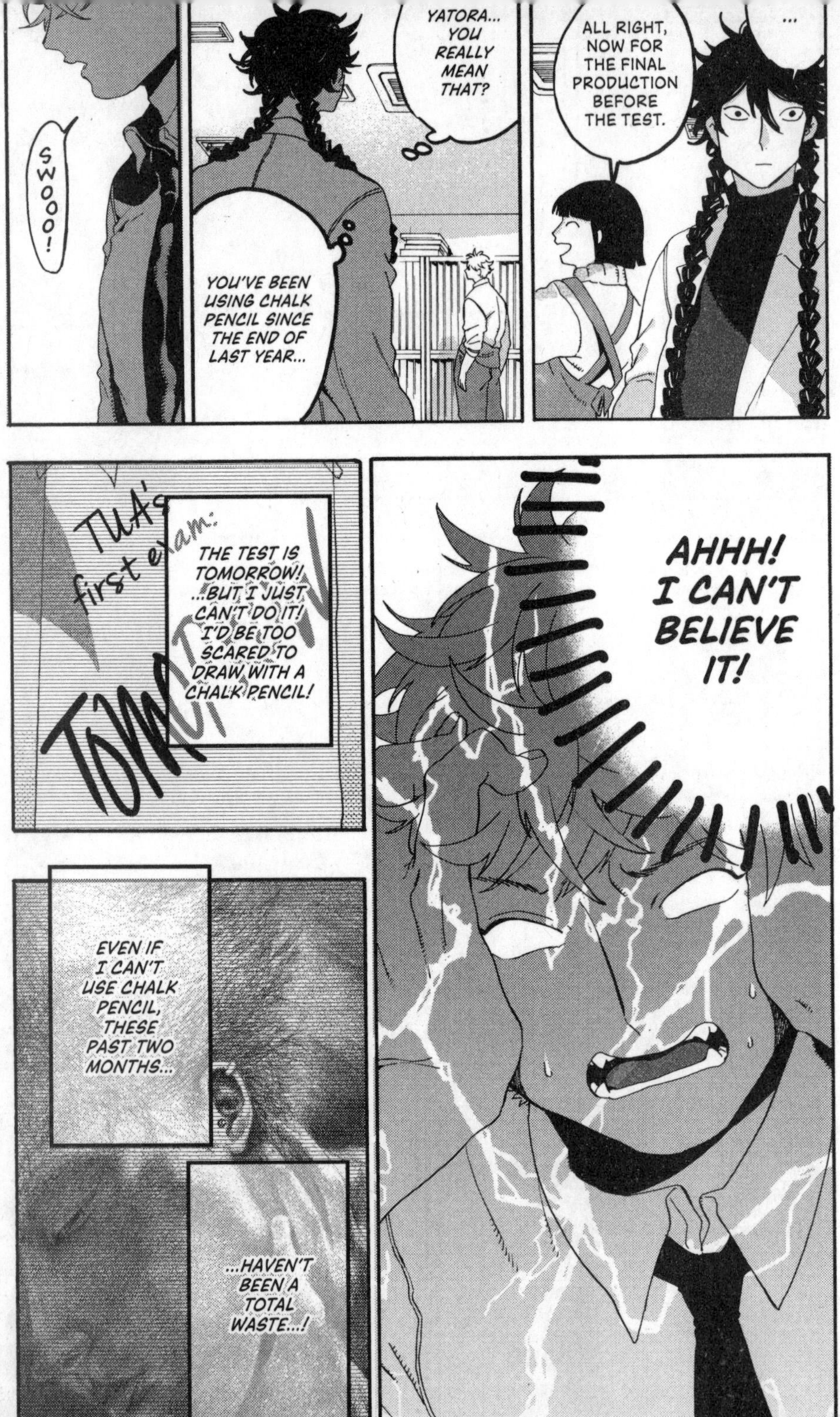
...
ALL RIGHT, NOW FOR THE FINAL PRODUCTION BEFORE THE TEST.
YATORA... YOU REALLY MEAN THAT?
YOU'VE BEEN USING CHALK PENCIL SINCE THE END OF LAST YEAR...
SWOOO!
AHHH! I CAN'T BELIEVE IT!
TUA's first exam:
THE TEST IS TOMORROW! ...BUT I JUST CAN'T DO IT! I'D BE TOO SCARED TO DRAW WITH A CHALK PENCIL!
EVEN IF I CAN'T USE CHALK PENCIL, THESE PAST TWO MONTHS...
...HAVEN'T BEEN A TOTAL WASTE...!

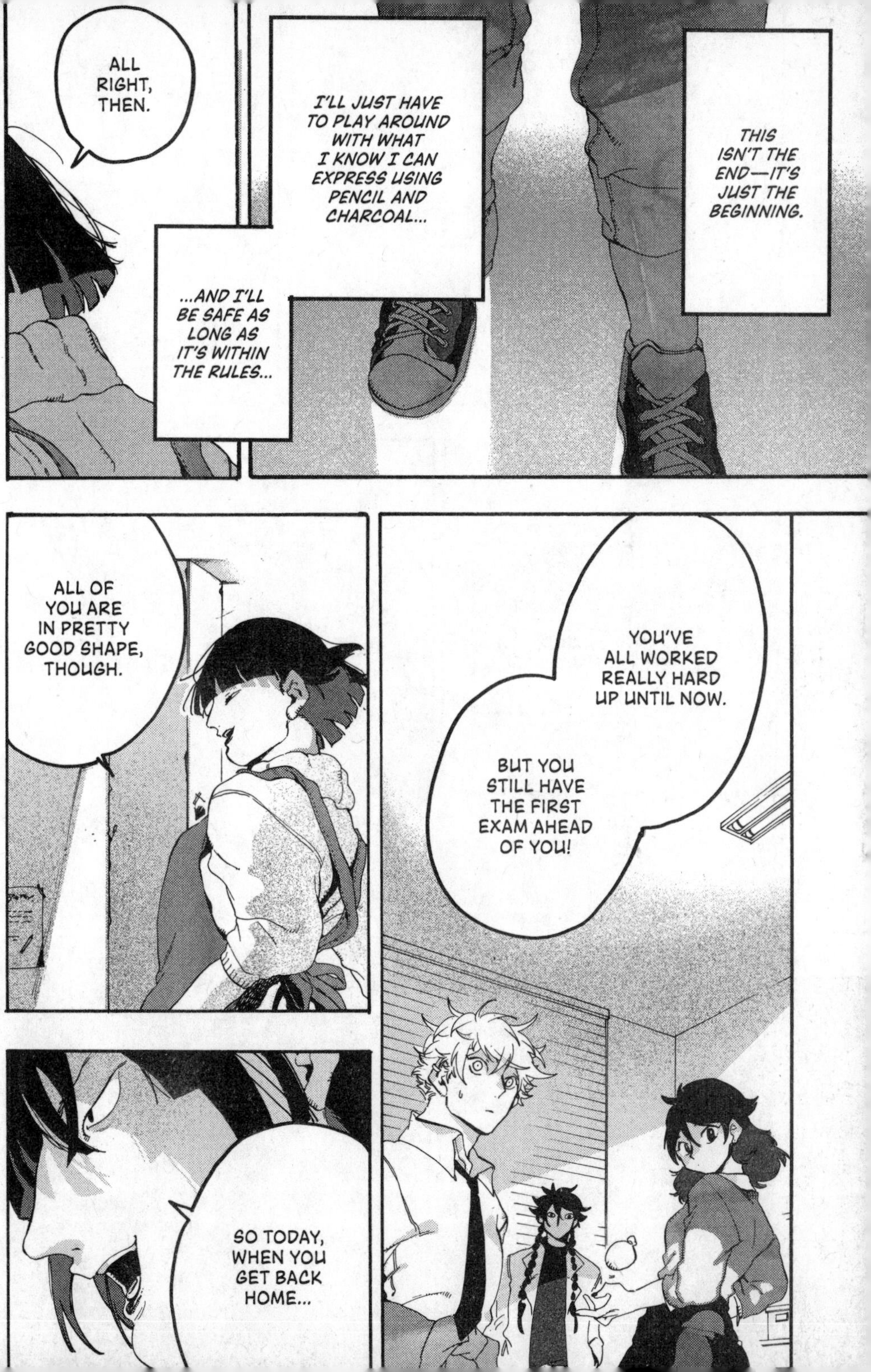

I'LL JUST HAVE TO PLAY AROUND WITH WHAT I KNOW I CAN EXPRESS USING PENCIL AND CHARCOAL...
...AND I'LL BE SAFE AS LONG AS IT'S WITHIN THE RULES...
THIS ISN'T THE END—IT'S JUST THE BEGINNING.
ALL RIGHT, THEN.
YOU'VE ALL WORKED REALLY HARD UP UNTIL NOW.
BUT YOU STILL HAVE THE FIRST EXAM AHEAD OF YOU!
ALL OF YOU ARE IN PRETTY GOOD SHAPE, THOUGH.
SO TODAY, WHEN YOU GET BACK HOME...

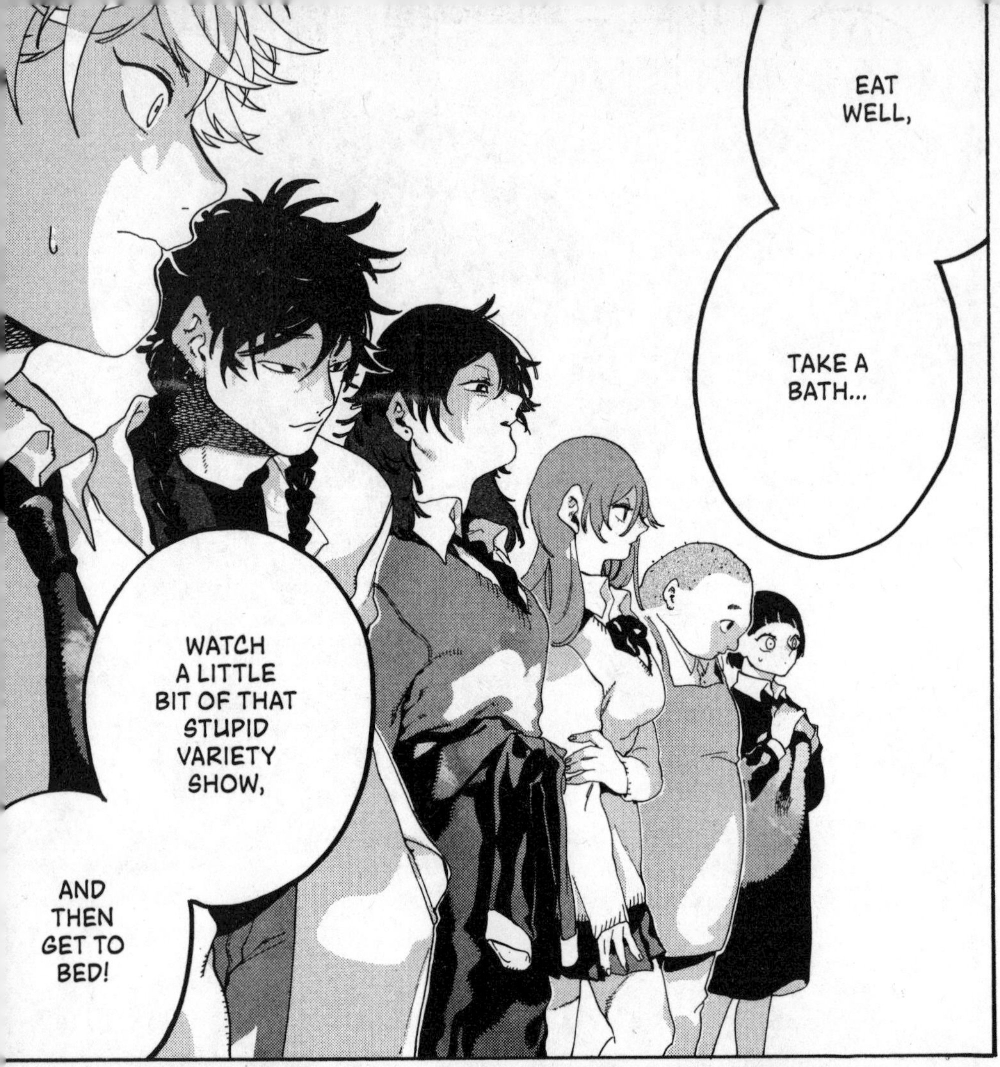
EAT WELL,
TAKE A BATH...
WATCH A LITTLE BIT OF THAT STUPID VARIETY SHOW,
AND THEN GET TO BED!
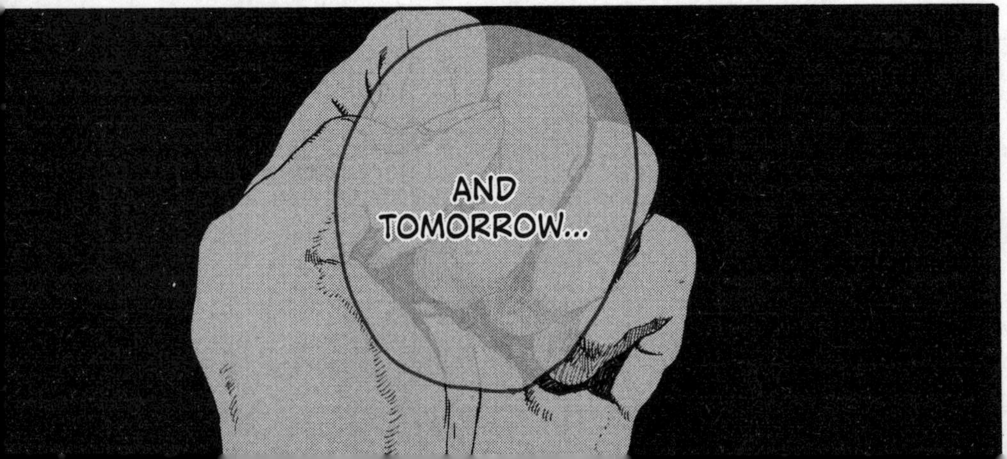
AND TOMORROW...

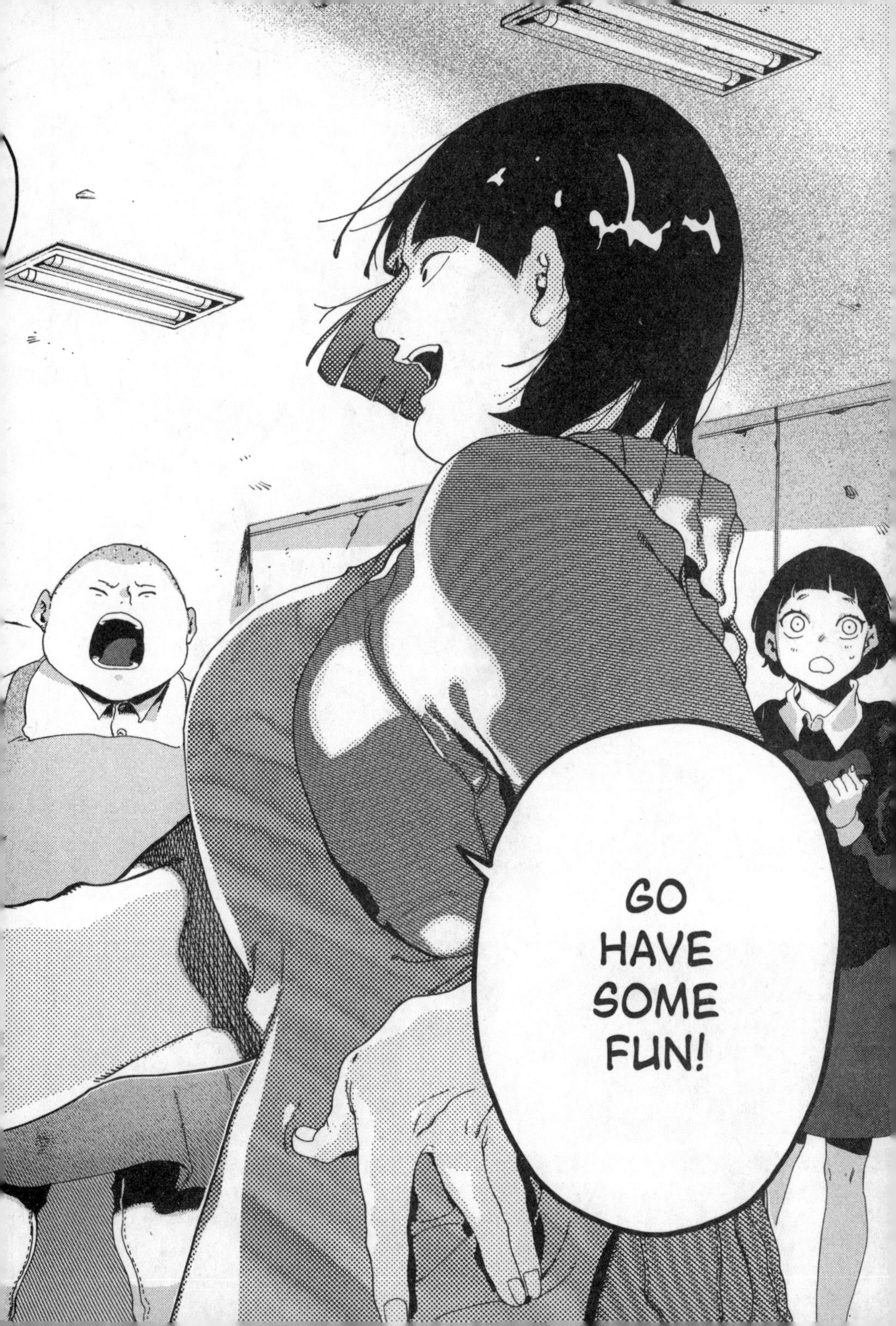
GO HAVE SOME FUN!

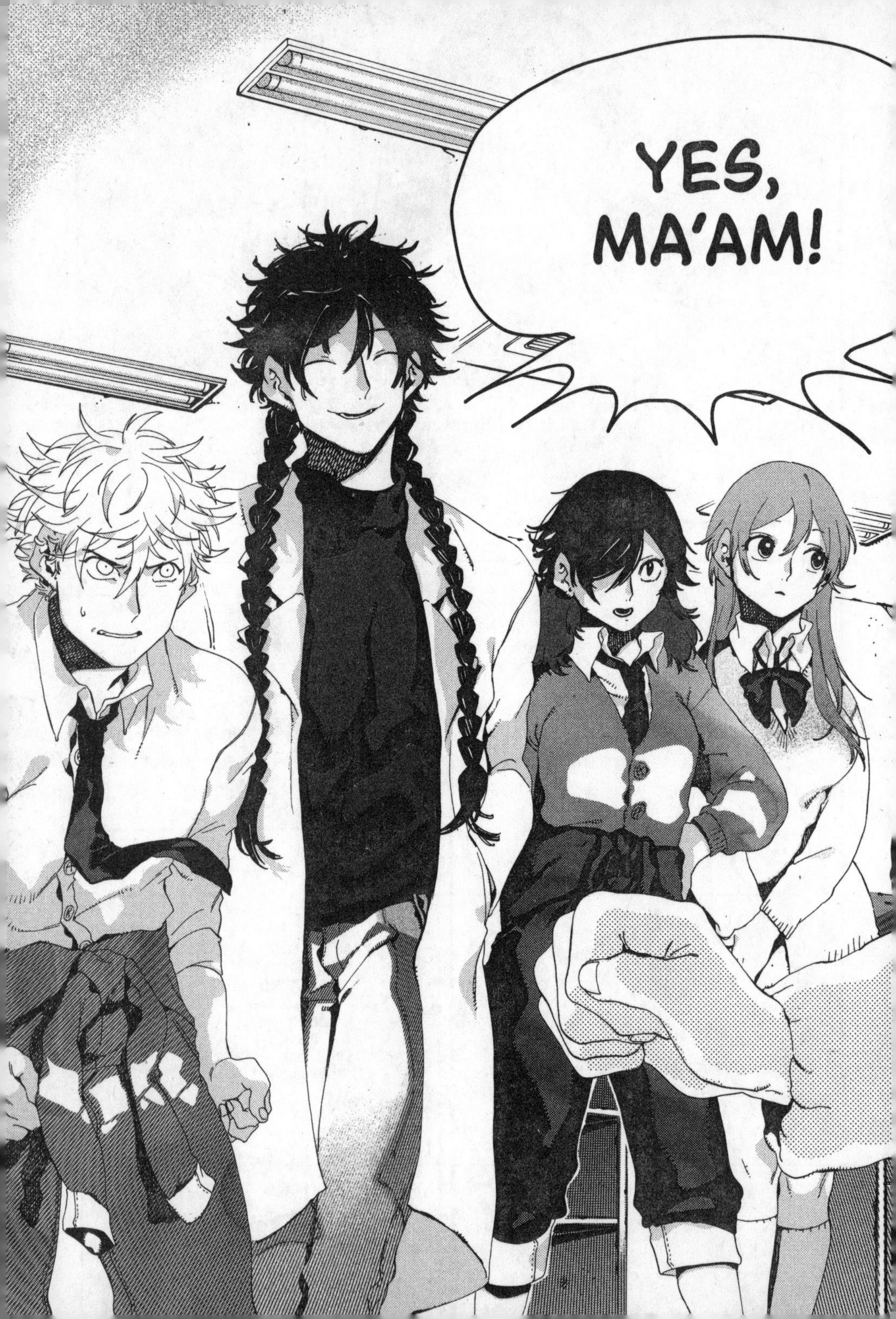
YES, MA'AM!

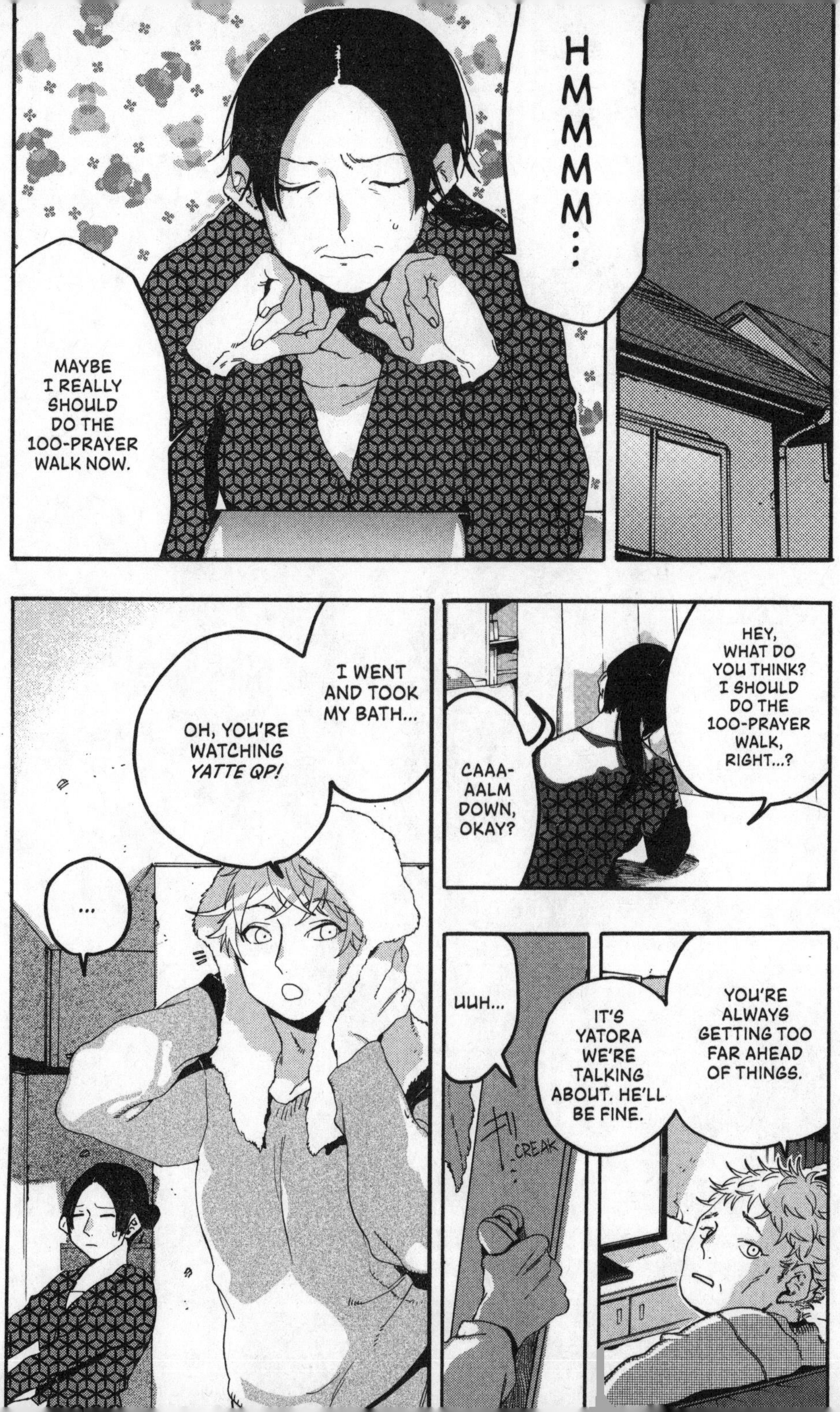
HMMMM...
MAYBE I REALLY SHOULD DO THE 100-PRAYER WALK NOW.
HEY, WHAT DO YOU THINK? I SHOULD DO THE 100-PRAYER WALK, RIGHT...?
CAAA-AALM DOWN, OKAY?
YOU'RE ALWAYS GETTING TOO FAR AHEAD OF THINGS.
IT'S YATORA WE'RE TALKING ABOUT. HE'LL BE FINE.
UUH...
CREAK
I WENT AND TOOK MY BATH...
OH, YOU'RE WATCHING *YATTE QP!*
...

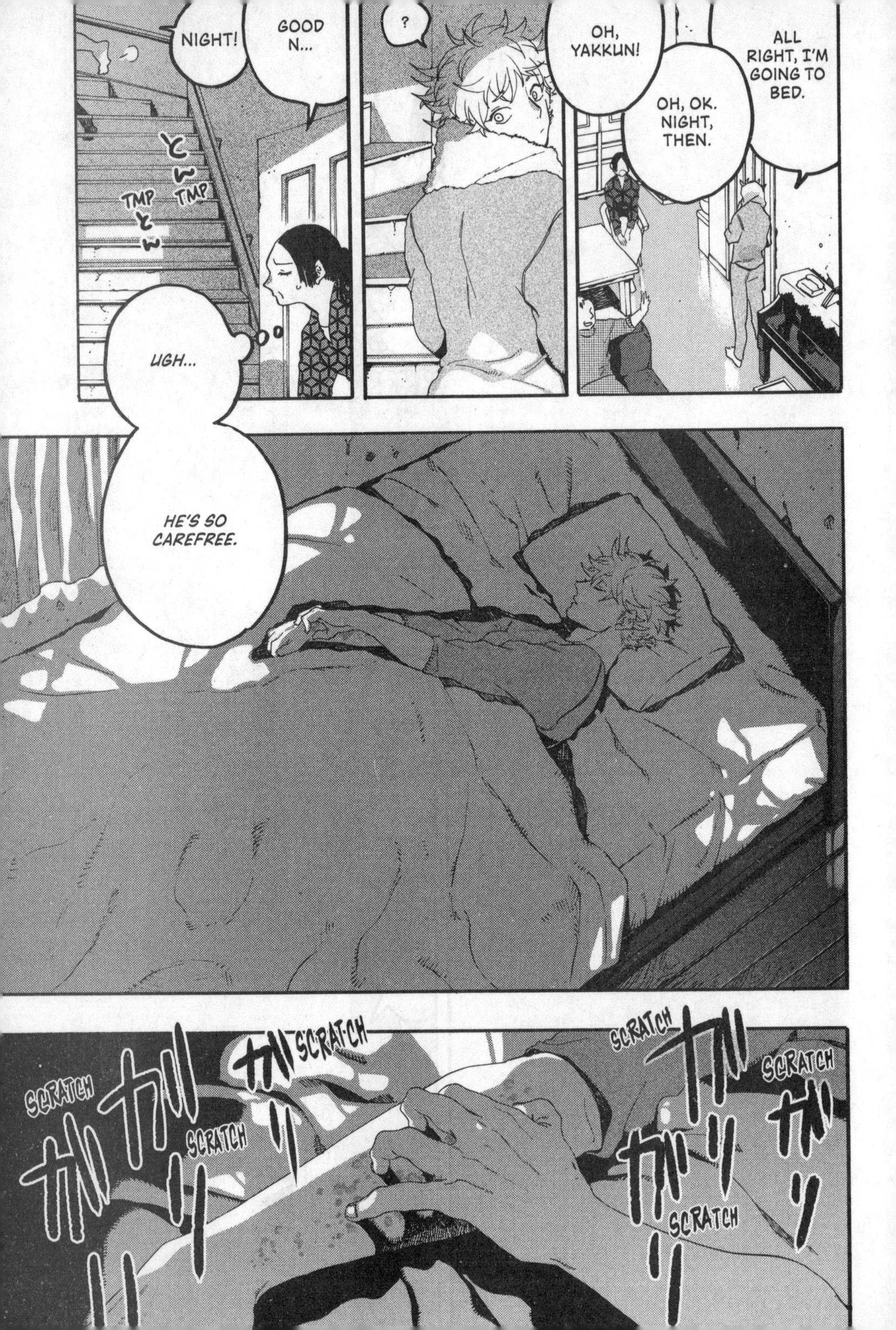
ALL RIGHT, I'M GOING TO BED.
OH, OK. NIGHT, THEN.
OH, YAKKUN!
?
GOOD N...
NIGHT!
TMP TMP
UGH...
HE'S SO CAREFREE.
SCRATCH
SCRATCH
SCRATCH
SCRATCH
SCRATCH
SCRATCH

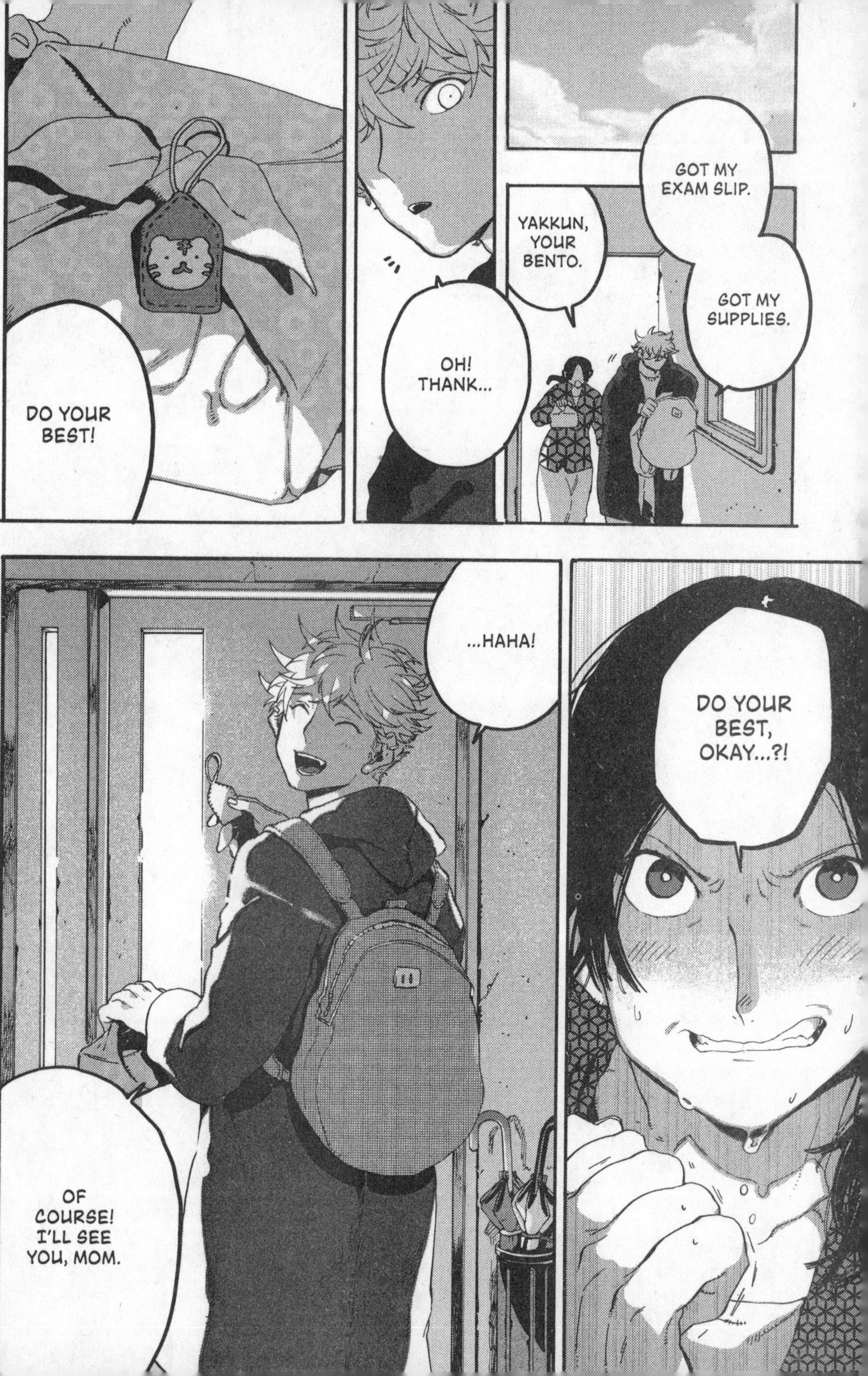
GOT MY EXAM SLIP.
GOT MY SUPPLIES.
YAKKUN, YOUR BENTO.
OH! THANK...
DO YOUR BEST!
DO YOUR BEST, OKAY...?!
...HAHA!
OF COURSE! I'LL SEE YOU, MOM.

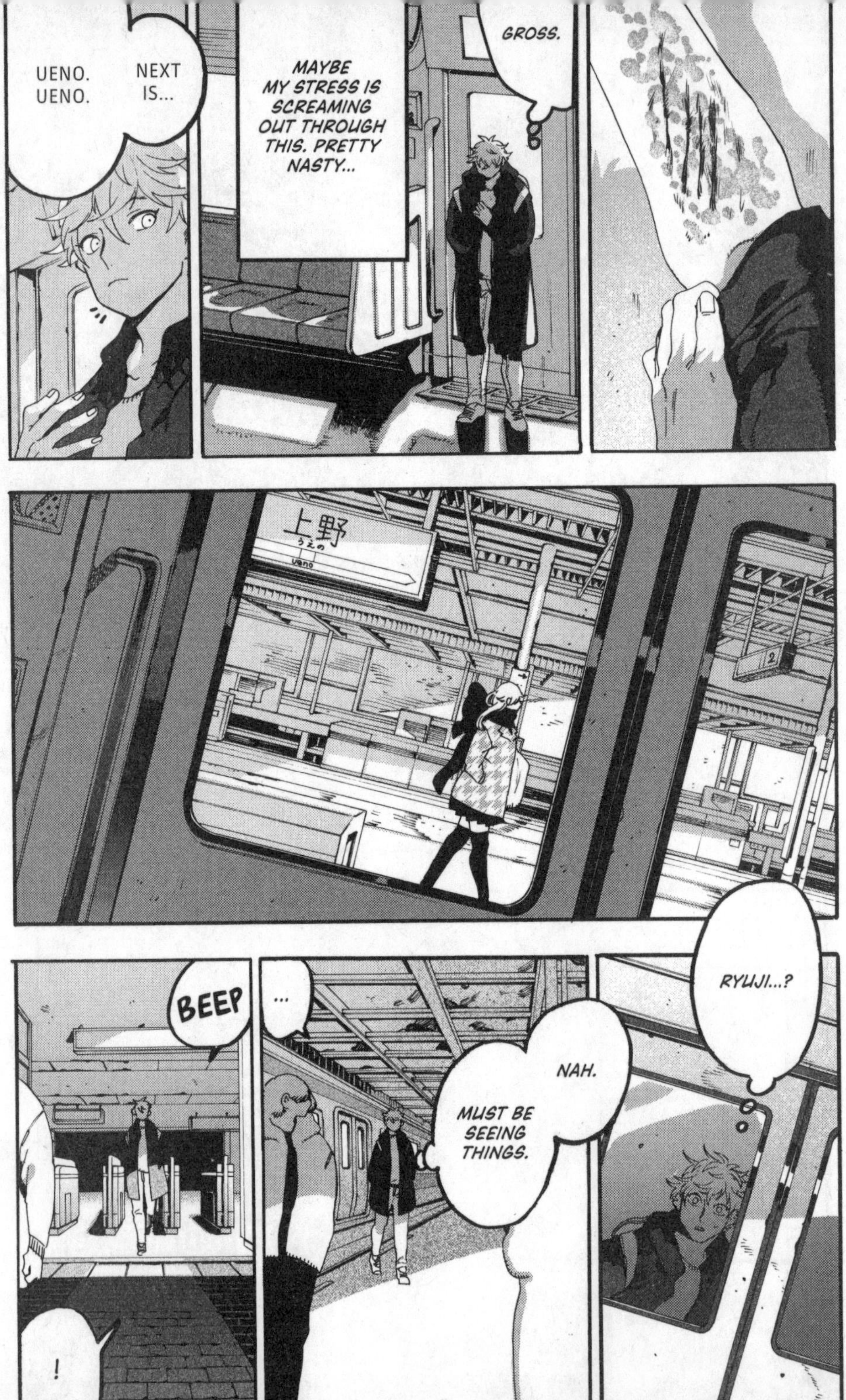
GROSS.
MAYBE MY STRESS IS SCREAMING OUT THROUGH THIS. PRETTY NASTY...
NEXT IS...
UENO. UENO.
上野
うえの
ueno
RYUJI...?
NAH.
MUST BE SEEING THINGS.
...
BEEP
!

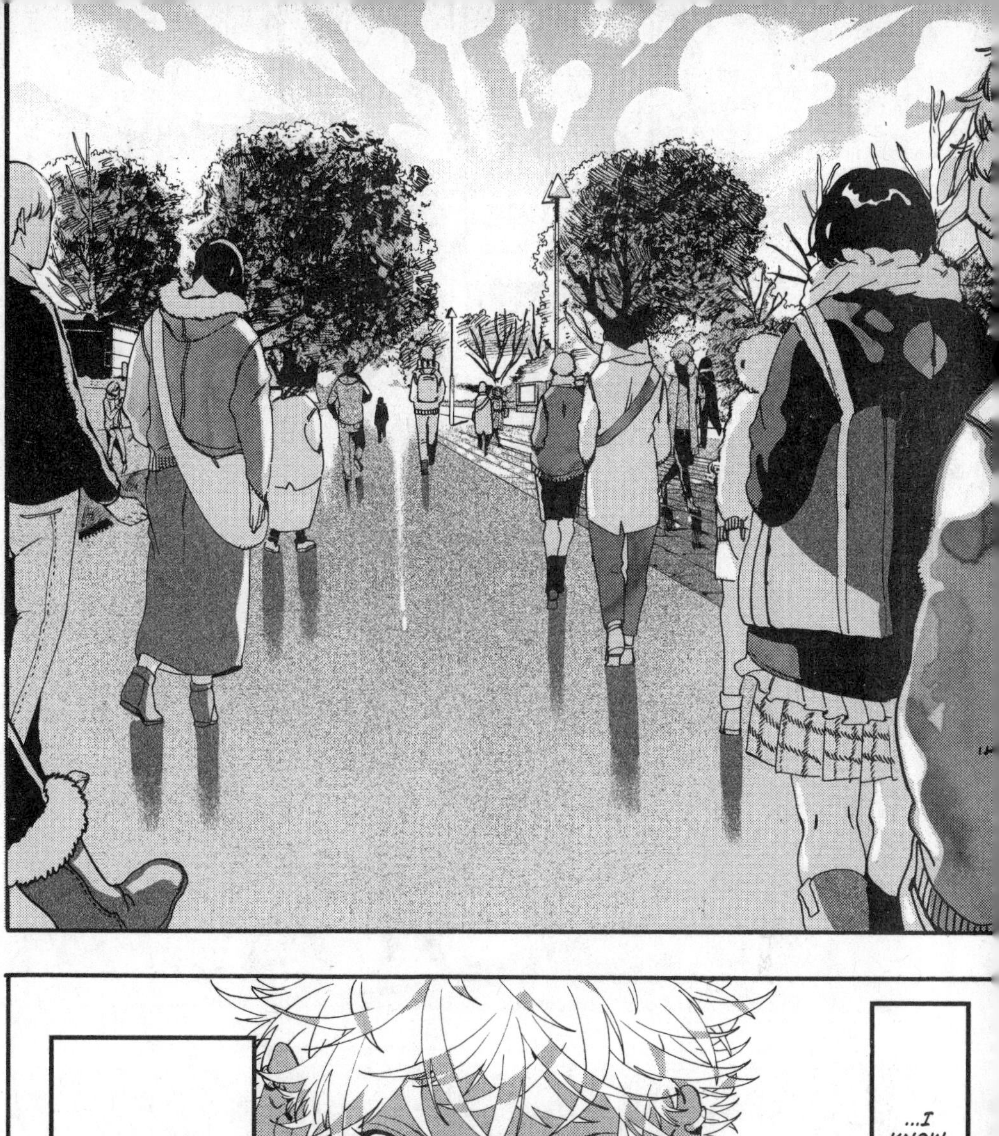

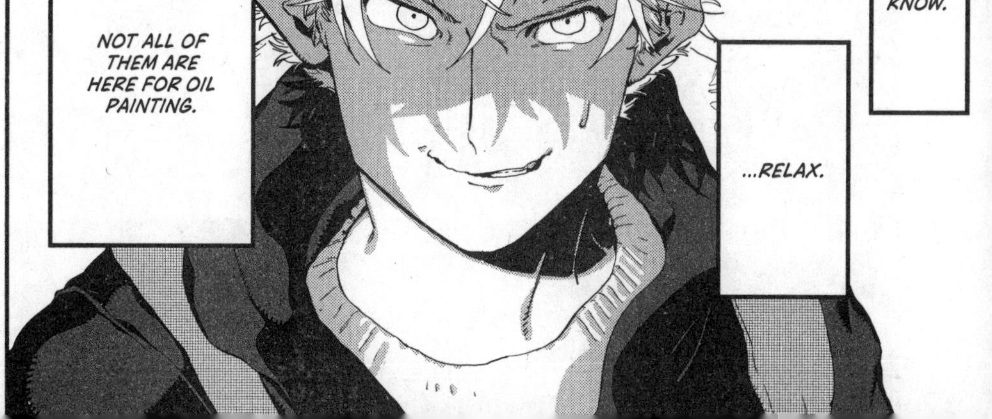
...I KNOW.
...RELAX.
NOT ALL OF THEM ARE HERE FOR OIL PAINTING.

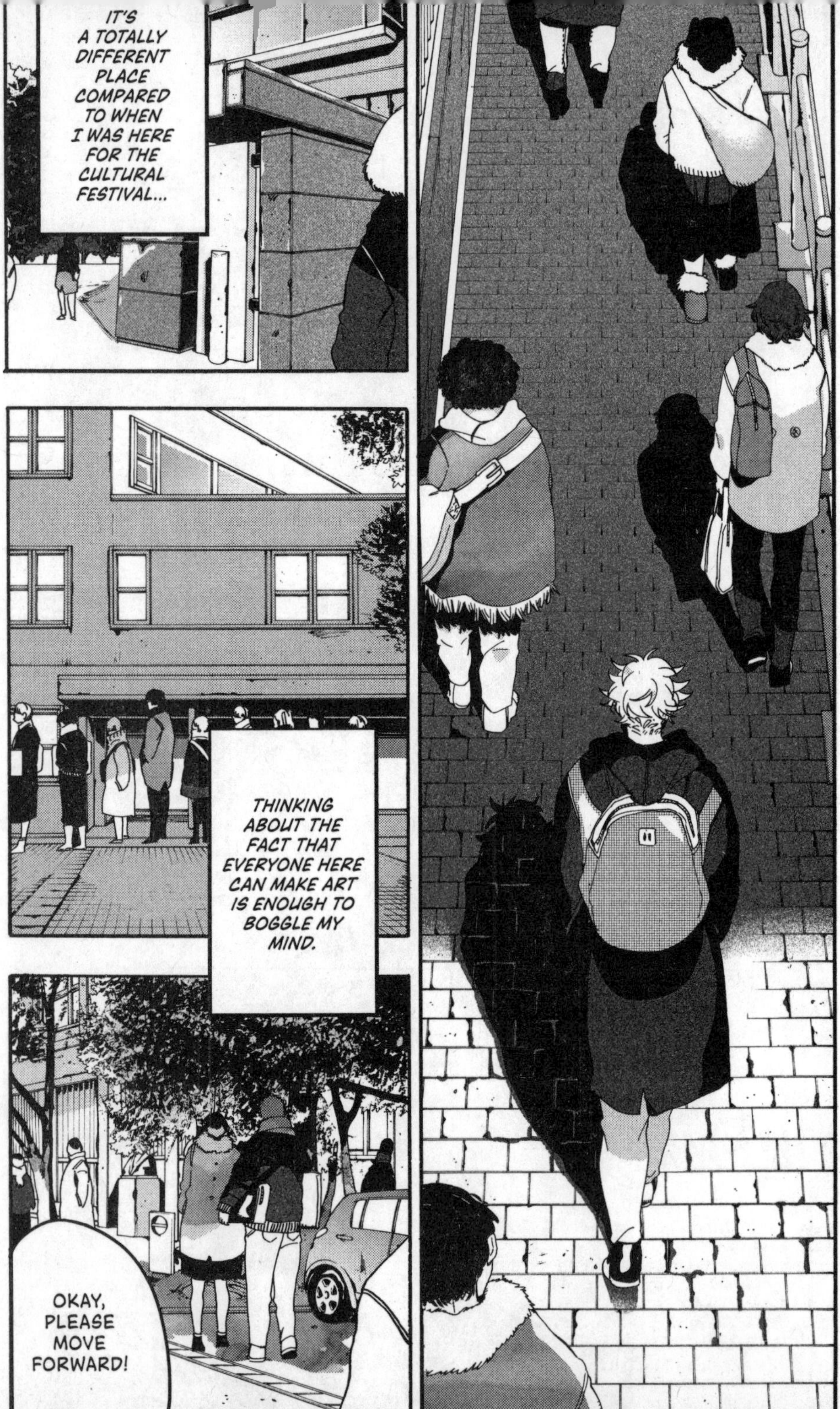
IT'S A TOTALLY DIFFERENT PLACE COMPARED TO WHEN I WAS HERE FOR THE CULTURAL FESTIVAL...
THINKING ABOUT THE FACT THAT EVERYONE HERE CAN MAKE ART IS ENOUGH TO BOGGLE MY MIND.
OKAY, PLEASE MOVE FORWARD!

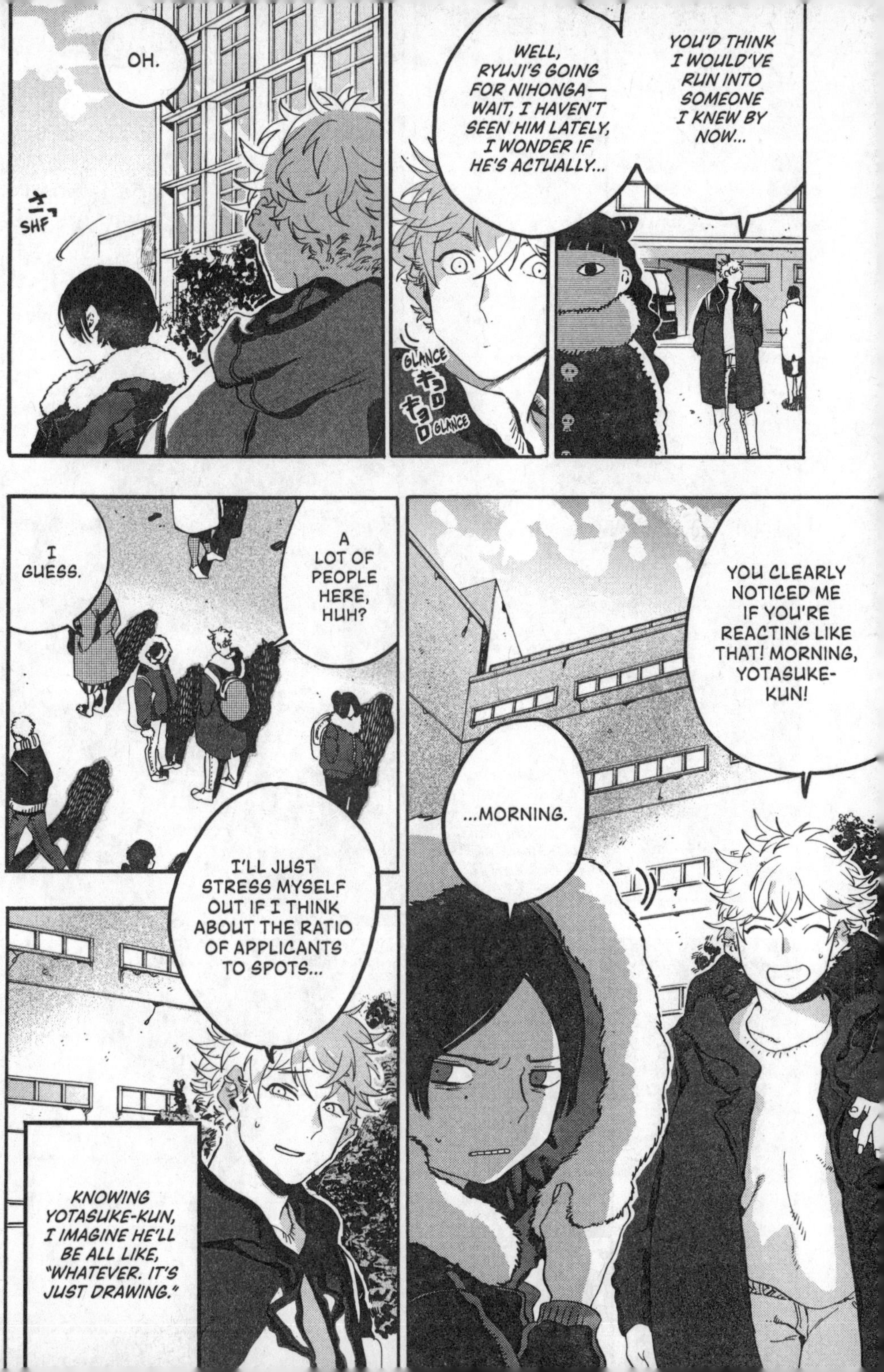
YOU'D THINK I WOULD'VE RUN INTO SOMEONE I KNEW BY NOW...
WELL, RYUJI'S GOING FOR NIHONGA— WAIT, I HAVEN'T SEEN HIM LATELY, I WONDER IF HE'S ACTUALLY...
キョロ GLANCE
キョロ GLANCE
OH.
SHF
YOU CLEARLY NOTICED ME IF YOU'RE REACTING LIKE THAT! MORNING, YOTASUKE-KUN!
...MORNING.
A LOT OF PEOPLE HERE, HUH?
I GUESS.
I'LL JUST STRESS MYSELF OUT IF I THINK ABOUT THE RATIO OF APPLICANTS TO SPOTS...
KNOWING YOTASUKE-KUN, I IMAGINE HE'LL BE ALL LIKE, "WHATEVER. IT'S JUST DRAWING."

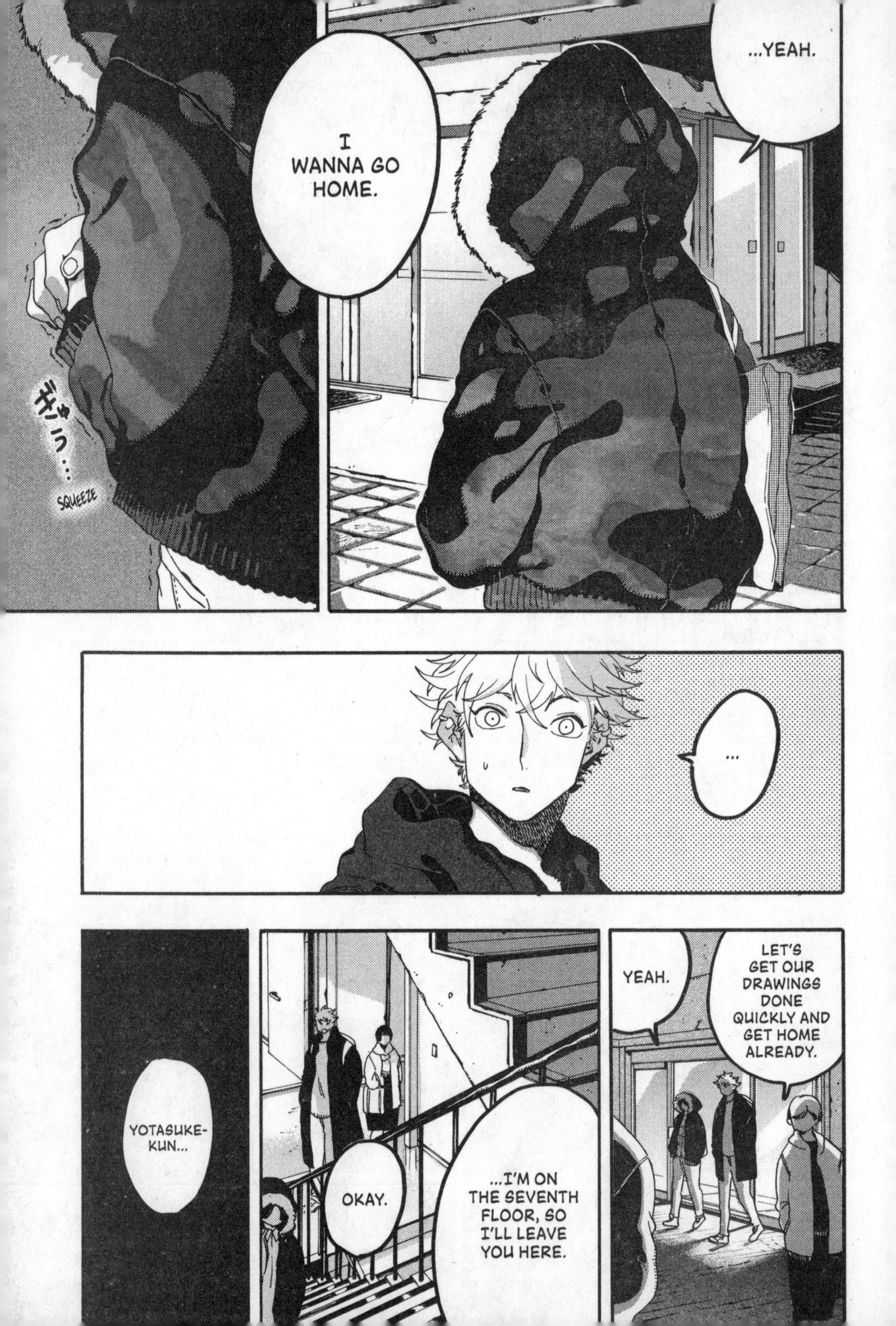
...YEAH.
I WANNA GO HOME.
ぎゅう…
SQUEEZE
...
LET'S GET OUR DRAWINGS DONE QUICKLY AND GET HOME ALREADY.
YEAH.
...I'M ON THE SEVENTH FLOOR, SO I'LL LEAVE YOU HERE.
OKAY.
YOTASUKE-KUN...

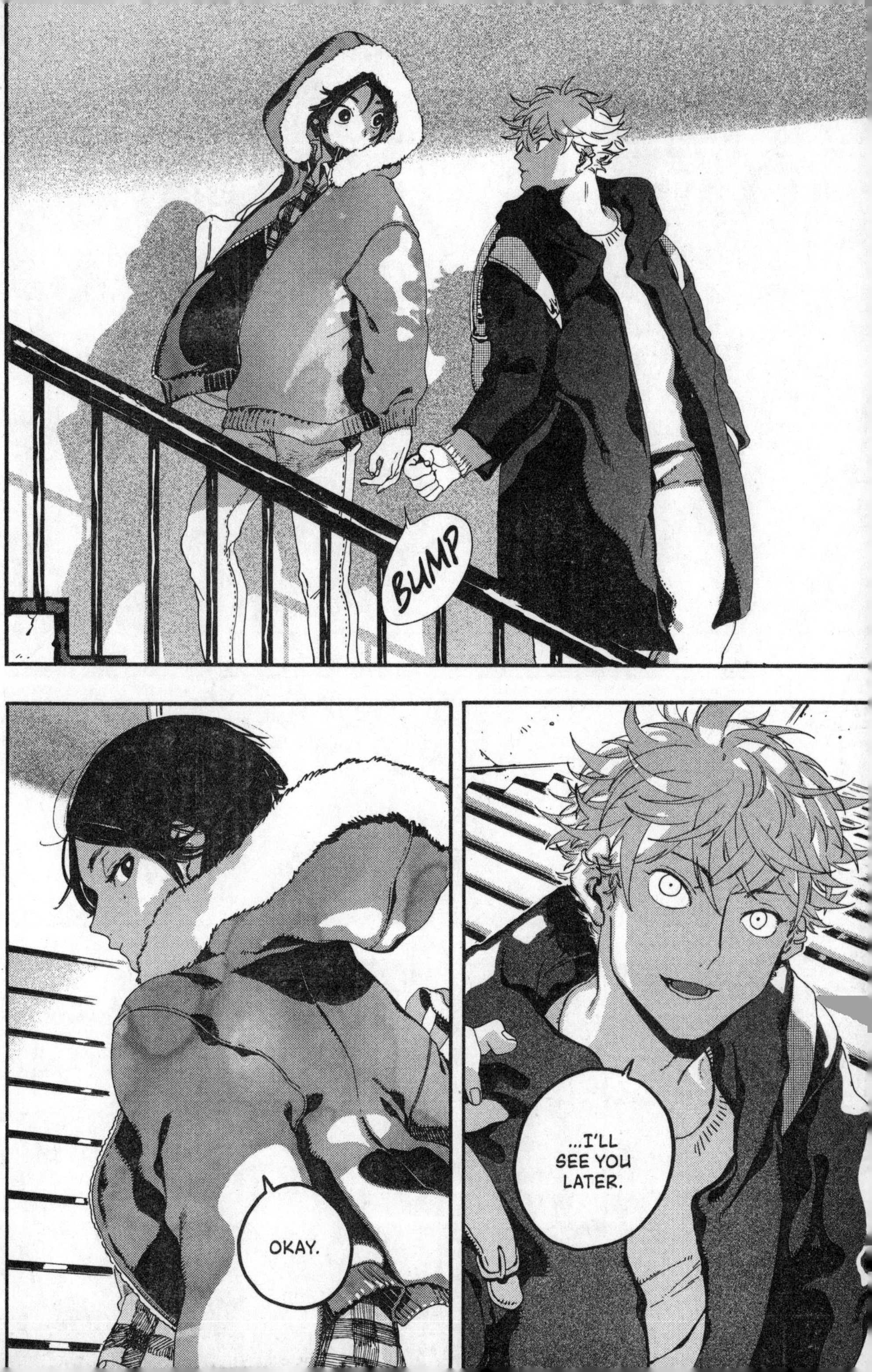
BUMP
...I'LL SEE YOU LATER.
OKAY.

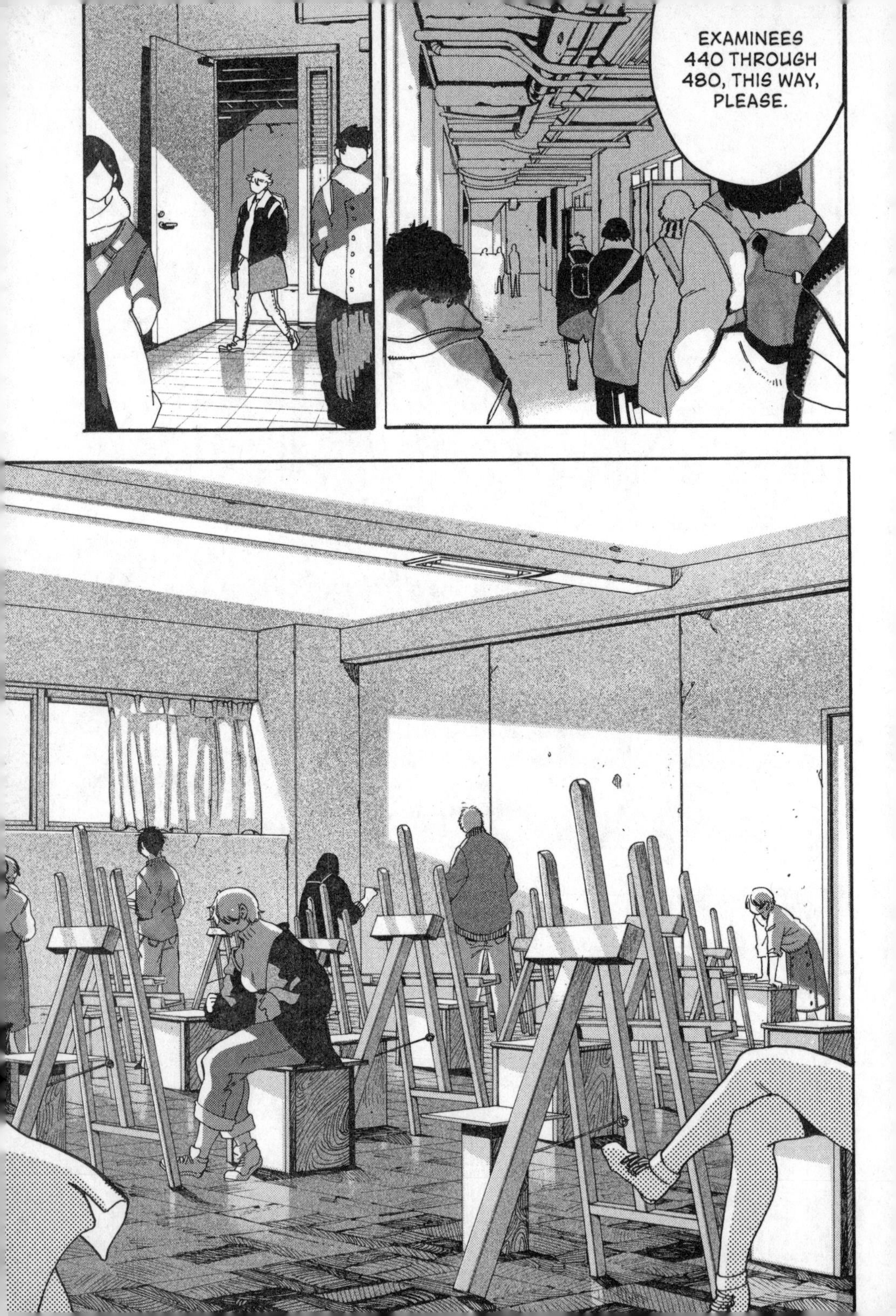
EXAMINEES 440 THROUGH 480, THIS WAY, PLEASE.

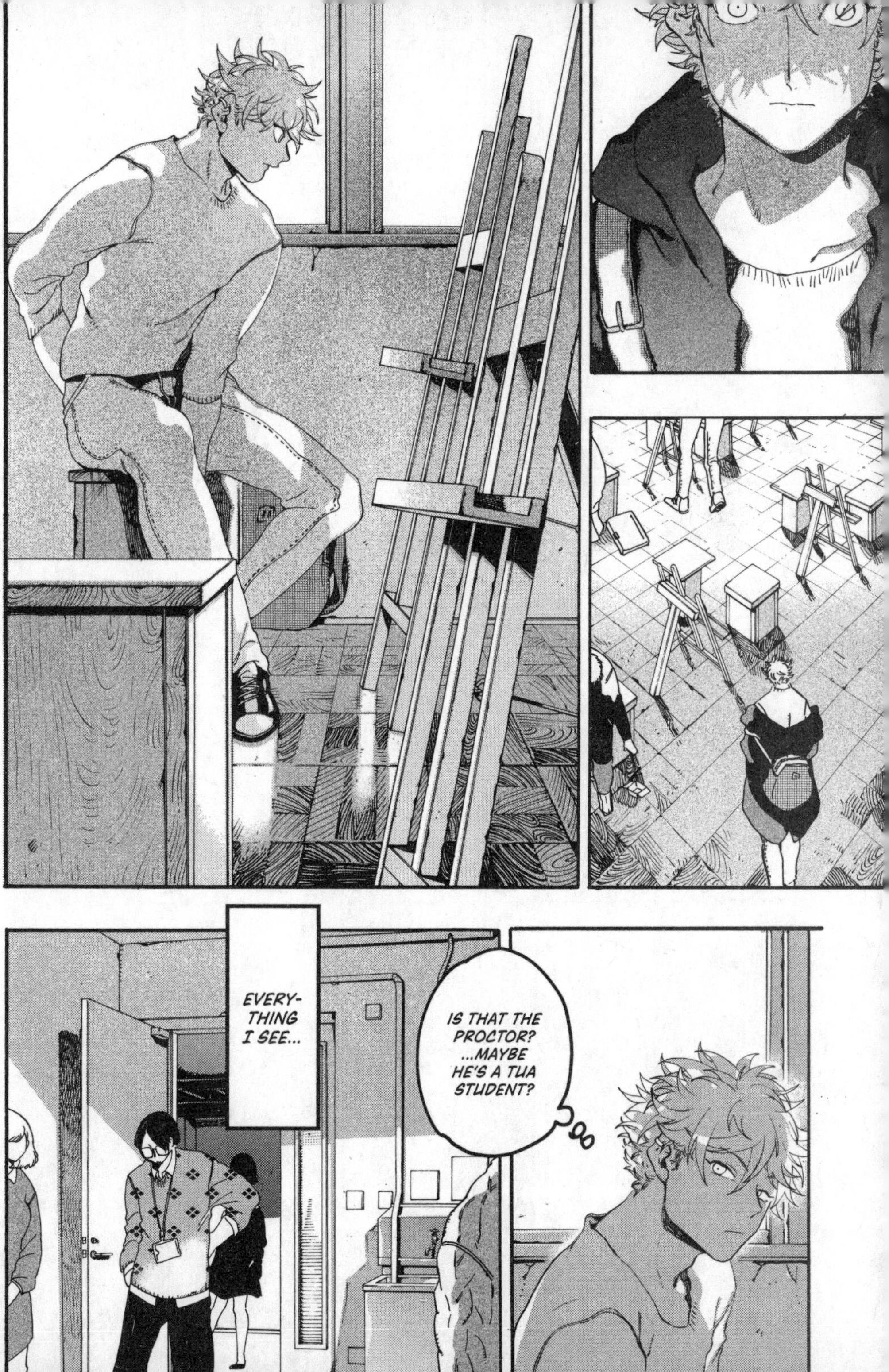
IS THAT THE PROCTOR? ...MAYBE HE'S A TUA STUDENT?
EVERY-THING I SEE...

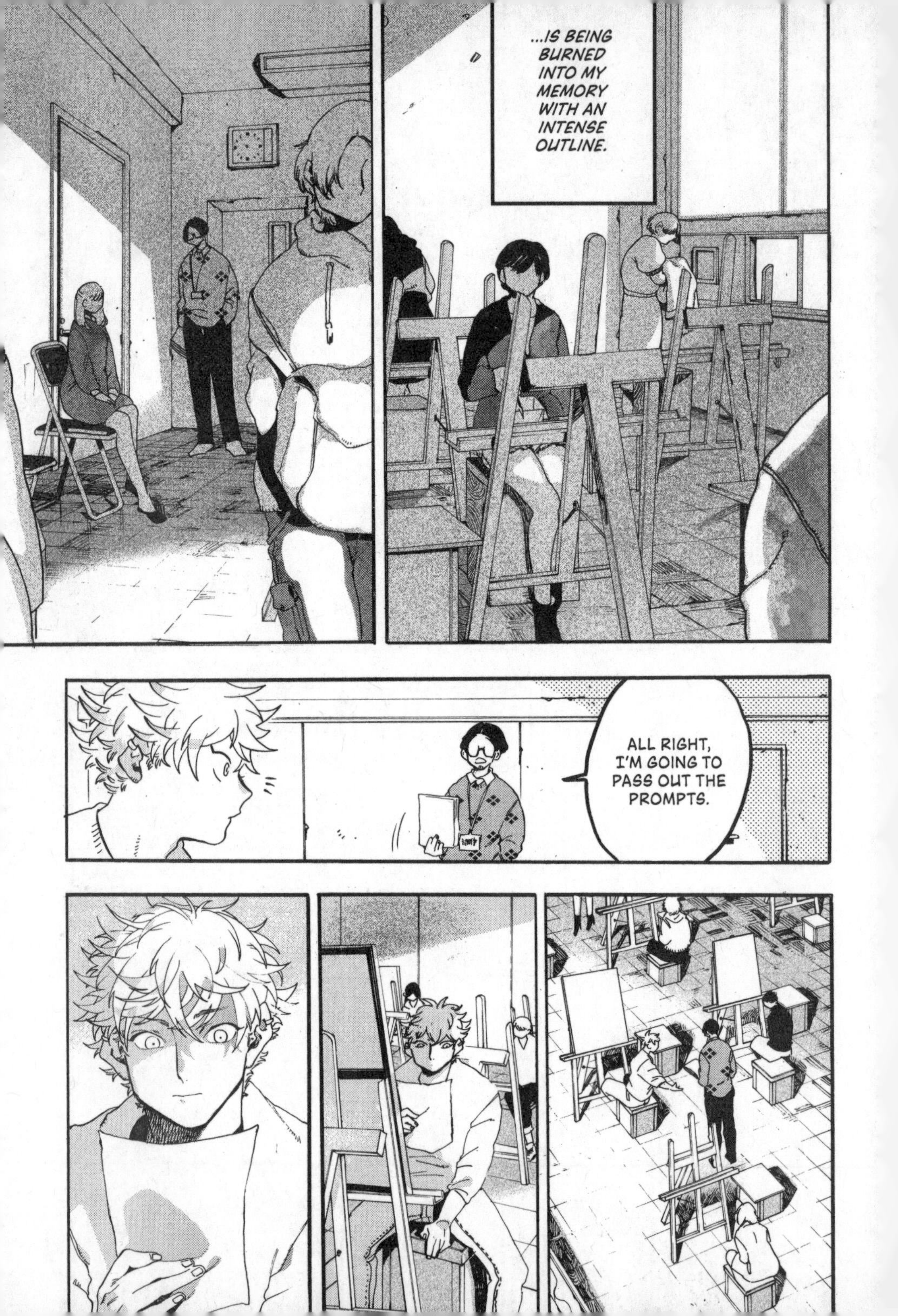
...IS BEING BURNED INTO MY MEMORY WITH AN INTENSE OUTLINE.
ALL RIGHT, I'M GOING TO PASS OUT THE PROMPTS.

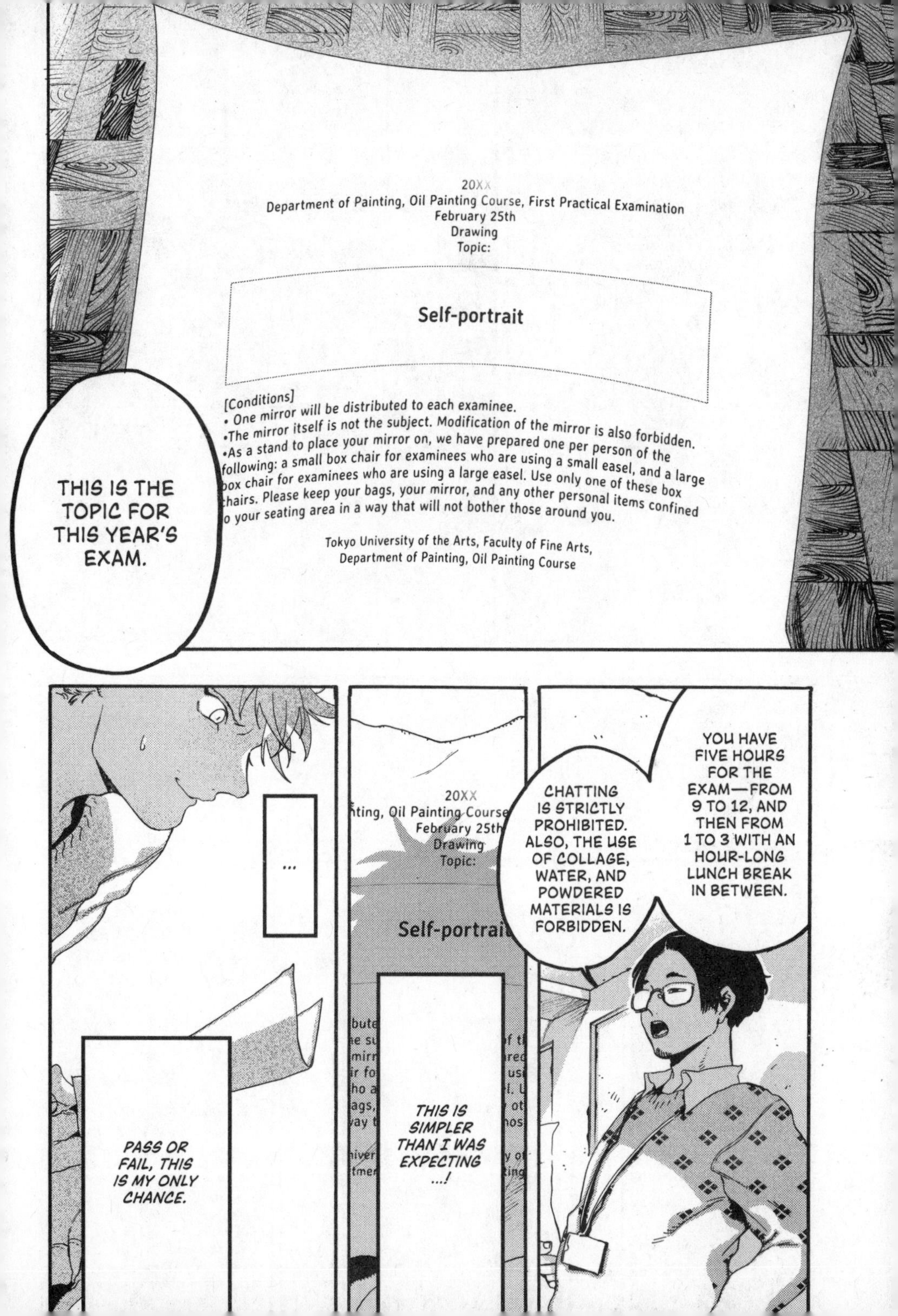
20XX
Department of Painting, Oil Painting Course, First Practical Examination
February 25th
Drawing
Topic:
Self-portrait
[Conditions]
• One mirror will be distributed to each examinee.
•The mirror itself is not the subject. Modification of the mirror is also forbidden.
•As a stand to place your mirror on, we have prepared one per person of the following: a small box chair for examinees who are using a small easel, and a large box chair for examinees who are using a large easel. Use only one of these box chairs. Please keep your bags, your mirror, and any other personal items confined to your seating area in a way that will not bother those around you.
Tokyo University of the Arts, Faculty of Fine Arts,
Department of Painting, Oil Painting Course
THIS IS THE TOPIC FOR THIS YEAR'S EXAM.
YOU HAVE FIVE HOURS FOR THE EXAM—FROM 9 TO 12, AND THEN FROM 1 TO 3 WITH AN HOUR-LONG LUNCH BREAK IN BETWEEN.
CHATTING IS STRICTLY PROHIBITED. ALSO, THE USE OF COLLAGE, WATER, AND POWDERED MATERIALS IS FORBIDDEN.
20XX
February 25th
Drawing
Topic:
Self-portrait
THIS IS SIMPLER THAN I WAS EXPECTING ...!
...
PASS OR FAIL, THIS IS MY ONLY CHANCE.

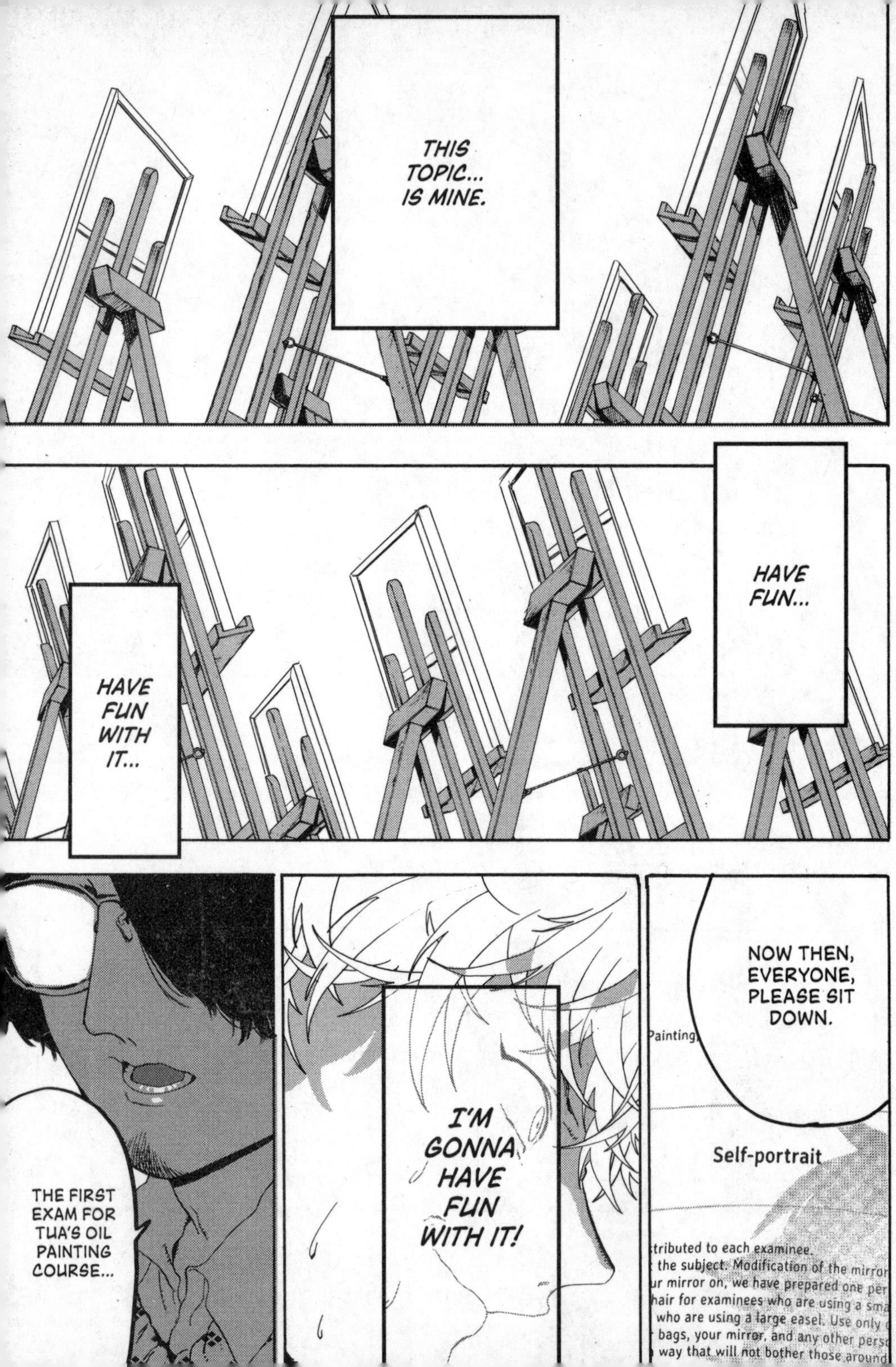
THIS TOPIC... IS MINE.
HAVE FUN...
HAVE FUN WITH IT...
NOW THEN, EVERYONE, PLEASE SIT DOWN.
Painting)
Self-portrait
tributed to each examinee.
the subject. Modification of the mirror
ur mirror on, we have prepared one per
hair for examinees who are using a sma
who are using a large easel. Use only
bags, your mirror, and any other pers
way that will not bother those around
I'M GONNA HAVE FUN WITH IT!
THE FIRST EXAM FOR TUA'S OIL PAINTING COURSE...

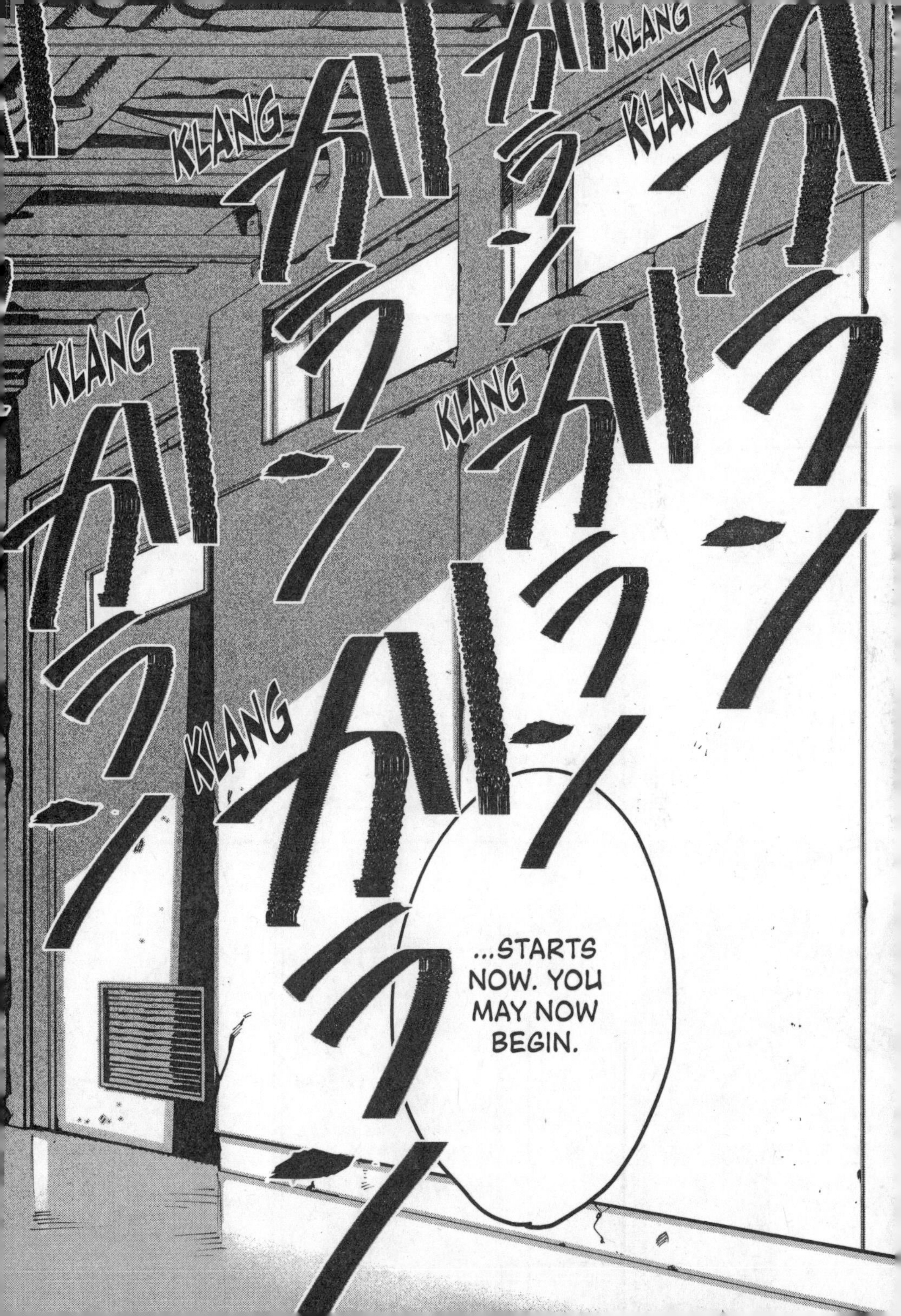
KLANG
KLANG
KLANG
KLANG
KLANG
KLANG
KLANG
...STARTS NOW. YOU MAY NOW BEGIN.

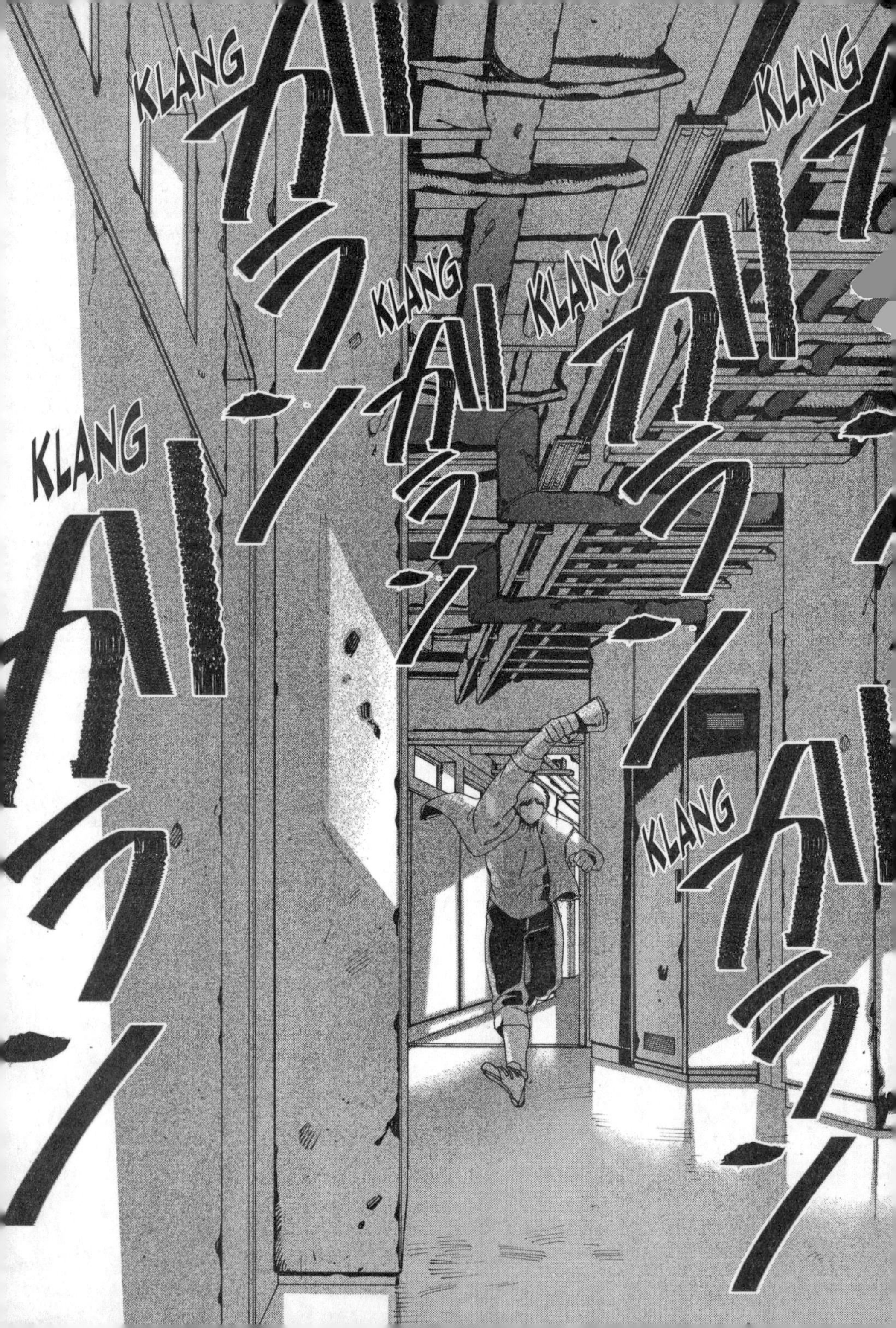
KLANG
KLANG
KLANG
KLANG
KLANG
KLANG

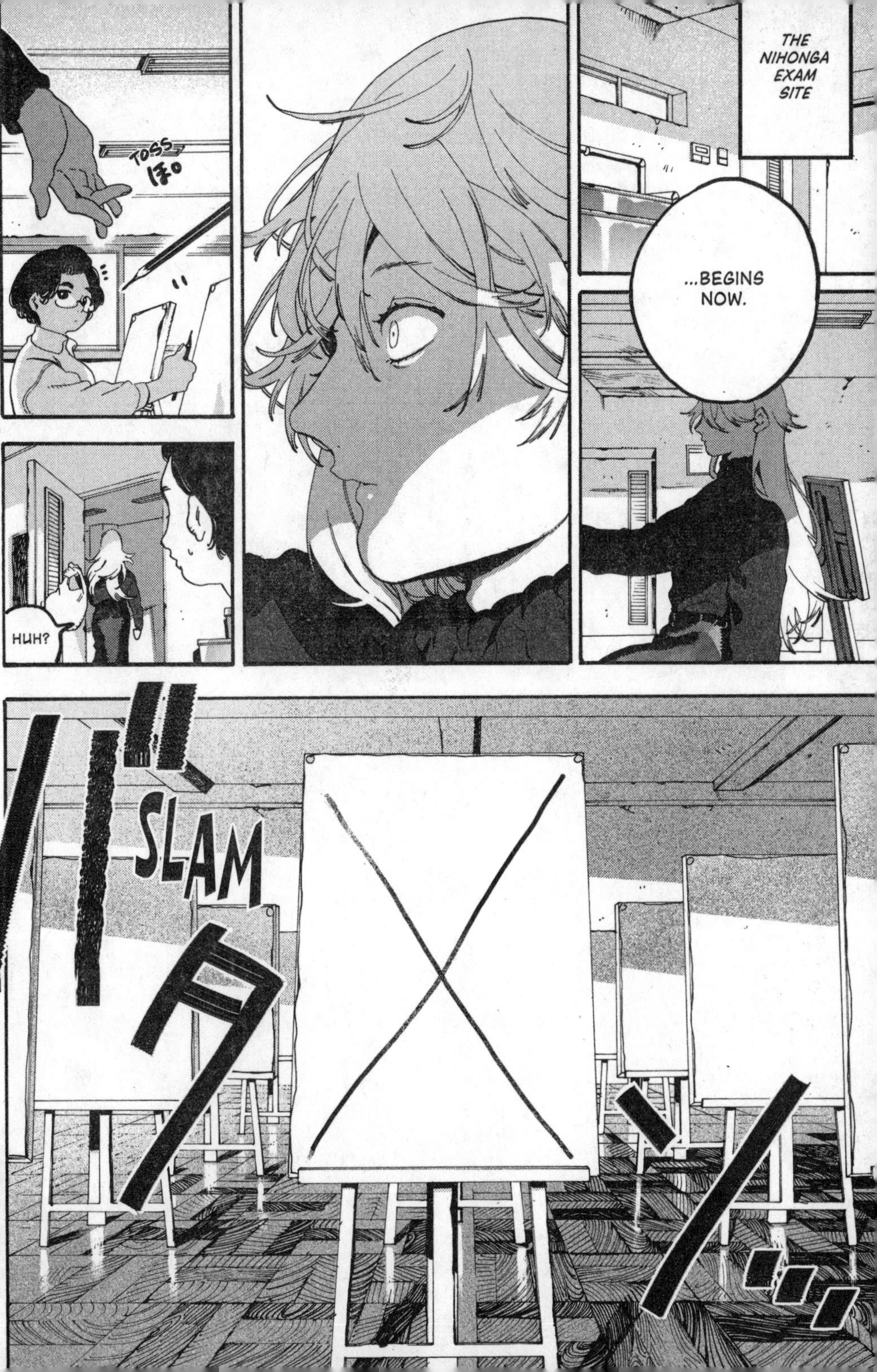
THE NIHONGA EXAM SITE
...BEGINS NOW.
TOSS
ほ
HUH?
SLAM

STROKE 15 END

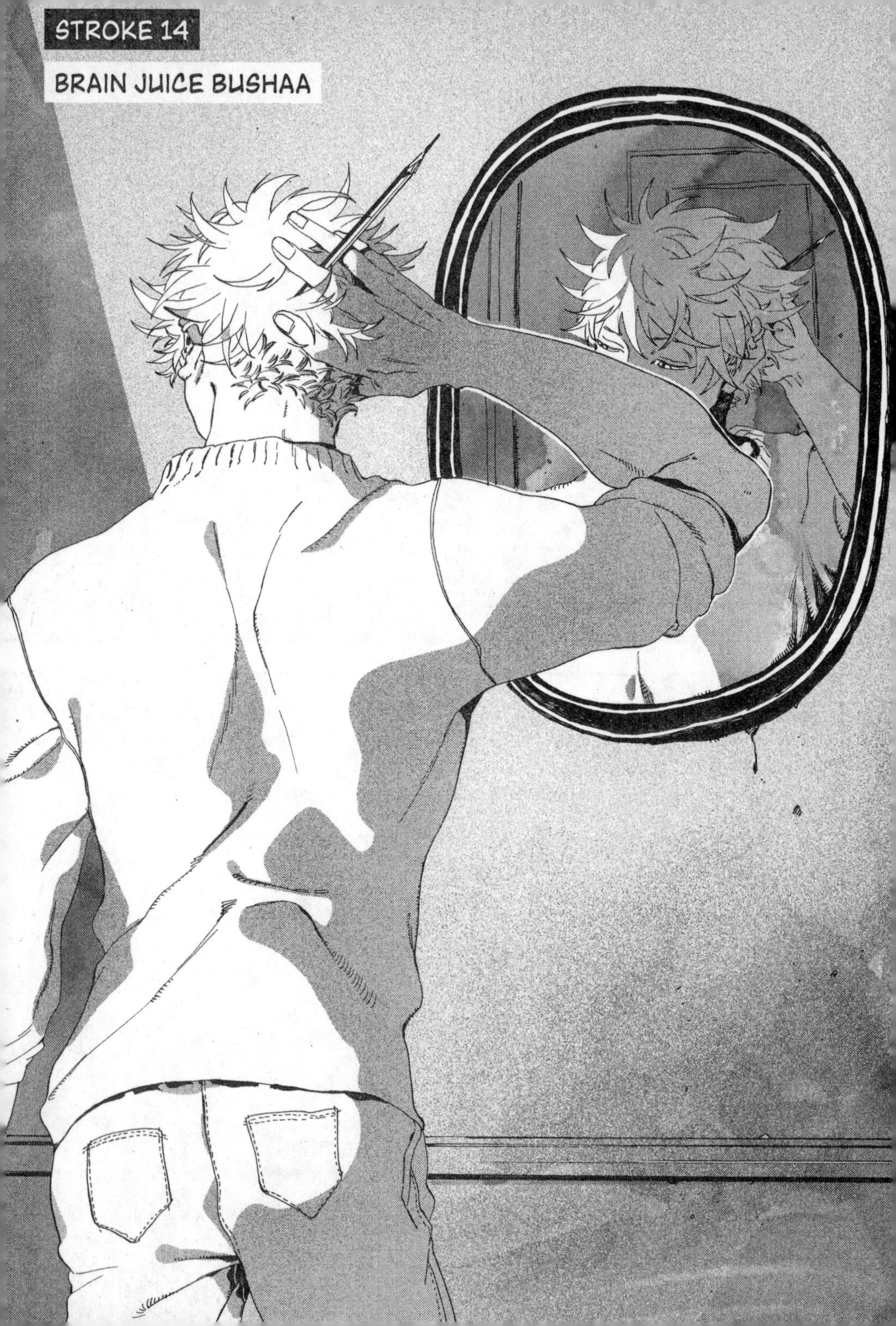

STROKE 14
BRAIN JUICE BUSHAA

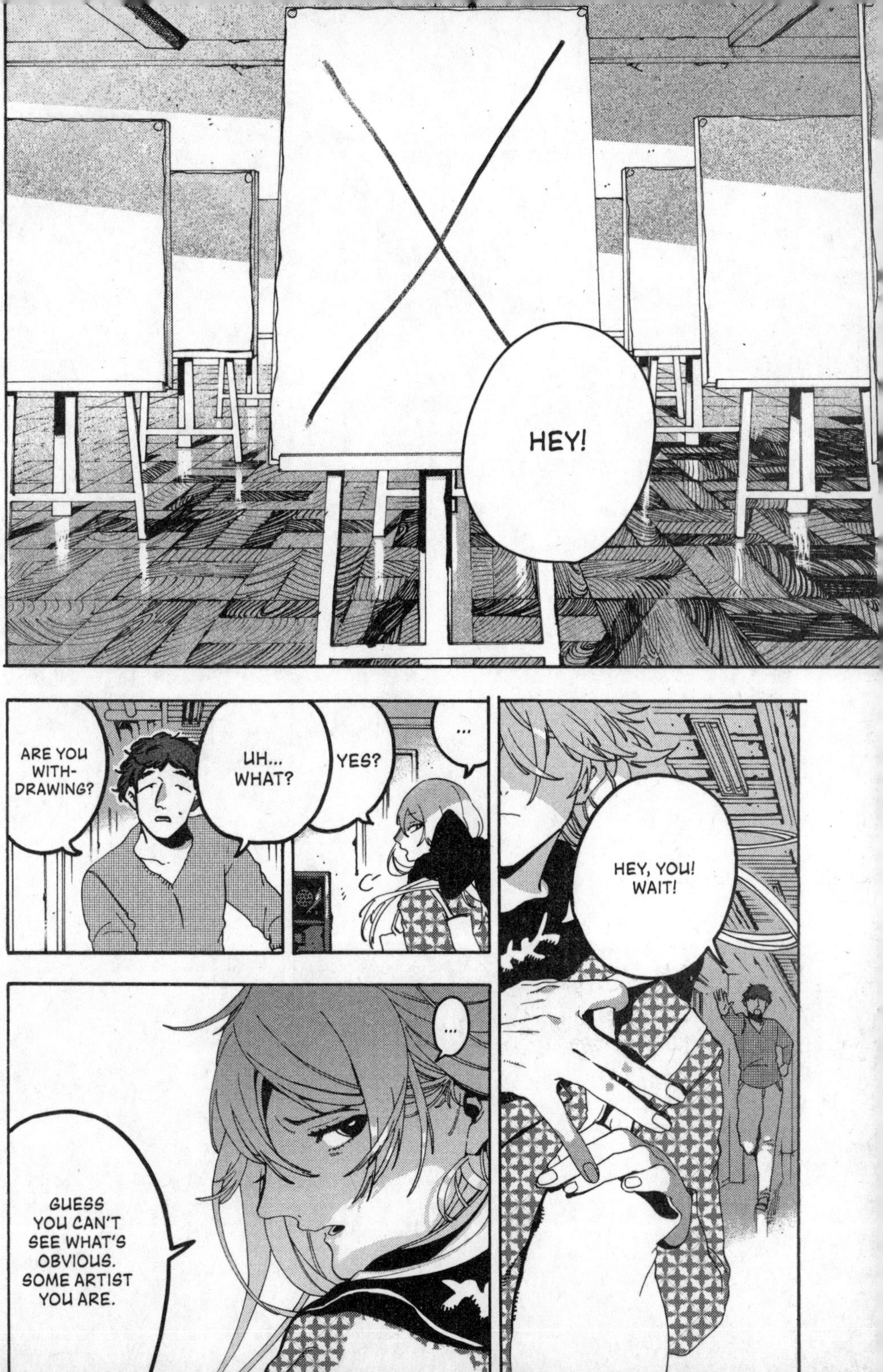
HEY!
HEY, YOU! WAIT!
...
YES?
UH... WHAT?
ARE YOU WITH-DRAWING?
...
GUESS YOU CAN'T SEE WHAT'S OBVIOUS. SOME ARTIST YOU ARE.

WHAT ELSE DOES IT LOOK LIKE I'M DOING?

KLANG

KLANG

KLANG

KLANG

SWOO

KTNK

KTNK

FLAP

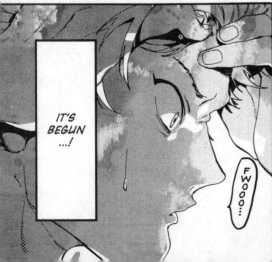

IT'S BEGUN ...!

FWOOO...

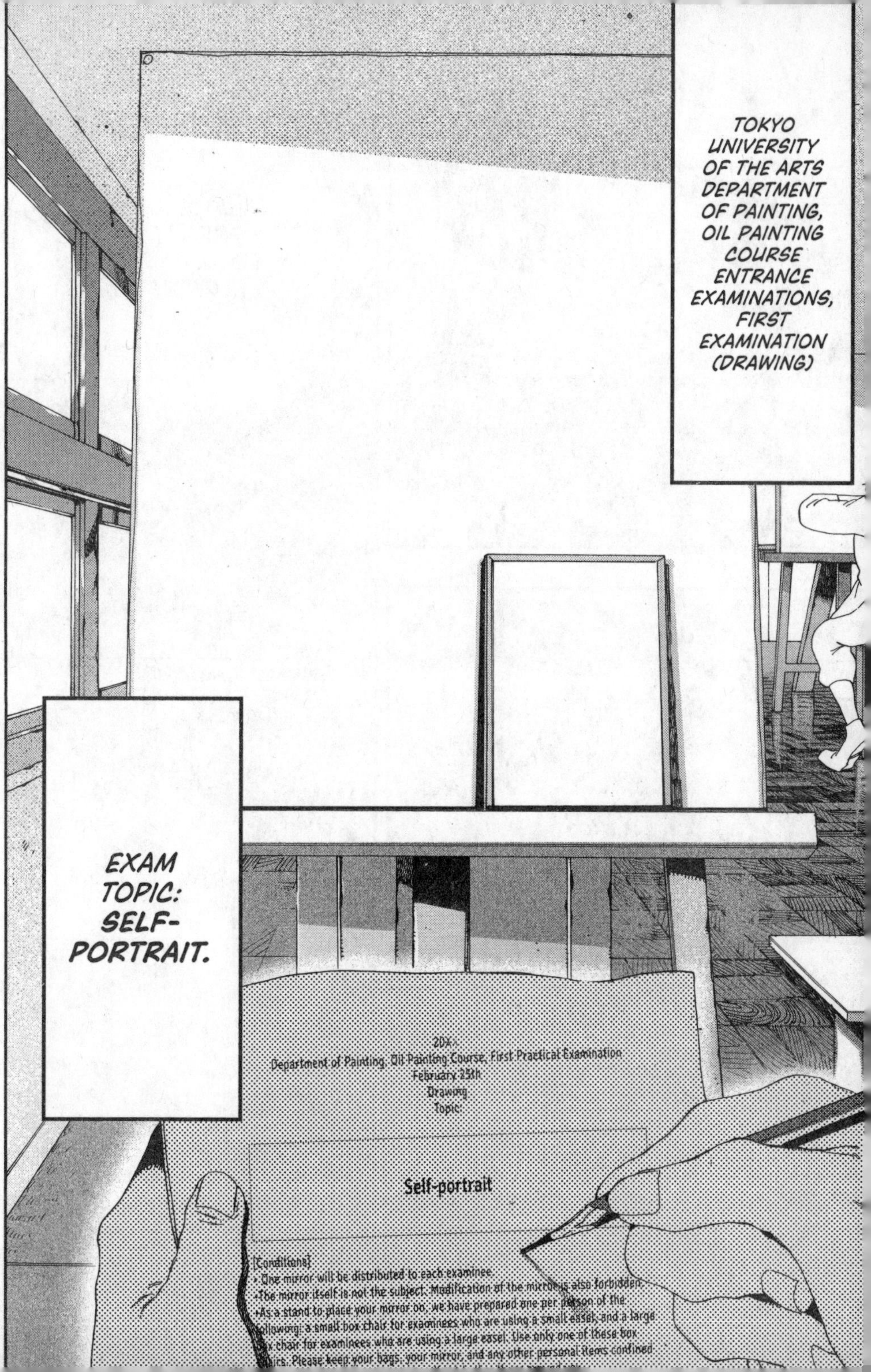
TOKYO UNIVERSITY OF THE ARTS DEPARTMENT OF PAINTING, OIL PAINTING COURSE ENTRANCE EXAMINATIONS, FIRST EXAMINATION (DRAWING)
EXAM TOPIC: SELF-PORTRAIT.
20XX
Department of Painting, Oil Painting Course, First Practical Examination
February 25th
Drawing
Topic:
Self-portrait
[Conditions]
• One mirror will be distributed to each examinee.
•The mirror itself is not the subject. Modification of the mirror is also forbidden.
•As a stand to place your mirror on, we have prepared one per person of the
following: a small box chair for examinees who are using a small easel, and a large
x chair for examinees who are using a large easel. Use only one of these box
irs. Please keep your bags, your mirror, and any other personal items confined

20XX
Department of Painting, Oil Painting Course, First Practical Examination
February 25th, Drawing
Topic: Self-portrait

Distributed item(s): Mirror

[Conditions]
• One mirror will be distributed to each examinee.
•The mirror itself is not the subject. Modification of the mirror is also forbidden.
•As a stand to place your mirror on, we have prepared one per person of the following: a small box chair for examinees who are using a small easel, and a large box chair for examinees who are using a large easel. Use only one of these box chairs. Please keep your bags, your mirror, and any other personal items confined to your seating area in a way that will not bother those around you.

Duration: 5 hours
9:00-12:00, 13:00-15:00 (with one-hour lunch break)

Prohibited items: The use of collage, water, and powdered art materials is forbidden.

A SELF-PORTRAIT SHOULD BE SIMPLE.

...NO, IT'S THAT SIMPLICITY...

...THAT MAKES IT SUCH A DIFFICULT TOPIC.

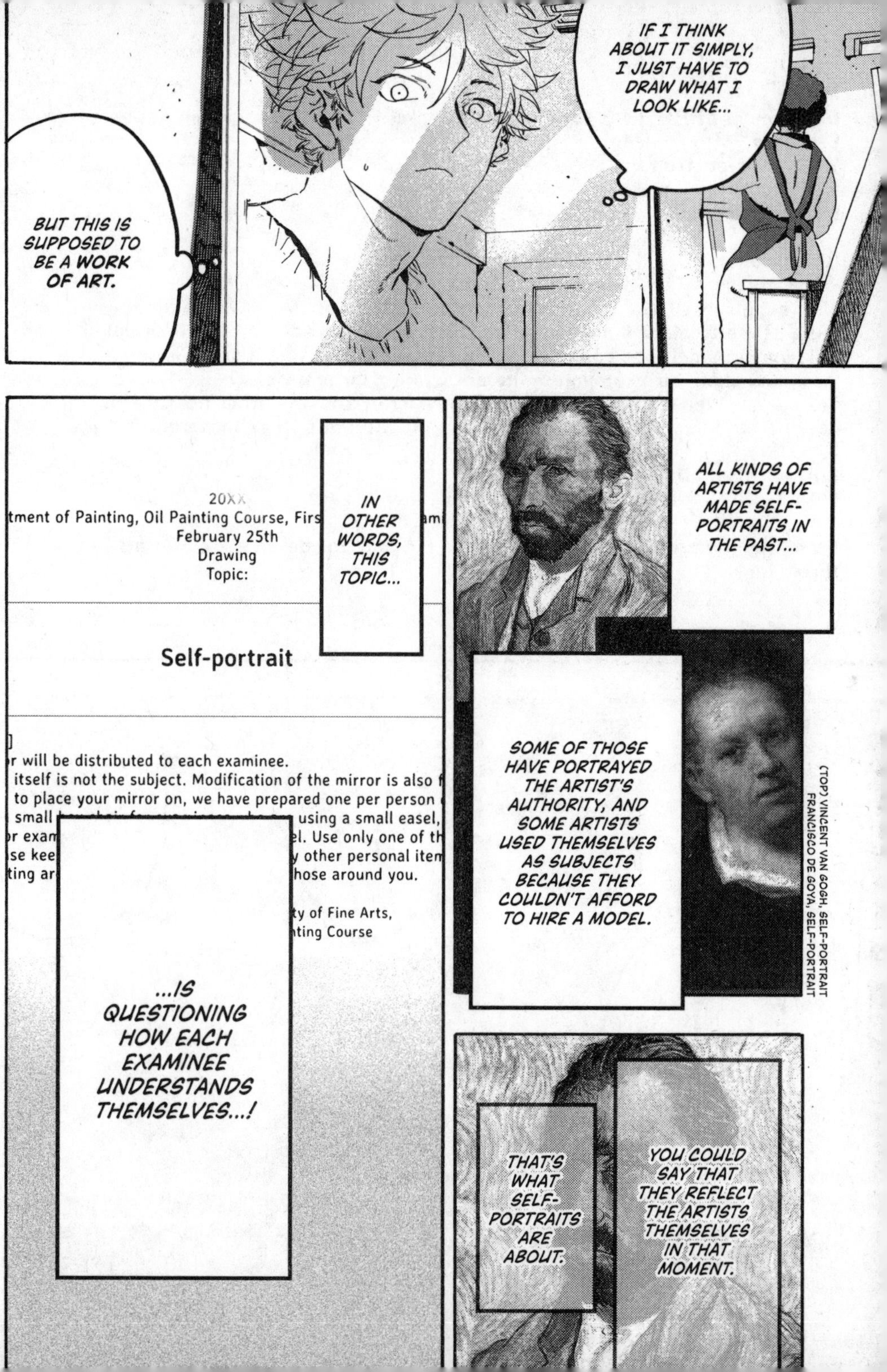
IF I THINK ABOUT IT SIMPLY, I JUST HAVE TO DRAW WHAT I LOOK LIKE...
BUT THIS IS SUPPOSED TO BE A WORK OF ART.
ALL KINDS OF ARTISTS HAVE MADE SELF-PORTRAITS IN THE PAST...
SOME OF THOSE HAVE PORTRAYED THE ARTIST'S AUTHORITY, AND SOME ARTISTS USED THEMSELVES AS SUBJECTS BECAUSE THEY COULDN'T AFFORD TO HIRE A MODEL.
YOU COULD SAY THAT THEY REFLECT THE ARTISTS THEMSELVES IN THAT MOMENT.
THAT'S WHAT SELF-PORTRAITS ARE ABOUT.
20XX
tment of Painting, Oil Painting Course, Firs
ami
February 25th
Drawing
Topic:
Self-portrait
r will be distributed to each examinee.
itself is not the subject. Modification of the mirror is also f
to place your mirror on, we have prepared one per person
small
using a small easel,
r exam
el. Use only one of th
se kee
y other personal item
ting ar
hose around you.
ty of Fine Arts,
nting Course
IN OTHER WORDS, THIS TOPIC...
...IS QUESTIONING HOW EACH EXAMINEE UNDERSTANDS THEMSELVES...!
(TOP) VINCENT VAN GOGH, SELF-PORTRAIT
FRANCISCO DE GOYA, SELF-PORTRAIT

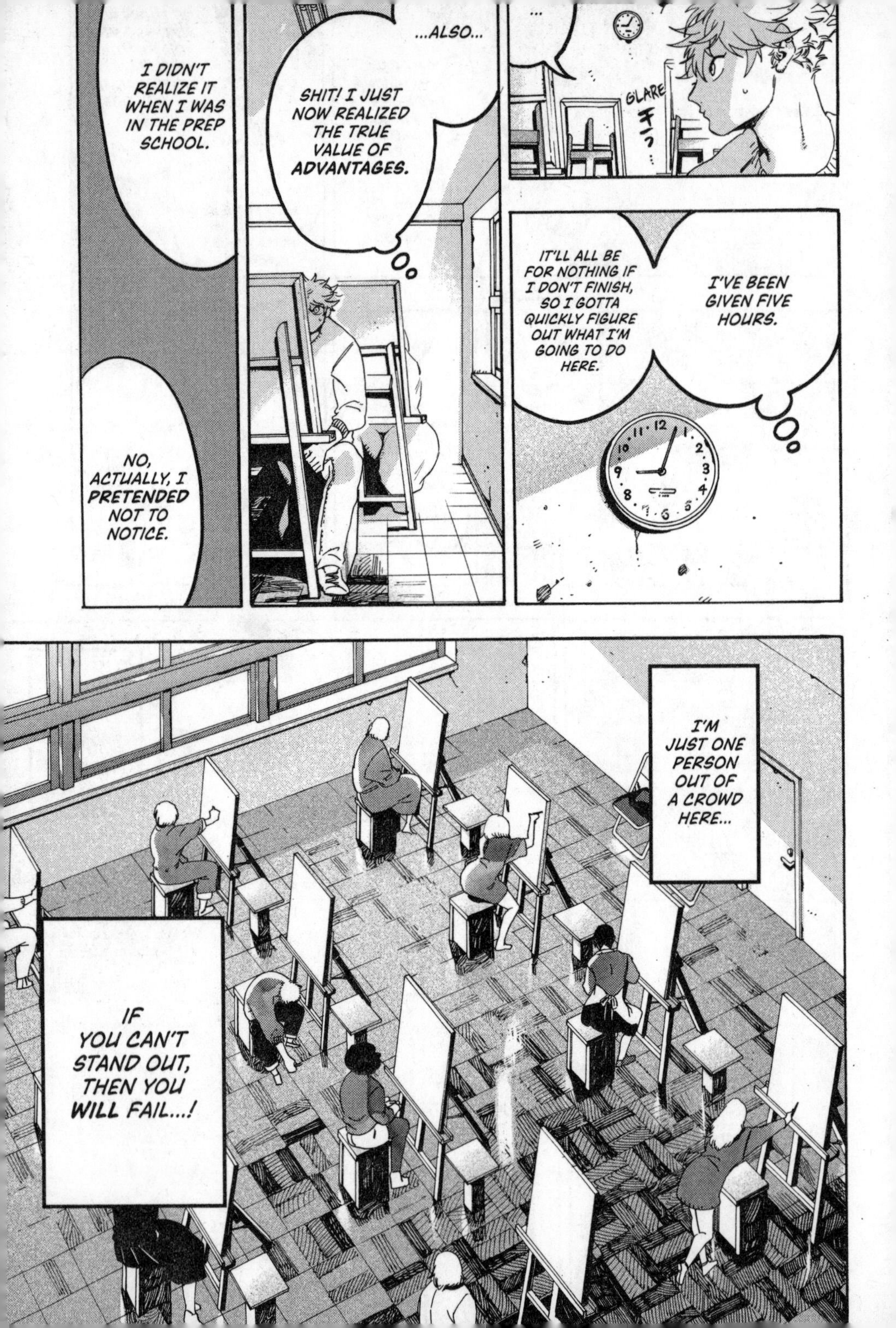
...
GLARE
I'VE BEEN GIVEN FIVE HOURS.
IT'LL ALL BE FOR NOTHING IF I DON'T FINISH, SO I GOTTA QUICKLY FIGURE OUT WHAT I'M GOING TO DO HERE.
...ALSO...
SHIT! I JUST NOW REALIZED THE TRUE VALUE OF **ADVANTAGES.**
I DIDN'T REALIZE IT WHEN I WAS IN THE PREP SCHOOL.
NO, ACTUALLY, I **PRETENDED** NOT TO NOTICE.
I'M JUST ONE PERSON OUT OF A CROWD HERE...
IF YOU CAN'T STAND OUT, THEN YOU **WILL** FAIL...!

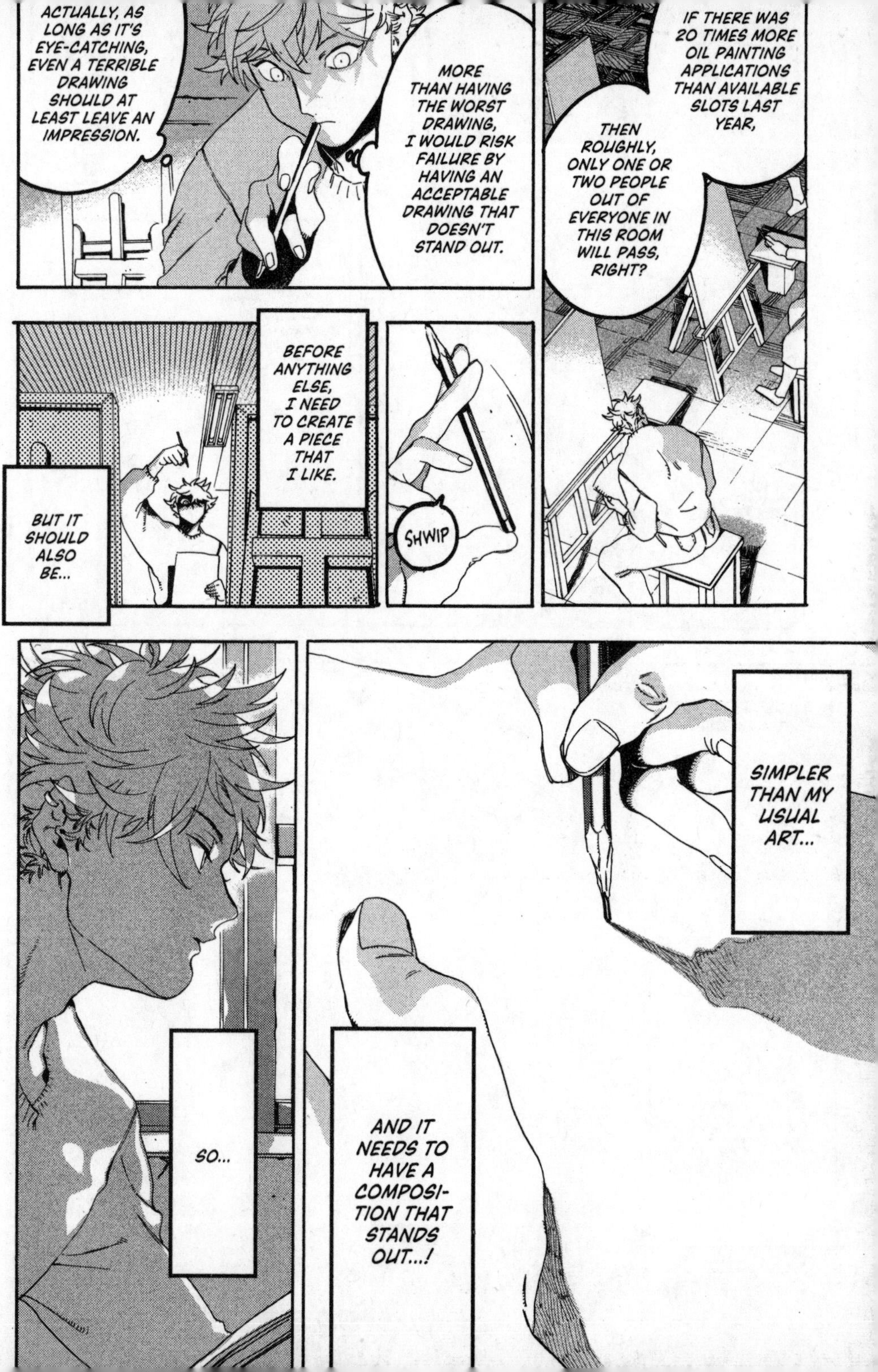
IF THERE WAS 20 TIMES MORE OIL PAINTING APPLICATIONS THAN AVAILABLE SLOTS LAST YEAR,
THEN ROUGHLY, ONLY ONE OR TWO PEOPLE OUT OF EVERYONE IN THIS ROOM WILL PASS, RIGHT?
ACTUALLY, AS LONG AS IT'S EYE-CATCHING, EVEN A TERRIBLE DRAWING SHOULD AT LEAST LEAVE AN IMPRESSION.
MORE THAN HAVING THE WORST DRAWING, I WOULD RISK FAILURE BY HAVING AN ACCEPTABLE DRAWING THAT DOESN'T STAND OUT.
BEFORE ANYTHING ELSE, I NEED TO CREATE A PIECE THAT I LIKE.
SHWIP
BUT IT SHOULD ALSO BE...
SIMPLER THAN MY USUAL ART...
AND IT NEEDS TO HAVE A COMPOSITION THAT STANDS OUT...!
SO...

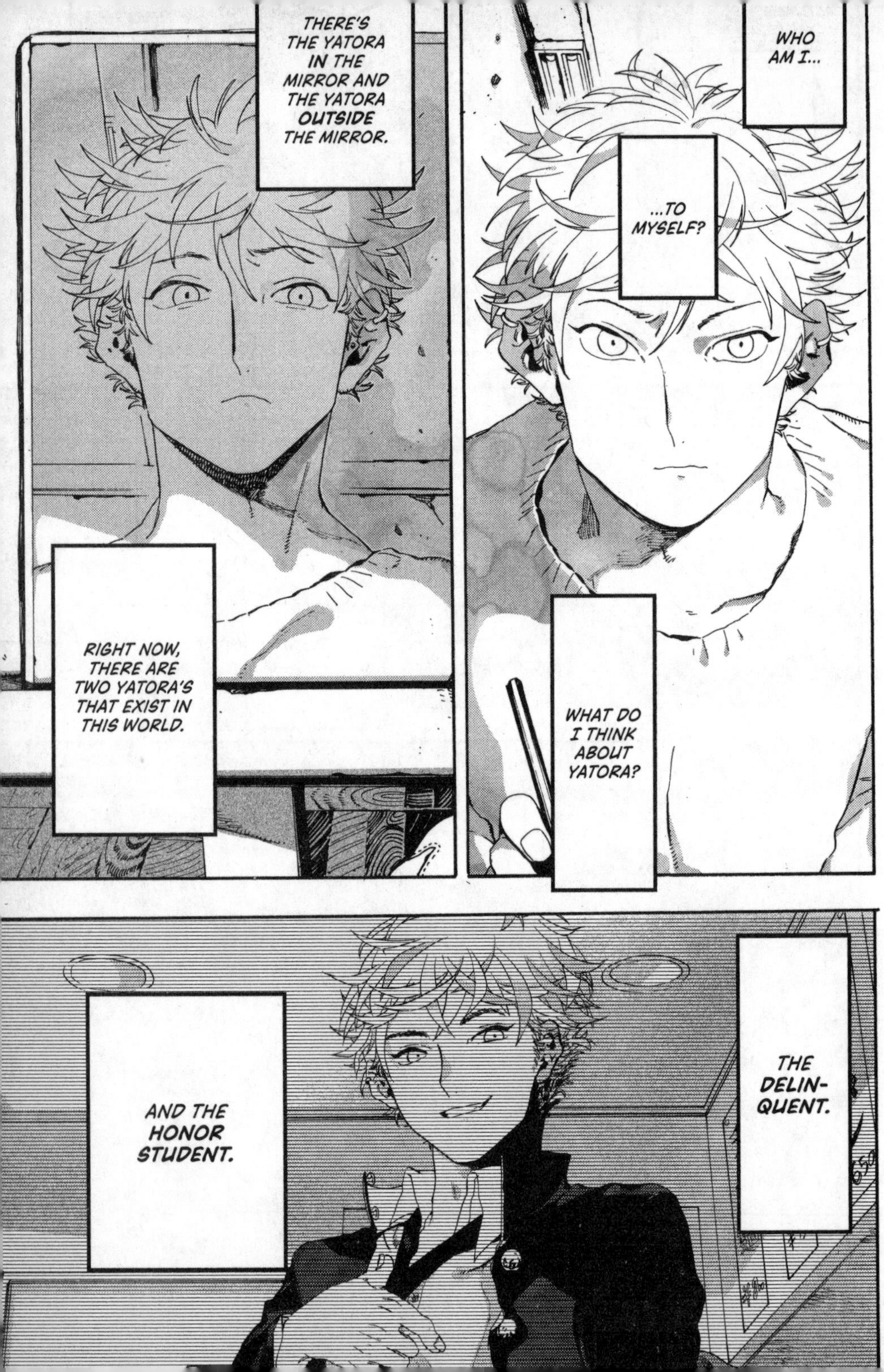
WHO AM I...
...TO MYSELF?
WHAT DO I THINK ABOUT YATORA?
THERE'S THE YATORA IN THE MIRROR AND THE YATORA OUTSIDE THE MIRROR.
RIGHT NOW, THERE ARE TWO YATORA'S THAT EXIST IN THIS WORLD.
THE DELINQUENT.
AND THE HONOR STUDENT.

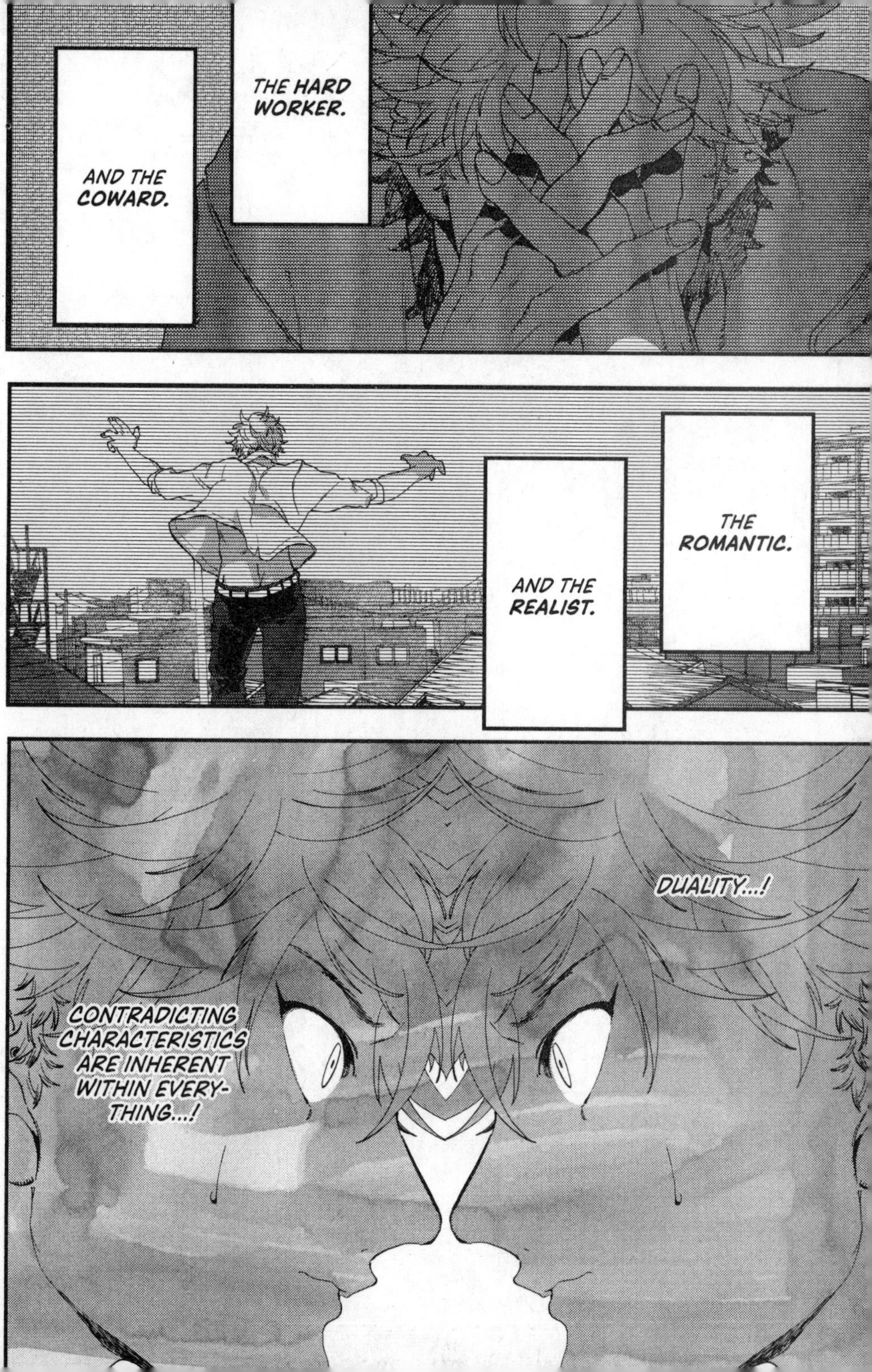
THE HARD WORKER.
AND THE COWARD.
THE ROMANTIC.
AND THE REALIST.
DUALITY...!
CONTRADICTING CHARACTERISTICS ARE INHERENT WITHIN EVERY-THING...!

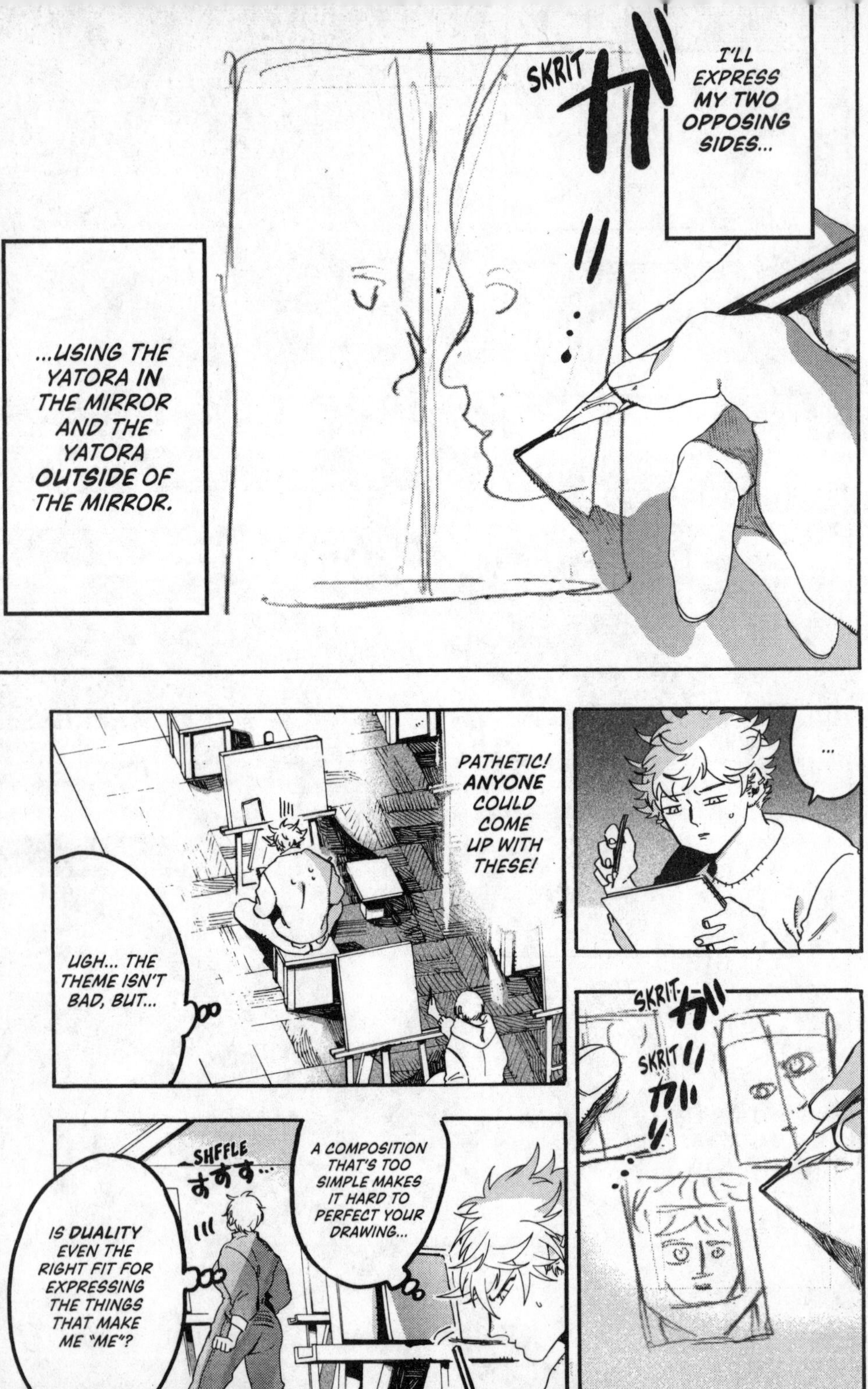
I'LL EXPRESS MY TWO OPPOSING SIDES...
SKRIT
ガ
...USING THE YATORA IN THE MIRROR AND THE YATORA OUTSIDE OF THE MIRROR.
...
PATHETIC! ANYONE COULD COME UP WITH THESE!
UGH... THE THEME ISN'T BAD, BUT...
SKRIT
ガ
SKRIT
ガリ
A COMPOSITION THAT'S TOO SIMPLE MAKES IT HARD TO PERFECT YOUR DRAWING...
SHFFLE
すすす...
IS DUALITY EVEN THE RIGHT FIT FOR EXPRESSING THE THINGS THAT MAKE ME "ME"?

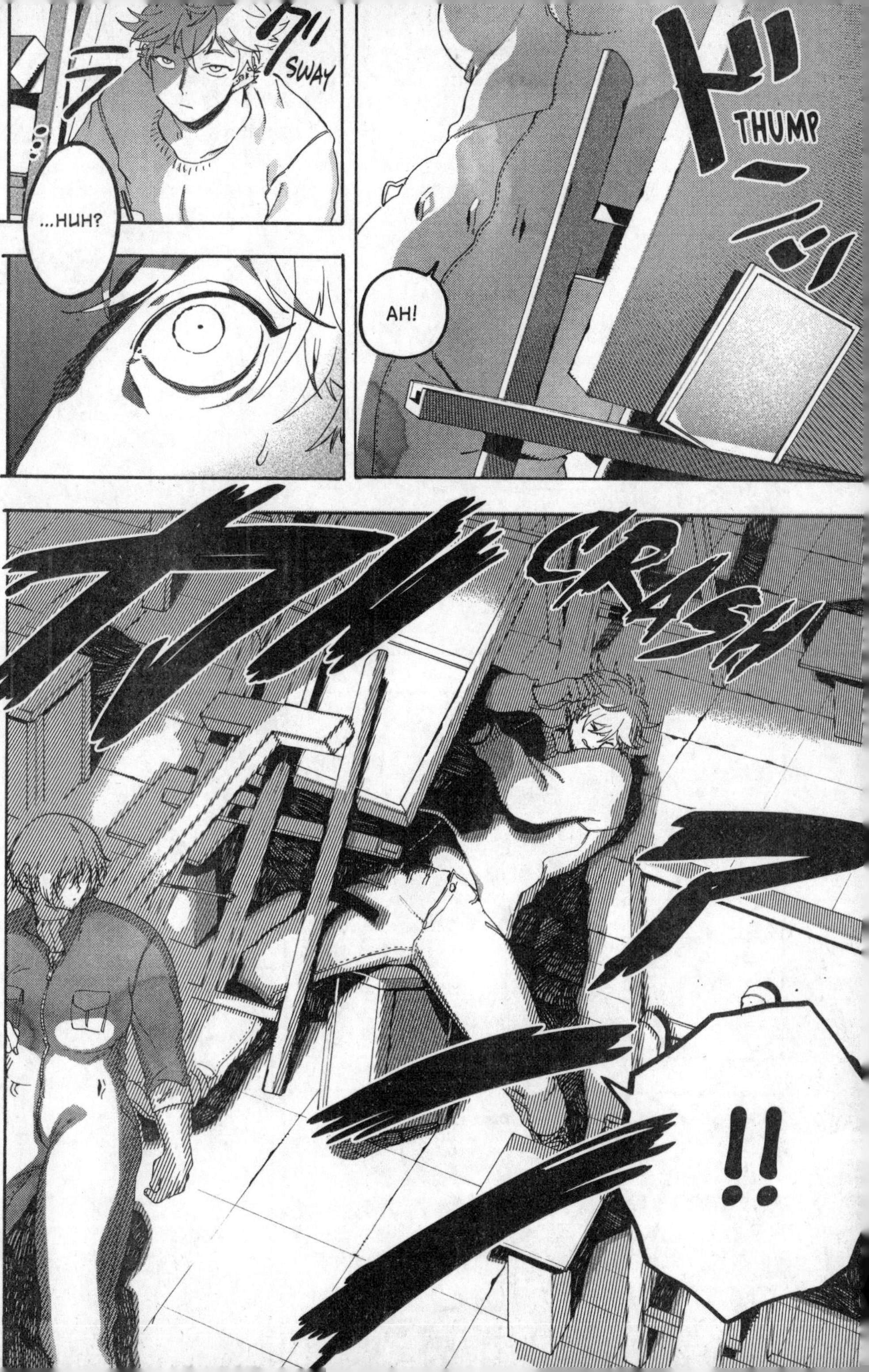
THUMP
AH!
SWAY
...HUH?
CRASH
!!

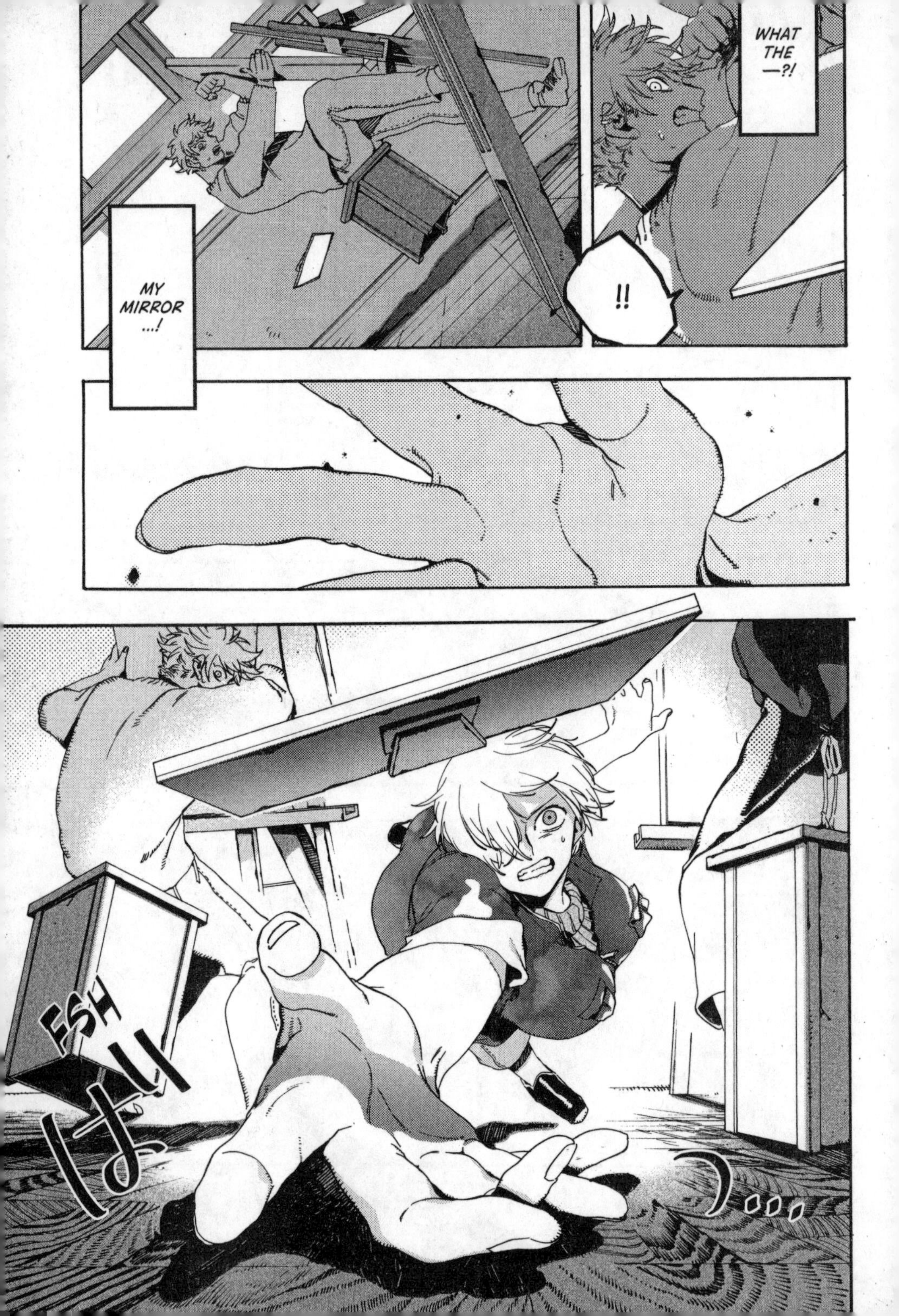
WHAT THE—?!
!!
MY MIRROR ...!
FSH

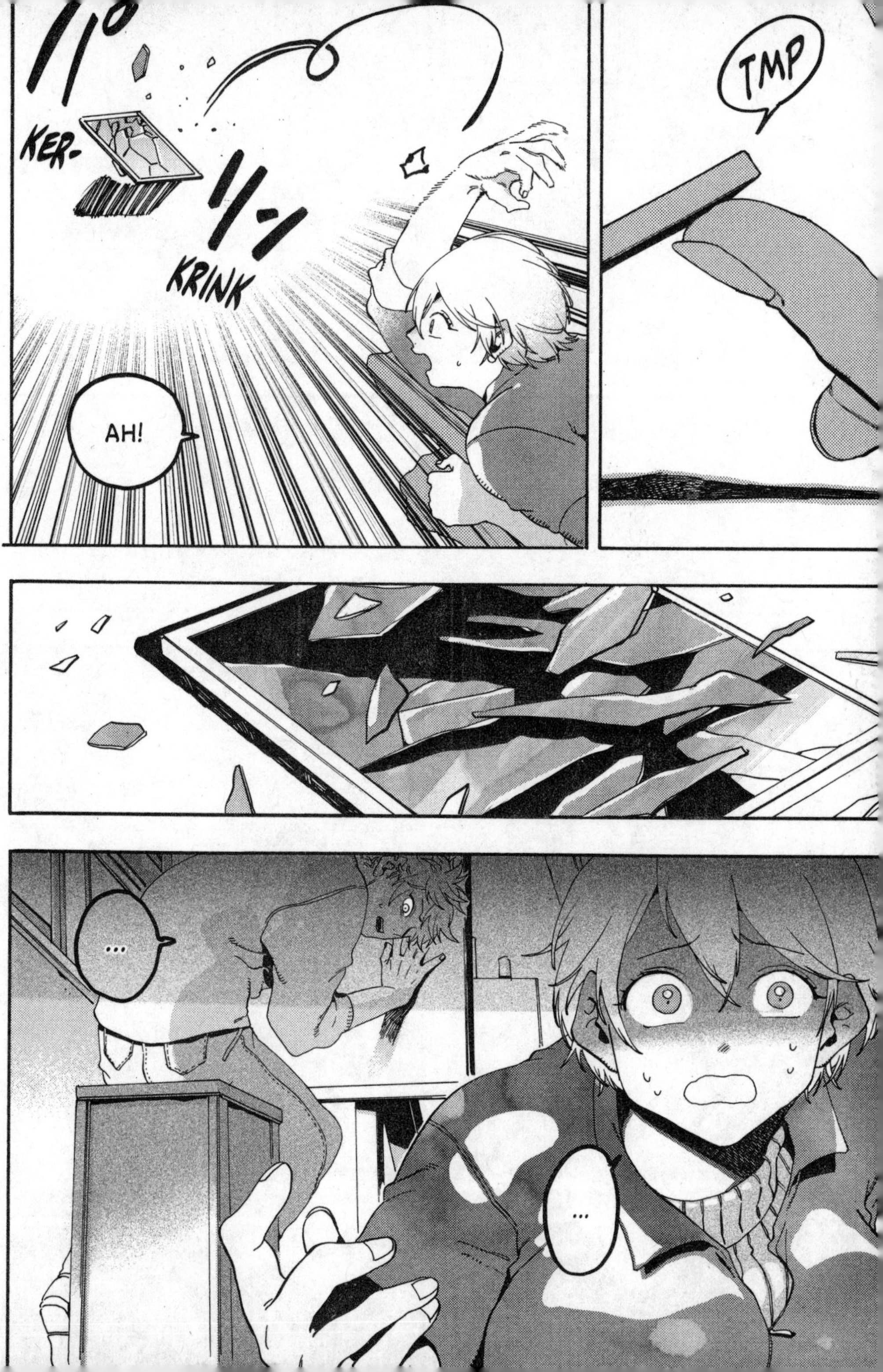
TMP
KER-
KRINK
AH!
...
...

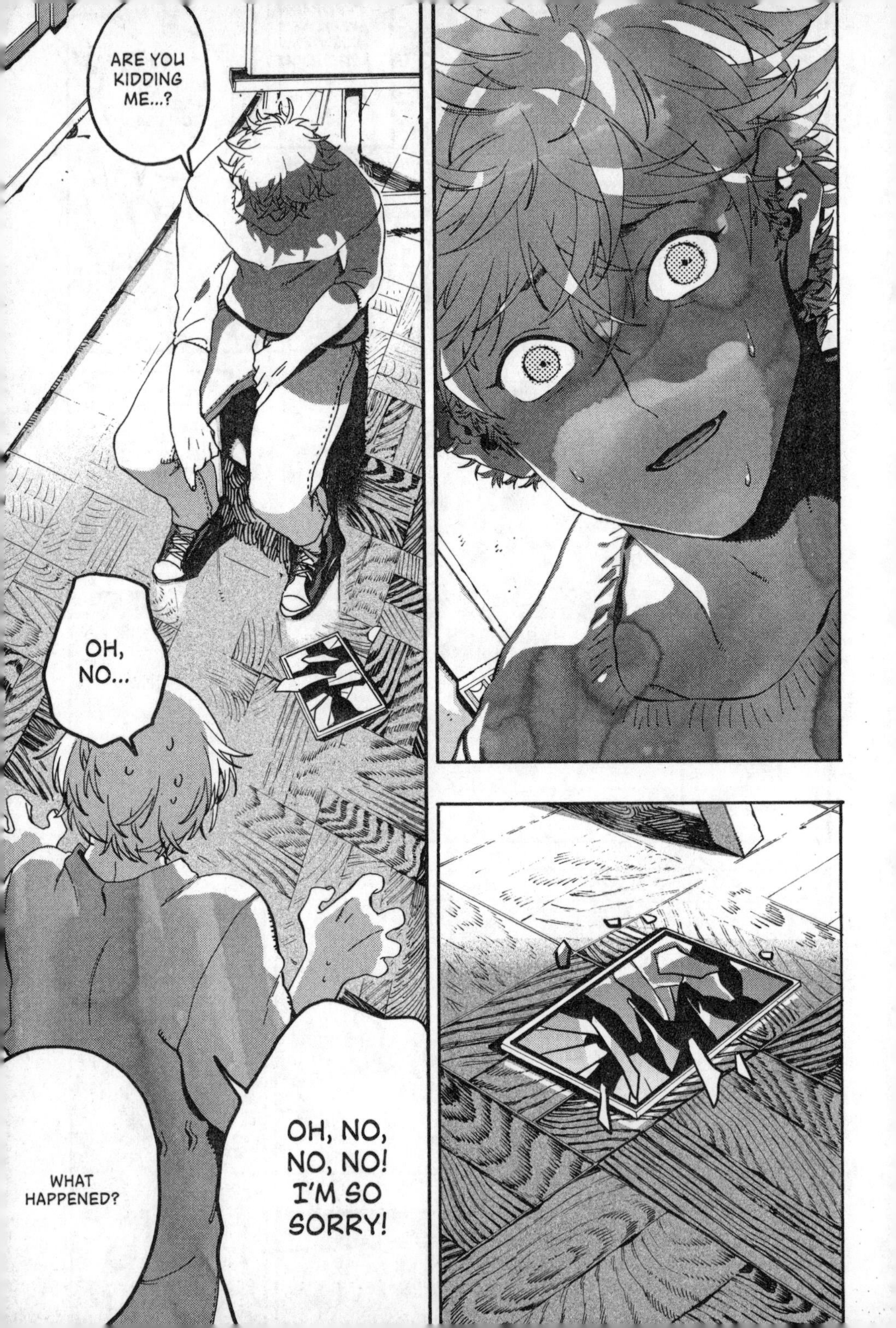
ARE YOU KIDDING ME...?
OH, NO...
OH, NO, NO, NO! I'M SO SORRY!
WHAT HAPPENED?

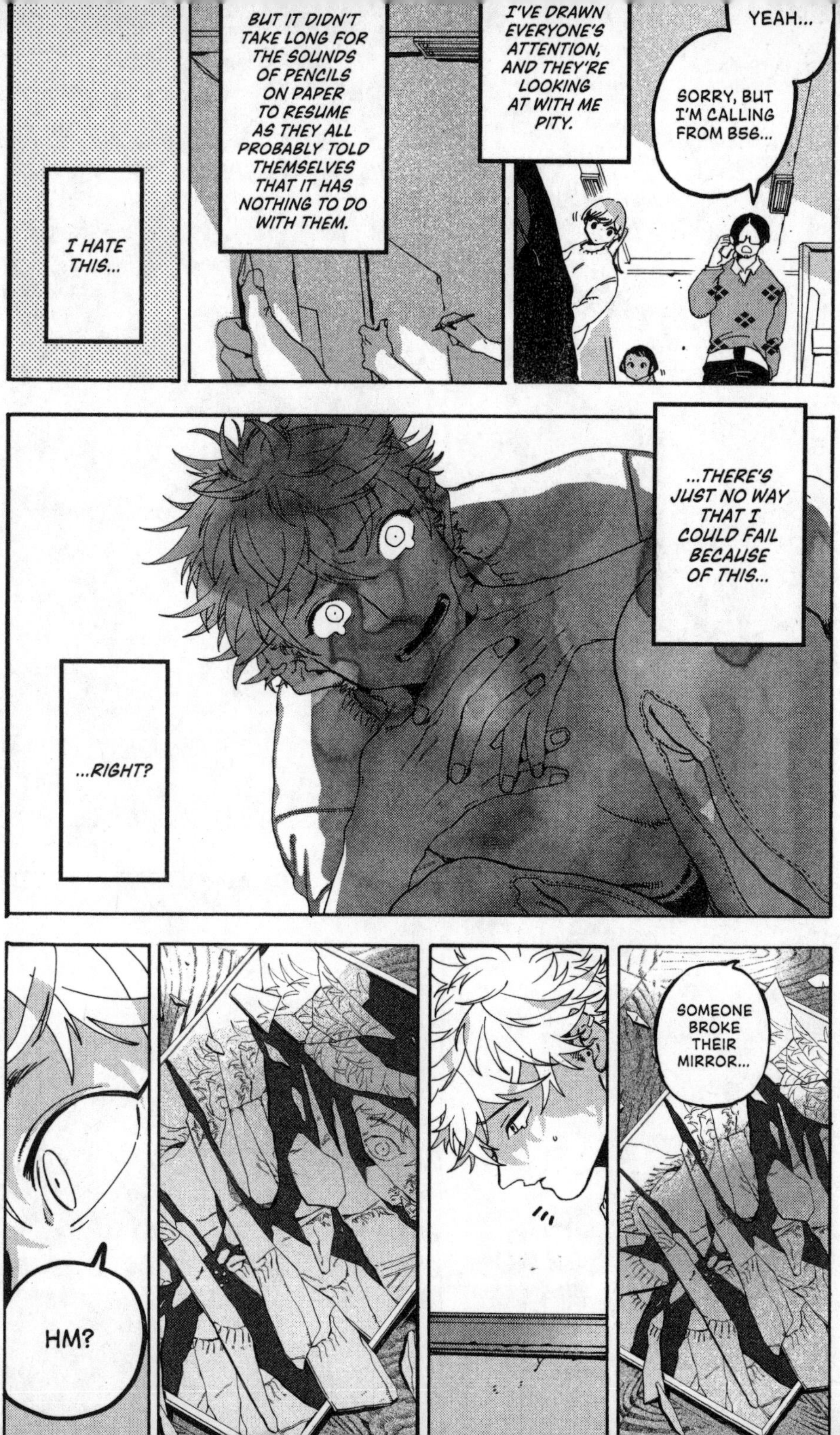
YEAH...
SORRY, BUT I'M CALLING FROM B56...
I'VE DRAWN EVERYONE'S ATTENTION, AND THEY'RE LOOKING AT WITH ME PITY.
BUT IT DIDN'T TAKE LONG FOR THE SOUNDS OF PENCILS ON PAPER TO RESUME AS THEY ALL PROBABLY TOLD THEMSELVES THAT IT HAS NOTHING TO DO WITH THEM.
I HATE THIS...
...THERE'S JUST NO WAY THAT I COULD FAIL BECAUSE OF THIS...
...RIGHT?
SOMEONE BROKE THEIR MIRROR...
HM?

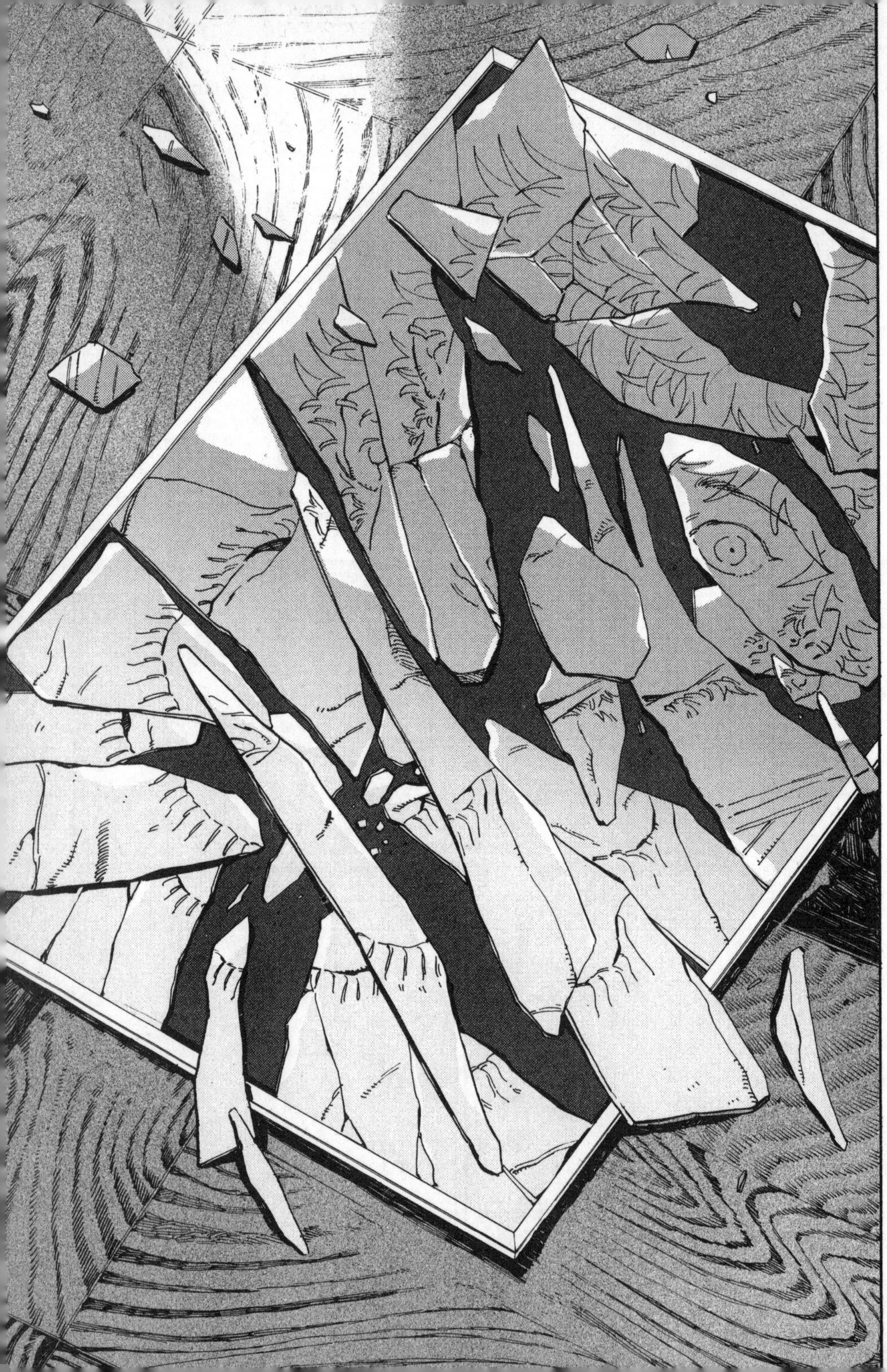

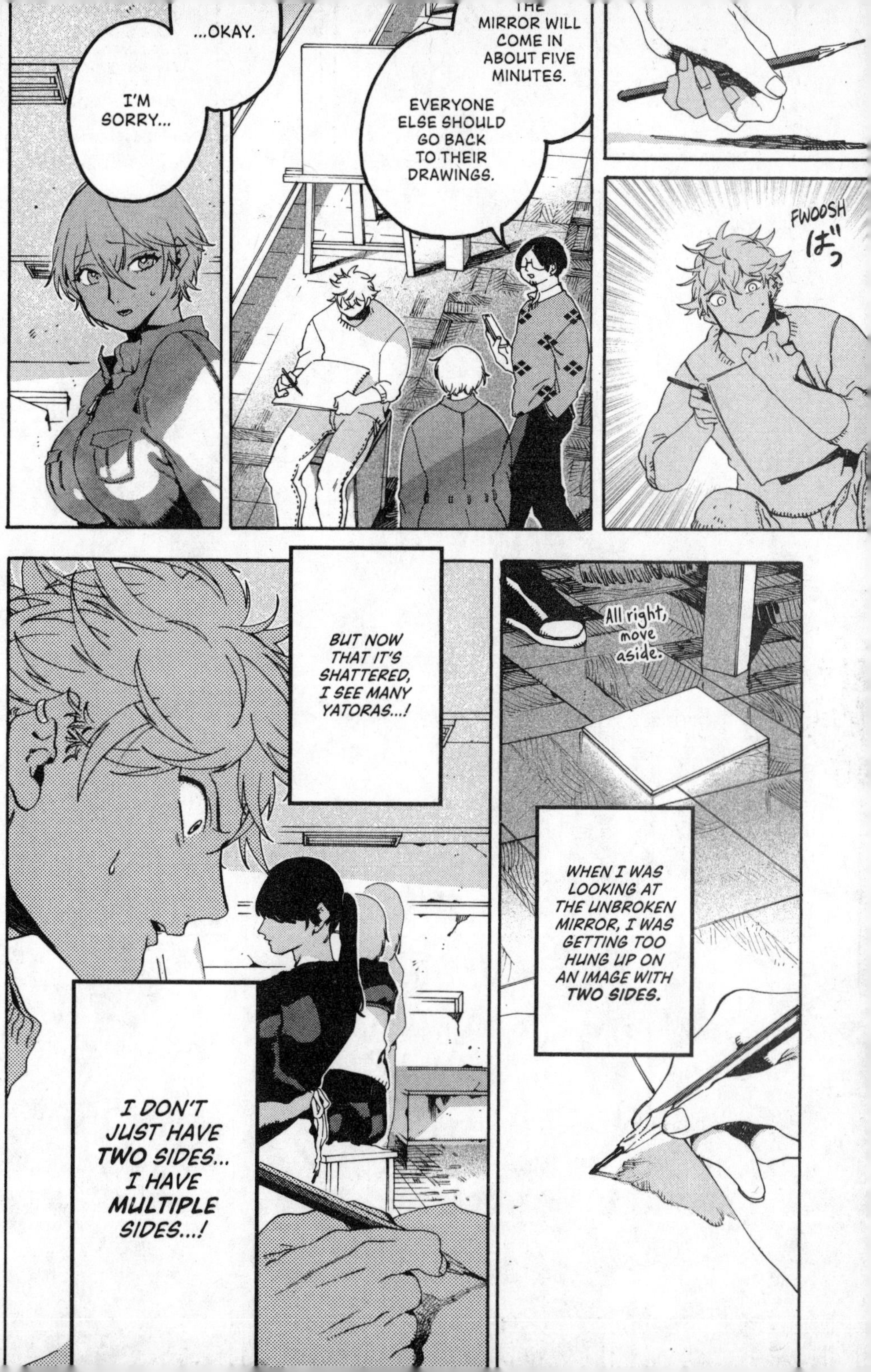
FWOOSH
ばっ
THE MIRROR WILL COME IN ABOUT FIVE MINUTES.
EVERYONE ELSE SHOULD GO BACK TO THEIR DRAWINGS.
...OKAY.
I'M SORRY...
All right, move aside.
WHEN I WAS LOOKING AT THE UNBROKEN MIRROR, I WAS GETTING TOO HUNG UP ON AN IMAGE WITH TWO SIDES.
BUT NOW THAT IT'S SHATTERED, I SEE MANY YATORAS...!
I DON'T JUST HAVE TWO SIDES... I HAVE MULTIPLE SIDES...!

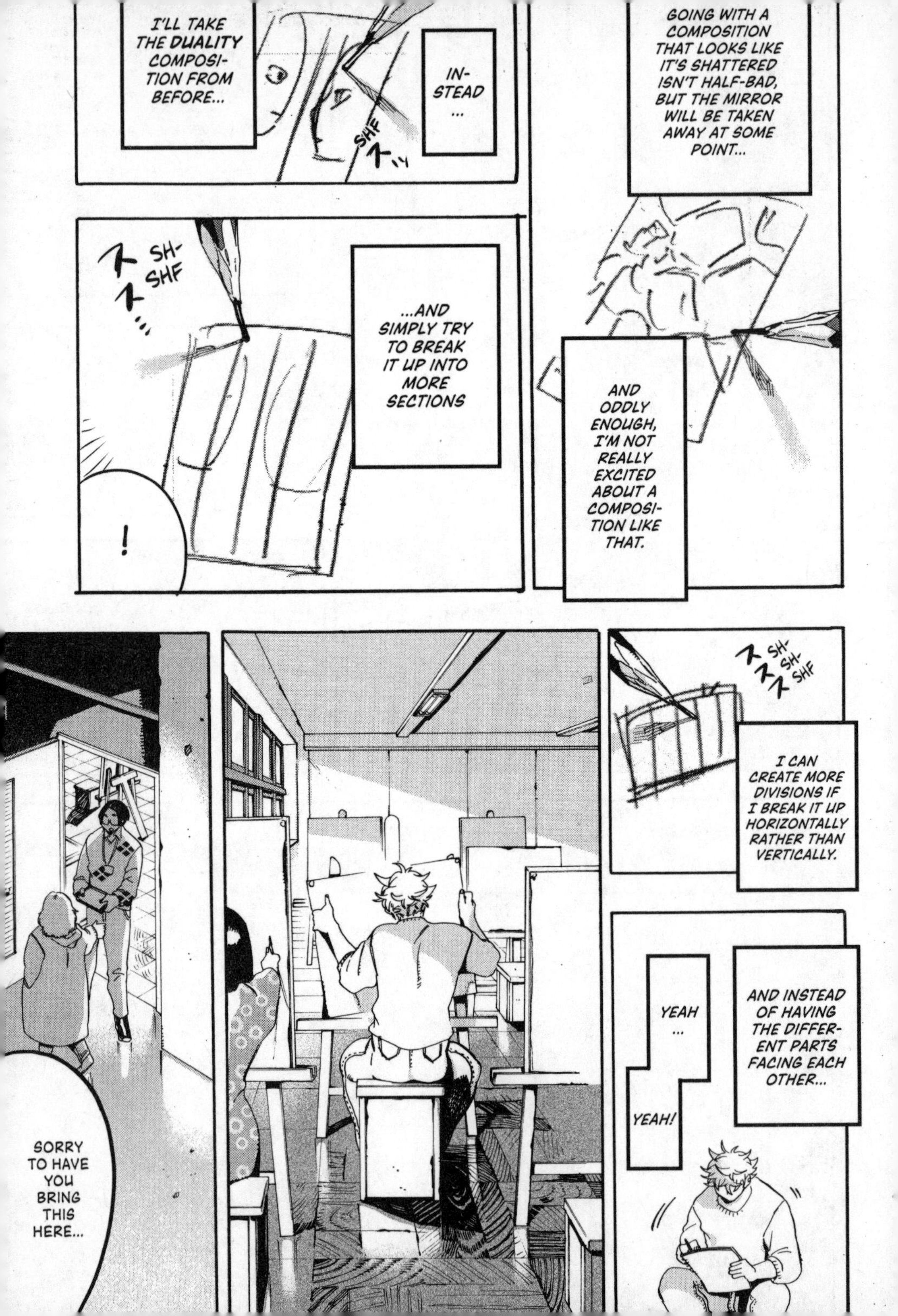
GOING WITH A COMPOSITION THAT LOOKS LIKE IT'S SHATTERED ISN'T HALF-BAD, BUT THE MIRROR WILL BE TAKEN AWAY AT SOME POINT...
AND ODDLY ENOUGH, I'M NOT REALLY EXCITED ABOUT A COMPOSITION LIKE THAT.
IN-STEAD...
SHF
I'LL TAKE THE DUALITY COMPOSITION FROM BEFORE...
...AND SIMPLY TRY TO BREAK IT UP INTO MORE SECTIONS
SH-SHF
!
SH-SH-SHF
I CAN CREATE MORE DIVISIONS IF I BREAK IT UP HORIZONTALLY RATHER THAN VERTICALLY.
AND INSTEAD OF HAVING THE DIFFER-ENT PARTS FACING EACH OTHER...
YEAH...
YEAH!
SORRY TO HAVE YOU BRING THIS HERE...

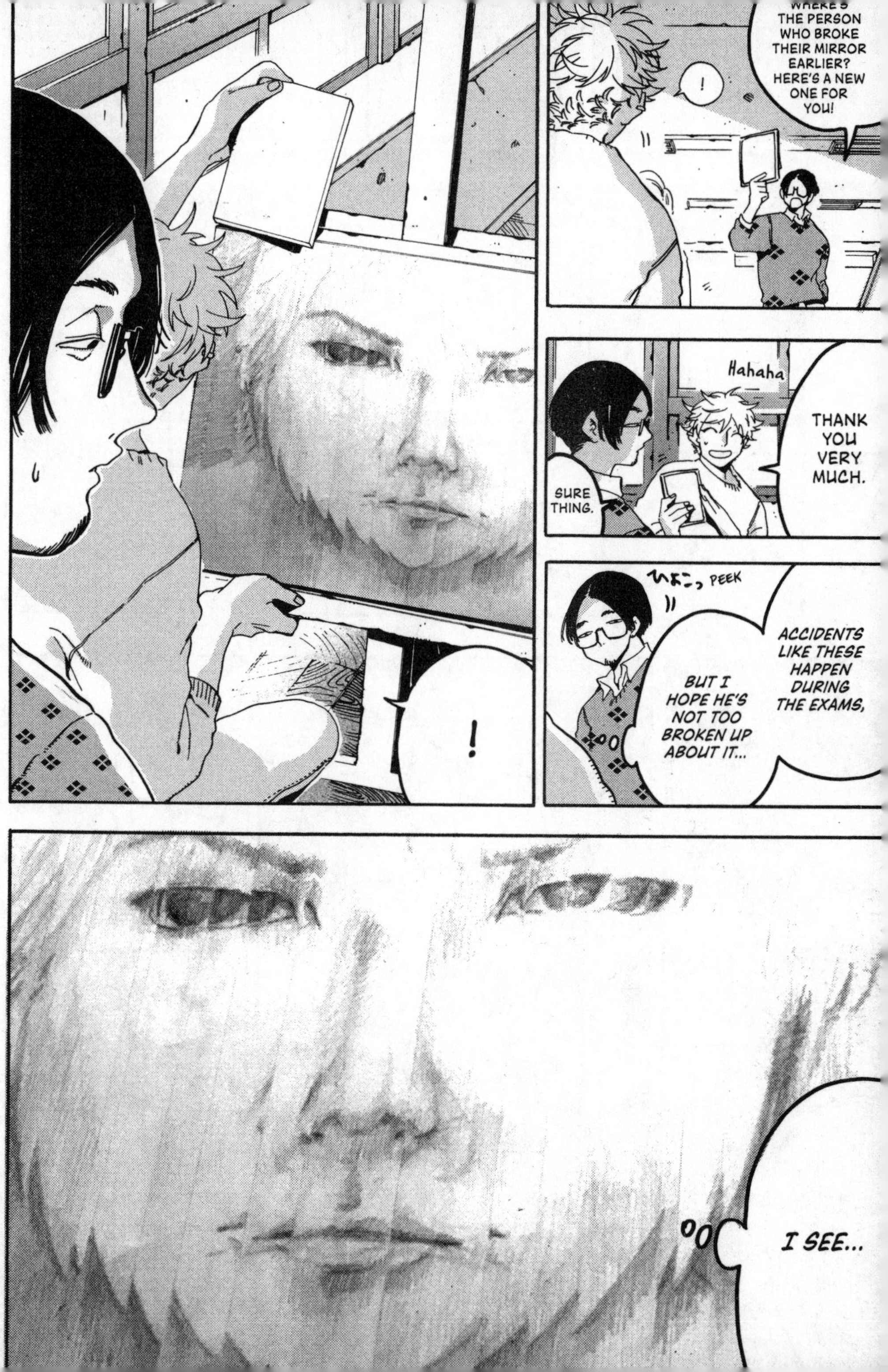
WHERE'S THE PERSON WHO BROKE THEIR MIRROR EARLIER? HERE'S A NEW ONE FOR YOU!
!
Hahaha
THANK YOU VERY MUCH.
SURE THING.
ひょこっ PEEK
ACCIDENTS LIKE THESE HAPPEN DURING THE EXAMS,
BUT I HOPE HE'S NOT TOO BROKEN UP ABOUT IT...
!
I SEE...

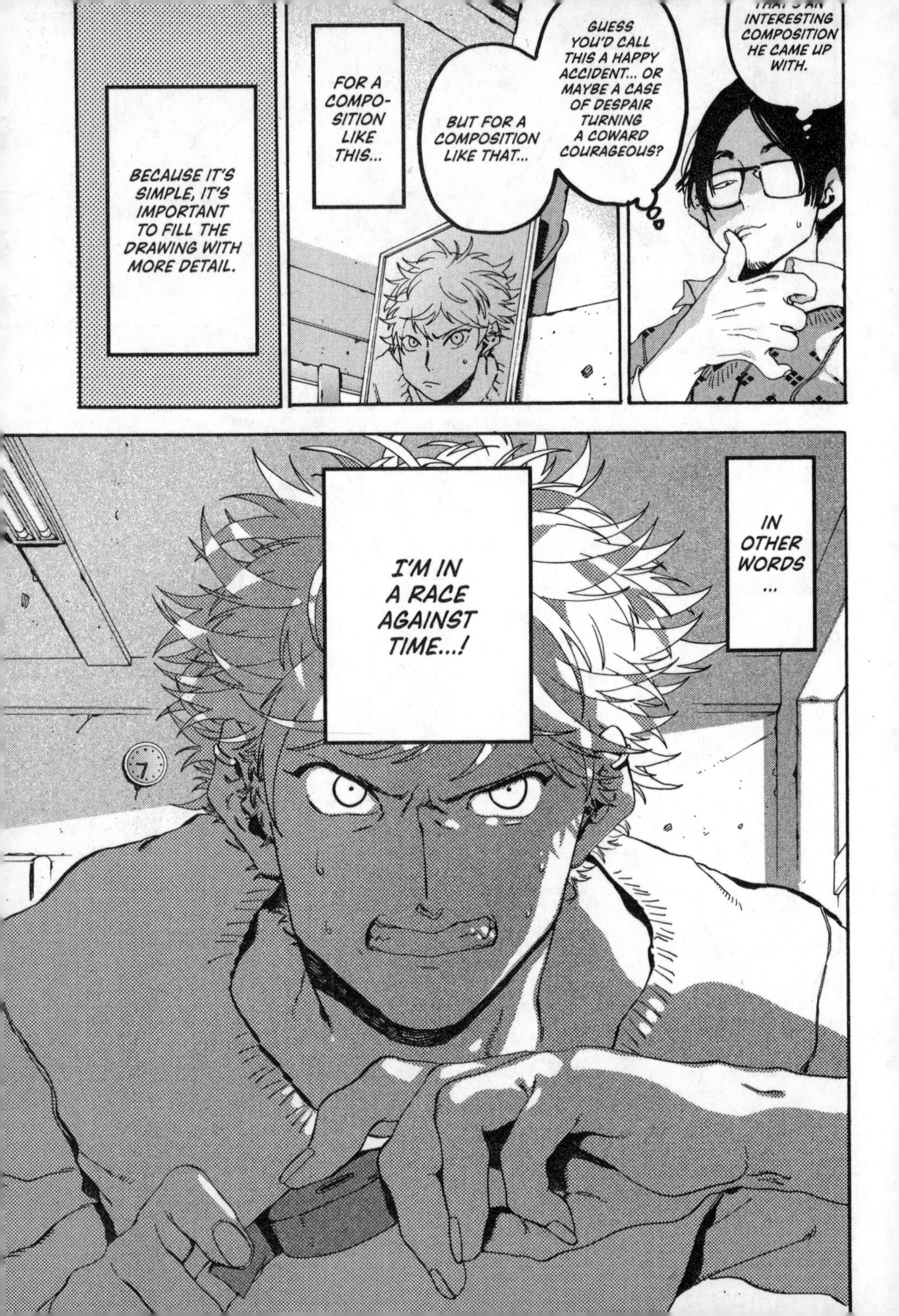
INTERESTING COMPOSITION HE CAME UP WITH.
GUESS YOU'D CALL THIS A HAPPY ACCIDENT... OR MAYBE A CASE OF DESPAIR TURNING A COWARD COURAGEOUS?
BUT FOR A COMPOSITION LIKE THAT...
FOR A COMPOSITION LIKE THIS...
BECAUSE IT'S SIMPLE, IT'S IMPORTANT TO FILL THE DRAWING WITH MORE DETAIL.
IN OTHER WORDS...
I'M IN A RACE AGAINST TIME...!

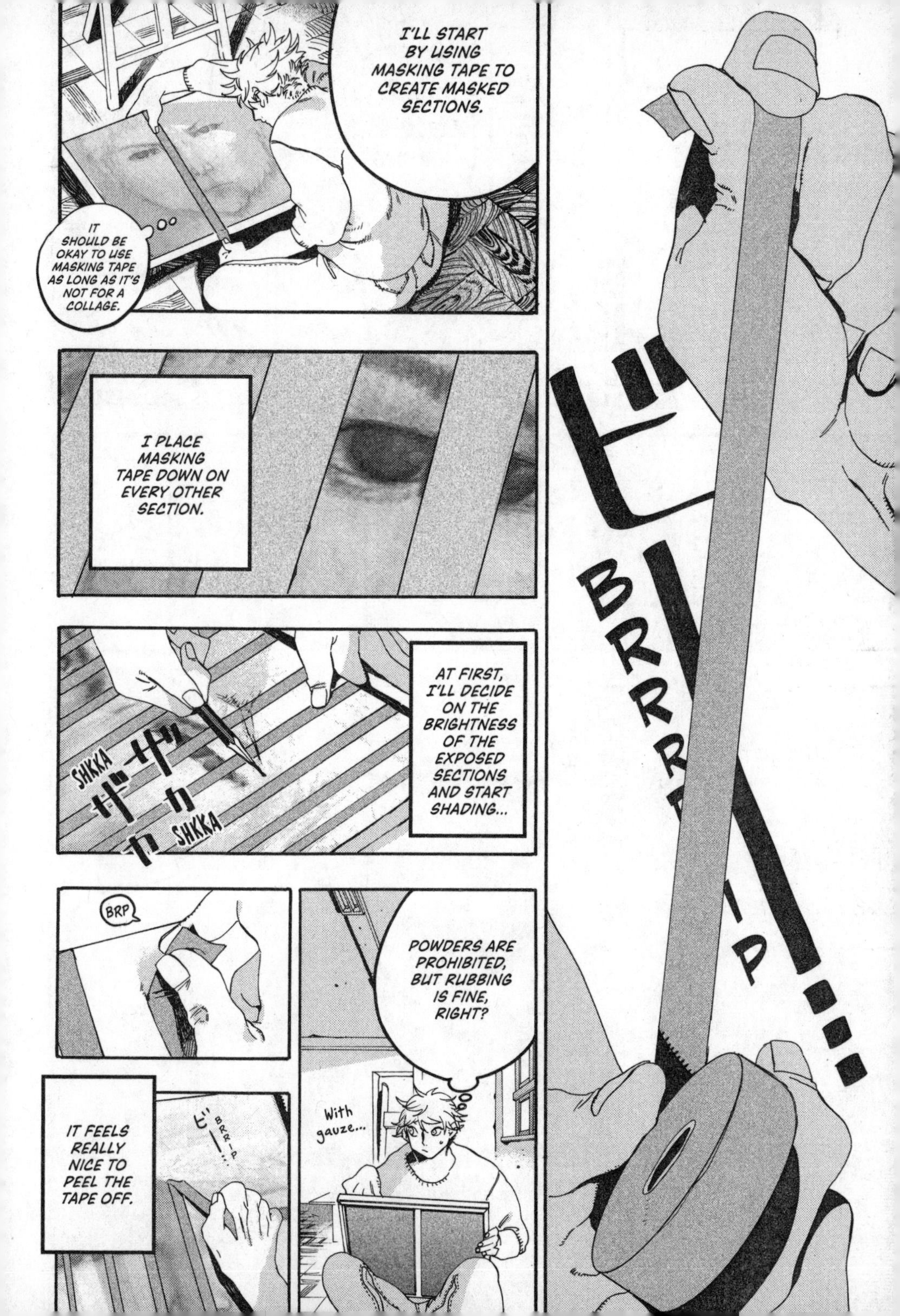
BRRRRIP...
I'LL START BY USING MASKING TAPE TO CREATE MASKED SECTIONS.
IT SHOULD BE OKAY TO USE MASKING TAPE AS LONG AS IT'S NOT FOR A COLLAGE.
I PLACE MASKING TAPE DOWN ON EVERY OTHER SECTION.
AT FIRST, I'LL DECIDE ON THE BRIGHTNESS OF THE EXPOSED SECTIONS AND START SHADING...
SHKKA
SHKKA
POWDERS ARE PROHIBITED, BUT RUBBING IS FINE, RIGHT?
With gauze...
BRP
IT FEELS REALLY NICE TO PEEL THE TAPE OFF.
BRRIP

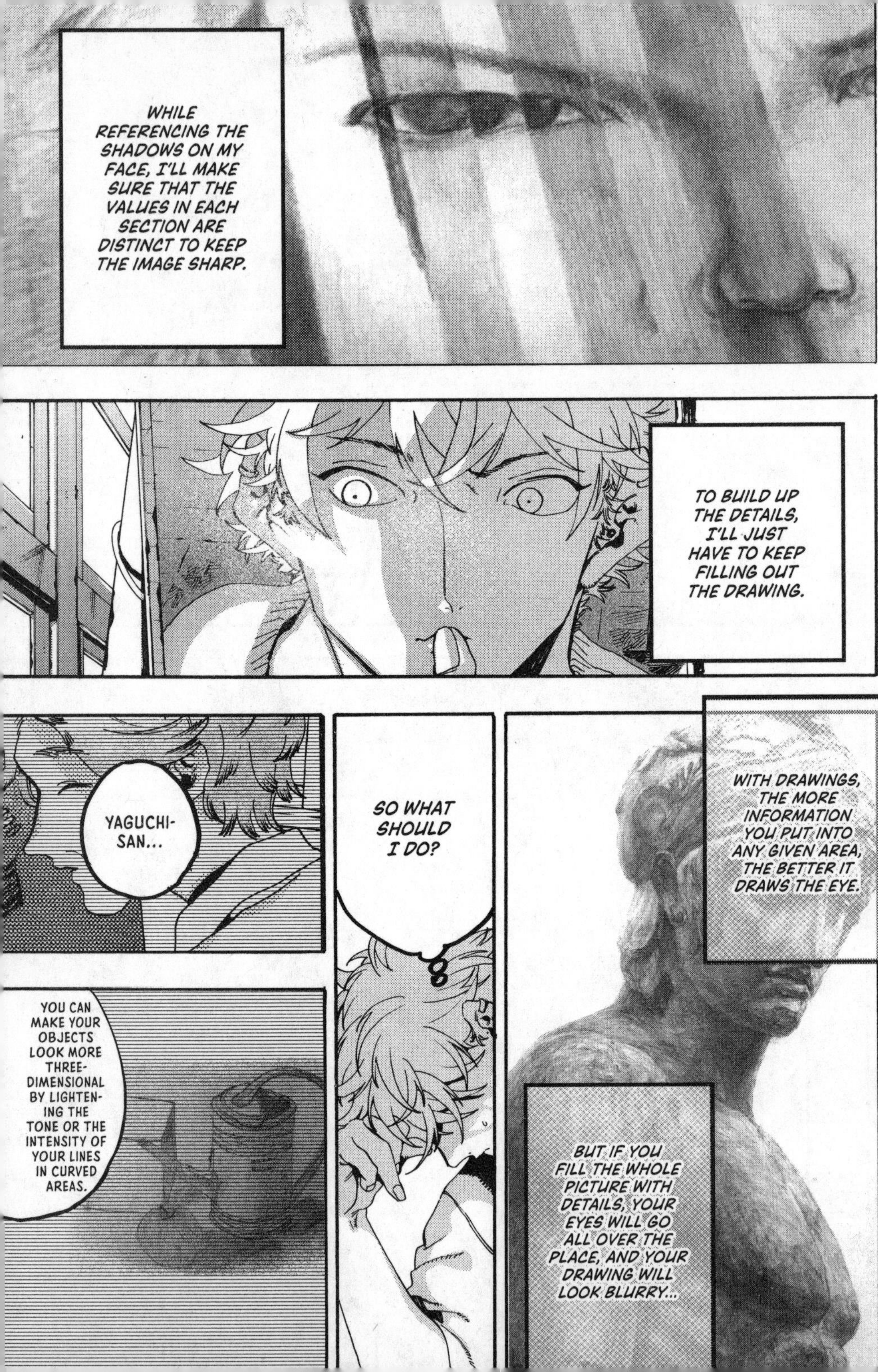
WHILE REFERENCING THE SHADOWS ON MY FACE, I'LL MAKE SURE THAT THE VALUES IN EACH SECTION ARE DISTINCT TO KEEP THE IMAGE SHARP.
TO BUILD UP THE DETAILS, I'LL JUST HAVE TO KEEP FILLING OUT THE DRAWING.
WITH DRAWINGS, THE MORE INFORMATION YOU PUT INTO ANY GIVEN AREA, THE BETTER IT DRAWS THE EYE.
BUT IF YOU FILL THE WHOLE PICTURE WITH DETAILS, YOUR EYES WILL GO ALL OVER THE PLACE, AND YOUR DRAWING WILL LOOK BLURRY...
SO WHAT SHOULD I DO?
YAGUCHI-SAN...
YOU CAN MAKE YOUR OBJECTS LOOK MORE THREE-DIMENSIONAL BY LIGHTENING THE TONE OR THE INTENSITY OF YOUR LINES IN CURVED AREAS.

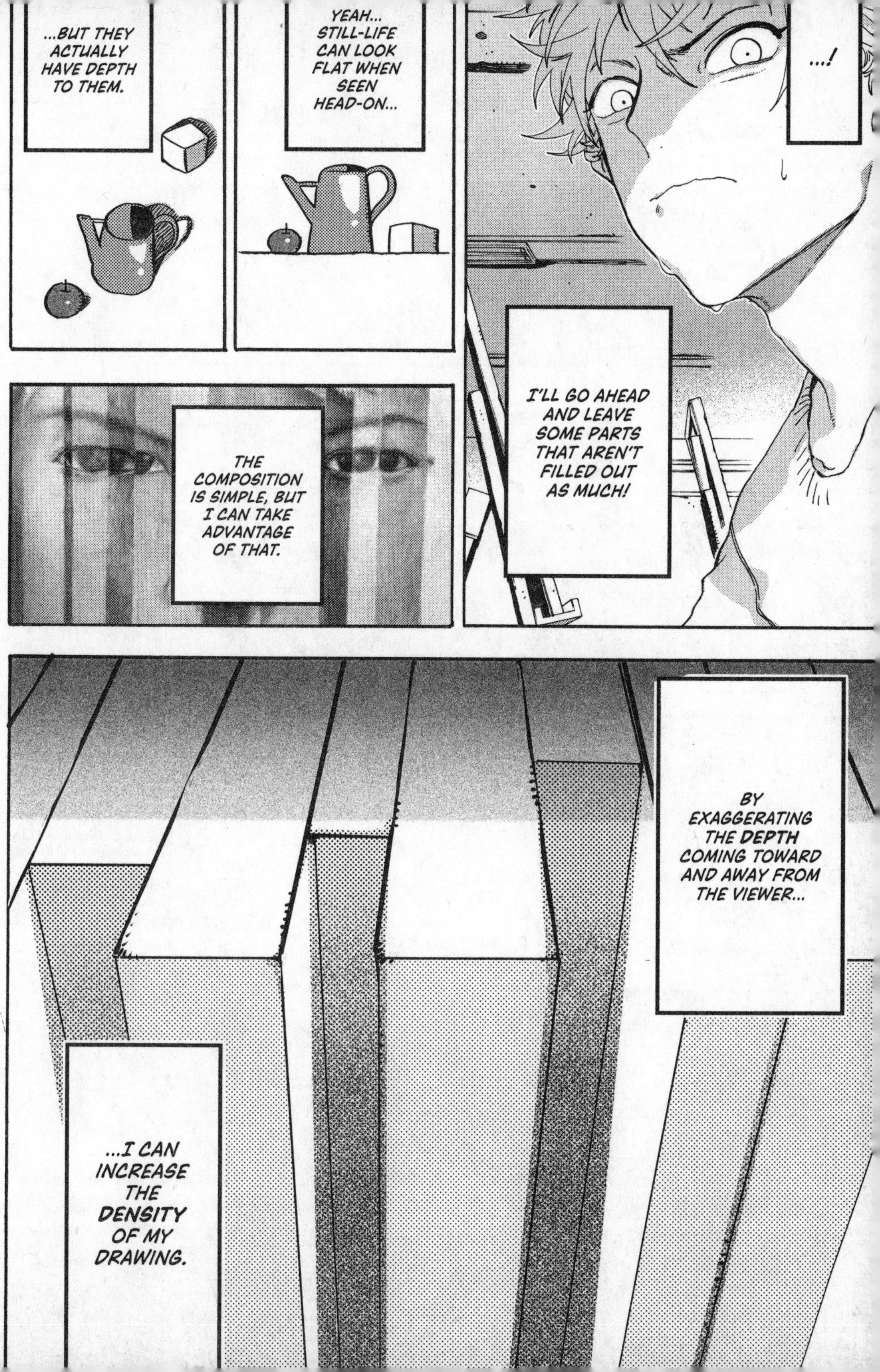
...!
I'LL GO AHEAD AND LEAVE SOME PARTS THAT AREN'T FILLED OUT AS MUCH!
YEAH... STILL-LIFE CAN LOOK FLAT WHEN SEEN HEAD-ON...
...BUT THEY ACTUALLY HAVE DEPTH TO THEM.
THE COMPOSITION IS SIMPLE, BUT I CAN TAKE ADVANTAGE OF THAT.
BY EXAGGERATING THE DEPTH COMING TOWARD AND AWAY FROM THE VIEWER...
...I CAN INCREASE THE DENSITY OF MY DRAWING.

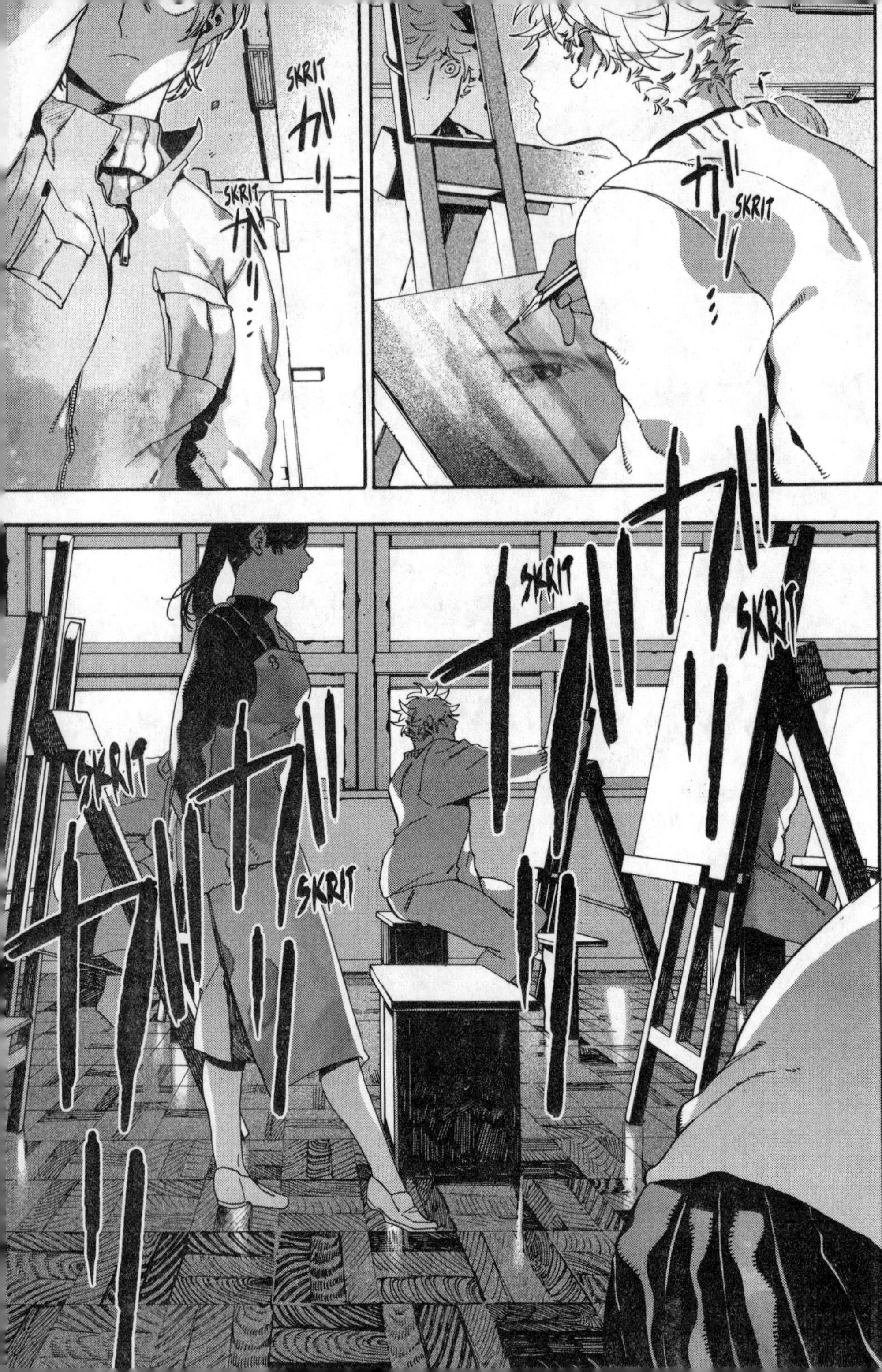
SKRIT
SKRIT
SKRIT
SKRIT
SKRIT
SKRIT
SKRIT

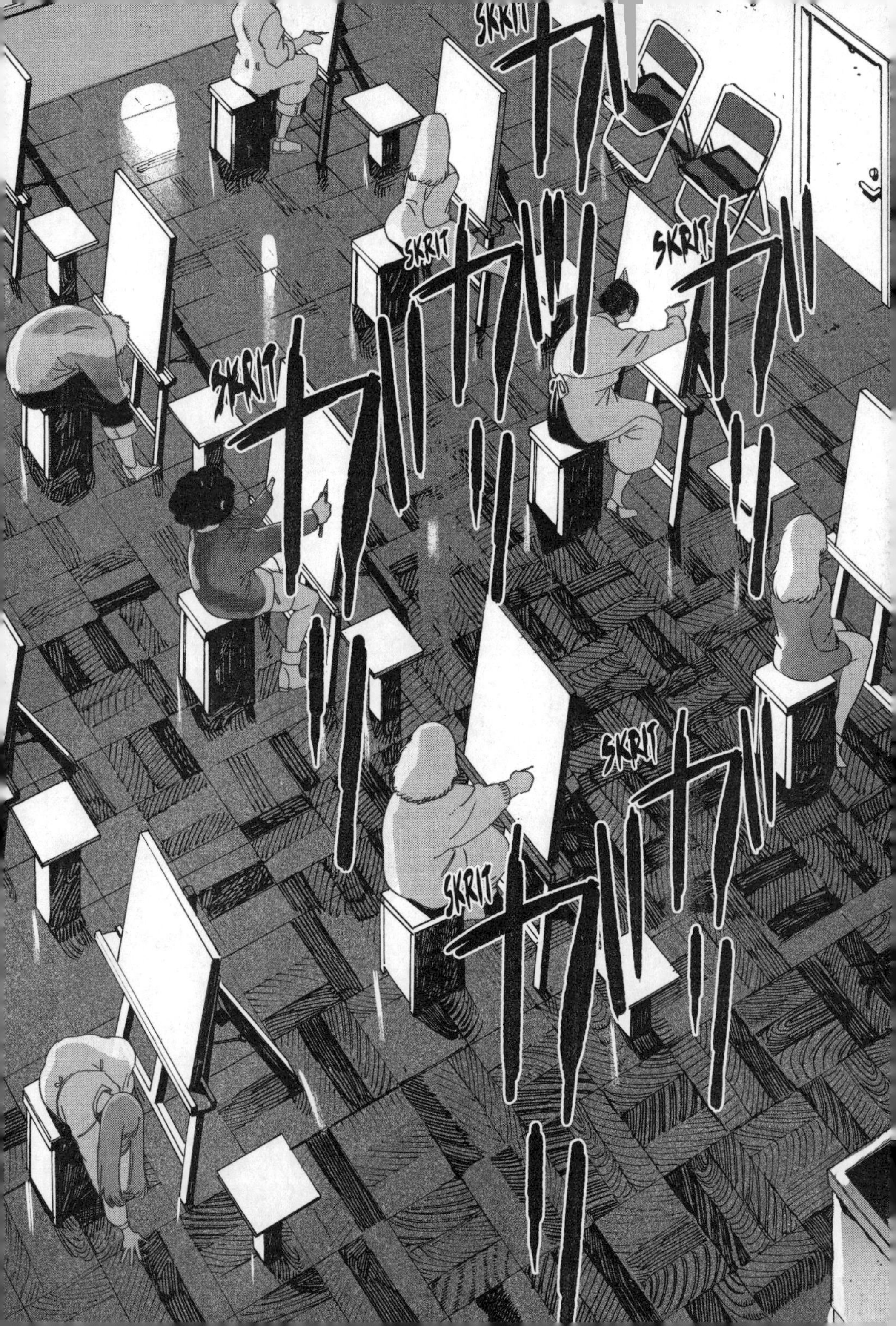
SKRIT
SKRIT
SKRIT
SKRIT
SKRIT
SKRIT

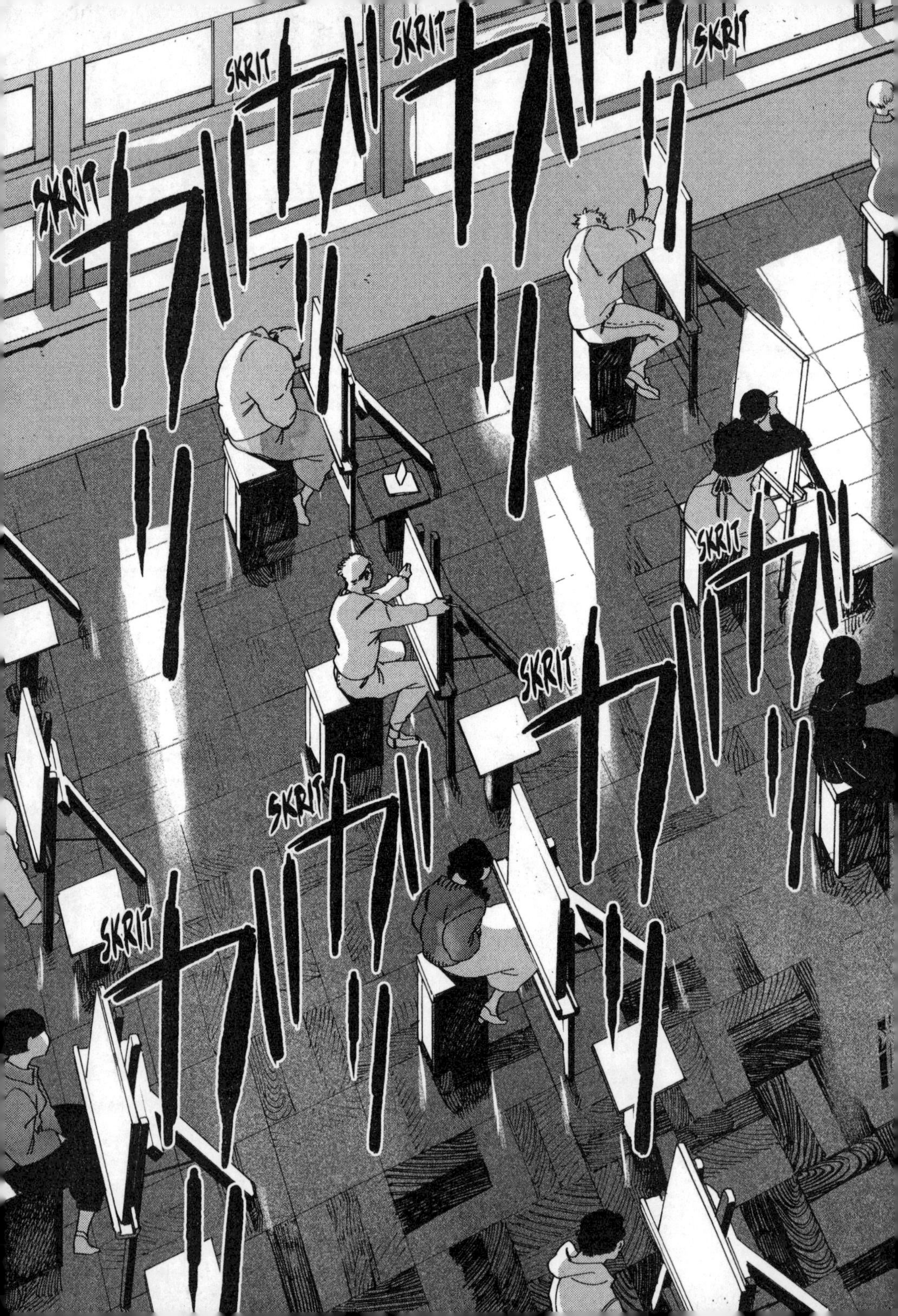
SKRIT
SKRIT
SKRIT
SKRIT
SKRIT
SKRIT
SKRIT
SKRIT

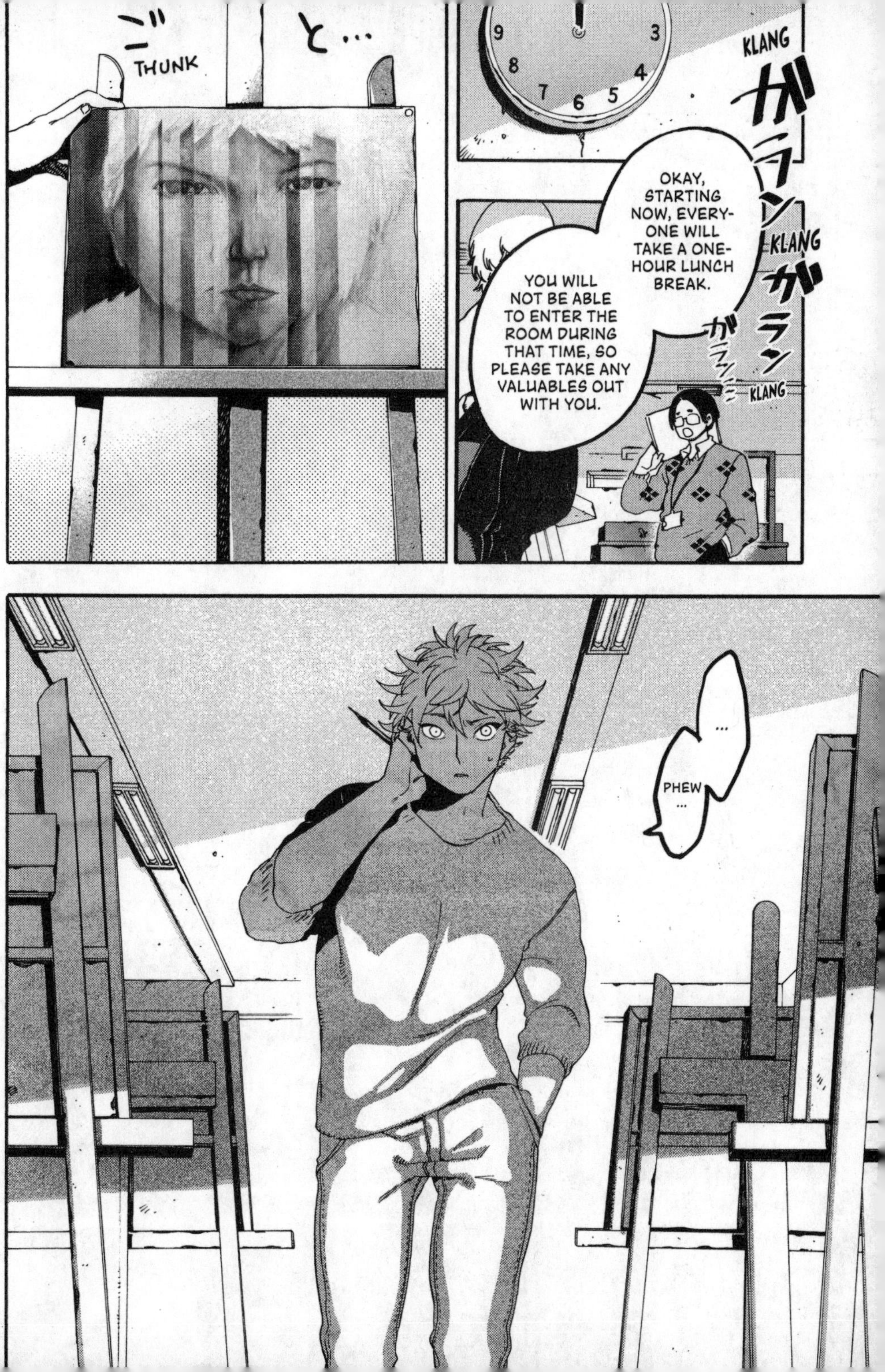
KLANG
ガラン
KLANG
ガラン
ガラン
KLANG
OKAY, STARTING NOW, EVERYONE WILL TAKE A ONE-HOUR LUNCH BREAK.
YOU WILL NOT BE ABLE TO ENTER THE ROOM DURING THAT TIME, SO PLEASE TAKE ANY VALUABLES OUT WITH YOU.
と…
ゴ
THUNK
...
PHEW ...

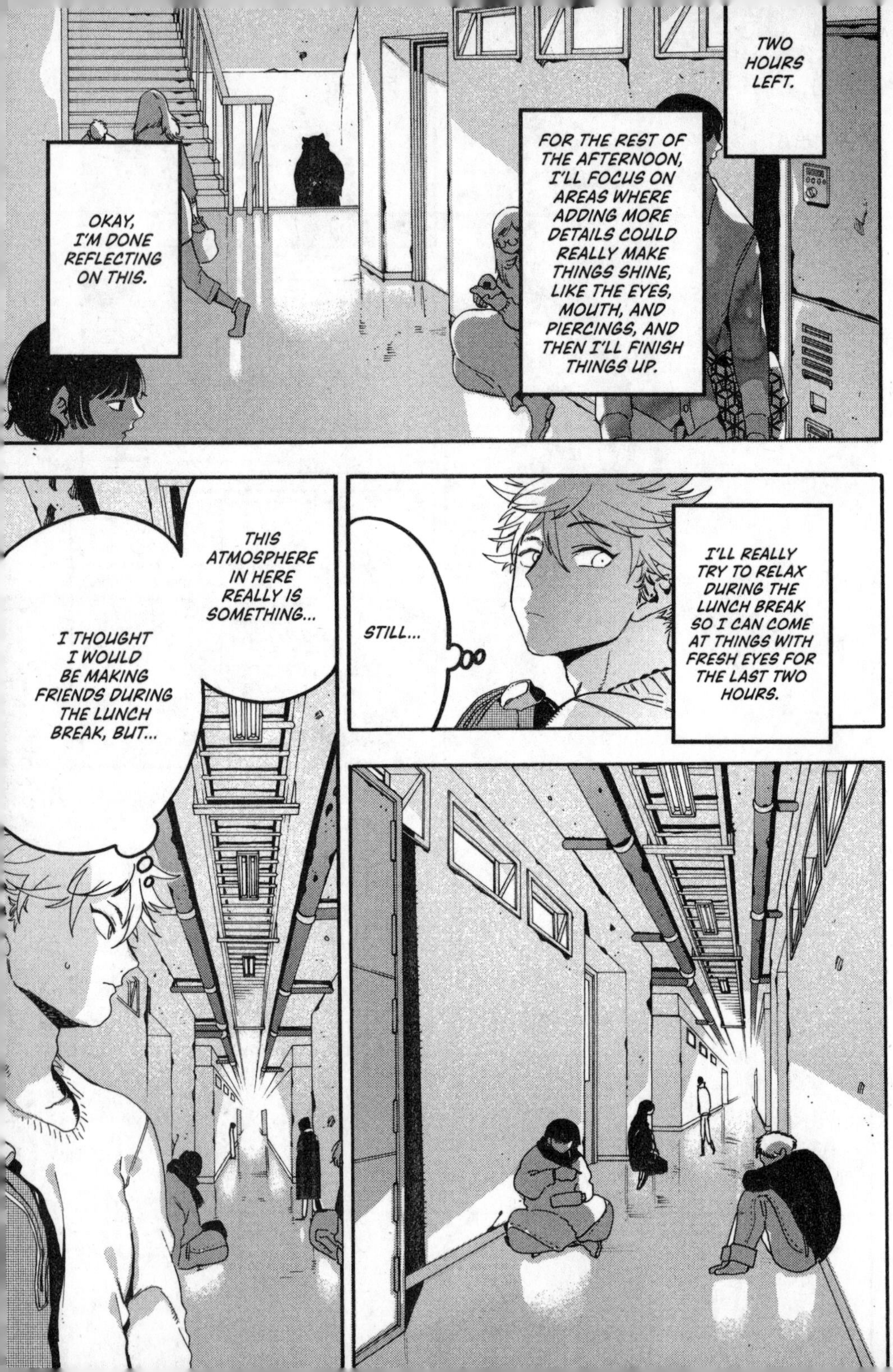
TWO HOURS LEFT.
FOR THE REST OF THE AFTERNOON, I'LL FOCUS ON AREAS WHERE ADDING MORE DETAILS COULD REALLY MAKE THINGS SHINE, LIKE THE EYES, MOUTH, AND PIERCINGS, AND THEN I'LL FINISH THINGS UP.
OKAY, I'M DONE REFLECTING ON THIS.
I'LL REALLY TRY TO RELAX DURING THE LUNCH BREAK SO I CAN COME AT THINGS WITH FRESH EYES FOR THE LAST TWO HOURS.
STILL...
THIS ATMOSPHERE IN HERE REALLY IS SOMETHING...
I THOUGHT I WOULD BE MAKING FRIENDS DURING THE LUNCH BREAK, BUT...

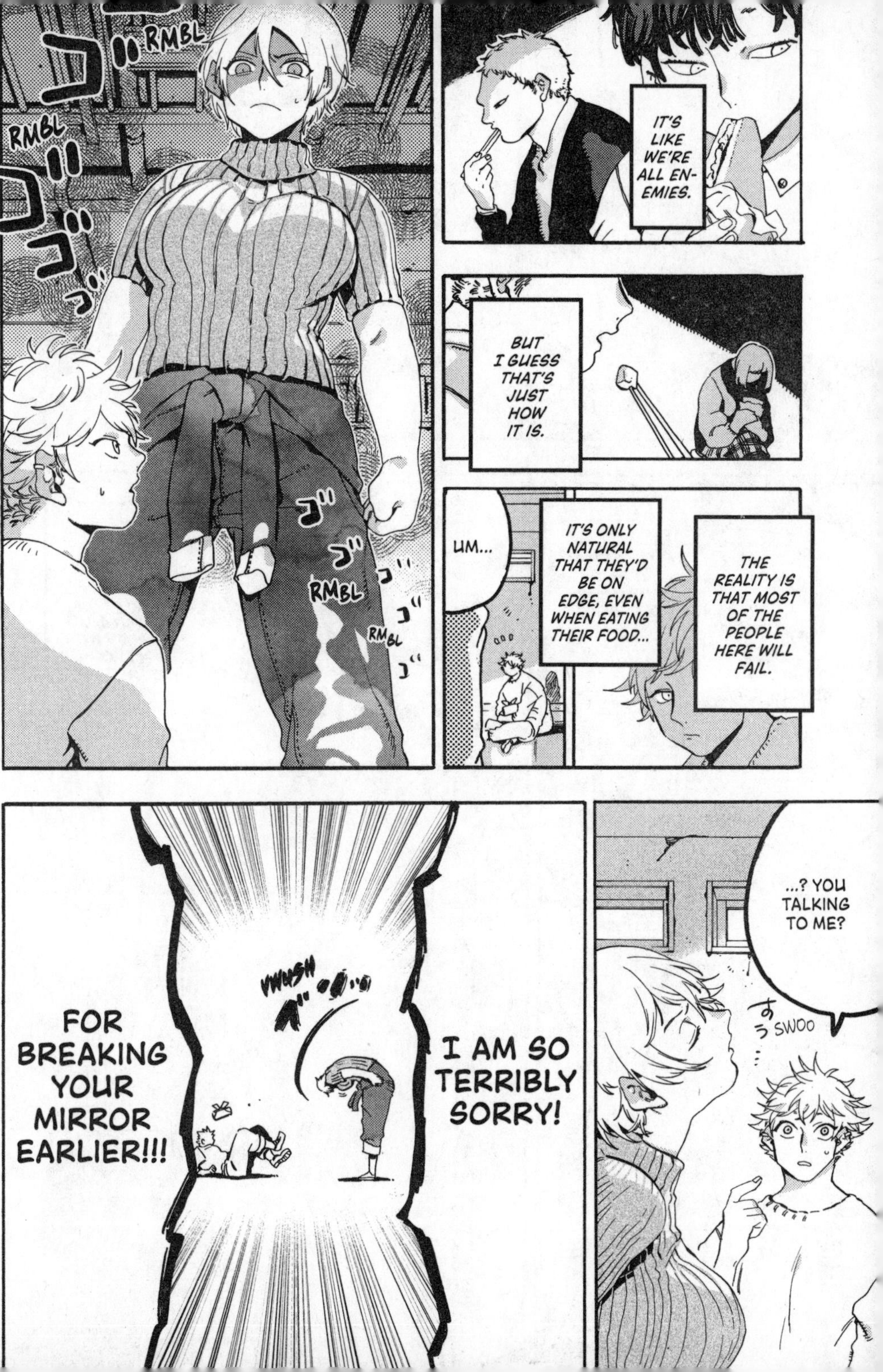
IT'S LIKE WE'RE ALL EN-EMIES.
BUT I GUESS THAT'S JUST HOW IT IS.
THE REALITY IS THAT MOST OF THE PEOPLE HERE WILL FAIL.
IT'S ONLY NATURAL THAT THEY'D BE ON EDGE, EVEN WHEN EATING THEIR FOOD...
UM...
RMBL
RMBL
RMBL
RMBL
...? YOU TALKING TO ME?
SWOO
I AM SO TERRIBLY SORRY!
VWUSH
FOR BREAKING YOUR MIRROR EARLIER!!!

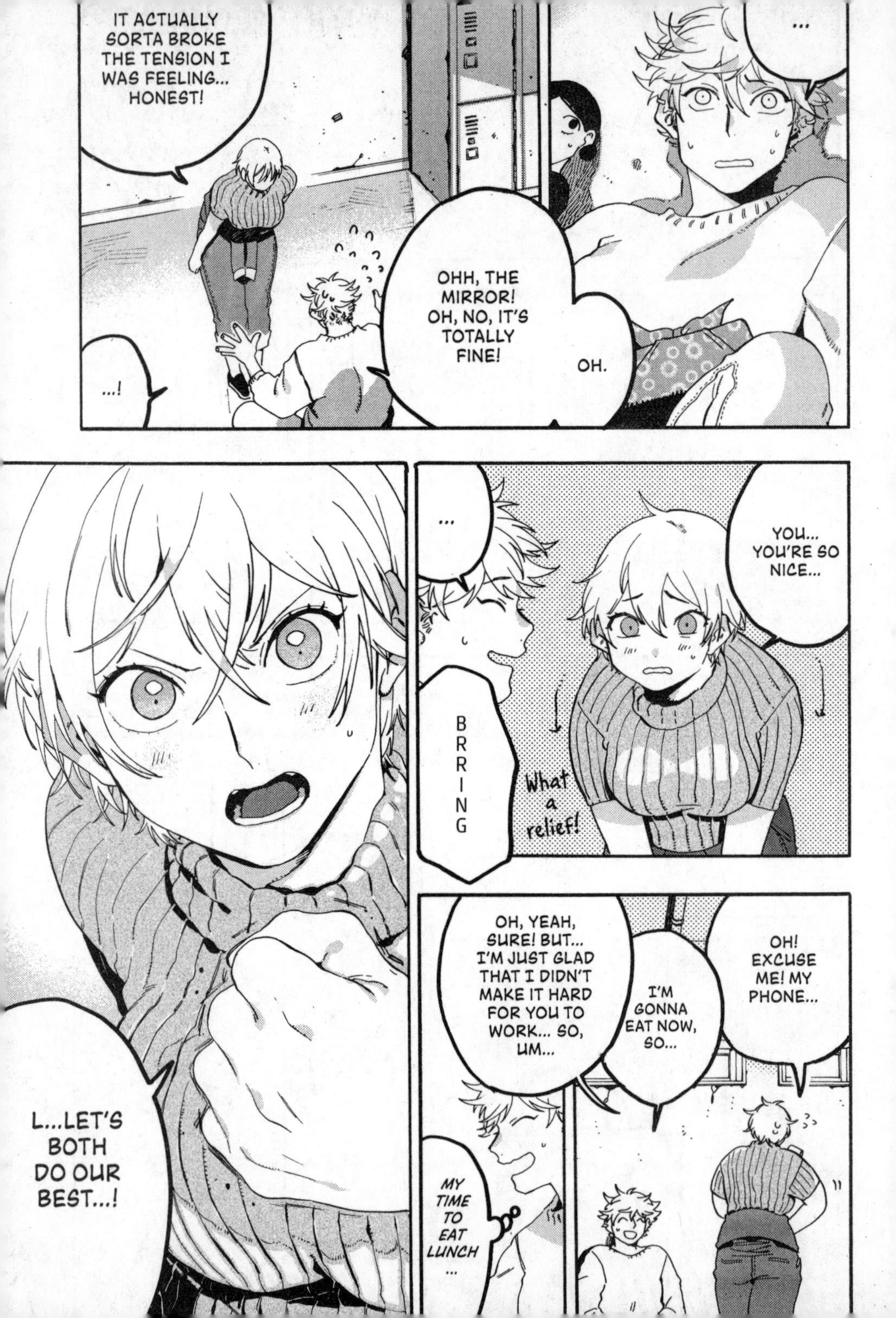
...
OH.
OHH, THE MIRROR! OH, NO, IT'S TOTALLY FINE!
IT ACTUALLY SORTA BROKE THE TENSION I WAS FEELING... HONEST!
...!
YOU... YOU'RE SO NICE...
What a relief!
BRRING
...
OH! EXCUSE ME! MY PHONE...
I'M GONNA EAT NOW, SO...
OH, YEAH, SURE! BUT... I'M JUST GLAD THAT I DIDN'T MAKE IT HARD FOR YOU TO WORK... SO, UM...
MY TIME TO EAT LUNCH ...
L...LET'S BOTH DO OUR BEST...!

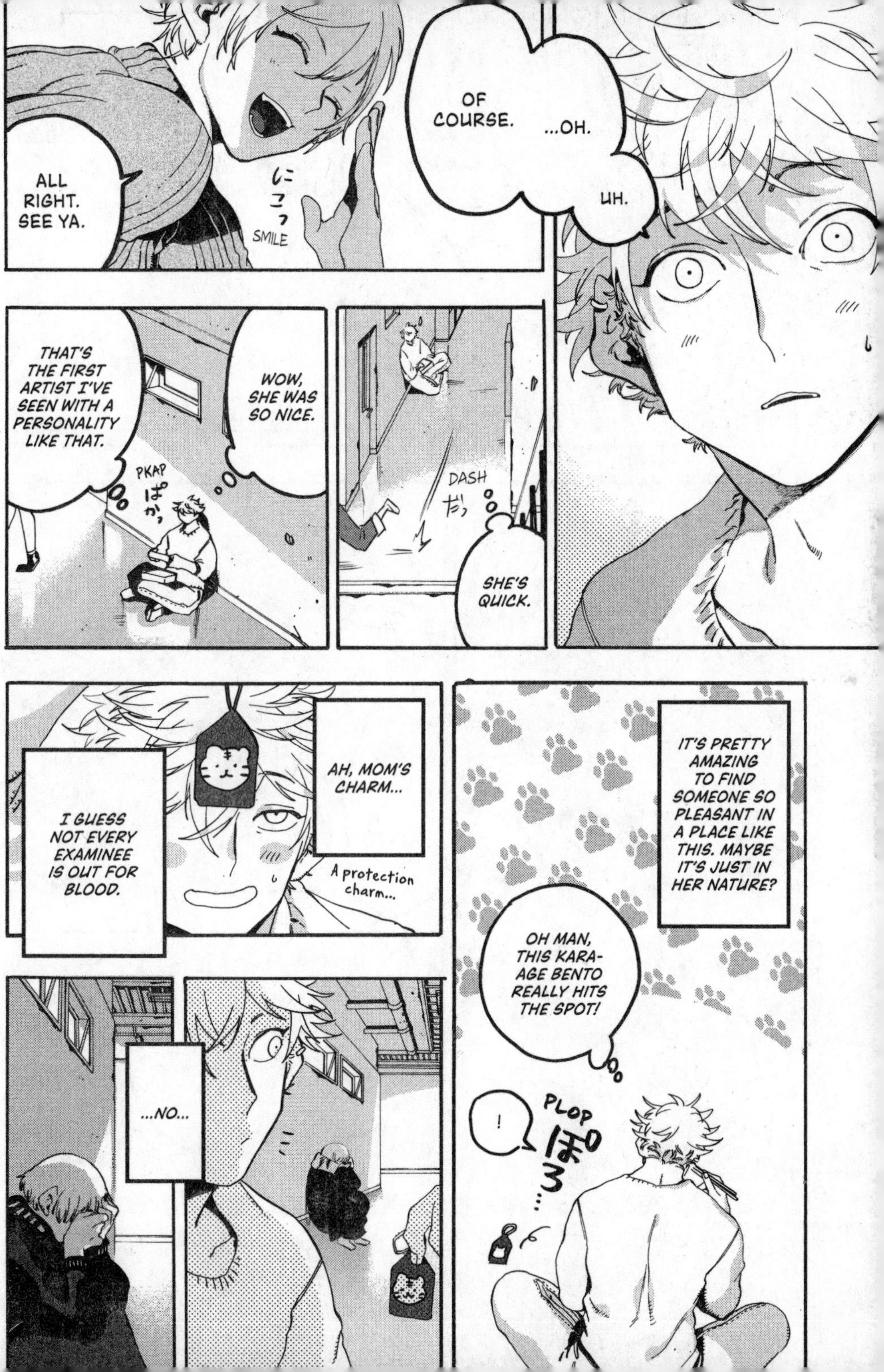

ALL RIGHT. SEE YA.
にこっ
SMILE
OF COURSE.
...OH.
UH.
DASH
だっ
SHE'S QUICK.
WOW, SHE WAS SO NICE.
THAT'S THE FIRST ARTIST I'VE SEEN WITH A PERSONALITY LIKE THAT.
PKAP
ぱかっ
IT'S PRETTY AMAZING TO FIND SOMEONE SO PLEASANT IN A PLACE LIKE THIS. MAYBE IT'S JUST IN HER NATURE?
OH MAN, THIS KARA-AGE BENTO REALLY HITS THE SPOT!
PLOP
ぽろ…
!
AH, MOM'S CHARM...
I GUESS NOT EVERY EXAMINEE IS OUT FOR BLOOD.
A protection charm...
...NO...

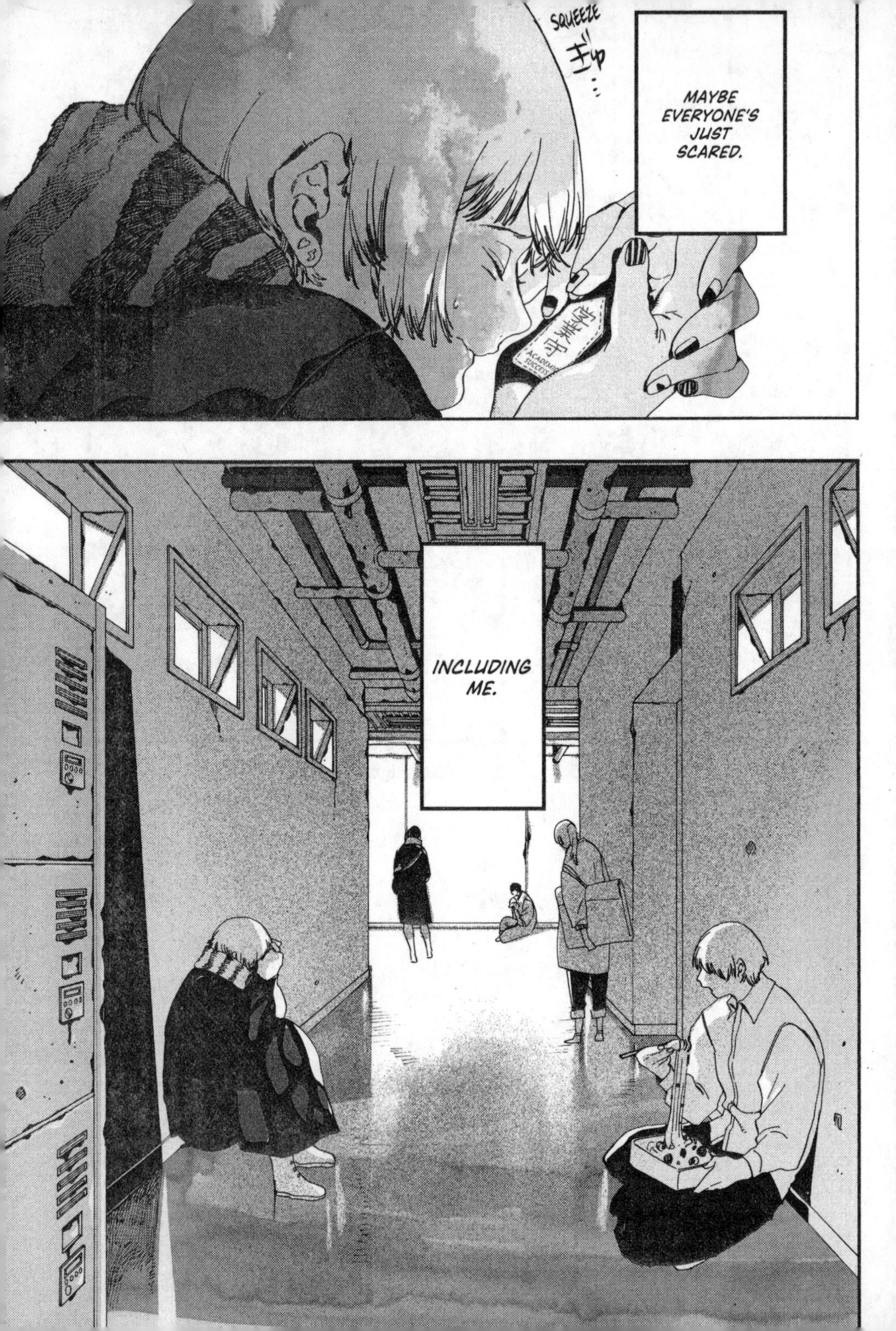
MAYBE EVERYONE'S JUST SCARED.
SQUEEZE
ギュ…
ACADEMIC SUCCESS
INCLUDING ME.

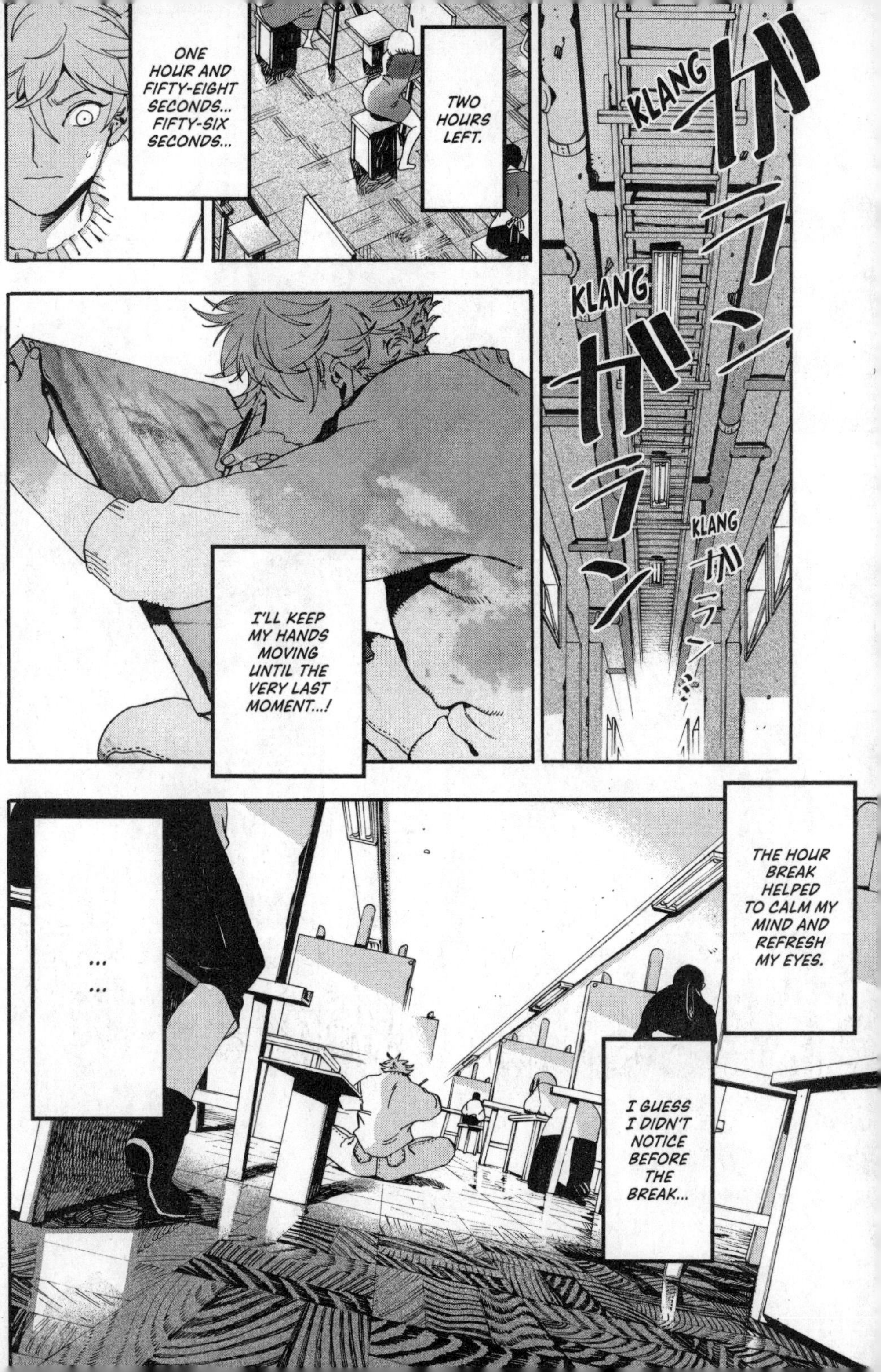
KLANG
ガラン
KLANG
ガラン
KLANG
ガラン
TWO HOURS LEFT.
ONE HOUR AND FIFTY-EIGHT SECONDS... FIFTY-SIX SECONDS...
I'LL KEEP MY HANDS MOVING UNTIL THE VERY LAST MOMENT...!
THE HOUR BREAK HELPED TO CALM MY MIND AND REFRESH MY EYES.
I GUESS I DIDN'T NOTICE BEFORE THE BREAK...
...
...

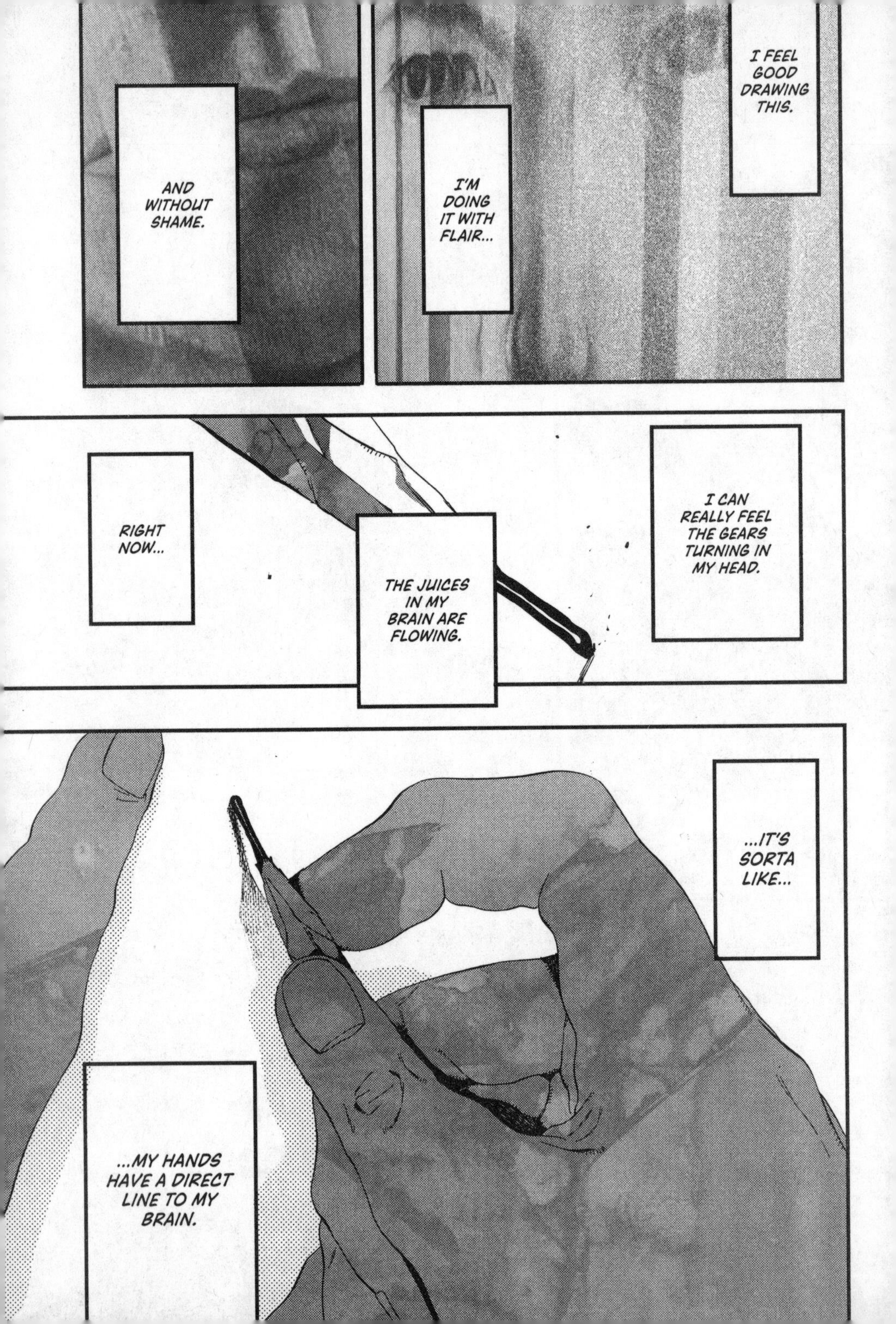
I FEEL GOOD DRAWING THIS.
I'M DOING IT WITH FLAIR...
AND WITHOUT SHAME.
I CAN REALLY FEEL THE GEARS TURNING IN MY HEAD.
THE JUICES IN MY BRAIN ARE FLOWING.
RIGHT NOW...
...IT'S SORTA LIKE...
...MY HANDS HAVE A DIRECT LINE TO MY BRAIN.

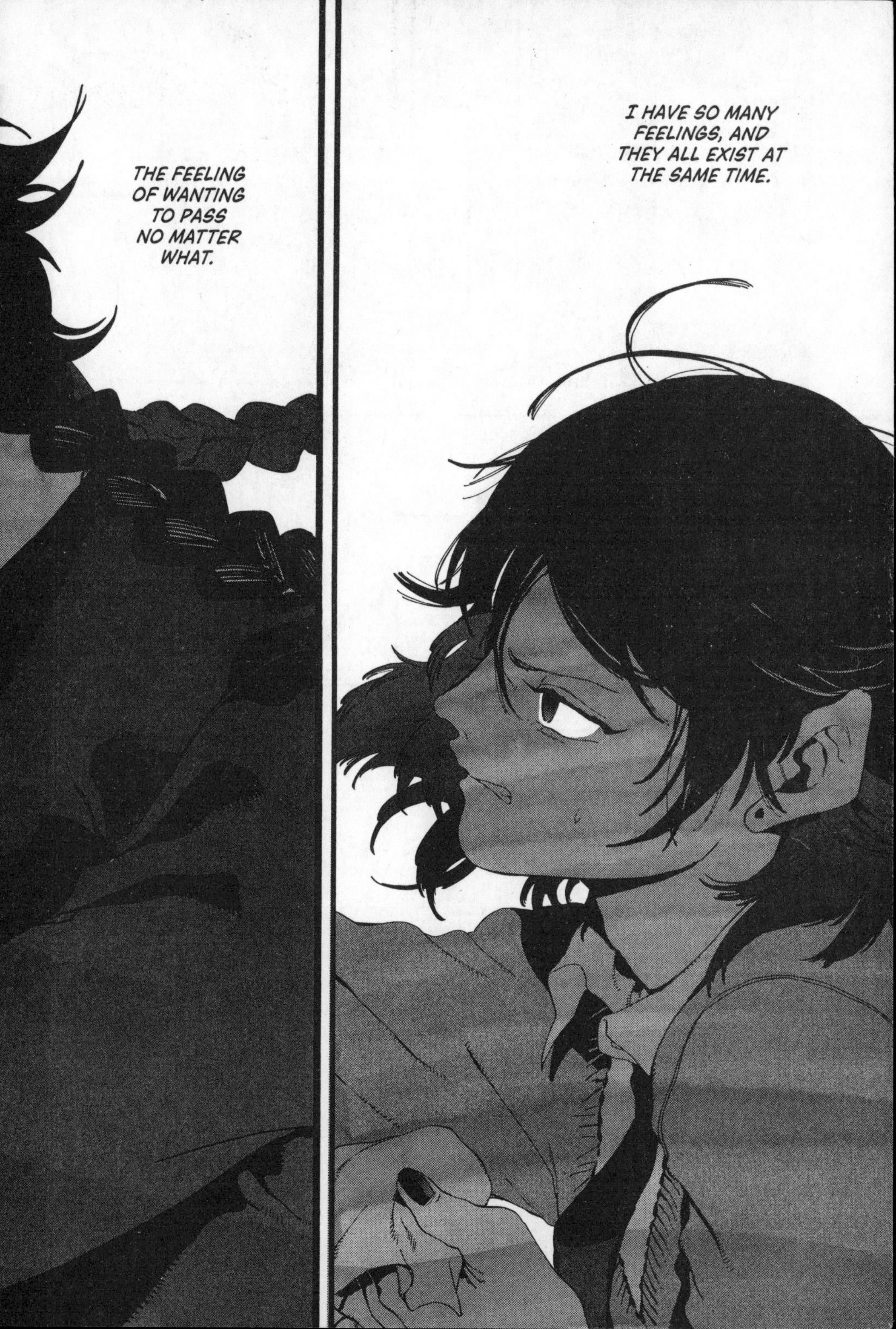
I HAVE SO MANY FEELINGS, AND THEY ALL EXIST AT THE SAME TIME.
THE FEELING OF WANTING TO PASS NO MATTER WHAT.

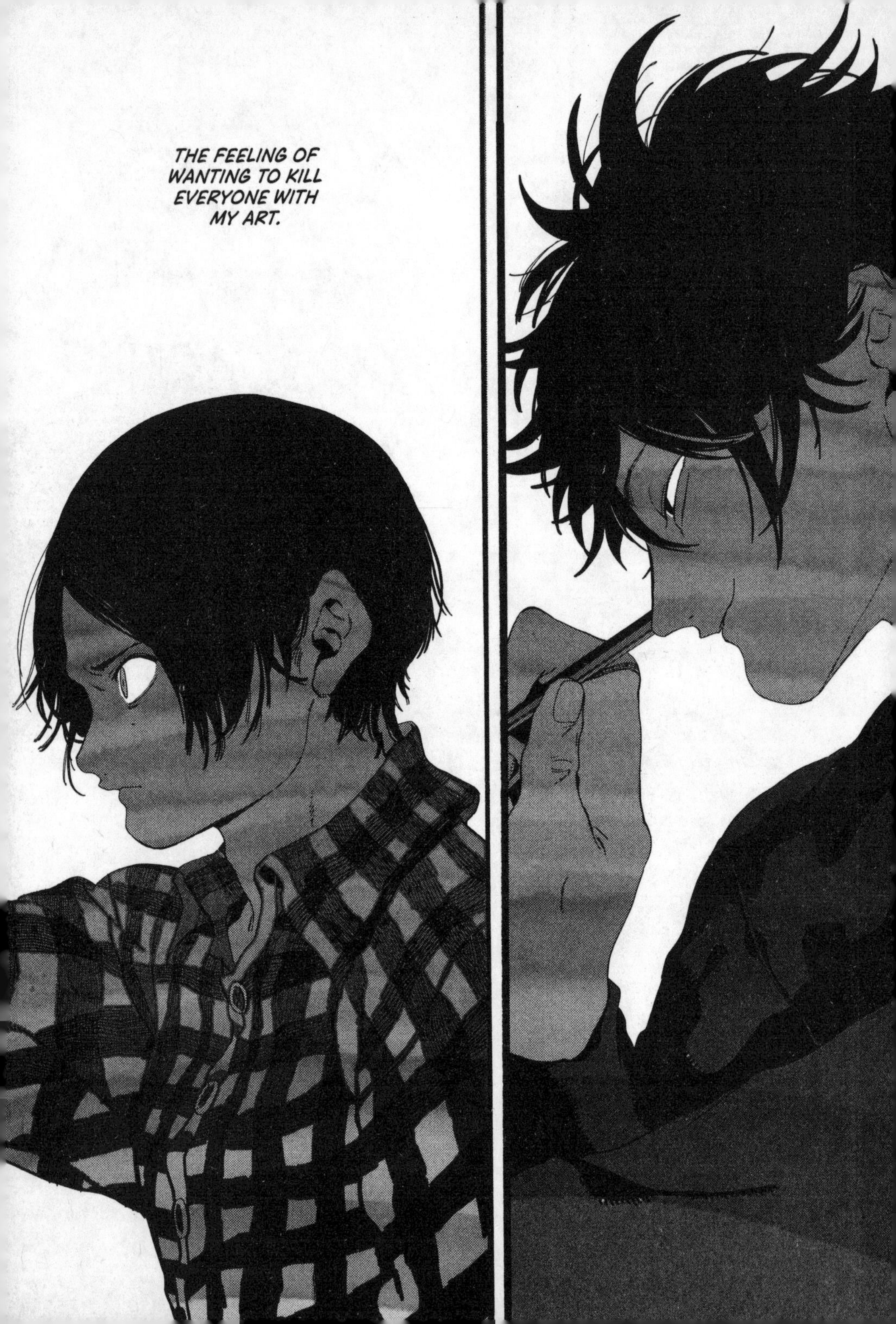
THE FEELING OF WANTING TO KILL EVERYONE WITH MY ART.

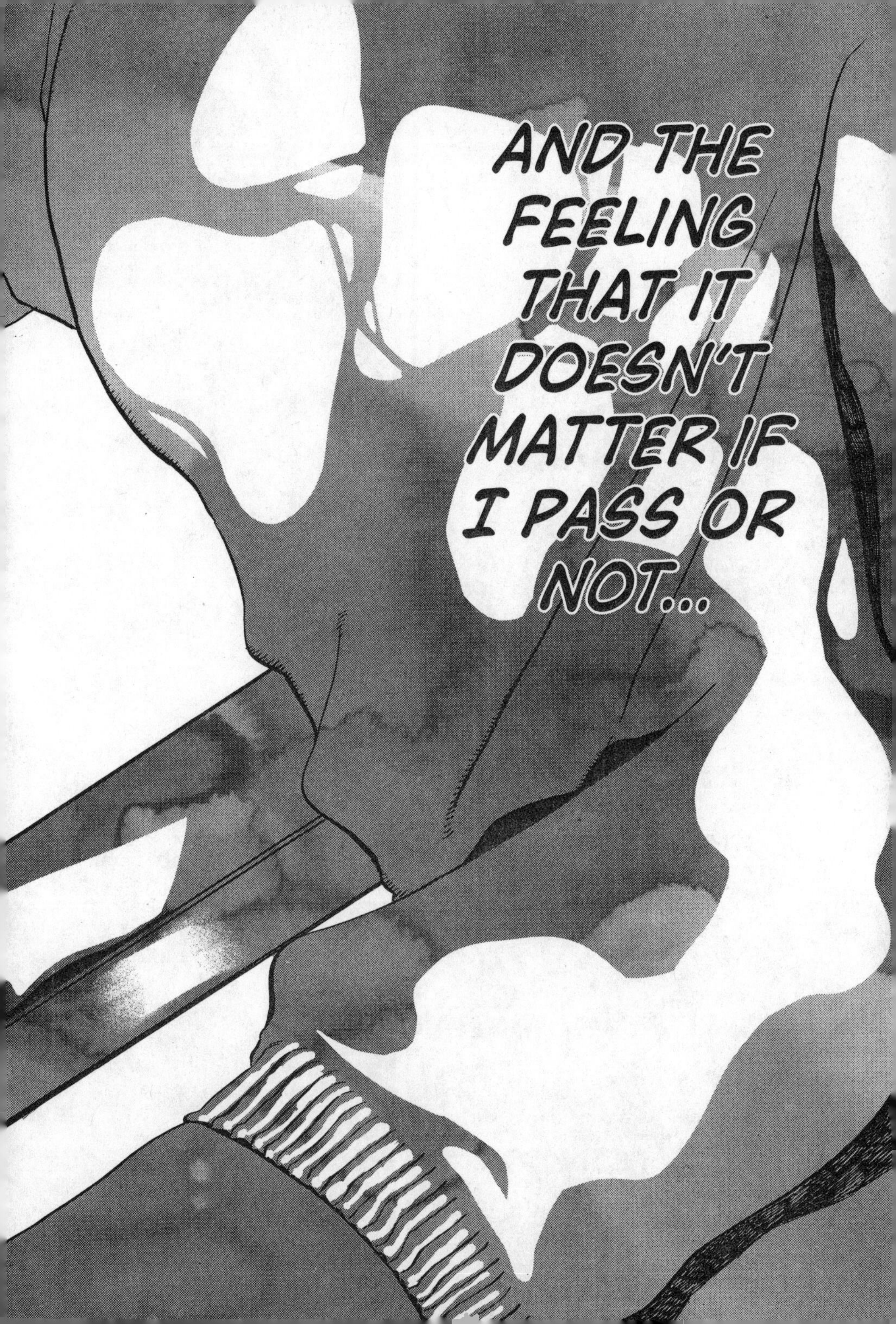
AND THE FEELING THAT IT DOESN'T MATTER IF I PASS OR NOT...

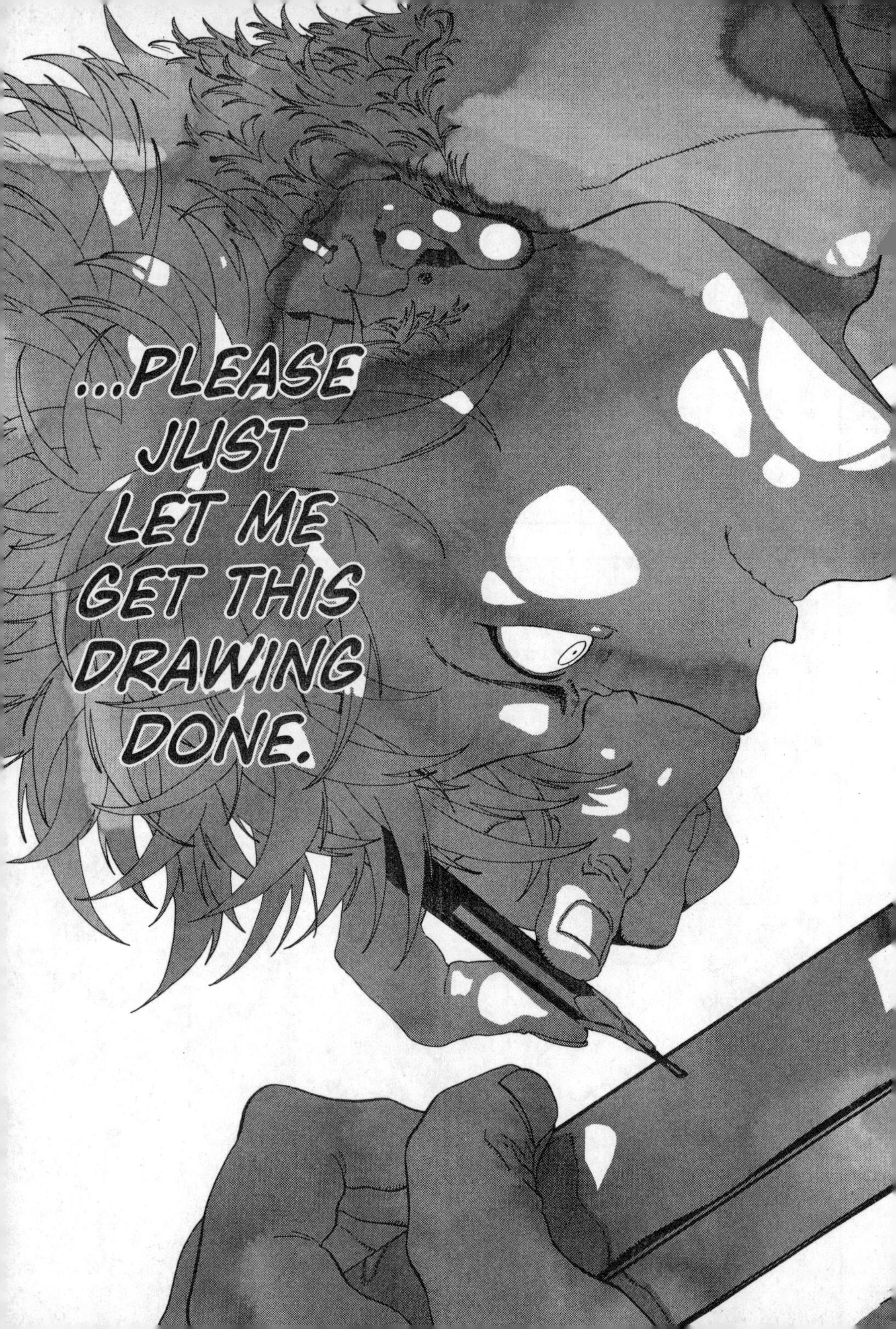
...PLEASE JUST LET ME GET THIS DRAWING DONE.

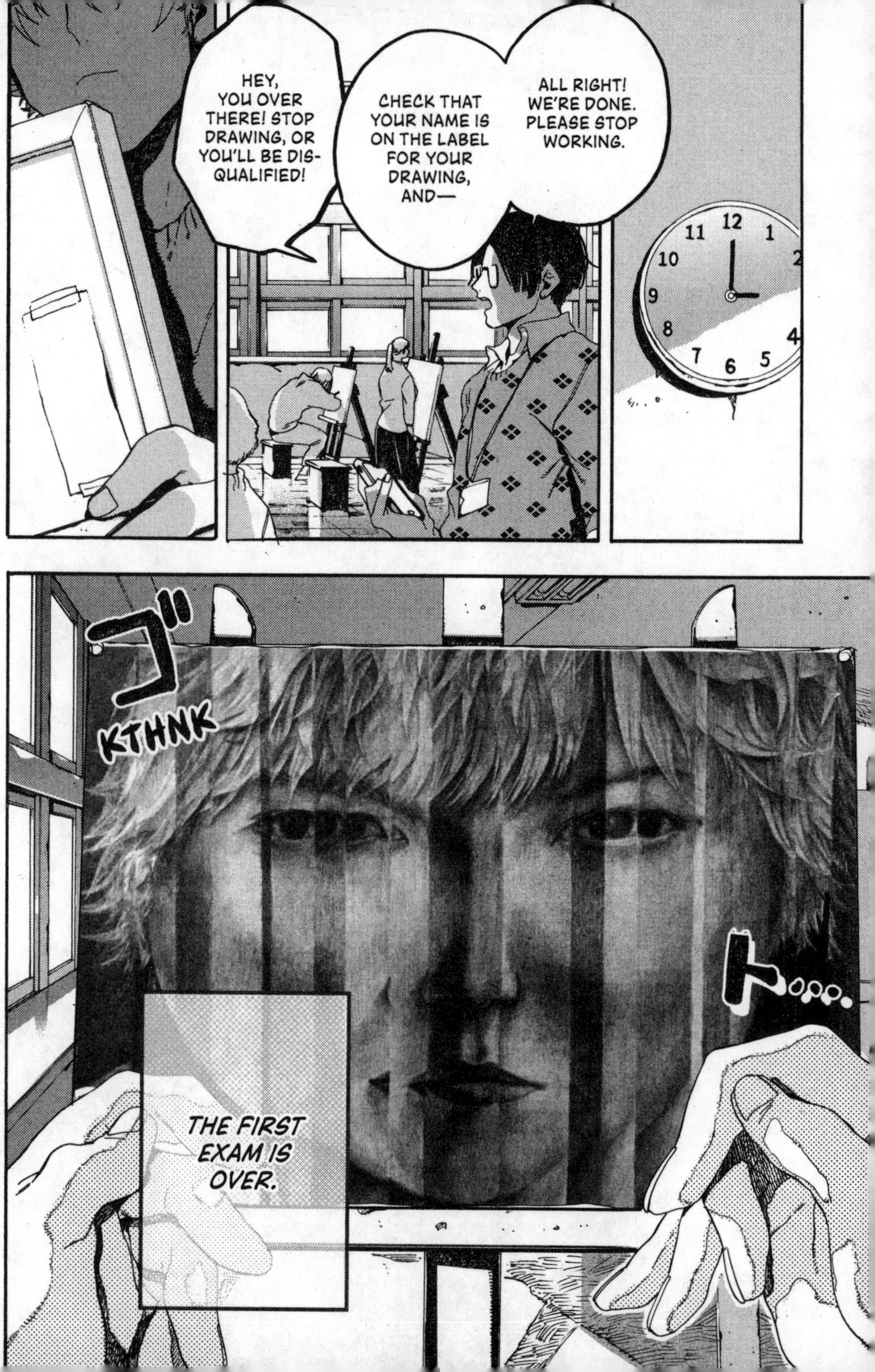

ALL RIGHT! WE'RE DONE. PLEASE STOP WORKING.
CHECK THAT YOUR NAME IS ON THE LABEL FOR YOUR DRAWING, AND—
HEY, YOU OVER THERE! STOP DRAWING, OR YOU'LL BE DIS-QUALIFIED!
ゴ
KTHNK
ト....
THE FIRST EXAM IS OVER.

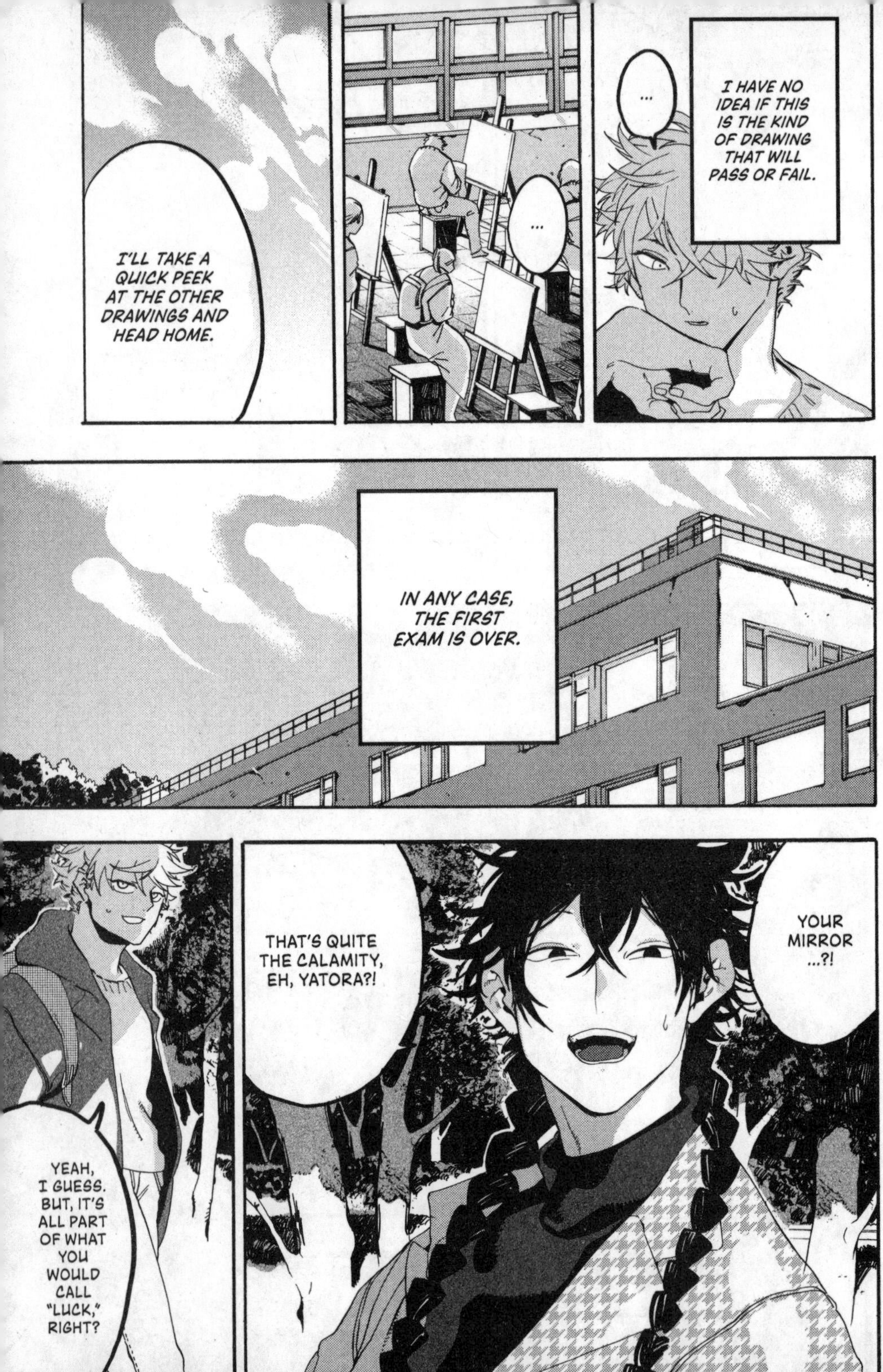

I HAVE NO IDEA IF THIS IS THE KIND OF DRAWING THAT WILL PASS OR FAIL.
...
...
I'LL TAKE A QUICK PEEK AT THE OTHER DRAWINGS AND HEAD HOME.
IN ANY CASE, THE FIRST EXAM IS OVER.
YOUR MIRROR ...?!
THAT'S QUITE THE CALAMITY, EH, YATORA?!
YEAH, I GUESS. BUT, IT'S ALL PART OF WHAT YOU WOULD CALL "LUCK," RIGHT?

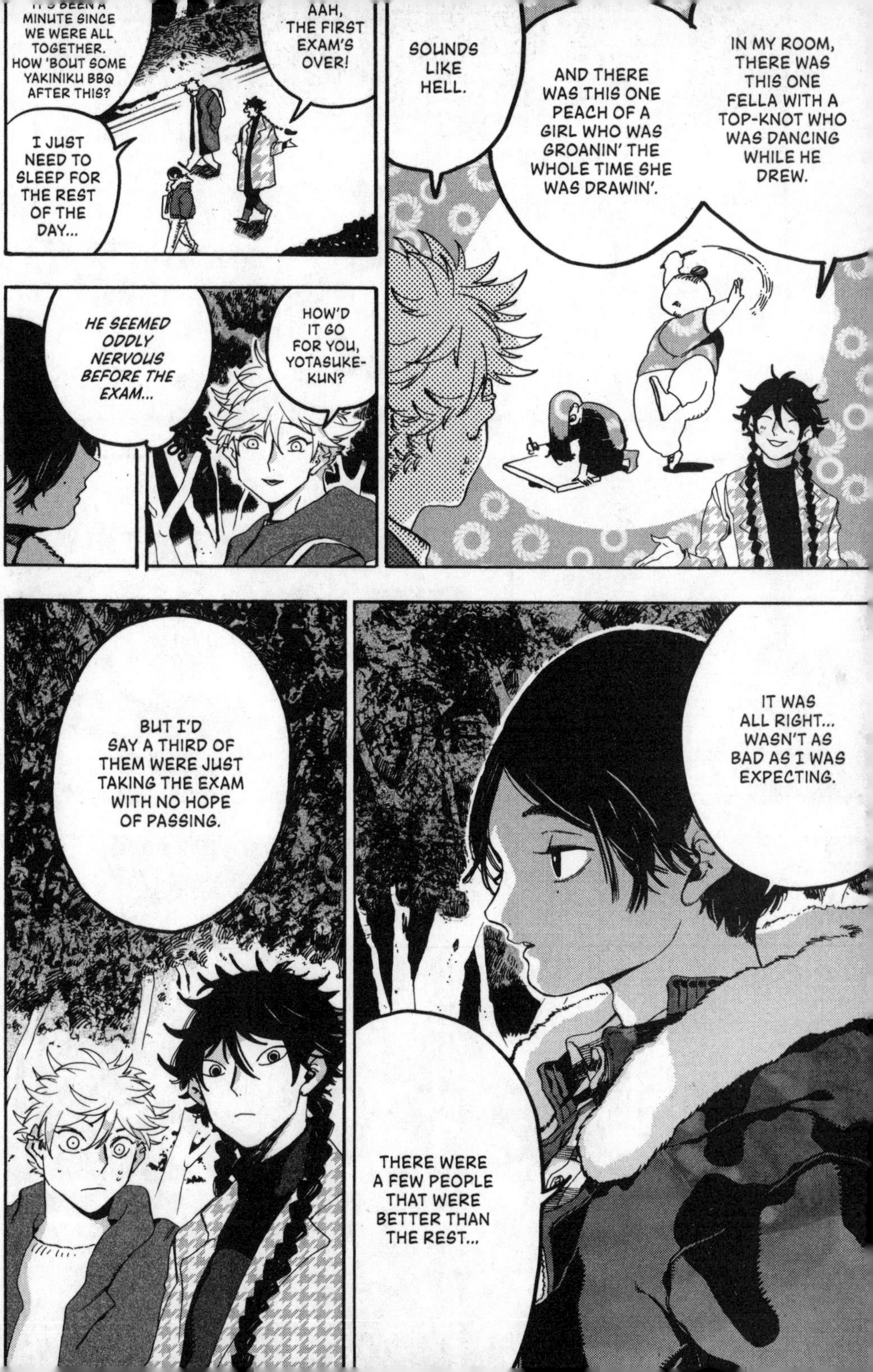
IN MY ROOM, THERE WAS THIS ONE FELLA WITH A TOP-KNOT WHO WAS DANCING WHILE HE DREW.
AND THERE WAS THIS ONE PEACH OF A GIRL WHO WAS GROANIN' THE WHOLE TIME SHE WAS DRAWIN'.
SOUNDS LIKE HELL.
AAH, THE FIRST EXAM'S OVER!
IT'S BEEN A MINUTE SINCE WE WERE ALL TOGETHER. HOW 'BOUT SOME YAKINIKU BBQ AFTER THIS?
I JUST NEED TO SLEEP FOR THE REST OF THE DAY...
HOW'D IT GO FOR YOU, YOTASUKE-KUN?
HE SEEMED ODDLY NERVOUS BEFORE THE EXAM...
IT WAS ALL RIGHT... WASN'T AS BAD AS I WAS EXPECTING.
THERE WERE A FEW PEOPLE THAT WERE BETTER THAN THE REST...
BUT I'D SAY A THIRD OF THEM WERE JUST TAKING THE EXAM WITH NO HOPE OF PASSING.

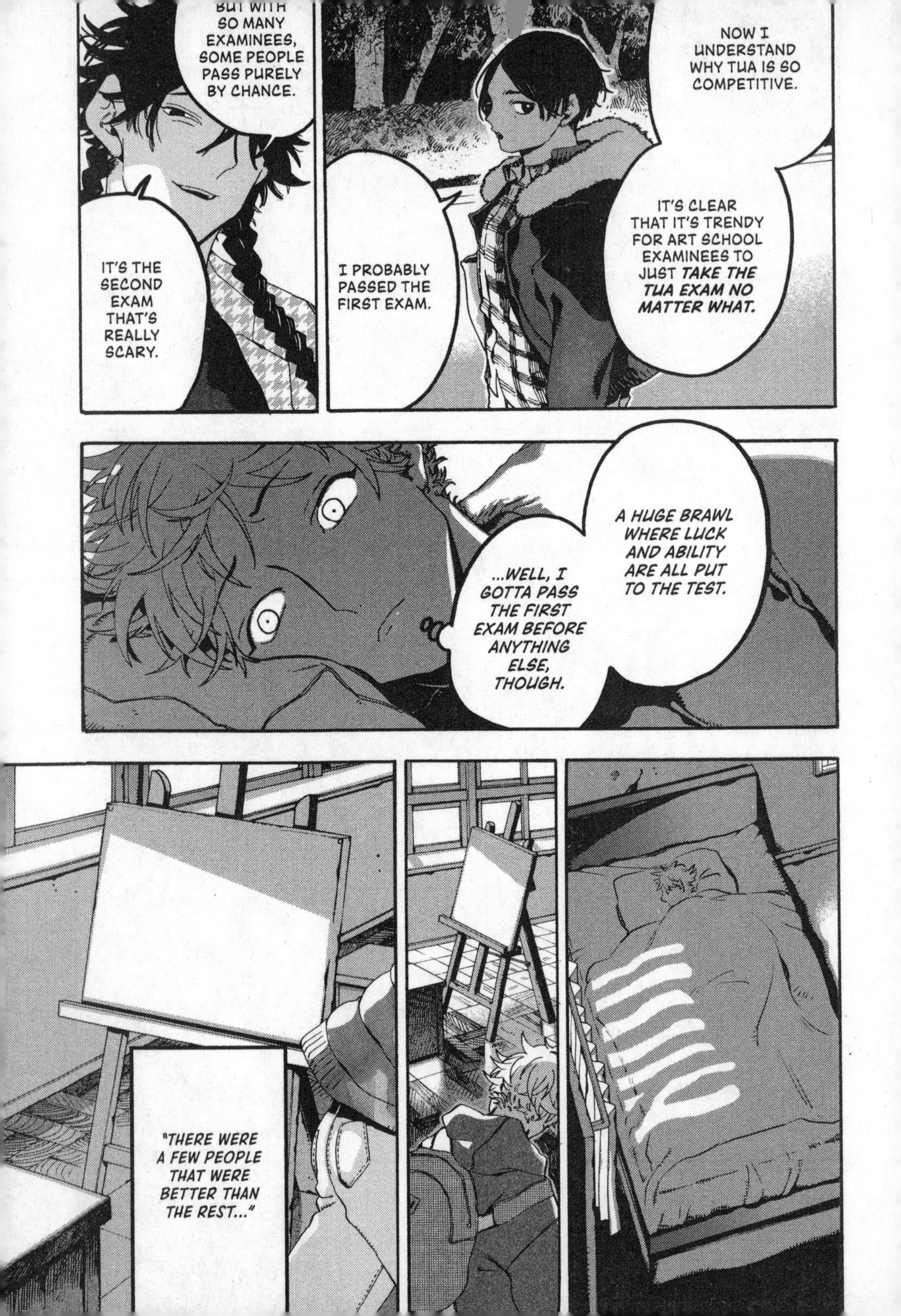
NOW I UNDERSTAND WHY TUA IS SO COMPETITIVE.
IT'S CLEAR THAT IT'S TRENDY FOR ART SCHOOL EXAMINEES TO JUST *TAKE THE TUA EXAM NO MATTER WHAT.*
I PROBABLY PASSED THE FIRST EXAM.
BUT WITH SO MANY EXAMINEES, SOME PEOPLE PASS PURELY BY CHANCE.
IT'S THE SECOND EXAM THAT'S REALLY SCARY.
A HUGE BRAWL WHERE LUCK AND ABILITY ARE ALL PUT TO THE TEST.
...WELL, I GOTTA PASS THE FIRST EXAM BEFORE ANYTHING ELSE, THOUGH.
"THERE WERE A FEW PEOPLE THAT WERE BETTER THAN THE REST..."

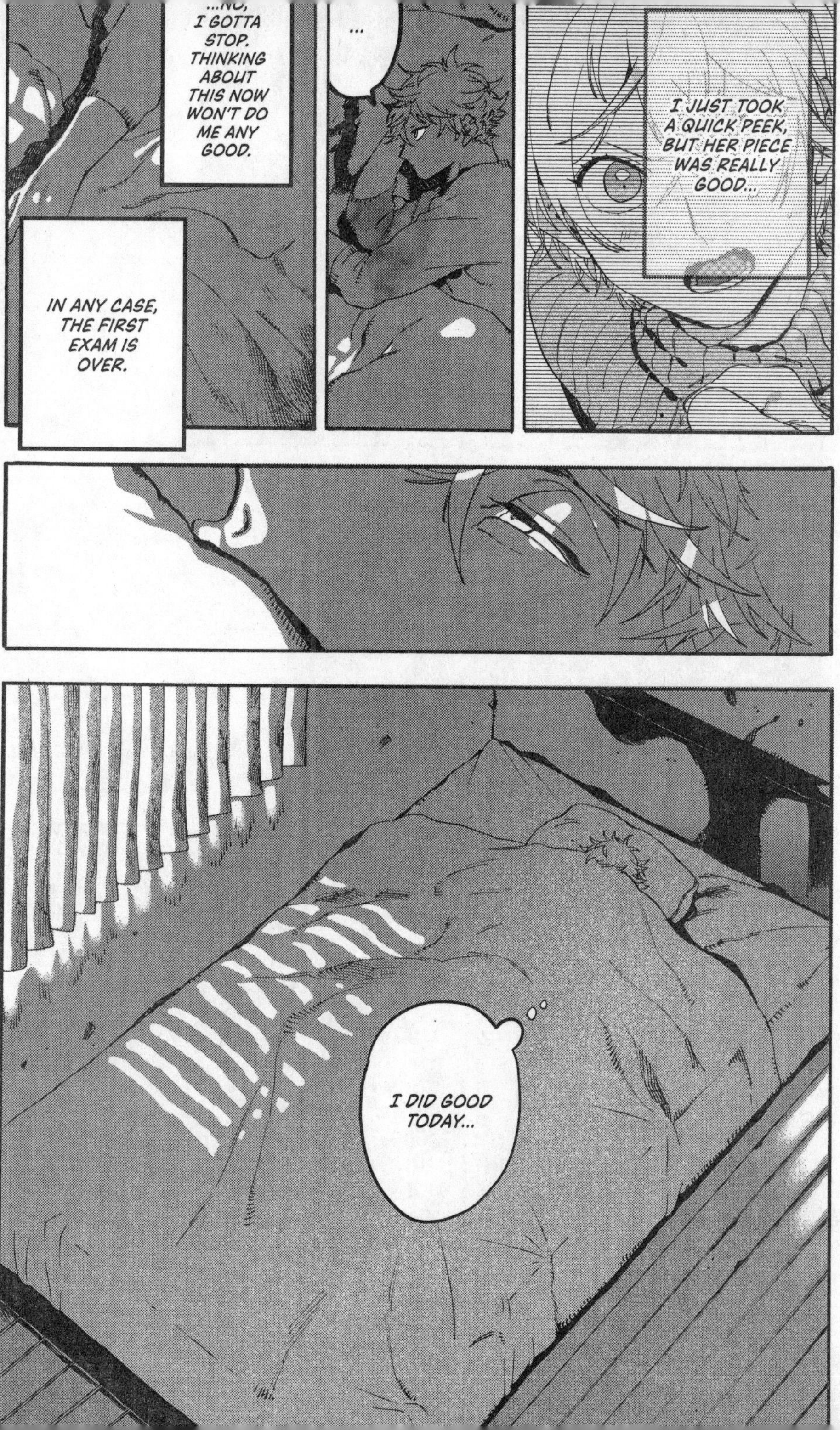
I JUST TOOK A QUICK PEEK, BUT HER PIECE WAS REALLY GOOD...
...
...NO, I GOTTA STOP. THINKING ABOUT THIS NOW WON'T DO ME ANY GOOD.
IN ANY CASE, THE FIRST EXAM IS OVER.
I DID GOOD TODAY...

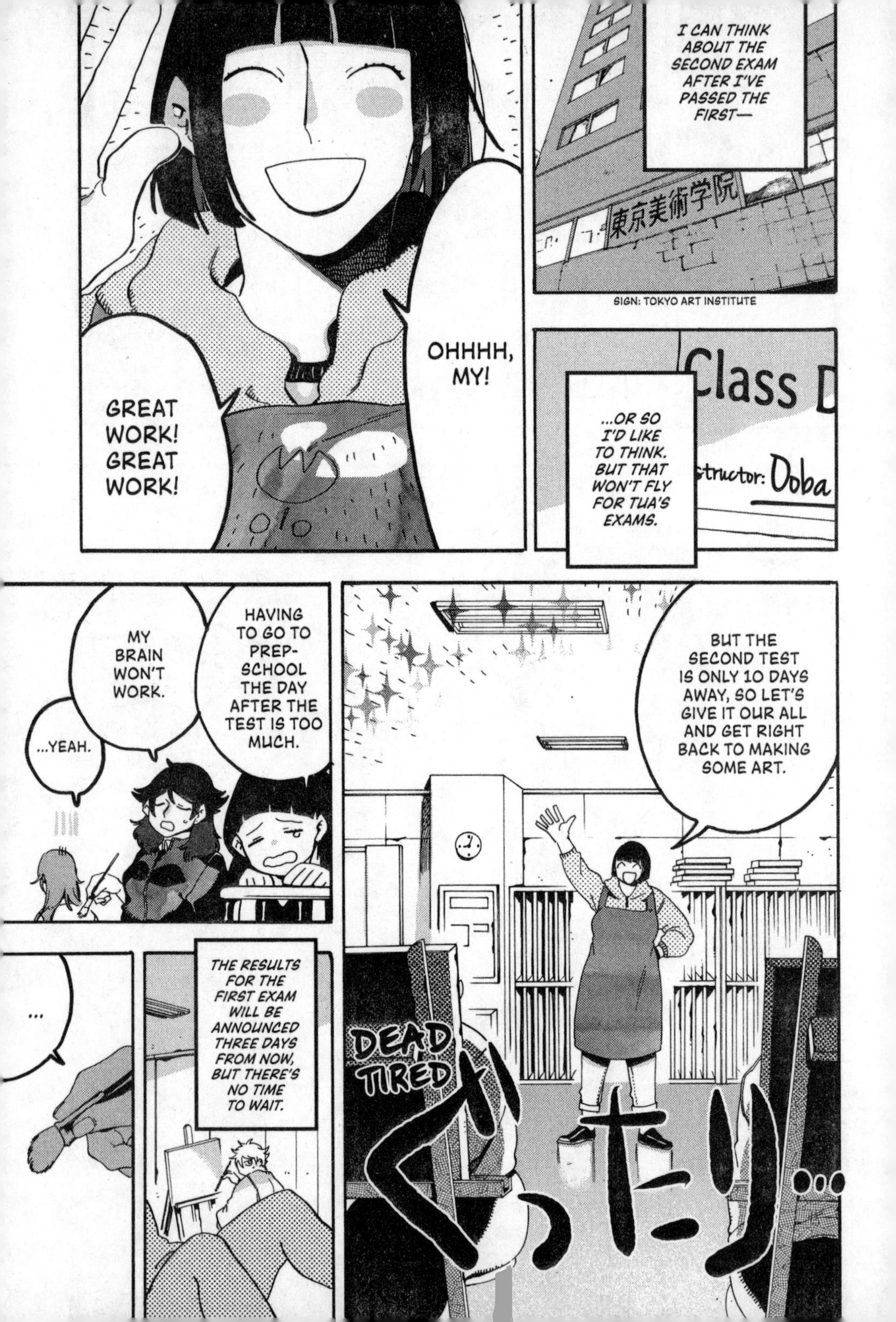
I CAN THINK ABOUT THE SECOND EXAM AFTER I'VE PASSED THE FIRST—
東京美術学院
SIGN: TOKYO ART INSTITUTE
Class D
structor: Ooba
...OR SO I'D LIKE TO THINK. BUT THAT WON'T FLY FOR TUA'S EXAMS.
OHHHH, MY!
GREAT WORK! GREAT WORK!
BUT THE SECOND TEST IS ONLY 10 DAYS AWAY, SO LET'S GIVE IT OUR ALL AND GET RIGHT BACK TO MAKING SOME ART.
DEAD TIRED
HAVING TO GO TO PREP-SCHOOL THE DAY AFTER THE TEST IS TOO MUCH.
MY BRAIN WON'T WORK.
...YEAH.
THE RESULTS FOR THE FIRST EXAM WILL BE ANNOUNCED THREE DAYS FROM NOW, BUT THERE'S NO TIME TO WAIT.
...

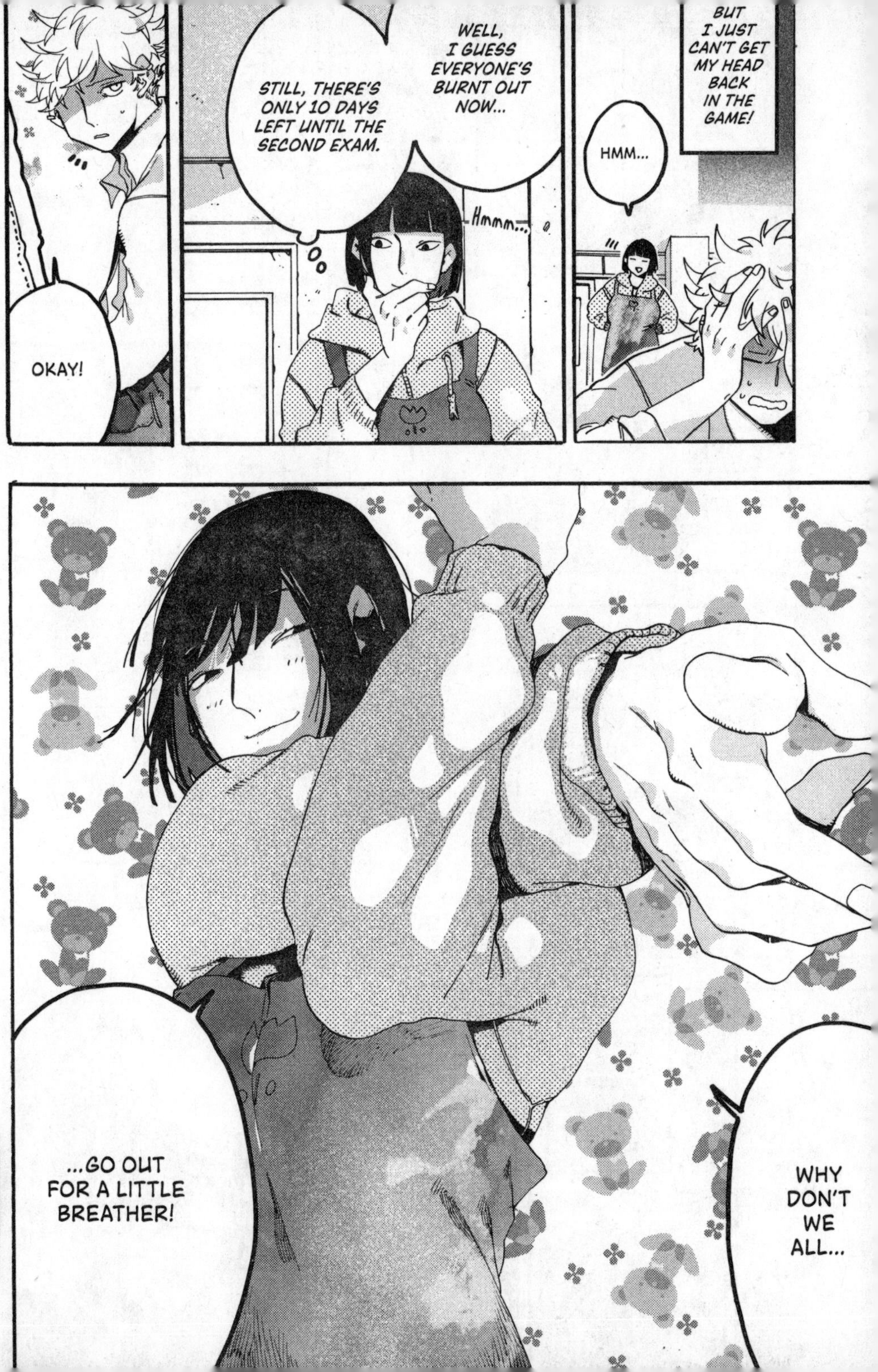
BUT I JUST CAN'T GET MY HEAD BACK IN THE GAME!
HMM...
WELL, I GUESS EVERYONE'S BURNT OUT NOW...
STILL, THERE'S ONLY 10 DAYS LEFT UNTIL THE SECOND EXAM.
Hmmm...
OKAY!
WHY DON'T WE ALL...
...GO OUT FOR A LITTLE BREATHER!

STROKE 16 END

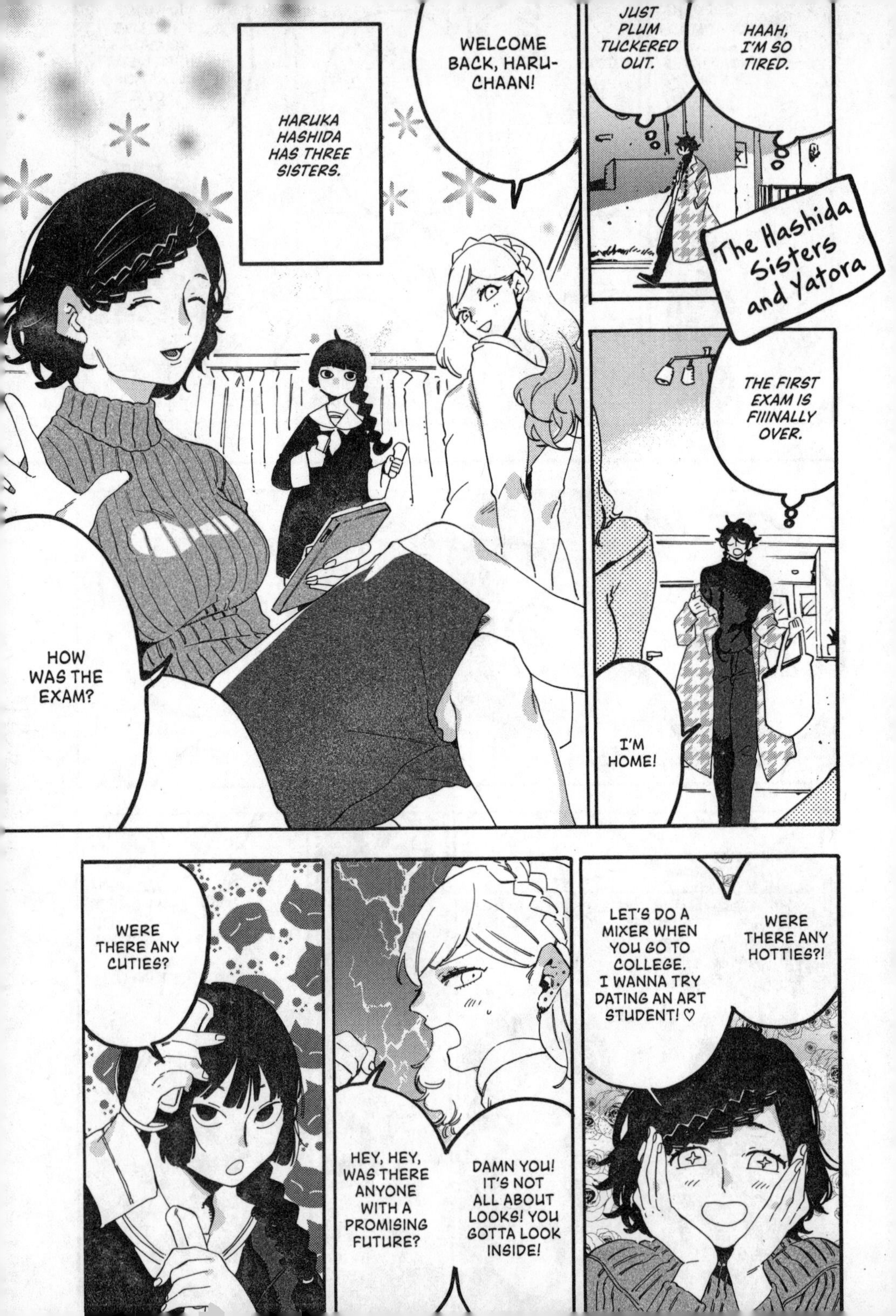
HAAH, I'M SO TIRED.
JUST PLUM TUCKERED OUT.
The Hashida Sisters and Yatora
THE FIRST EXAM IS FIIIINALLY OVER.
I'M HOME!
WELCOME BACK, HARU-CHAAN!
HARUKA HASHIDA HAS THREE SISTERS.
HOW WAS THE EXAM?
WERE THERE ANY HOTTIES?!
LET'S DO A MIXER WHEN YOU GO TO COLLEGE. I WANNA TRY DATING AN ART STUDENT! ♡
DAMN YOU! IT'S NOT ALL ABOUT LOOKS! YOU GOTTA LOOK INSIDE!
HEY, HEY, WAS THERE ANYONE WITH A PROMISING FUTURE?
WERE THERE ANY CUTIES?

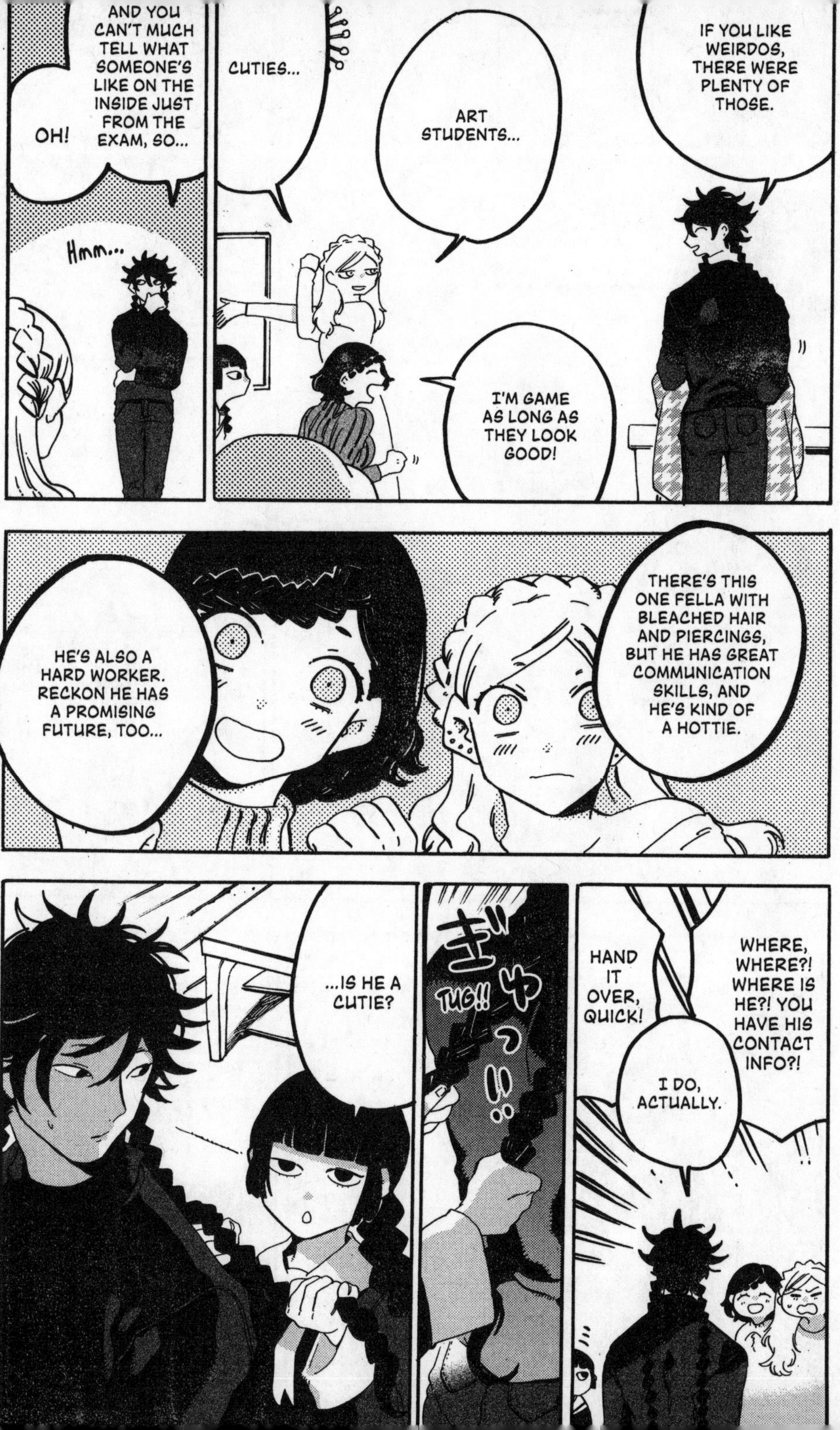
IF YOU LIKE WEIRDOS, THERE WERE PLENTY OF THOSE.
ART STUDENTS...
CUTIES...
I'M GAME AS LONG AS THEY LOOK GOOD!
AND YOU CAN'T MUCH TELL WHAT SOMEONE'S LIKE ON THE INSIDE JUST FROM THE EXAM, SO...
OH!
Hmm...
THERE'S THIS ONE FELLA WITH BLEACHED HAIR AND PIERCINGS, BUT HE HAS GREAT COMMUNICATION SKILLS, AND HE'S KIND OF A HOTTIE.
HE'S ALSO A HARD WORKER. RECKON HE HAS A PROMISING FUTURE, TOO...
WHERE, WHERE?! WHERE IS HE?! YOU HAVE HIS CONTACT INFO?!
HAND IT OVER, QUICK!
I DO, ACTUALLY.
ぎゅっ!!
TUG!!
...IS HE A CUTIE?

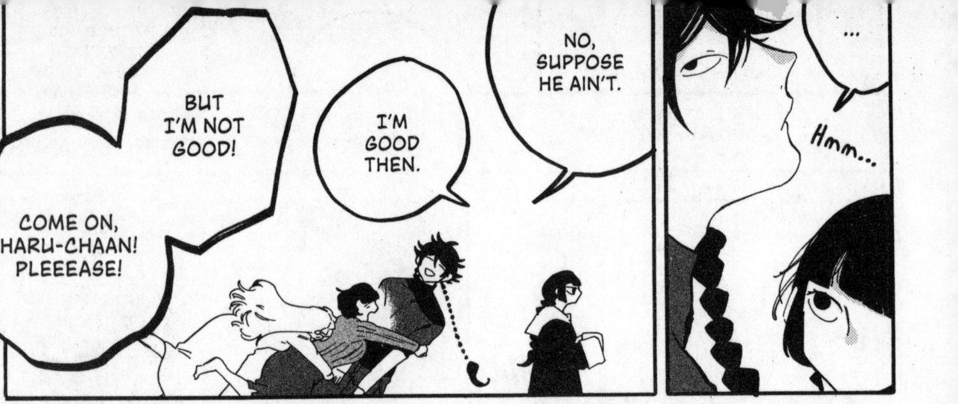
...
Hmm...
NO, SUPPOSE HE AIN'T.
I'M GOOD THEN.
BUT I'M NOT GOOD!
COME ON, HARU-CHAAN! PLEEEASE!

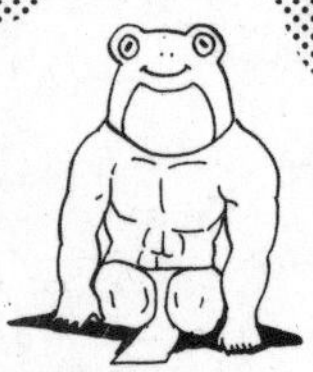

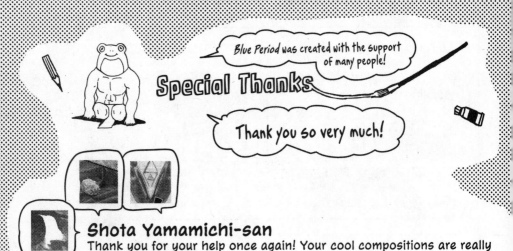

Blue Period was created with the support of many people!

Special Thanks

Thank you so very much!

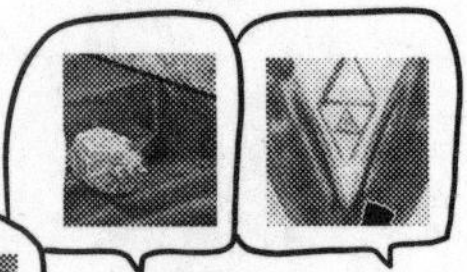

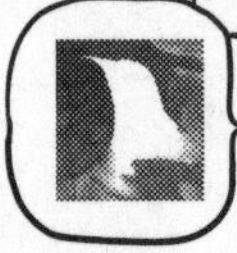

Shota Yamamichi-san

Thank you for your help once again! Your cool compositions are really impressive.

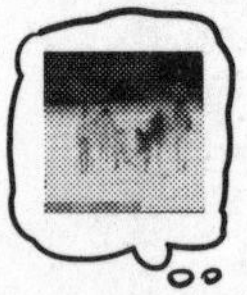

Moeko Natsui-san

Your piece really brings me back! Thanks for letting me borrow it! Let's go drinking... I mean it...

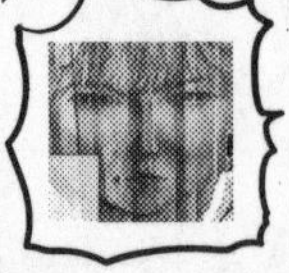

Yuko Yamazaki-san

Thank you so, so, so much for working so hard...! I am nothing but grateful to you for making such an incredibly convincing drawing...

THE EVER-CHANGING CIRCUMSTANCES OF THE EXAMS

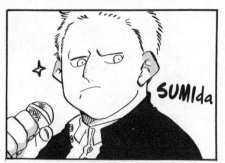

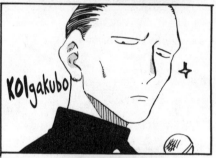

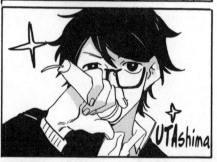

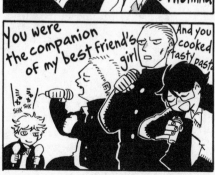

THE 2019 TUA OIL PAINTING EXAM HAD AN INTER-VIEW, YOU KNOW.
HUH?
OH, SHIT!
SO WE SHOULD PRACTICE FOR INTER-VIEWS, TOO...
YEAH, YATORA, BUT...
...THE CONTENTS OF THE EXAMS SOMETIMES CHANGE.
IN THE PAST, THE NIHONGA COURSE ALSO HAD INTERVIEWS.
BUT THEN THEY GOT RID OF THEM.
AND 10 YEARS AGO, THE OIL PAINTING COURSE HAD A WATERCOLOR CHALLENGE.
20 YEARS AGO, THEY DIDN'T HAVE THE SKETCHBOOK CHALLENGE.
HUH, BUT...
WHO KNOWS WHAT KIND OF CHALLENGES THEY'LL HAVE 10 YEARS FROM NOW?

THESE ARE THE SAME CONTENTS AS THOSE ON THE 2017 EXAMS WHEN THIS MANGA BEGAN SERIALIZATION. PLEASE UNDERSTAND THAT THE CONTENTS OF THE EXAMS IN *BLUE PERIOD* MAY DIFFER FROM THE ACTUAL CONTENTS DEPENDING ON THE YEAR.

KARAOKE

SUMIda
KOIgakubo
UTAshima
And you cooked tasty pasta
You were the companion of my best friend's girl
SHK
SHK

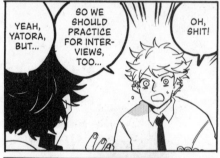

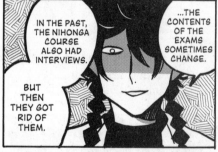

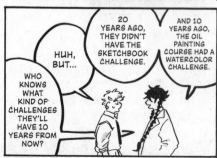

AFTER CHAPTER 1

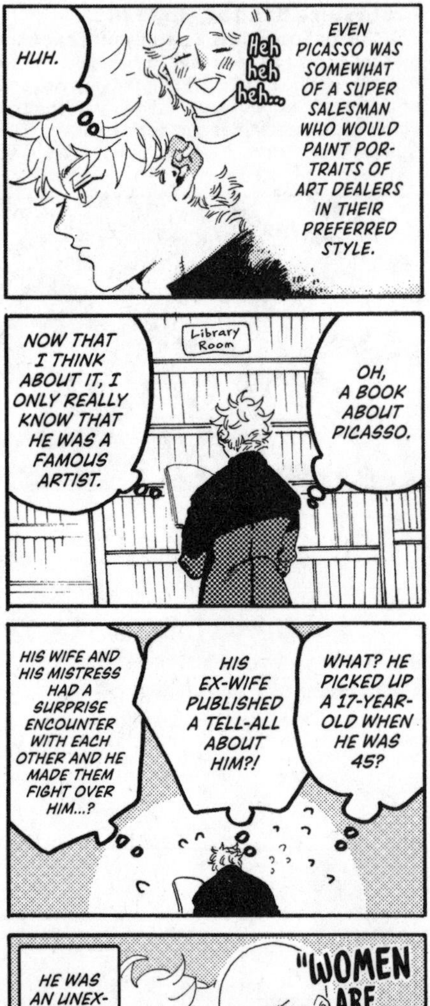
EVEN PICASSO WAS SOMEWHAT OF A SUPER SALESMAN WHO WOULD PAINT POR-TRAITS OF ART DEALERS IN THEIR PREFERRED STYLE.
Heh heh heh...
HUH.
OH, A BOOK ABOUT PICASSO.
Library Room
NOW THAT I THINK ABOUT IT, I ONLY REALLY KNOW THAT HE WAS A FAMOUS ARTIST.
WHAT? HE PICKED UP A 17-YEAR-OLD WHEN HE WAS 45?
HIS EX-WIFE PUBLISHED A TELL-ALL ABOUT HIM?!
HIS WIFE AND HIS MISTRESS HAD A SURPRISE ENCOUNTER WITH EACH OTHER AND HE MADE THEM FIGHT OVER HIM...?
"WOMEN ARE MACHINES FOR SUFFERING." by Picasso
HE WAS AN UNEX-PECTEDLY TERRIBLE GUY.
Picasso
His paintings were super good when he was 14.

NOT SIMILAR BUT SIMILAR

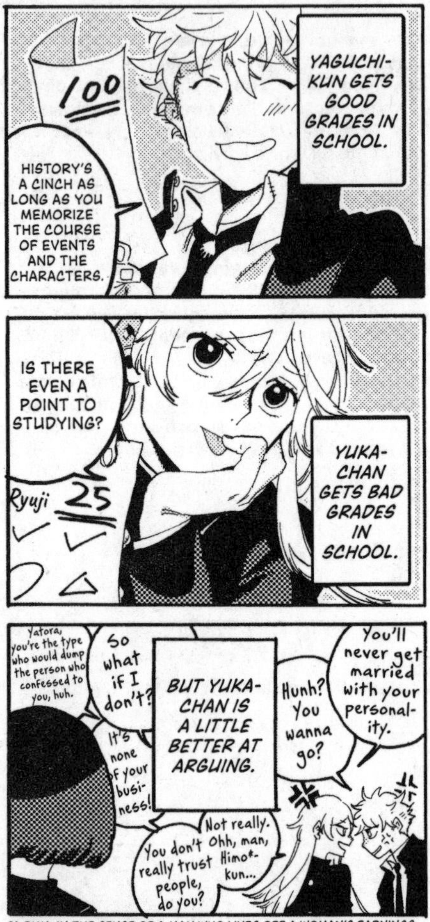
YAGUCHI-KUN GETS GOOD GRADES IN SCHOOL.
100
HISTORY'S A CINCH AS LONG AS YOU MEMORIZE THE COURSE OF EVENTS AND THE CHARACTERS.
YUKA-CHAN GETS BAD GRADES IN SCHOOL.
IS THERE EVEN A POINT TO STUDYING?
Ryuji 25
You'll never get married with your personal-ity.
Hunh? You wanna go?
BUT YUKA-CHAN IS A LITTLE BETTER AT ARGUING.
So what if I don't?
Yatora, you're the type who would dump the person who confessed to you, huh.
It's none of your business!
Not really. Ohh, man, Himo*-kun...
You don't really trust people, do you?

*A BUM, IN THE SENSE OF A MAN WHO LIVES OFF A WOMAN'S EARNINGS.

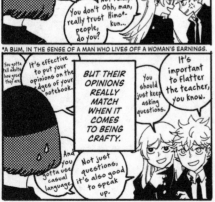

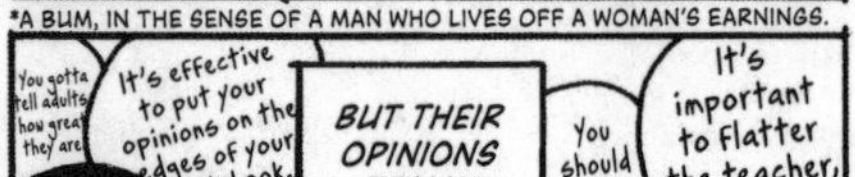
It's important to flatter the teacher, you know.
You should just keep asking questions.
BUT THEIR OPINIONS REALLY MATCH WHEN IT COMES TO BEING CRAFTY.
It's effective to put your opinions on the edges of your notebook.
You gotta tell adults how great they are.
Not just questions, it's also good to speak up.
And you gotta use casual language.

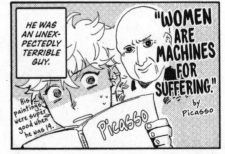

TRANSLATION NOTES

Brain Juice Bushaa, page 143
The title of Stroke 16 is a parody of "Pear Juice Bushaa," one of the catchphrases of a Japanese mascot known as Funassyi. Funassyi is a *yuru-chara* (essentially a promotional mascot) that represents the pear-producing region of Funabashi in Chiba, Japan. Funassyi has become one of the most famous mascots in Japan, and they are famous for their high-energy, frenetic mannerisms as well as their catchphrase *"Nashijiru bushaa!"* (officially translated as "Pear Juice Bushaa" but "bushaa" can be interpreted as the sound of gushing or spraying).

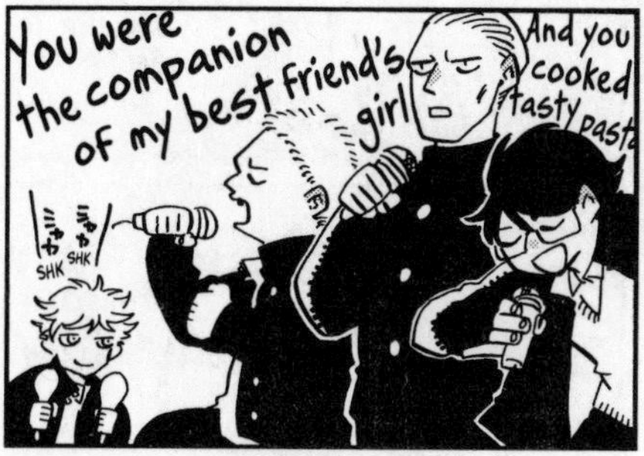
And you cooked tasty pasta
You were the companion of my best friend's girl
SHK SHK

Karaoke song, page 192
Yatora's friends are singing is *Junrenka (Pure Love Song)*, the 2006 hit song from the reggae-influenced Japanese band known as Shonan no Kaze. The song is a fairly standard tale of young love, and apparently, the line "And you cooked tasty pasta" added to its popularity at the time because it was a trend among young people to believe that cooking pasta with someone you like would grant one's desire to be a couple.

BLUE PERIOD

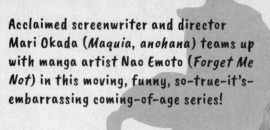

Acclaimed screenwriter and director Mari Okada (*Maquia*, *anohana*) teams up with manga artist Nao Emoto (*Forget Me Not*) in this moving, funny, so-true-it's-embarrassing coming-of-age series!

When Kazusa enters high school, she joins the Literature Club, and leaps from reading innocent fiction to diving into the literary classics. But these novels are a bit more...*adult* than she was prepared for. Between euphemisms like fresh dewy grass and pork stew, crushing on the boy next door, and knowing you want to do that *one thing* before you die—discovering your budding sexuality is no easy feat! As if puberty wasn't awkward enough, the club consists of a brooding writer, the prettiest girl in school, an agreeable comrade, and an outspoken prude. Fumbling over their own discomforts, these five teens get thrown into chaos over three little letters: *S...E...X...!*

O Maidens in your Savage Season

NOW AN ANIME!

Mari Okada   Nao Emoto

KC
KODANSHA
COMICS

Akiko Higashimura

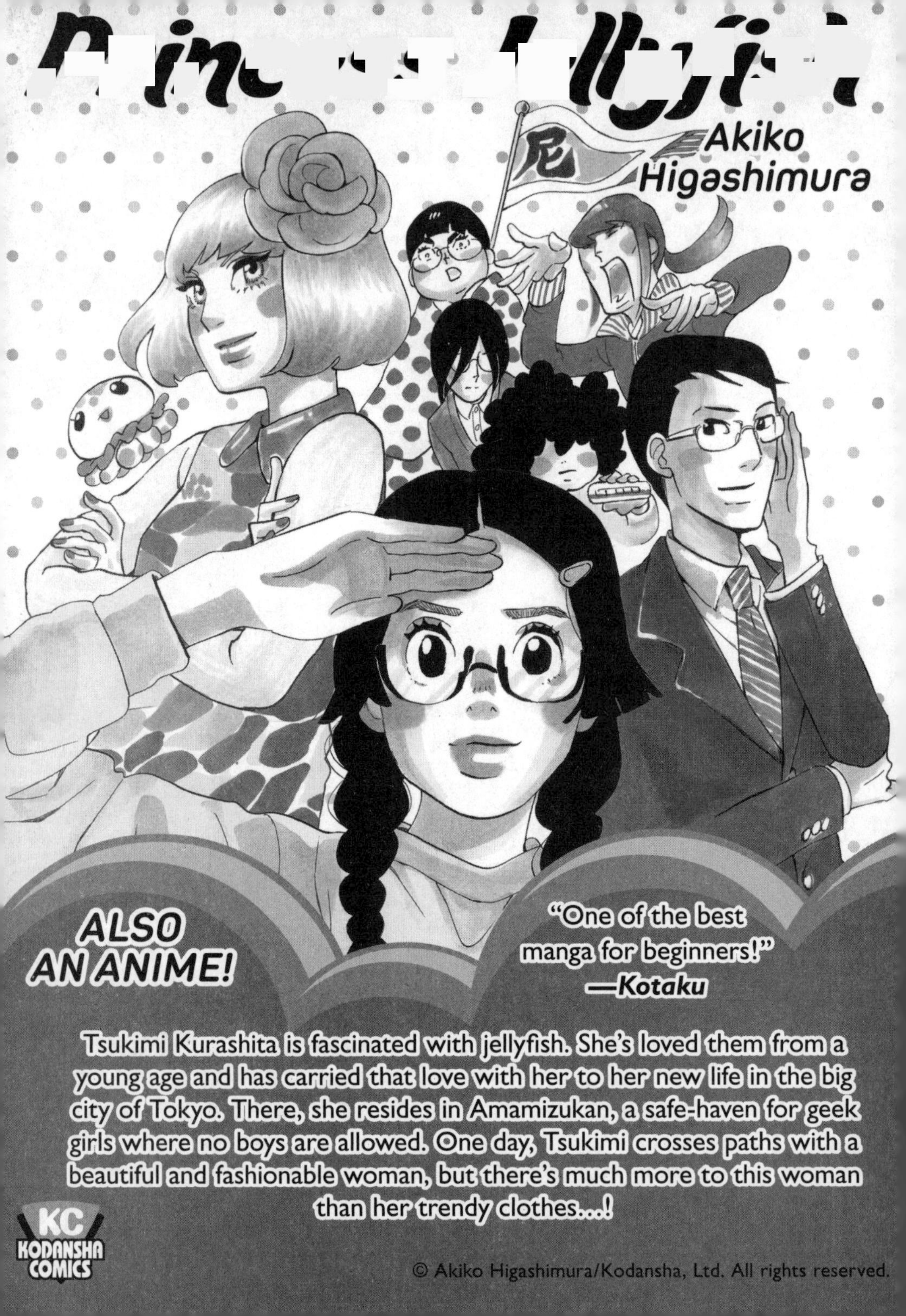
尼

ALSO AN ANIME!

"One of the best manga for beginners!"
—*Kotaku*

Tsukimi Kurashita is fascinated with jellyfish. She's loved them from a young age and has carried that love with her to her new life in the big city of Tokyo. There, she resides in Amamizukan, a safe-haven for geek girls where no boys are allowed. One day, Tsukimi crosses paths with a beautiful and fashionable woman, but there's much more to this woman than her trendy clothes...!

KC KODANSHA COMICS

◄ KAMOME ►
SHIRAHAMA

Witch Hat Atelier

A magical manga
adventure for
fans of Disney
and Studio
Ghibli!

Witch Hat Atelier © Kamome Shirahama/Kodansha Ltd.

The magical adventure that took Japan by storm is finally here, from acclaimed DC and Marvel cover artist Kamome Shirahama!

In a world where everyone takes wonders like magic spells and dragons for granted, Coco is a girl with a simple dream: She wants to be a witch. But everybody knows magicians are born, not made, and Coco was not born with a gift for magic. Resigned to her un-magical life, Coco is about to give up on her dream to become a witch...until the day she meets Qifrey, a mysterious, traveling magician. After secretly seeing Qifrey perform magic in a way she's never seen before, Coco soon learns what everybody "knows" might not be the truth, and discovers that her magical dream may not be as far away as it may seem...

Having lost his wife, high school teacher Kōhei Inuzuka is doing his best to raise his young daughter Tsumugi as a single father. He's pretty bad at cooking and doesn't have a huge appetite to begin with, but chance brings his little family together with one of his students, the lonely Kotori. The three of them are anything but comfortable in the kitchen, but the healing power of home cooking might just work on their grieving hearts.

"This season's number-one feel-good anime!" —Anime News Network

"A beautifully-drawn story about comfort food and family and grief. Recommended." —Otaku USA Magazine

sweetness & lightning

By Gido Amagakure

SAINT☆YOUNG MEN

A LONG AWAITED ARRIVAL IN PREMIUM 2-IN-1 HARDCOVER

After centuries of hard work, Jesus and Buddha take a break from their heavenly duties to relax among the people of Japan, and their adventures in this lighthearted buddy comedy are sure to bring mirth and merriment to all!

"Brilliant…the physical comedy and facial expressions will make you literally LOL."
—Sam Humphries
(host of *DC Daily*;
writer, *Green Lanterns, Legendary Star-Lord*)

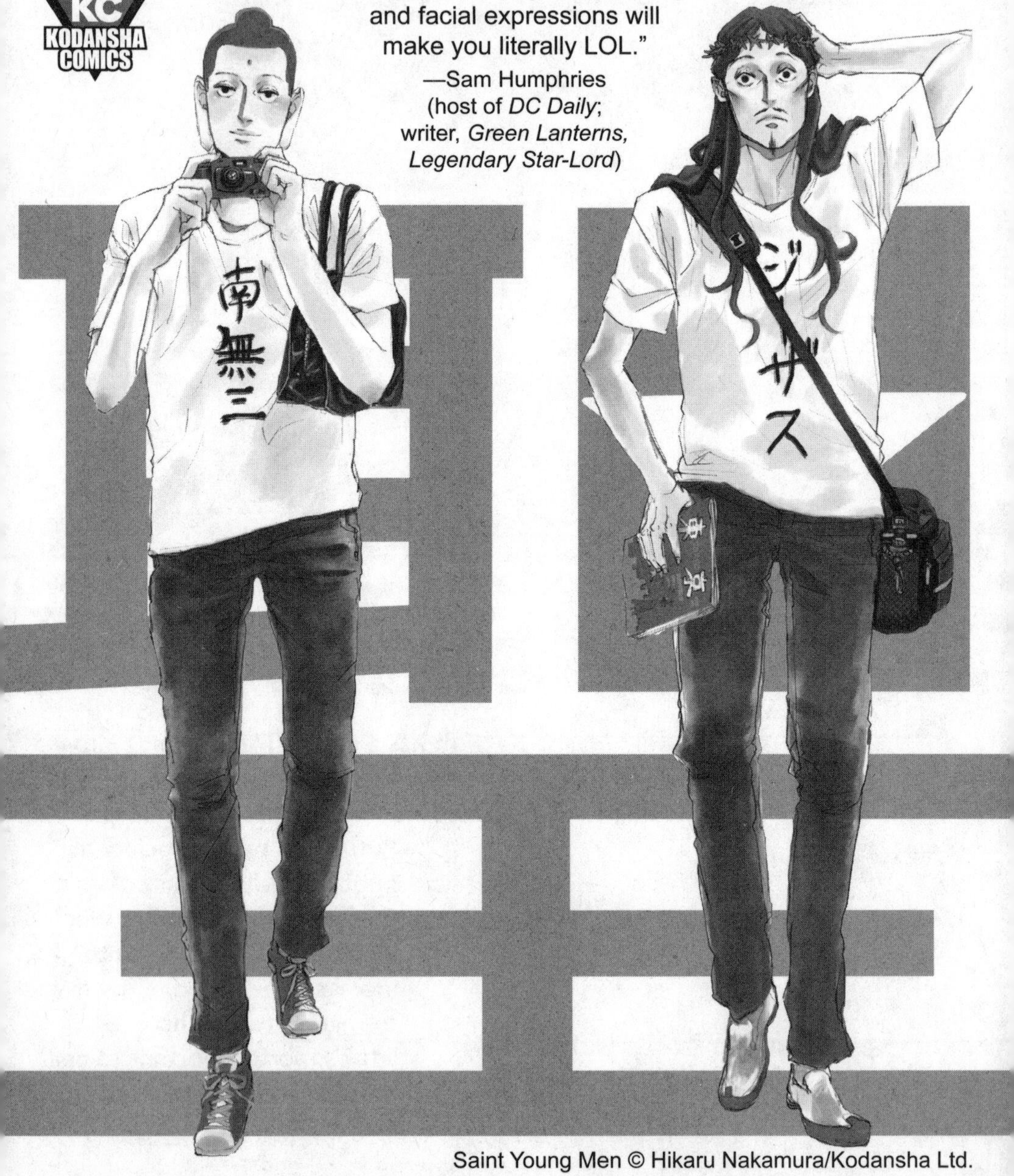
南無三

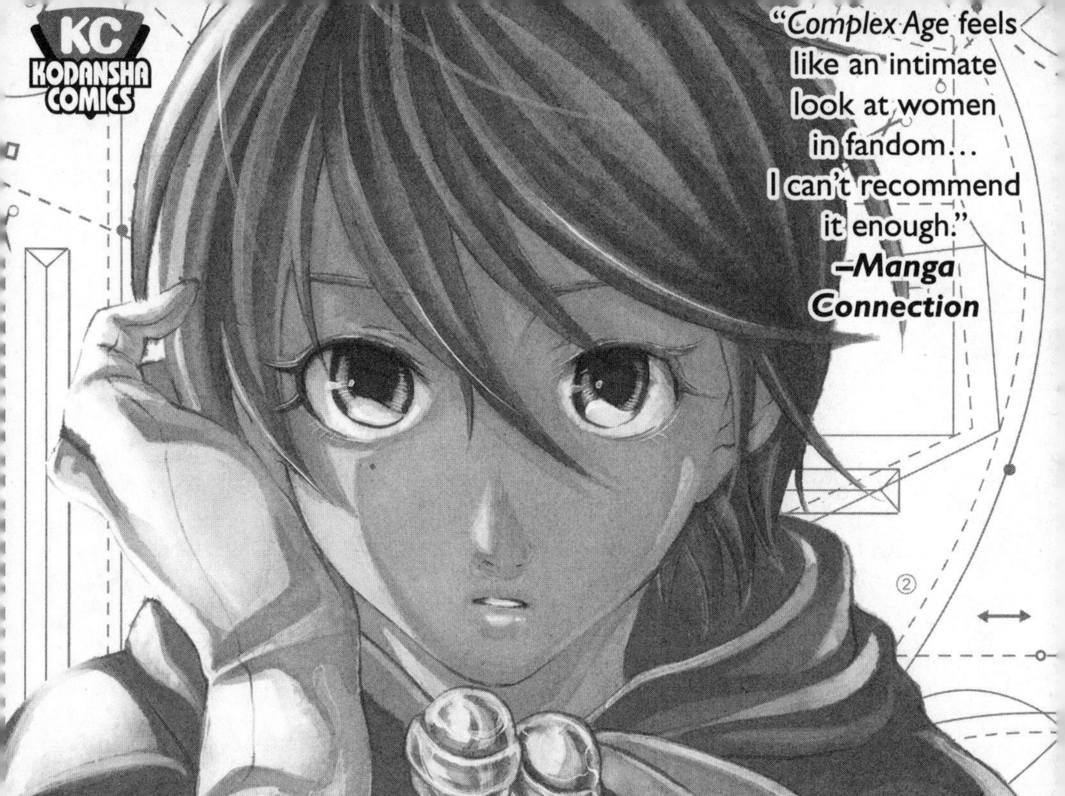
KC
KODANSHA COMICS
"*Complex Age* feels like an intimate look at women in fandom… I can't recommend it enough."
–Manga Connection
complex age
yui sakuma

26-year-old Nagisa Kataura has a secret. Transforming into her favorite anime and manga characters is her passion in life, and she's earned great respect amongst her fellow cospayers. But to the rest of society, her hobby is a silly fantasy. As demands from both her office job and cosplaying begin to increase, she may one day have to make a tough choice—what's more important to her, cosplay or being "normal"?

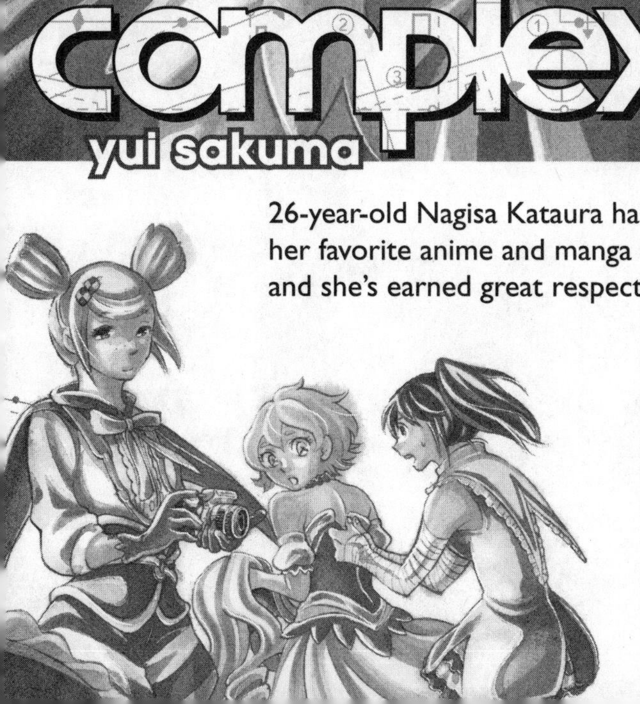

Knight of the Ice ©Yayoi Ogawa/Kodansha Ltd.

SKATING THRILLS AND ICY CHILLS WITH THIS NEW TINGLY ROMANCE SERIES!

A rom-com on ice, perfect for fans of *Princess Jellyfish* and *Wotakoi*. Kokoro is the talk of the figure-skating world, winning trophies and hearts. But little do they know... he's actually a huge nerd! From the beloved creator of *You're My Pet* (*Tramps Like Us*).

Chitose is a serious young woman, working for the health magazine *SASSO*. Or at least, she would be, if she wasn't constantly getting distracted by her childhood friend, international figure skating star Kokoro Kijinami! In the public eye and on the ice, Kokoro is a gallant, flawless knight, but behind his glittery costumes and breathtaking spins lies a secret: He's actually a hopelessly romantic otaku, who can only land his quad jumps when Chitose is on hand to recite a spell from his favorite magical girl anime!

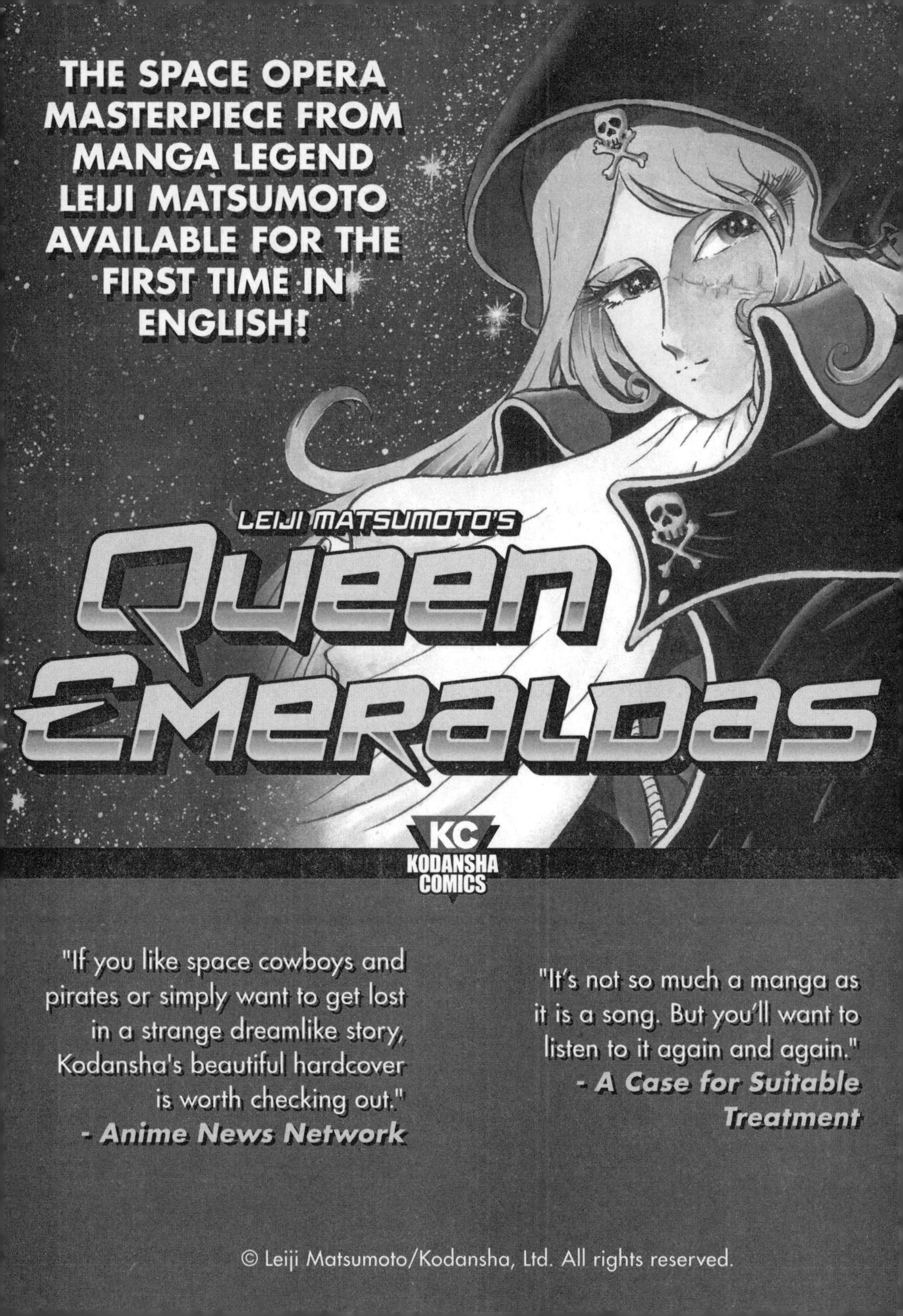
THE SPACE OPERA MASTERPIECE FROM MANGA LEGEND LEIJI MATSUMOTO AVAILABLE FOR THE FIRST TIME IN ENGLISH!
LEIJI MATSUMOTO'S
Queen Emeraldas
KC
KODANSHA COMICS

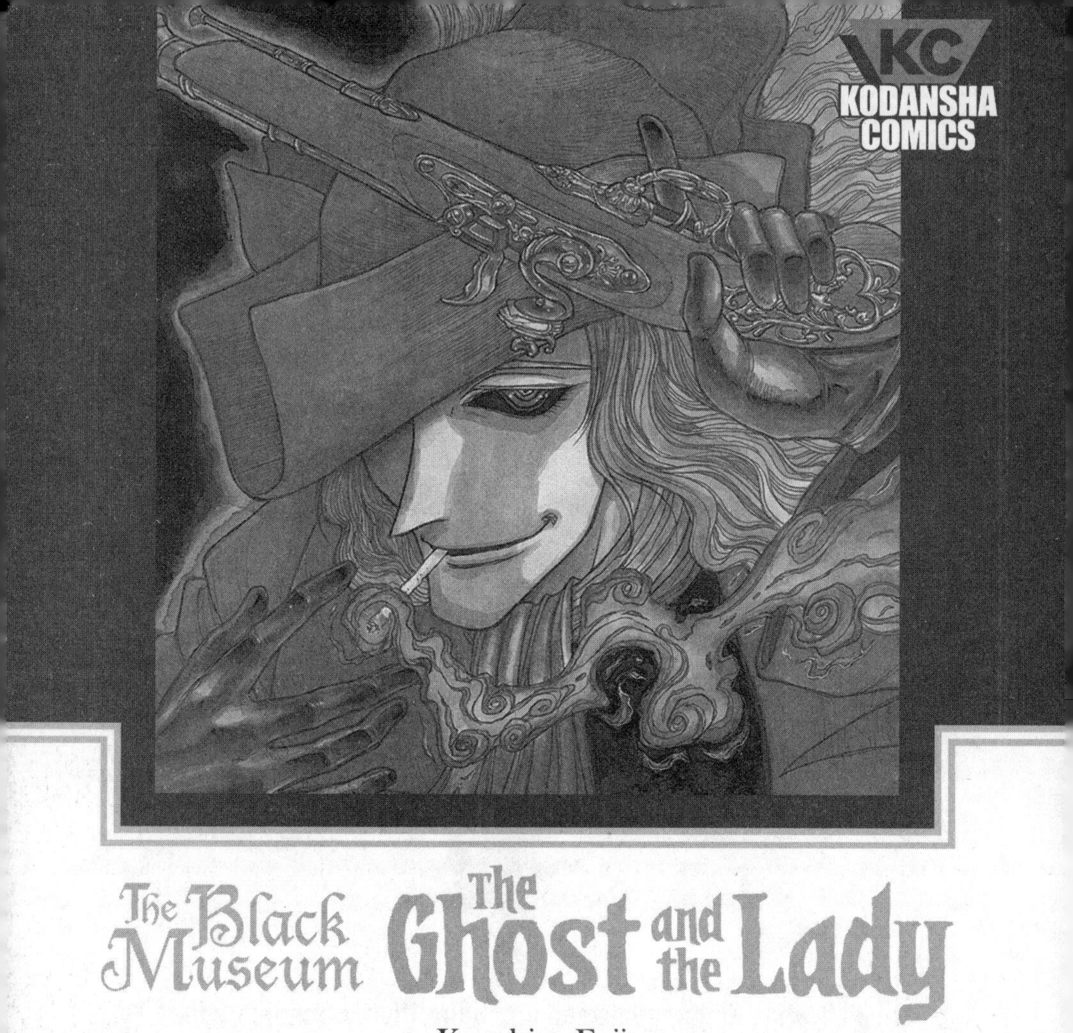

KODANSHA COMICS

The Black Museum The Ghost and the Lady

By Kazuhiro Fujita

Deep in Scotland Yard in London sits an evidence room dedicated to the greatest mysteries of British history. In this "Black Museum" sits a misshapen hunk of lead—two bullets fused together—the key to a wartime encounter between Florence Nightingale, the mother of modern nursing, and a supernatural Man in Grey. This story is unknown to most scholars of history, but a special guest of the museum will tell the tale of The Ghost and the Lady...

Praise for Kazuhiro Fujita's *Ushio and Tora*

"A charming revival that combines a classic look with modern depth and pacing... **Essential viewing both for curmudgeons and new fans alike.**" — Anime News Network

"**GREAT!** The first episode of Ushio and Tora captures the essence of '90s anime." — IGN

OTOMO 大友克洋
A GLOBAL TRIBUTE TO
THE MIND BEHIND AKIRA

A celebration of manga legend Katsuhiro Otomo from more than 80
world-renowned fine artists and comics legends
With contributions from:
- Stan Sakai
- Tomer and Asaf Hanuka
- Sara Pichelli
- Range Murata
- Aleksi Briclot
And more!
168 pages of stunning, full-color art

THE WORLD OF CLAMP!

Cardcaptor Sakura
Collector's Edition

Cardcaptor Sakura:
Clear Card

Magic Knight Rayearth
25th Anniversary Box Set

Chobits

TSUBASA Omnibus

TSUBASA WoRLD CHRoNiCLE

xxxHOLiC Omnibus

xxxHOLiC Rei

CLOVER Collector's Edition

Kodansha Comics welcomes you to explore the expansive world of CLAMP, the all-female artist collective that has produced some of the most acclaimed manga of the century. Our growing catalog includes icons like *Cardcaptor Sakura* and *Magic Knight Rayearth*, each crafted with CLAMP's one-of-a-kind style and characters!

Blue Period 4 is a work of fiction. Na[me]s, places, and incidents are the products of th[e] or are used fictitiously. Any resemblance to a[ctual] persons, living or dead, is entirely coincidental.

A Kodansha Comics Trade Paperback Original
Blue Period 4 copyright © 2019 Tsubasa Yamaguchi
English translation copyright © 2021 Tsubasa Yamaguchi

All rights reserved.

Published in the United States by Kodansha Comics, an imprint of
Kodansha USA Publishing, LLC, New York.

Publication rights for this English edition arranged through
Kodansha Ltd., Tokyo.

First published in Japan in 2019 by Kodansha Ltd., Tokyo.

ISBN 978-1-64651-126-6

Original cover design by Yohei Okashita (Inazuma Onsen)

Printed in the United States of America.

www.kodansha.us

3rd Printing
Translation: Ajani Oloye
Lettering: Lys Blakeslee
Editing: Haruko Hashimoto
Kodansha Comics edition cover design by Matthew Akuginow

Publisher: Kiichiro Sugawara

Director of publishing services: Ben Applegate
Associate director of operations: Stephen Pakula
Publishing services managing editors: Alanna Ruse, Madison Salters
Production managers: Emi Lotto, Angela Zurlo
Logo and character art ©Kodansha USA Publishing, LLC